2011
COACH OF THE YEAR CLINICS
FOOTBALL MANUAL

Edited by Earl Browning

COACHES CHOICE™

www.coacheschoice.com

ISBN: 978-1-60679-171-4

ISSN: 1534-925X

Telecoach, Inc. Transcription: Emmerson Browning, Kent Browning, and Tom Cheaney

Diagrams: Steve Haag and Travis Rose

Book layout and cover design: Bean Creek Studio

Cover photo (front): ©Matt Cohen/Southcreek Global/ZUMA Press.com

Cover photos (back): ©TCU Athletics Media Relations (top)
              ©Charles Baus/Cal Sport Media/ZUMA Press.com (bottom)

Special thanks to the Nike clinic managers for having the lectures taped.

Coaches Choice
P.O. Box 1828
Monterey, CA 93942
www.coacheschoice.com

Contents

THE PISTOL OFFENSE: AN UPDATE AND HISTORY

University of Nevada

How many pistol coaches are in here this morning? Let's see a show of hands. Good! When I finish, all of you will be running the pistol.

First, I want to give you some background of what I have done as a coach in terms of offense. I have always coached the quarterbacks. I continue to coach the quarterbacks today. When I went to Nevada in 1976, we were a Division II program. We ran the wing-T then. We ran the wing-T for 13 seasons. During that time, we went from Division II to Division I-AA. After three years of installing the wing-T offense, we became one of the better teams in the country. We were very good. It was us, Delaware, Georgia Southern, and Boise State, and we all played good football. I loved the wing-T. We threw the ball well out of the wing-T. We developed the one-back wing-T passing game. We used the motions with the passing game.

In the early 1990s, we evolved to the Division I-A league. I did not feel we could recruit the type of athlete we needed to compete with the I-A schools on our schedule each year. Therefore, we went to the one-back offense.

From 1993 to 1997 at that level, we were the top passing team in the country in Division I-A. Our quarterbacks led the country and threw for 4,300 yards. Our receivers caught between 120 and 129 passes per year. We were good at throwing the football. We ran the one-back with motion. We were good throwing the ball. We did a lot of different things from that offensive set.

We were not a true spread offense. We have always had a tight end. As we moved up to playing better competition, I felt we had to run the ball better to be successful. We had to be able to eat the clock. When we ran the wing-T, we ate the clock. When we became a good passing team, we still had 1,000-yard rushers every year. We would throw the ball 35 to 40 times per game at that time.

As we moved up in classification, the talent on the defensive side got better. The defenses could play more loosely, so to speak. At that time, I wanted to come up with something that would identify Nevada by itself, if there were such an animal. We wanted something that would be creative for us, and give us an identity. We were not concerned if it was something that would catch on across the country. That was not an issue, but it was a concern with our team.

Here is the reason we went to the pistol offense. At the time, I really liked what people were doing in the shotgun. The thing I did not like about the shotgun is the fact that the running game is east-west. You can watch the University of Oregon to see what I mean. They are as good a team as you are going to see. Their running game is east-west. I could not give you a percentage of the times they run the outside zone plays. They do a great job with their great speed. They read off the zone, and they throw the football. A lot of people think they just throw the ball, but they do run the ball extremely well.

We study a lot of their film to see where we are. We call the alignment, when the back is on the side, the hip alignment. As I talk today, you will see we do a little of the hip alignment. The back splits the leg of the onside tackle that he is closest to on the line. He is one yard back behind the quarterback and off the line of scrimmage. We do some of this, but not much.

The pistol is a two-phased thing. Here is the reason we went to the pistol and why I thought it was important for us to go to the offense.

We created the pistol to our liking. Let me show you what we wanted to do with the pistol. First, we wanted to be able to run the ball better. Here was my theory. In the one-back set, our deep back was always seven yards from the football. We never measured it from the quarterback. We measured it from the ball to the tip of the deep back's toes. That is the concept. You must remember there were no films we could collect to study. When I was growing up, you could not bring in something new like the pistol concept.

When we started working on the new concept in the spring of 1995, I told the staff what I wanted to do on offense. They all started working on their resumes. They thought I had really lost my marbles. They told me there was no way we could run the new offense. We really did not know what to expect because there was nothing to look at on film.

What we decided to do was this: when we are under center in the one-back set, or if we were in the I formation, because we could run it from the I formation, our deepest back was 7 to 7.5 yards deep. We decided not to move the deep back. We wanted to keep him consistent. However, we wanted to get him the football sooner and deeper. We worked on the concept, checking where we could get the ball to the deep back and get it to him as soon as possible.

We found out in the pistol we could get the deep back the ball at 5.5 yards. This gave the back a yard to a half yard to make his cut on the backside zone, or the frontside zone play. He could go either way he wanted to go.

The number-one thing in creating the pistol was to get the ball to the deep back sooner (Diagram #1). The deep back is three yards from the quarterback, and the toes of the quarterback are four yards deep from the ball. That is the true pistol.

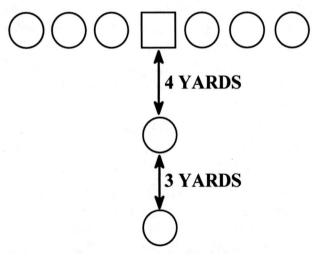

Diagram #1. True Pistol Alignment

Could we back the quarterback up to five yards as he is in the shotgun offense? Absolutely! However, the key is the timing of the back. The reason we came up with three yards between the quarterback and deep back was this: in the misdirection offense, we wanted enough room for the quarterback to rid the back and go outside. We wanted to have enough space between them so we could bring a man in motion behind them or in front of them. If you move the back closer, your ability to run the bootleg or misdirection is challenged.

We experimented in working with the alignment. We did it all. We moved the deep back, and we move the quarterback around at different depths. I took the assistant coaches in the locker room and worked on the alignment in our locker room before spring practice. I would play the role of the quarterback. The assistant coaches just did not think we could run the offense. They thought I was insane.

We found it was best to put the deep back three yards from the quarterback to run the misdirection. This gave us the ability to run what we wanted to run, and it gave us the best opportunities. Do we move the back up at times? We very seldom move the back up in the pistol offense. The quarterback's toes are at four yards, and the deep running back is three yards behind the quarterback. We want the quarterback to bring the ball back to the depth of the tailback.

When we look at the tailback, it increases his vision. What we are saying is this. If the running back gets the ball deeper, he has more vision to take the ball inside or to the outside. When we run the inside zone play, we cut it back a ton at times. That is because the read on the 3 technique or 1 technique as we double the down linemen when we do that. The depth of the deep back is important. The way we run the play, it hides the running back on those zone plays.

Our quarterback this year was a great one. He was 6'6"! Not all of our quarterbacks are like that. We were just fortunate with this quarterback. When you get a tailback three yards behind the quarterback, it makes it difficult for the linebackers to find the ball when we give it to the tailback. In the one-back or in the I-back formation, the tailback is at seven yards. Those linebackers can identify the ball going to the tailback on the counter plays and on misdirection plays. However, when we line the tailback three yards behind the quarterback, it is very difficult for the linebackers to identify the tailback on the counter steps and the counter plays.

We were not aware of this fact at the time we installed the pistol offense. We installed the pistol offense to get the ball to the tailback deeper and to have him run north-south. We wanted to run the ball downhill.

What I am going to show you here is the offense we install in first three days of spring football. This is what we installed on the first three days of 2005. It will be the same installation in 2011. It is what we build our offense around. The hiding of the tailback was a plus for us. We did not realize the opportunity it gave us at the time. It is hard for the linebackers to identify the tailback, and more difficult for the safeties to identify the tailback if you are running a delayed action play. It is the same if you are faking to the tailback in the isolation play, and putting the safety on a checkdown.

Defensive teams cannot set their front based on the offset back. When we run the hip alignment, the linebackers can set in position and read the backs without a lot of difficulty (Diagram #2). They can run their stunts, and it becomes easier to read when we have the back offset. Yes, we can run the sweep in that direction. You can run the inside zone play. Some teams will bring the hip back inside on a counter play. However, it is easier for the linebackers to I.D. the running back, and to adjust their sets to what they want to do defensively.

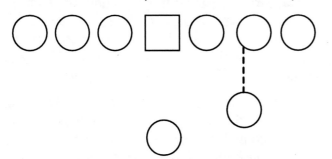

Diagram #2. Hip Alignment

As we started running the pistol, we are trying to create more misdirection. We want to get our quarterback more involved as a runner. In our system, our quarterback must be an athlete. The quarterback we had this year was a great runner.

You will be reading about Colin Kaepernick in the future. He will line up with the best quarterbacks in terms of running the football.

We are one of the few teams that allow the defense to hit our quarterbacks in the spring. We do not drop them, but we do allow the defense to hit them. We are a hard-nosed football team. We do not allow our quarterbacks to skip the live hitting part of practice. We do not hit them every down, but most of the time.

What we do in the pistol offense is this: if you are a power team, or a gap team, which is the weakside power plays, we run a select number of plays. This is what we ran in the 2004 season. When we were under the center with the quarterback, we ran the power play just as everyone else ran it. We ran it with a one-back set with a man in motion. We had the fullback kick-out on the play. We ran the gap play, where we pulled the guard and blocked down with the wingback. We ran the counter trey. That is what we ran.

As a result, when we installed the pistol in 2005, we ran those same plays. We just moved the quarterback four yards back, and we kept the tailback constant. We ran the same offense. The difference was the fact we got the ball to the tailback faster in the pistol. That is what we ran, the same offense. On our bootleg play-action passes, there was no contest in comparison to when we were under the center with the quarterback. None. We won our conference with that offense that first year. We came out of nowhere to win the conference. We controlled the football for 33 minutes per game the first year we ran the pistol.

Again, you must remember we did not have any game film to look at. There was not opportunity for us to say, "Here is what we are doing." We had to make some tough decisions when we started that first season with the pistol offense. We did not look very pretty. Then, all of a sudden, we could see the connection with the quarterback and the running back, and the misdirection with all of the motions you can use with the pistol.

I am going to show you our base offense. Here is the most important thing to me: the group you cannot confuse is the offensive front. If you are going to be a championship team, you must not confuse the front linemen. You do not genius size with the front line. You need to have blocking schemes, whether it be two, three, or four that you can practice every single day in repetitions.

What we developed in our pistol offense was the fact that our zone-blocking scheme allowed us to use the same blocking in multiple plays. We take that same scheme into our read plays, our down plays. On the read plays, the tackle does make an adjustment on his block. On the down plays, we pull the guard. Otherwise, the plays are the same scheme for everyone else, every single time. On play-action passes, the majority of time we actually duplicate what we are doing on the running the down scheme. This was critical for me. The players we will move and change their assignment are the quarterback, motion man, and the running back. This is where the misdirection comes into play in our offensive schemes.

As we evolved from the power, or gap offense into what we do now, which we call the two-man game, we are talking about the read. It does not matter if we are in the hip alignment or in the pistol offense. We also have the three-man game, which is the triple option. We only run five triple options per game, maybe. We run the two-man-game every which way you can. That is using our quarterback as a threat.

I am going to show you what we do in our base offense. Again, this is what we teach in the first three days of spring football. If you could see us during those first three days, you could get a feel for what we are trying to accomplish.

The first thing we work on is the zone play. Let me hit you with this. We give our linemen targets to block against the defense. It is critical to our offensive linemen that they know on a 3 technique on the inside zone play, we want them to have a target. Other teams may use different numbering systems on the zone plays. We tell our linemen the target on a 3 technique is the armpit of that defender. Because of what we do in the pistol offense, we see so many defensive fronts moving now. It is critical for our linemen to understand the six inches out and six inches up on our zone, is at the inside armpit of the 3 technique. It is critical to our offense.

With the movement inside, we can take it and drive the defensive man straight back. With the

movement outside, we drive the defensive man outside. We are a chest blocking—oriented team. We come out of our stance, and we "throw the bone." We are one of the schools that still talk about knocking the defensive line off the ball. We can get so involved with our techniques and the great things we do on offense, which is wonderful, but if you are going to win a championship with the execution of your offense, it all starts with your front line.

We tell our football team the offensive front is the most important group on the field. They are number one. Offensive linemen get no attention, and no glory. We make a big deal out of the offensive line. We call them the "union." We started this in 1986. The linemen get a union hat, and a big union card. If they walk around our campus with their union card, everyone on campus knows what that union card stands for. They all know the linemen are tough sons of guns. The union hat is a hard hat, and they wear those during their film session. When our other players see our linemen wearing the union hat, they know they knocked the crap out of someone. It is neat to our players; it really is. Our line coaches are bulldogs. They really work those offensive linemen.

I am going to show you the inside zone play. It is nothing special, but I want you to see what we can do off this play. Our quarterback is four yards from the ball, and the tailback is three yards from the quarterback. If the back is faster, we can line him up at 3.5 yards. That is what we start with. Our line splits are at two feet, and the tight end can split up to one yard (Diagram #3). This is how they line up every single time. The guards line up off the center. This sets our helmet alignment. It determines the depth of their alignment, with the guards' helmets at the bottom of the numbers of the center.

This is the true pistol formation. This is the inside zone play and the concept we have off the play (Diagram #4). You can see our splits, and they will be consistent. This is the inside zone to the strongside.

You can see the action of the quarterback. He is booting to the outside. You can see the quarterback looking back. That is where we are going set up the bootleg play. We are looking for the naked bootleg all of the time. You will see how we bring in our slice

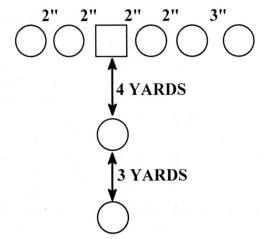

Diagram #3. Base Alignment

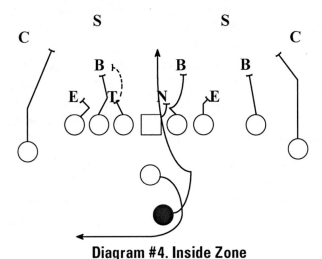

Diagram #4. Inside Zone

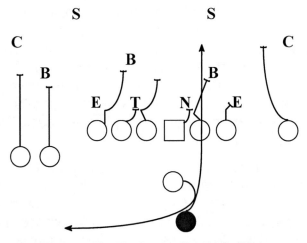

Diagram #5. Twins Left—Zone Right

to the inside of the leg of the guard. His second step will be directly parallel, perpendicular to the line of scrimmage. Then, he will read the defensive man in the gap. If it is a 3 technique or a 1 technique, we call it "hug it" on the 3 or 1 technique. He is expecting the play to go into the B gap.

We double the 1 technique. The center has the A gap, and the guard has the B gap responsibility. The back breaks the play back inside.

This is what is critical about the pistol offense. We tell the quarterback to get as deep as he can after he takes that snap. We want to hand the ball to the tailback as deep as we can to him and to let the tailback run to the opening. Our quarterback does not have a read. This is a zone play, and we are handing the ball to the tailback.

On the zone play, our players are blocking to the side of the call. It is all gaps blocking, wherever their target may be, to the side of the call. We are looking at the guy in the gap. The tailback is reading the first defensive down man to the playside. We are a real good weakside zone team.

When we run the zone to the strongside, the back is reading the 3 technique. Our center blocks off on the noseguard. The onside guard and tackle block the 3 technique and linebacker. The tailback reads the blocks and makes his cut off the blocks.

The question is: how big are our splits up front? That is a good question. We split two feet between the center and guard, and two feet between the guard and tackle. The tight end can split three feet.

When we ran the one-back offense, we split one yard all across the line. Trying to block back on a 3 technique was tough for us. When we went to the pistol, we made the splits inside at two feet. They do not have to be exactly at two feet, but we do not want then any tighter. This takes care of any seepage from tackle to tackle.

On the first day of practice, you can hear our offensive coaches telling the players, "No seepage, from tackle to tackle. We do not want anyone getting into the gaps." That is the philosophy of the offense. If the splits are bigger, this offense will not work. We want to coordinate the handoff with our front so the tailback can read the blocks. What we have found is when we have larger splits, we get a faster flow from the defense.

play into the sequence. Everyone in the Western United States has copied our slice play. This is our pure zone play (Diagram #5). We can run it from several different formations.

The aiming point for the deep back on our inside zone play is this: his first step is with his left foot

We run multiple formations. We are a team that runs unbalanced line, we run the wing-T, and we do it all. I am showing you the same play based from different formations. When you see the films, you may want to say the backside defensive end can make the play on the tailback by coming down the line very hard. You must remember we are a bootleg team. The defensive end is a real key for us. It helps us decide what we want to do on our read and zone plays.

Our whole offense starts with the inside zone play. Every scheme we have will come off those same actions with our tailback.

We use our slice play to help with the backside pressure. Slice means someone is going to come over to help with this pressure (Diagram #6). It can be a wide receiver, a wingback, or a double tight end. We are going to run a strongside zone play, and the man coming over is going to slice the defensive end. He is going to run the heel line of our offensive line and come inside the quarterback. His job is to slice or contain the end on the outside to prevent him from getting to the tailback on the zone play. Next, we go to our play-action passing game.

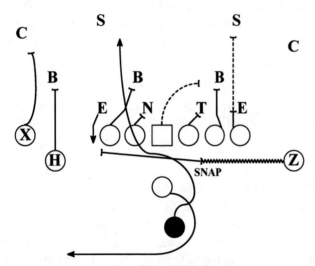

Diagram #6. Slice Play

When people come to see us in spring practice this is the play they adopt for their offense. If you are a two-back team, you can run the play with your second back. When we go into our deuce formation, we have the deep pistol back and another back set in the off alignment. The offset back will be the slicer. If we go into our quads formation, which means our tight end is off the ball, he will be the

slicer. We have different formations to block the end by using the slice technique to our play.

The action of the tailback and quarterback are exactly the same. When we tell our receivers they are going to block the defensive end, they know what we want. When we first told them we wanted them to block the end, they were scared they would get hurt. We tell the slice blocker all he has to do is to get a piece of the defensive end. Those ends weigh 250 to 260 pounds. Nevertheless, we do not need a tough, hard block on them. If the defensive end is coming uphill, we want to take him outside on the play. This sets up the boot pass.

Our wide receivers know they are expected to block the defensive ends. When we run the read play to the same side, the defensive end has two things to think about on the play. Our receivers are similar to other wide receivers, but they know we expect them to block on the defensive ends at times. As they get better, they take pride in blocking on the slice play.

We love the unbalanced set. A lot of teams study our unbalanced set. We run the regular slice with the wingback. It could be a tight end or a receiver. We may use our #2 tight end on the unbalanced line.

We tell our quarterback on the snap the ball is going to his third hand, which is his stomach. We do not want to confuse them with a lot of different steps and a lot of directions. We tell him to step back as deep as he can. We do not want to tell them to take a step at 45 degrees. When you tell them to take a 45-degree step, they open their shoulders, by stretching the play, so they can get depth. We do not tell them to step out.

The quarterback knows the aiming point of the tailback, which is the inside leg of the guard. If the quarterback steps out, he is not going to be able to make the handoff to the tailback. We tell the quarterback if he steps outside, he is not going to get the ball to the back, and secondly, if he does get the ball to the tailback, it is going to force him to go wide.

On our slice play, we have the ball snapped when the motion man is between the guard and tackle. Our quarterback hands the ball to the tailback as deep as possible. We want the defensive end guessing who is going to block him on the play. If the defensive end comes upfield, the slice blocker turns it up inside and looks for the next defender.

Once the zone scheme is in our offense, and it can be the slice or a base zone play, we block it that way on our two-man game and the three-man game. We run these plays from different formations. This will set up the pop pass. We will run the play the same way, and if the quarterback sees there is no rotation by the defense on the motion man going behind the tailback, he can throw the motion man a pass outside. Everyone else is running the slice play, the running play.

All this is for us is another way we can run a wing play. I am trying to illustrate to you the beauty of the offense. It gives us a combination of different slice plays, and we have other plays to run off the play as well including the passing game.

Again, I want to stress the importance on our blocking up front. It is not man-to-man blocking. It is gap blocking, and there is no seepage. From tackle to tackle, we do not want any penetration up front. That is what we tell our linemen. If we get seepage, then we are not running the play correctly.

On the slice play, we run the bootleg pass. We run the slice play, and the tailback runs his same path, and the quarterback bootlegs outside. We have a different array of pass routes we can run on the bootleg action. We run three routes on the bootleg action. We run a corner, comeback, and a drag route off the bootleg action. We put in this offense on the first day of practice.

The zone bluff play is the two-man read play (Diagram #7). This is what we have evolved to after the 2005 season. We added this play to help on the zone play. We run the zone play as well as anyone does in the country. Our zone play averaged 6.0 yards per carry last season. We run it out of every formation you can conceive in terms of having a slicer, or having a back coming back in motion. The bluff play or the two-man game is exactly that.

Most teams that run the read play run it from the hip alignment. You can only run the read play to one side if you are in the hip alignment. From the pistol, we can run the read to both sides. We block the read the same as we do on the zone play. We block everything the same except the defensive

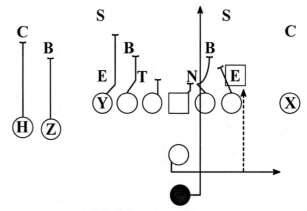

Diagram #7. Zone Bluff Play

end. We let him go completely free now. He is our read man on the two-man game.

The aiming point on the play to the far side would be this: The first step with the right foot is toward the inside leg of the onside guard so the play looks like the zone play. On the second step, with his left foot, would come back on the outside leg of the center. He is on the outside hip of the center when we run the two-man game.

If we are running the read to the right side, he lines up the same as he does on all plays with his toes to his instep just as he does when he is under the center for a snap. The final aiming point for the tailback is at the outside leg of the center to the playside. The back steps to the inside leg of the guard, just as he did on the zone play. On the second step, he is coming back to the outside leg of the center. The quarterback knows this. The quarterback takes the snap, and this is what we tell him. We want him to open up and to pivot. We do not want his shoulders at 90 degrees. They are not at 45 degrees. We want his left shoulder pointing toward the outside shoulder of the widest man on the line of scrimmage. It is that simple.

We do not talk about degrees. We do not run downhill as the quarterback does on the speed option (Diagram #8). We are going parallel to the line. Then we want the quarterback to take off running to the outside. He takes off parallel to the line and then make a decision where to take it upfield. We have a slice blocker coming to the alley to block for him.

We also run the arc block on the play. We want the blocker to arc block to the second level. We run our zone, slice, and bluff plays with different

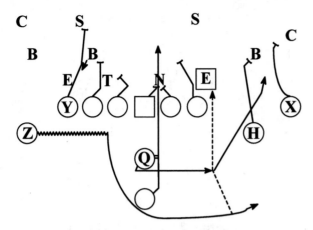

Diagram #8. Two-Man Read

motions, and from the unbalanced look. On the arc play, everyone blocks the same as they block on the zone play. We have the wide receiver or tight end arc block on the first man to show outside the end man on the line of scrimmage. That end man on the line is our read on the play. You may ask why the defensive end would come down inside on the play. The reason he does that is because he is trying to stop the zone play. That is one reason we call the option with the arc block. When we tie the zone play in with the read play, we still like to run the slice plays. The blocking is consistent for the front line. That is a key for us.

On the two-man game or the read, everyone is blocking down, or blocking back. If the defensive end comes down on the clavicle of the offensive tackle, he will wash him, and lock up with him hard and not let him go. The quarterback reads the play and hands the ball to the tailback.

On the two-man game, we ride the tailback and read the defensive end. The two outside receivers block the safety and corner on the play. The man we bring in motion is the man that blocks the alley. Alley means the offensive man blocks the first defender to show in that area. We are still reading the defensive end. If he comes upfield, we hand the ball to the tailback. If he stays on the line, we run the read play. We do not tell our wide receivers they have one or two to block. We tell them to block the cover defenders. The first man to show up, they block them.

On these plays I am talking about, we do not motion across the face of the quarterback. We talked about snapping the ball before the motion man reaches the quarterback on the slice play.

On the read plays, we have the motion man doing the back motion, or deep motion for the pitch on the play. Again, everything is the same for the front line. The difference is, on this particular play, the quarterback is reading the defensive end. We option off the defensive end. The line is blocking the same as they do on zone, slice, and the other plays.

Our practices on Tuesday and Wednesday are two hours and 20 minutes. Out of that time our thunder game, which is our run game, we have a thunder game period for 20 minutes, and we have a 10-minute inside thunder period. Our linemen are blocking the same for all of this time on the zone play except for a few down blocks. We do not have power or gap plays. They block it the same on the zone plays for about 30 minutes on those two days.

When the line and receivers are doing their stretching drills, we have the quarterbacks taking snaps. We have them working on their footwork during this time as well. We never allow the quarterback to do any drill without catching the snap of the football.

I am always concerned about time and distance, meaning this: how much time per week are we going to need to spend on this to get it done? Then on game day, what is the distance we can get out of the time we spend on something in practice? If you add a new play, you are going to have to spend seven minutes a day to perfect that play. We would spend four days working on a new play. So if we worked on the new play for four days, at seven minutes a day we would have 28 minutes invested in that new play. We would expect some distance out of that play. It makes you think when you start talking about adding new plays. We are a rep team. We are going to rep, rep, and rep. We want to be able to block anything the defense throws at us when we are on offense.

Since running the pistol, we have seen about every defense invented. We see it all with our schedule. Remember what I said about our blocking. From the inside of one tight end to the inside of the inside end on the other side, no one on defense penetrates. That is how we sell this to our front.

Look at our alignment. The front line is sticking a blow. They are not just pushing with their hands. They work their way up the field, and then they get their arms extended.

Our quarterback and tailback tandem of Colin Kaepernick and Vei Taua broke the NCAA rushing record for the two-man record of touchdowns and yardage of Eric Dickerson and Craig James of SMU. We were the only team in the history of the NCAA to have three backs rush for 1,000 yards in the same season. That was a year ago. This year, we had the two-man record for yards and touchdowns. We do run the football. We threw the ball for almost 3,100 yards this past year as well. We love to throw the ball and expect to throw it more next year.

Off the running offense, we have the play-action pass. The man running the motion continues out on the bubble, and we run curl and stop routes to the inside of the bubble. We are a no-huddle offense. All of our plays are by signals and words.

In the first three days of practice, you will not see our triple option. You will see the two-man game with the alley block. We do run a play-action pass that looks similar to our zone play. Remember between the arc actions and the motions and the slice plays is where all of this comes into play. I want to get your imagination working. Look at the different plays you can run with the different formation. We do use the bunch formation as well. The thing I like about the pistol is the fact you can run most of the offense you are using now in our offense. We want our backs to run the football. They are not fast, but they are tough, and they are north-south runners.

We do run the pocket pass as well. We can run the pocket pass from the two-man game and the slice game. We do not cut on the pocket pass. We stay up and block. Pocket pass means to our front line that the quarterback is going to set up usually, on the outside leg of our guard, depending if it is an even or odd side call. We see the defense on the outside so much; we bring them inside with the pocket pass. We do see a lot of seven-man fronts. We can run this off the bluff action as well.

I have been a little long, but I have enjoyed it. If you have any questions let me know. Thank you.

ZONE PRESSURE DEFENSIVE SCHEME

University of Louisville

Part of what we do is based on the coaches around us. Anytime you can come to a clinic and better yourself, that is what you want to do. The things we are going to talk about today are things we believe in. There are many ways to do them and they are all the right way. I hope I can give you something that will help you better yourself and give you something you can take back to your team. If you do, it will give you a good opportunity to be successful on the field.

UNIVERSITY OF LOUISVILLE DEFENSIVE STATISTIC COMPARISON

Category	2010	2009
Total defense	311.7	371.1
Points per game	19.4	26.2
Third down percentage	34%	40%
Sacks	39	23
Tackles for loss	86	69

#12 total defense in the country
#9 pass defense in the country
#15 scoring defense in the country

I want to show you the difference between the 2009 and 2010 seasons for our team. The difference in the total defense is better by 60 yards, but the points per game is the most important statistic. The rest of the chart is good clinic material and looks good. However, if we can average giving up only 19.4 points a game, we have a chance to win. The defense gave the offense a chance to win because our defense kept the games close.

Our third down percentage was better and we got off the field more times this past season. That is not what we wanted to achieve, but it was an improvement from the year before. Our sack totals were up by 16 sacks. The tackles for loss really

jumped from the previous year. You can see our national ranking for total defense, pass defense, and scoring defense was something we wanted to see. Those stats mean you have a chance to win.

That improvement was not because we have great coaching. We got the players to believe in what we were doing. If you look at our first game against the University of Kentucky, we were not very good. Coach Strong and I were talking as the game went on. It was 14-0 after three plays of defense. We thought it was going to be a long year and that was how we felt. As the players bought into what we were doing, we got better.

We could not play base defense and not move around. We had to turn the dogs loose. When you pressure the way we did, you will give up big plays. We gave up some big plays but as the season went on, we cut the number of big plays down. That gave us a chance to be successful.

BLITZES

- We want to cause confusion in the offense's blocking schemes.
  - ✓ What is the offense doing?
  - ✓ Does the tight end free release? Where is the center blocking? Where is the back blocking (tight end or splitside)?
- Does the offense sight adjust in the passing game? Bring two or three from one side.
- Versus the run—create an eight-man front. Zone blitzes are another form of man free defense.
- Create mismatches—defensive line and backers in a 1-on-1 situation.

We are a pressure team. We pressure for a number of reasons. The first thing pressure does is to cause confusion with the offensive line. We want to give the offensive line different looks and bring different players from those looks. We do not want a defensive lineman getting double-teamed the entire game. In college football, a double-team block is 600 pounds of bodies. If the defensive lineman faces that for the entire game, he has no chance to play well. That is bad coaching if you allow that to happen. You cannot do that to your players. We will not sit there and let that happen. We move the defensive linemen a lot in our scheme to avoid those types of situations.

To pressure, you have to know what the offense is doing. We must know if they are trying to run the ball or throw it. If they throw the football, we want to know which way they turn the center in the pass protection scheme. We need to know where the running back is blocking. Is he blocking toward the tight end side or the splitside of the formation?

We have to know what the offensive line is doing. We need to know who the strong blockers are. Sometimes, we want to take advantage of a 1-on-1 match-up with the offensive linemen.

In the passing game, we must know if the receivers and quarterback are sight adjusting what they read in the secondary. We want to know if they throw quickly from a certain defensive look. If they do, we want to take those things away from them.

Our players must understand pressure is not just to stop the passing game. When we use zone pressure, we create an eight-man front. We design the pressure to stop the rush as well as to pressure the quarterback. The pressure game is a different way of playing an eight-man front. When we pressure, we want to create mismatches in personnel. We want our defensive line and linebackers to get into a 1-on-1 or 1-on-none situation. We have to do a better job of recruiting the types of players that can win in a 1-on-1 situation.

We try to get our best defensive player on the offensive line's worst player. If you can do that, it will win many games for you. To win on defense, these are the things we have to do.

We play a lot of field defense at the University of Louisville. On defense, you have to align your players correctly. Early in the year, we struggled with that. We try to match up with the offense. Early in the year, we had a hard time doing that. We

went to a field concept that helped our players. The field end, nose, and boundary defensive tackle aligned in the same alignments regardless of formation. The field end aligned in a 5 technique on the outside shoulder of the offensive tackle. The nose aligned in a shade to the fieldside of the formation, and the boundary tackle aligned in a 3 technique on the offensive guard.

Against the pro set into the field, the Sam linebacker dropped into a 9 technique on the tight end (Diagram #1). The Fox linebacker aligned in a 5 technique on the outside shoulder of the boundary side offensive tackle. The Mike linebacker plays a 40 technique head-up the offensive tackle five yards off the ball. The Will linebacker aligns in a 30 technique on the outside shoulder of the boundary side guard five yards off the ball. We play the strong safety into the field and the free safety into the boundary. We also have a field and boundary corner in our alignment.

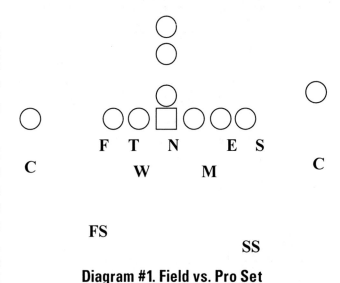

Diagram #1. Field vs. Pro Set

If the offensive set puts the tight end into the boundary, the alignment for the defensive end, nose, and tackle does not change (Diagram #2). They aligned in a 5 technique and shade technique to the field and a 3 technique into the boundary. The Sam linebacker stacks behind the 5-technique end and the Fox linebacker moves out to a 9 technique on the tight end into the boundary. The Mike and Will linebackers adjust into their 40 and 30 techniques. The strong safety aligns to the openside of the set and the free safety aligns to the boundary. The corners apply their field and boundary positions.

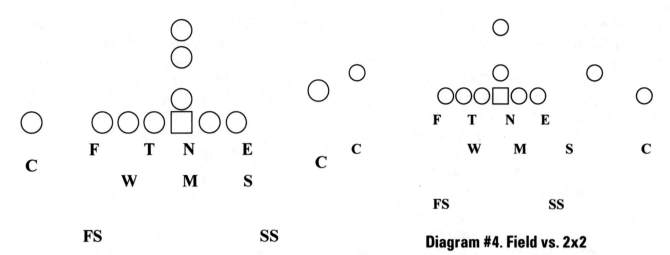

Diagram #2. Field vs. Open Set

If there is a twins set into the field, the adjustments are similar (Diagram #3). Nothing changes for the end, nose, and tackle. The end and nose play their techniques into the field, and the tackle plays his boundary technique over the offensive guard. Since the Sam linebacker has no tight end and has a second receiver to his side, he widens his alignment. Instead of stacking behind the defensive end, he widens into a walkaway position on the slot receiver. The safeties align in their field and boundary positions. The boundary corner has no wide receiver and moves down to one yard outside the tight end. His depth from the tight end will vary from one to five yards depending on the situation.

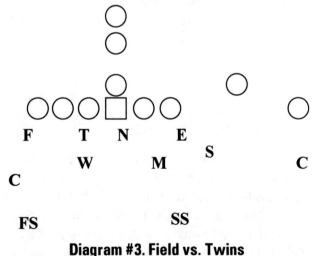

Diagram #3. Field vs. Twins

If the formation is a 2x2 formation with the tight end into the boundary, the alignment is similar to the pro set with the tight end into the boundary (Diagram #4). The alignment for the end, nose, and tackle are the same. The Fox linebacker plays a

Diagram #4. Field vs. 2x2

9 technique on the boundary side tight end. The Sam linebacker plays the walkaway alignment on the slot to the two-receiver side. The secondary aligns using their rules.

In all the defensive adjustments, the Mike and Will linebackers align according to the field and boundary positions of the defense. This allowed our defense to align properly and we started to eliminate mistakes in the defense. Too many times coaches overcoach and try to see how smart they are. They want to match up personnel and confuse their players. I am not that smart of a football coach. All I want to do is get my players aligned correctly without confusing them.

You have to play with the players you have. If they cannot do what you ask, what are you going to do? You have to help the players and make it simple for them. The players we have are the players we have to play. If they cannot do something, find something they can do. Get your players aligned and let them play hard and fast. Simplify your scheme and give them a chance to be successful.

I am not the sharpest tool in the toolshed; however, I know I must get the players aligned to have a chance to play defense. We have many smart young coaches on our coaching staff. They constantly ask me about adding something. My answer is the same every time they ask. If you want to add something, what do you want to take out of the scheme? You cannot continually add to the scheme and not subtract anything. If you do, your package gets too large and we get confused. That does not help your players play fast and hard. *Keep it simple.*

The blitz I want to show you is field Steeler three fire. It is a universal field stunt (Diagram #5). On this blitz, we bring the Sam and Mike linebackers. It is a five-man pressure scheme, with the Fox linebacker dropping into coverage. We play a basic man-to-man scheme in the secondary and with the linebackers. The defensive line slants away from the fieldside into the boundary. The defensive end aligns in a 5 technique into the field and long sticks to the inside A gap.

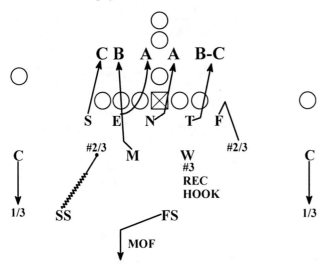

Diagram #5. Field Steeler Three Fire

Position	Alignment	Key	Run To
Fox	W-5 SE 6 to TE	OT ball	Block scheme
Field end	5 to field	OT ball	Long stick
3 tech	3 to BS contain	OG ball	Rip B to C gap
Nose	1 to field	OC ball	Rip BS A gap
Sam	9 tech	TE ball	Contain
Mike	40	Ball	Blitz B spill F-Ball
Will	30	Flow of backs	B gap

The defensive end plays across all blocks as he moves to the inside. The nose rips across the center into the boundary side A gap. The boundary tackle rips across the offensive tackle into a 5-technique alignment and has containment on a dropback pass. He has chase containment from the backside, checks for the bootleg, and plays any reverse coming to him.

Position	Run Away	Pass	Run Away
Fox	Fold to ball	#2 to boundary	#2 displaced hook play run first
Field end	Veer to A gap	Veer A rush across G	Cross all blocks
3 tech	Chase contain, boot, reverse	Contain B to C	Pursue
Nose	Secure BS A gap	Secure BS A gap	Cross all blocks
Sam	Same as 3 tech	Rush contain	Pursue
Mike	Blitz B gap	Blitz B gap	Pursue
Will	Fast flow	Find #3	Pursue

The Sam linebacker with a tight end plays a 9 technique on the tight end. He is run containment and is the chase defender if the ball goes away. He comes hard off the outside on a dropback pass. The Mike linebacker blitzes the B gap. If the play is a run to him, he spills the ball to the outside. If it is a pass, he attacks the quarterback. The Will linebacker plays the #3 receiver. If there is no #3 receiver, he drops to the hook.

If the play goes away from the Mike linebacker on a run, he does not run through the B gap. He redirects his charge and flows with the play. However, he has to make sure the play is going away and not a counter or misdirection type of play.

The Fox linebacker drops and plays the #2 receiver to the #3 receiver. If there are two receivers to his side, he plays the #2 receiver, which is the slot or second receiver from the sideline. If there is a #3 receiver in the backfield or a triple formation, he could end up taking him. He plays from the #2 receiver to the #3 receiver.

To the fieldside of the formation, the strong safety has the same type of coverage. He plays the #2 receiver to the #3 receiver to his side. The corners play the deep outside thirds, and the free safety is the middle-of-the-field deep player. If we match in man coverage, the corners match the #1 receivers and the free safety is free.

When we play man coverage, the coverage to the boundary side is like 3-on-3 basketball.

The safety, Will linebacker, and Fox linebacker play 3-on-3 with the #2 and #3 receivers. The Fox and Will linebackers play the #2 and #3 receivers with in-and-out coverage. The safety is free in the middle. The Fox linebacker aligns on the #2 receiver but he sees the #3 receiver. If #2 runs a curl pattern and #3 runs to the flat, the Fox linebacker takes the #3 receiver.

The Will linebacker reads the #3 receiver but looks for the #2 receiver coming in. If the #3 receiver runs to the flat, the Will linebacker runs to the #2 receiver coming inside on the curl.

This is a universal blitz where the defensive line angles to the boundary and the Mike linebacker runs the Steeler stunt to the fieldside. We ran this blitz 50 times this year. I was surprised how well this blitz worked for us this year.

We run another blitz off the same look (Diagram #6). Everyone on the blitz does the same thing except for three players. We call this "field smash three fire." The field defensive end, instead of spiking to the A gap, fires up the field. The Sam linebacker folds inside into the B gap and the Mike linebacker fires the A gap.

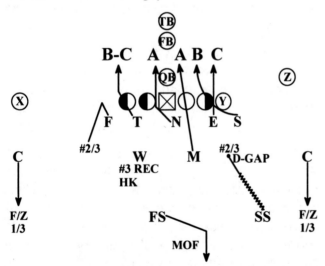

Diagram #6. Field Smash Three Fire

Everyone else on this blitz does the same thing he did on the Steeler. We made a minor change to the blitz but it looks vastly different to the offensive line. It is simple to make that adjustment. Sometimes as coaches, we want to tell our players that A squared plus B squared equals C squared, when all we have to say is one plus one equals two.

Position	Alignment	Key	Run To
Fox	5 SE 6 TE	OT ball	Blocking scheme to ball
Field end	5 tech to field	OT ball	Contain
3 tech	3 tech to boundary	OG ball	Rip B to C gap
Nose	1 tech to field	OC ball	Rip BS A gap
Sam	9 tech	TE ball	Long stick
Mike	40 tech	Ball	Blitz A gap spill FB
Will	30 tech	Flow	B gap

Position	Run Away	Pass	Run Away
Fox	Fold to ball	#2 to boundary	#2 displace hook
Field end	Chase contain, boot, reverse	Rush contain	Pursue
3 tech	Same as field end	Contain B to C gap	Pursue
Nose	Secure boundary A gap	Secure boundary A gap	Cross all blocks
Sam	Veer B	Veer B Rush across OT	Cross all Blocks
Mike	Blitz A gap	Blitz A gap	Pursue
Will	Fast flow	Find #3	Pursue

That is first grade math, which gives us a chance. In college, we have to adjust to the players we recruit. That is all football is. It is being simple so players can understand.

My dad was a high school coach. He is 78, and I am 52 years old. He has been coaching longer than I have been born. I learned from him. I am from the state of Texas and I live by a simple rule: KISS. That means *keep it simple stupid*. We have to bring ourselves down to the level of our players and coach them up. That way, we can get the best out of them and have a chance to be successful. That is the only thing that matters in football. At the end of the day, the only thing that matters is whether you win or lose. You want your players to play 60 minutes with extreme effort. If they did not do that, you need to look at yourself. That is coaching.

If you need me to slow down, let me know. This meeting is not about me. It is about you learning something. While you are here, let us get something done. Otherwise, you have no reason to be here. The two blitzes I showed you let us teach the same things repeatedly. That builds repetitions into what we do. The Steeler and smash blitzes are the same techniques for everyone except three players. The other eight players are doing the same thing on both blitzes. That gives them a chance to improve.

The next blitz, which was good to us, was field Bronco (Diagram #7). The *B* in Bronco stands for backer. The blitz is a smash blitz by the Mike and Will linebackers. The defensive end charges up the field as he did on the smash blitz. The Mike linebacker blows the A gap as he did on the smash blitz. The Will linebacker blows the fieldside B gap instead of the Sam linebacker.

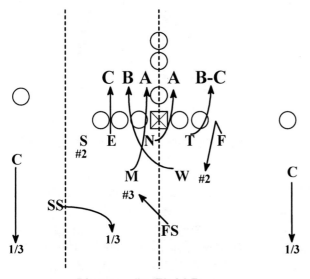

Diagram #7. Field Bronco

The Mike linebacker is the penetrator on this blitz. He adjusts his alignment from a 40 to a 30 alignment on the offensive guard. The Will linebacker loops from the backside of the blitz to the frontside and fires the B gap. With every blitz we run, we always talk about being gap *sound*. Everyone has a gap, a run fit, and a responsibility on every blitz. It does not matter what the offense does, we have to be gap sound. The nose has to get across the center into the backside A gap. He cannot let the center block him. The tackle has to get into the C gap and contain the quarterback if he is bootlegging the ball. When we zone pressure, we blitz into an eight-man front.

Position	Alignment	Key	Run To
Fox	Loose 5	OT	Force fold
Field end	5 field	OT	C gap
3 tech	3 tech	OG ball	Rip B to C gap
Nose	1 tech field	OC ball	Rip to bench A
Sam	On #2 to field	#2 to field ball	#2 force
Mike	30 to field	Ball	Blitz field A cross all blocks
Will	30 to bench	Ball	Blitz field B cross all blocks

Position	Run Away	Pass	Run Away
Fox	Fold	Match #2 to bench	Hook vs. 1 back 2 back displace
Field end	Chase contain	Contain	Never let ball outside
3 tech	Rip B to C chase contain	Contain	
Nose	Rip to bench A	Rip to bench A	
Sam	#2 fold	Match #2 to field	
Mike	Same as run to	Same	
Will	Same as run to	Same	

If the offense gives us a one-back triple set, the strong safety adjusts to the tripleside of the formation (Diagram #8). The droppers are the only ones affected by this formation. The strong safety comes to the three-receiver side and the Sam linebacker falls back inside. He plays over the tight end and the safety aligns on the slot receiver. This keeps everything simple.

The experts picked us to win three games. We won seven games because the players bought into what we were doing. The one thing we told them was to be aggressive. If the offense hit a big play,

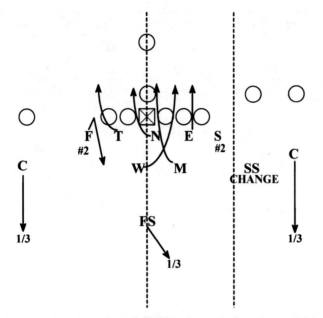

Diagram #8. Field Bronco vs. Triple

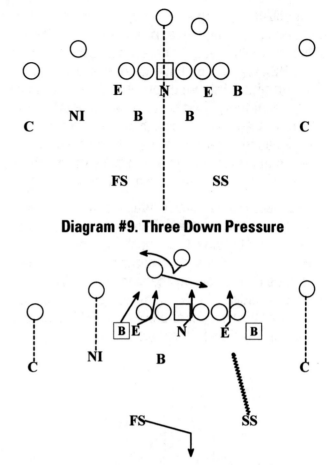

Diagram #9. Three Down Pressure

Diagram #10. Three Down vs. Zone Play

life goes on and I did a bad job of coaching. During the course of the game, it is never the players' fault. They did a good job and I did a bad job of coaching. However, on Sunday, they may get their butts torn up. I will tell them the way it is. If they want to call mommy and go home, I can deal with that too.

Off the same look is one of our major packages. We call it "three down pressure" (Diagram #9). If we play against the spread package with a 2x2 tight end formation, the defense is balanced. We get into an odd look with the nose head-up the center. If you cut the defense down the middle, we have five and a half players on each side of the ball. The nose aligned in the 0 technique counts as half a player to each side. From this look, we can run the blitzes I just showed you with almost the same calls. The three down linemen are two 4-technique defensive ends and a 0 technique by the nose. We have three linebackers and a nickel back in the game. One linebacker plays a 9 technique on the tight end. If there is no tight end in the game, he plays a 5 technique on the fieldside offensive tackle.

In the secondary, we always show a cover 2 look but one of the secondary players rolls down somewhere within the defense. We see many spread offenses. One thing the spread coaches do not like to see is the 3-4 look. What we make from this front against a one-back set is a 3-4 look.

In this look, we want to get an overhang on each side. We do that with our linebackers (Diagram #10).

With the quarterback in the shotgun and one back, this allows us to get an extra hitter to the side of the back. The three down linemen angle away from the back. People that run the zone read play, run it right into the direction of our angle. The overhang player to the back can play the dive back on the zone or the quarterback on the keep. We use the scouting report to keep people guessing as to what he does.

If there is a tight end in the game as there is in the diagram, the strong safety rolls down to take the place of the displaced linebacker. We want to get the safety down as much as we can. We want to get as many players around the box as we possibly can.

When you play against college teams, there may be one good receiver in the game. We played 13 games and played four teams with a quarterback who could throw the ball from the boundary hash mark outside the hash mark to the wideside of the field. We do not think the quarterback can take advantage of a corner playing the wide receiver with an outside alignment. They will tell you they can throw the slant on the corner all day long. I found out the quarterbacks have trouble throwing the slant consistently.

I coached six years in the NFL and the quarterbacks at that level can beat you all over the field. When I came back to college football, it took me three games to realize that most quarterbacks cannot make that throw. When I coach the corner in our man coverage, I coach him to get inside the receiver once he gets four yards outside the hash mark. The quarterback cannot throw the ball that far on an out breaking pattern. We feel the quarterbacks we play against cannot make that throw. We want to gang up on the running game and dare the quarterback to make the throws.

When we go to the three down package, we align the defensive ends head-up the offensive tackle. He has a three-way go on the tackle. He can come straight ahead, inside, or outside. When the offensive tackle starts to guess where the defender is going, he becomes less aggressive. We move our defensive linemen a lot.

I learned a simple way to teach zone pressure from the Pittsburgh Steelers. I feel they are the best in the NFL as far as zone pressure. We teach our three down linemen in angle patterns (Diagram #11). The angle patterns go back to the old slant and angle defenses. We simply slant the three down linemen right or left. In the diagram, they slant left. We call that a "Liz" stunt because they are going left. The left defensive end comes straight up the field. The nose slants into the left A gap and the right defensive end long sticks into the right A gap. The overhang linebacker to that side comes up the field and the inside linebacker blows the C gap behind the slant of the defensive end.

We make our calls on the single back in the backfield. We want the linebacker to pressure the back. We bring line pressure away from the back. To the side of the back, we have two linebackers coming. If the quarterback gives the ball to the back, he runs into the slant of the defensive line. If the quarterback keeps the ball, we have someone in his face immediately. This is a simple scheme.

Another slant pattern involves the nickel coming off the edge (Diagram #12). In the diagram, the offensive back sets to the openside of the

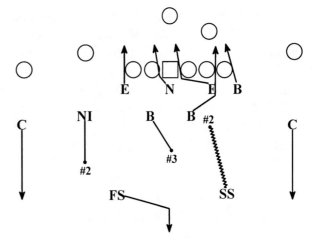

Diagram #11. Three Down Angle

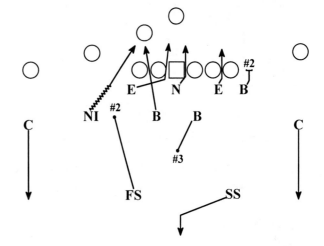

Diagram #12. Three Down Slant Nickel

formation. We slant the defensive line to the right and bring the nickel back off the edge. The left defensive end long sticks into the A gap and the linebacker to that side fires the B gap. We have the same pattern. We have the line slanting to the zone play and two defenders in the quarterback's face.

In the first diagram, the free safety goes to the deep middle with the safety coming down to replace the linebacker. In the second diagram, the free safety rolls up and plays the nickel back's responsibility and the strong safety rolls to the middle of the field. The pass coverage played underneath relates to the #2 and #3 receivers. The inside linebacker not involved in the stunt plays the #3 receiver. One of the overhang linebackers plays the #2 receiver and either the free safety or strong safety plays the #2 receiver to the other side. Both of these blitzes come off the slant pattern for the defensive line.

The next pattern we run is the long stick pattern (Diagram #13). Both of the 4-technique defensive ends long stick into the A gaps. The nose goes opposite the call made by the linebackers. If the linebacker calls right, the nose goes left around the charge of the defensive end coming on the long stick. The linebacker blitzes the right C gap. The right outside linebacker comes up the field.

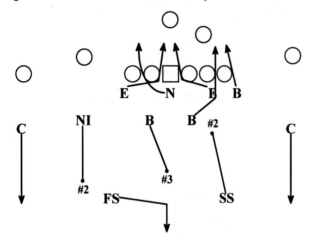

Diagram #13. Long Stick Pattern

One week we may run the slant pattern and the next week run the long stick pattern. However, in both defensive line patterns, the linebacker pressure is to the side of the single back in the backfield. There are different ways of teaching those patterns. You need to find the simplest way to teach it and let your players play. If you get your players going fast, you can implement a defense that they can play.

The jet pattern gets the defensive ends in an outside charge coming up the field hard from their 4-technique alignment (Diagram #14). The nose slants into the A gap, away from the linebacker's call. The linebackers run through the A gap and B gap to the side of the call. The frontside linebacker goes through the A gap and the backside linebacker goes through the B gap. This is similar to the Bronco blitz.

We put this next pattern in and ran it 10 times in a game. It worked 9 out of the 10 times we ran it. It should have worked 10 out of 10 but the defender missed the tackle. The defense gave up a 35-yard run on that play.

This is a good blitz for us. The Sam and Mike linebackers went inside on the smash blitz. We call this the "joker package" (Diagram #15). We call

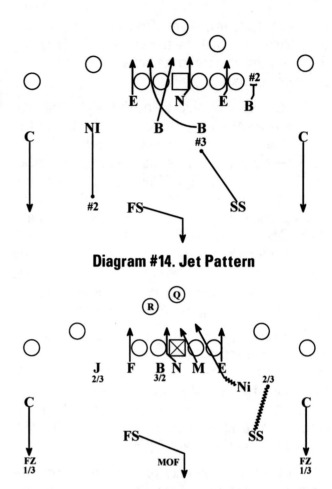

Diagram #14. Jet Pattern

Diagram #15. Joker Field Texas Three Fire

this blitz "joker field Texas three fire." We have different personnel on the field. We play with a nickel back and the joker instead of linebackers. The joker is a boundary side linebacker playing like a nickel back. We play with the Fox linebacker as a defensive end. He aligns to the boundary side in a loose 5 technique on the offensive tackle. The field end aligns to the field in a 5 technique. The nose aligns head-up the center and slants into the boundary A gap.

This is the same blitz as the smash blitz. The difference is instead of a Sam linebacker running the blitz, the nickel back runs the blitz. The field end goes up the field and the nickel back comes under him into the B gap. In this package, we change the name of the Will linebackers. The Will linebacker becomes the Buck linebacker. The linebackers align pressing the line of scrimmage with the Buck in a 2i technique and the Mike in a 3 technique. The Mike on this blitz blows the A gap to his side. We play with three down linemen, three linebackers, and five defensive backs.

Position	Alignment	Key	Run Responsibility
Field end	5 tech	OT ball	C gap
Fox	Loose 5	OT ball	C gap
Nose	0 tech	CTR	Boundary A gap
Joker	Split the difference	End man	Run to D-gap run away fast flow
Mike	3 tech	OG	Blitz A
Buck	2i tech	OG	Run to B run away fold
Nickel	Split the difference	OT	Blitz B gap

Position	Pass	Notes
Field end	Contain rush	
Fox	Contain rush	
Nose	Boundary A	
Joker	#2/#3 dropper	Disguise alignment
Mike	Blitz A gap	Disguise alignment
Buck	#3 dropper	Disguise alignment
Nickel	Blitz B gap	Disguise alignment

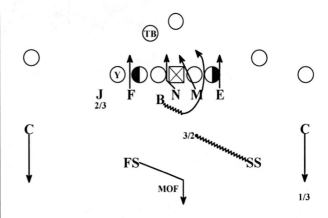

Diagram #16. Joker Bronco Three Hole

and Buck linebacker alignments are the same in the joker package. The Buck linebacker is a 3 technique to the boundary and the Mike linebacker aligns in a 2i technique to the field. The defensive line runs a jet pattern up the field with the nose in the boundary side A gap.

The Mike linebacker blitzes the field A gap and the Buck linebacker fires the field B gap. The call of the Bronco blitz is the same but the look is different to the offense. This defense is a 3-4 look as opposed to a 4-3 look. It is all about confusing the offensive linemen.

I worked at the University of Florida under Urban Meyer and he loved to see a 4-3 defense. The reason was he knew where the 3 technique and the 1 technique were on every play. He won two national championships in five years. However, he did not like to see 3-4 defenses.

The one thing all these packages have in common is we are aggressive all the time. We want to turn the defender loose and get after the ball. In these defenses, we move and penetrate. We want to cause havoc in the backfield. That is why we improved defensively this year.

Are there any questions? If there is anything I can do to help you or your staff, make sure to let us know. Thank you for your attention and time. It has been a pleasure being here.

When we teach this package, the teaching is the same as the base defense for our players. That keeps it simple for the defensive linemen and linebackers. We roll the secondary down to the blitz side. The strong safety rolls down and covers for the nickel back on the blitz.

We have a field Bronco from our base defense. We also have a joker Bronco (Diagram #16). The alignment is the joker alignment. The Fox linebacker plays a loose 5 technique to the boundary, and the field end plays a 5 technique into the field. The Mike

ELITE FIGHTING FORCE: THE SPECIAL TEAMS

The University of Tulsa

Thank you very much for that kind introduction. I played quarterback back in the day at The University of Tulsa. That puts things in perspective if you understand the era and time when I played at Tulsa. I tell my players about the difference between players today and back when I played. When I showed up at The University of Tulsa, I was one of 11 quarterbacks. I remember calling home at 10:00 at night to get the cheap rates. There were no cell phones. I told my Dad I was number 11 on the depth chart. They thought that was a good number. I played back in an era where you could not redshirt as a freshman.

We had a freshman team and I spent the first year playing freshman football. My second year was my redshirt year. We had enough quarterbacks so that each defensive assistant had his own quarterback to work in his drill work. I was the scout team quarterback for the linebackers for two years. I learned more about playing linebacker in all the individual drills than I did about playing quarterback.

I want to talk about special teams today. It is ironic to my friends because I was not a special teams player. I was a quarterback and I never held for extra points or anything like that. All the years I coached in high school, I was so offense driven and passionate about the offense, I did everything I could to stay away from coaching the special teams. I did not like kickers and wanted nothing to do with that part of the game. I thought it was God's revenge on me because I ended up having to coach them for three years.

From my experiences in high school, I knew how all the great coaches broke down offenses and defenses. For some reason, most of those coaches depended on schemes for special teams. Coaches always went to clinics and talked about how important the kicking game was. For three

years I got the opportunity to be special teams coordinator. I really did not know what to do. I started talking to friends and other coaches in the NFL and college about how to organize this part of the game.

I am a believer that the way you do anything is the way you do everything. If someone gives me a responsibility, it is important to me to do the best job I can. I am no different from most coaches in this room. When I got the job, I put my head down and went to work.

The first thing I figured out was our ability to get the right personnel on the field. There are several different philosophies for special teams. You can play your starters or play substitutes, but it all starts with getting the right players on the field. The big thing about coaching special teams is you have to inspire. I had to convince the coaches that special teams was not something that we just did. We came up with a name and we called it the "Elite Fighting Force." I do not mean this next statement as any disrespect to any of our Special Forces units. I know that in no way, shape, or form does what we do compare to anything the SEALs, Rangers, or Green Berets do. However, we wanted to model after and adapt some of the principles that those groups teach.

The first slide I use is about statistics. I do not like to use statistics, but this justifies what we did with our teams. I want to tell you about our national ranking in the five areas the NCAA ranks. We finished first in punt return defense. That means we covered punts well. We gave up 1.53 yards per return through 13 games. We finished ninth in net punt return and tenth in kickoff returns coverage. We finished 21st in punt return. The worst thing we did was kickoff return, which we finished 48th in the country. We felt those were good statistics for 120 teams in the Division I category.

The reason we do these statistics is to find out where we are and where we need to be. At this time every year, most programs break down everything in their program and set goals of improvement for the next season. The thing we looked at is the kickoff return average. In our conference, the leader returned the ball 27.78 yards per return. That gives us something to try to achieve.

PUNTING GAME

Most of the things I am going to show you today are how to sell your players on the importance of the kicking game. The punt is the "most *important* play in football." We preach that to our players because we feel it is important to everything we do. If you break down the practice in relation to amount of time spent in each drill, you spend more time on offense and defense than you do on special teams. Every head coach will tell you it is one-third of the game, but they will not give you one-third of the practice time. The challenge for the special teams coach is how to maximize the time so we can teach all the techniques we need.

If I use the techniques that the defensive backs coach, the running backs coach, and the linebackers coach are already using, I can maximize the time I need. Everything we do defensively at The University of Tulsa has the following principles:

- Alignment—perfect every time
- Protect—communicate the count
- Get-off—key the ball
- Speed—speed, speed, speed,
- Leverage—inside and in front

In the punting game, the first thing you have to do is align. Protection in the punting game is the most important thing you do. To protect, you must communicate in that scheme. We are a man protection team. Everything on special teams involves the get-off. In every phase of the kicking game, there is a get-off. In the kicking game, get-off is tied to keying the ball. Everyone on special teams knows what leverage is and how to get it. In the punting game, it is simple. You keep the ball inside and in front of you.

KICKOFF COVERAGE

The kickoff is the "most *violent* play in football." If the player thinks he really tough, he needs to get on the kickoff coverage team and prove it. We look for players that will play violently on kickoff.

- Alignment—perfect every time
- Get-off—be onside
- Speed zone—identify location and return
- Leverage—inside and in front

The terminology we use for get-off is to be "onside." We talk from a positive standpoint. We do not say, "Do not be offside." We want to reinforce the idea of being onside. If you tell a pitcher not to hang the curve ball or a quarterback not to throw interceptions, you get what you are saying. We talk about being onside and making sure to secure the ball. We do not talk about offside and fumbles. In the speed zone, we want to identify the location of the ball and identify the return.

Types of Kickoffs

- Deep left
- Deep right
- Squib
- Must onside
- Surprise onside
- Bunt

These are the things that we rep in practice and make sure we have in our arsenal when we have to kickoff. There is a teaching progression in the kicking game. It starts with alignment and covers running lanes and leverage.

Key Terms

- Escape
- Fight pressure
- Lane integrity
- Spatial awareness

There are key phrases and terms you want the coaching staff to use in teaching techniques with the kickoff team. We use these terms repeatedly to emphasize what we want the coverage team to do. We use the term "escape" instead of "avoid." Frankly, I thing avoid sounds soft as if you were running away from something. The term escape is a macho term. We do not avoid blocks, we escape blocks. We want this to be a violent action. When we get into the contact zone, it is the attack zone.

We want to attack blockers and the ballcarrier. Spatial awareness is an understanding and feeling to be four yards away.

Kickoff Return

The kickoff return is the "most *exciting* play in football." If you want the crowd involved in the game quickly, get a big return. If you want to fire up the stadium, you do it with a big return.

- Alignment—perfect every time
- Get-off—see the ball leave the tee
- Snap key—locate your returner
- Technique—no stupid penalties
- Excite the stadium—take it to the house

Every time our players take the field for a kickoff return, they tell themselves two things. Every coach reinforces those two things. They want to see the ball leave the tee and make no stupid penalties. We went two years with only one penalty on the kickoff return team. That does not include the penalty for kicking the ball out of bounds. That is tremendously important. If you receive a penalty for blocking in the back, the offense starts from inside the 15-yard line or worse. Nine times out of 10, the illegal blocks in the back occur inside your 30-yard line. If we get that penalty, we stabbed the offensive team in the heart.

The cause of that penalty is laziness and discipline. We believe and we coach our players that they are better off getting out of the way than making that type of block. You may think that is crazy, but there are percentages that support the facts. On special teams, we do not accept players that we cannot trust. The snap key is important in the kickoff return. When the blocker sees the ball kicked, he snaps his head around and finds the returner. He does not follow the flight of the ball. The returner will tell him the angle he must go.

PBR

The next part of the kicking game is "PBR," which stands for punt, block, and return. This is the "most *devastating* play in football." This is a two-phase deal. It is not about just blocking punts. It is also about returning punts. On this team, we start on defense but play offense after the ball goes. You either return a punt for big yardage or block a punt, which destroys a team. You need to look at the statistics of this fact. Statistically, if you block a punt, you will win the game. You have to be careful how you communicate that fact because it could happen to you. You do not want your players to think they cannot overcome a blocked punt and still win the game.

We try to put the focus on our side of the play and not so much on the opponent's side. That is a thin line.

- Alignment—perfect every time
- Get-off—key the ball
- Pressure—attack three and under, speed, knife
- Technique—hawk, mug, mob
- Devastate—your opponent

The coaching point we emphasize with this team is to play defense first. Do not let the punt team pick up a first down by a fake. We want no stupid penalties on a punt return. They need to know where the ball is and listen to the return for alerts to get away. Secure the ball before anything else. Possession of the ball is the primary goal of the punt return team. We do not want to give the ball back to the offense after a 40-yard gain by fumbling the ball. We want to return the ball 10 yards. Ten yards is a first down and a greater change in field position. The punt return can devastate the opponent by scoring on a punt return or setting up a score with a long return.

The biggest thing you can take away from the lecture that will help your team is the point on penalties. The penalties in the kicking game kill momentum quicker than anything you can do. If you get the big return, make it stand up by not committing a stupid penalty. Jumping offside, which gives the offense the ball back, is another killer penalty. When the yardage for the first down is less than five yards, it is imperative that you do not jump offside. There is nothing more important than the possession of the ball. When the defense turns the ball over, do not give it back because of a stupid mistake.

If all the returner did was catch the ball, we would be ahead. If he caught every ball with a fair catch, that would be great for the return team—he secured possession of the ball. If you do not catch the ball and it rolls, that is precious field position.

That is an overview of the kicking game. I want to show you some things as to how we teach and improve on what we do. There are hundreds of drills you can do related to the kicking game. I have some great friends that are offensive line coaches. They can spend two hours talking about a drive block. How are we supposed to teach the skills for special teams in a 10-minute period? On special teams, we are looking for players to play in space. We have to teach those fundamentals. The players on special teams have to block and tackle in space. That is a different skill set than most drill work. The biggest mistake is coaches assume their best athletes can play in space. That may be a bad assumption.

One of the first drills we teach is the shimmy drill. We do it in the spring and we do it in the fall. We got this from the University of Texas. If you think you have an original idea about drills, you probably have a short memory. We get drills from everyone.

SHIMMY DRILL COACHING POINTS

- Speed
- Come to balance (shimmy down)
- Get your feet in the grass
- Get leverage (inside and in front)
- Shoulders square—two-hand punch to outside hip of ballcarrier

The drill is set up with four cones that form a 10-yard square (Diagram #1). The cones are 10 yards apart. The coach is five yards past the second cone in the middle of the square. The coverage player starts at one cone and sprints to the other cone. The first element of the drill is speed. When he reaches the second cone, he squeezes inside on the coach and comes to balance. As he comes to balance, he starts to feel his feet in the grass. He squeezes to the coach. We want the coverage player to keep the ball inside and in front of him. When he reaches the coach, he punches the outside hip with two hands.

We film the drill and grade it after practice. In the spring, we put every player that is a runner and hitter in these drills. We divided the players into groups and gave them names. We called them

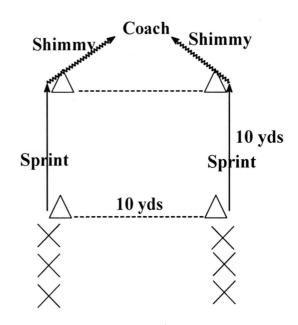

Diagram #1. Shimmy Drill

SEALs or Rangers. We had groups of big players and groups of players that were not so big. We posted the players in groups on the bulletin board. After two or three days of doing the drills, we started to draw lines through names on the board. We cut them from the drill. We ended up with the best players on our team at playing in space. We ended up with the players I trusted to play on special teams. That is how we started to make special teams special. We did not take a player out because he did the drill wrong one time. If he repeatedly did the drill wrong, we cut him. If you put a player in the game that does things wrong in practice, he will do them wrong in a game.

The next drill is a 2-on-1 drill (Diagram #2). We do the shimmy drill and 2-on-1 drill in shorts. This drill is a shimmy drill, except we have a returner in the drill instead of a coach or manager. This is an evaluation drill. We put potential return players running the ball. We evaluate the return players in the shimmy drill also. We evaluate them as a return player and a coverage player. A punt return specialist could cover kicks for you. He may be the best return player, but he may be the best bullet we have.

We have someone throw the ball to the return player. We have seven minutes to do the drill and do not need to chase bad punts all over the field. The coach tells the coverage players when to go. They sprint down the field. We time the throw so that the ball arrives with the coverage players 7 to 10

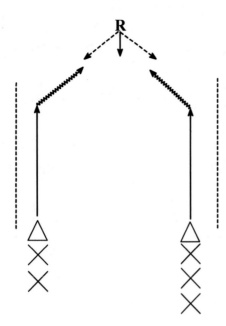

Diagram #2. 2-on-1 Drill

yards in front of the return player. The distance for the coverage personnel is 30 yards. The coverage players come down the field 10 yards apart and run the shimmy drill on the returner. We tell the returner that the hash marks are out of bounds. He can split the defender or get around them using any move that he can. We want the return player to use extreme cuts to get around or through the defenders. The coverage players have to keep the ball in front and inside. If they do that, we consider that a tackle.

If the defender thinks he is inside and in front of the returner, he should not have to extend his arms to reach the runner. If the defender is inside and has to reach outside to touch the returner, he is beat. It is alright if the defender is outside the returner and reaches inside. If you film this drill, make sure you get an end zone shot. You can tell who is in position and who is not in position.

When we send our bullets down the field, we want them to take a shot on the returner before he gets a chance to run. If the returner catches the ball, the terminology we use is "in phase" or "out phase." If the returner catches the ball, he is out phase and the bullet becomes an inside-and-in-front coverage player. If the ball is in phase, the bullet can time up the hit and tackle the returner as the ball arrives. In that case, he does not come to balance, he runs through the returner. The first defenders

down want to create mayhem and get the ball. The farther you are from the ballcarrier, the wider your pursuit to the ball is.

I want to switch gears and talk about the rabbit drill. For us, the rabbit drill is a kickoff return drill. This is how we teach the single blocks on kickoff return. We teach everybody in the spring the rabbit drill. The idea of doing that is to find out who can do the drill. I have to tell you about the kickoff cover team before you can understand how hard this skill is. The kickoff coverage team runs 40 yards before they get to the contact zone. We ask a blocker to turn around, find a defender that has a 40-yard head start, and block him.

The principles of kickoff coverage and kickoff return are the same. To do either skill you must win the single battles. In the NCAA, we cannot wedge block any more. That makes this team more violent. The double-teamed defenders are blocked. You do not cover kicks because you defeat the doubles. You cover kicks because you win the single blocks. The opposite of that principle is kickoff return. You win in the kickoff return because you tie on the singles. If you win, that is great.

We teach the rabbit drill off the sideline (Diagram #3). We work the drill between the hash marks and the sideline. We use the yard lines as cover lanes for the coverage team. We try to give players some teaching points so they can carry over the principles. The thing that screws up the drill is the rabbits, which is the coverage team. They are scout team players and we must teach them

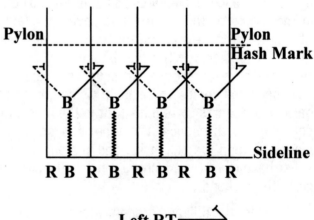

Diagram #3. Rabbit Drill

not to outrun the blocker. We want them to start slow and then speed up as the drill continues.

Both the blocker and rabbit start at the sideline with the blocker facing out of bounds. On the command, they both move toward the middle of the field. The rabbit goes slowly and the blocker goes at full speed. He has to get to a point to start his drop into his leverage spot. The blocker has to get depth and leverage on the defender. The blocker has to drop to the inside of the line because he wants to have leverage on the running lane. The first time we do the drill, the blockers do not block the defender. All we are doing is trying to get into position. If a blocker stops on the line, he does not have leverage. If the blocker straddles the line, he does not have leverage. The blocker gets depth, establishes leverage, and when the defender evades his space, he locks on to him. The blocker uses the defender's momentum to run him to the back pylon. We do the drill every day we are in fall camp and it is still hard for our players.

From this drill, we go to the other side of the ball and talk about kickoff coverage. When we do the rabbit drill in the spring, we do the gauntlet drill at the same time. We have half the team working the rabbit drill and the other half doing the gauntlet drill. We switch them at some time during the drill. If we do not get a chance to switch the groups on that day, the next day we switch the groups. We want to maximize the time.

We work the gauntlet drill across the field (Diagram #4). We use the yard lines as coverage lanes. The coverage team aligns on the sideline. At the numbers on the field is the first dummy holder. The coverage team skins the bag with all of them

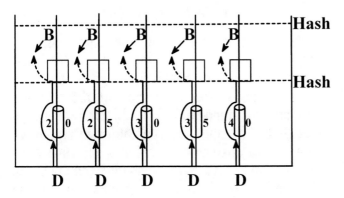

Diagram #4. Gauntlet Drill

taking the same side of the bag. We want them to return to the line immediately. We are evaluating them as to the speed at which they get back on the line. At the hash marks is the second group of dummy holders. The coverage team accelerates into the block, cages, and separates from the blocker. They separate from the blocker by snatching the blocker in a violent downward movement.

On the opposite hash marks are ballcarriers. The coverage team attacks the last blocker, and the ballcarrier moves up the field. The coverage team does their shimmy drill and makes the tackle on the ballcarrier. It is a form type of tackle. I use the kicker and punter in this drill as bag holders and ballcarriers. However, we do get the kickoff man involved in some of these drills because he has to make tackles as part of his job. In an actual situation, the coverage team has to assess the position of the ballcarrier to the last blocker. If the ballcarrier is out phase, the coverage escapes the block and shimmies on the ballcarrier. If the ballcarrier is in phase, the coverage attacks through the blocker to the ballcarrier.

We directional kick the ball on our kickoff. In the speed zone, all the defenders escape the blocker to the same side to maintain the lane integrity. Once they escape the blocker, they want to stack him behind them. He wants to get his shoulders in front of the blocker. That way the blocker cannot come back and block the defender without a block in the back.

When the coverage gets to the contact zone, represented by the second set of dummies, they want to attack the dummies. The dummies try to block the coverage with the shields. The coverage wants to rip and bring pressure back in the direction the blocker tries to bring pressure. We emphasize speed above everything else. If players come down the middle running hard, the blocker will not touch them. Schemes do not matter on the coverage teams. If you do not have speed and the right personnel, it does not matter what scheme you use.

In the spring, we never work the full kickoff in practice. We work get-off to time the run to the ball. We work speed zone for escape moves, we work contact zone to attack blockers, and shimmy to tackle. We evaluate in the spring and find players to put on these teams. On a kickoff return, if the returner hesitates or breaks stride, we have him. You are in trouble when the returner fires through the first line of tacklers at full speed.

The next drill is a combination of the rabbit drill and the gauntlet. We have four blockers on four coverage people. We call it "4-on-4" (Diagram #5). We have four coverage defenders running down in their lanes. They run the gauntlet drill. The object for them is to escape blocks and keep the ball inside and in front of them. The four blockers run the rabbit drill. We tell them their running lanes. The blocker to the side of the return runs one yard outside the hash and the outside blocker runs midway between the hash and the numbers. The backside is in the middle of the field and one yard inside the backside hash mark. I stand behind the coverage team and give the blockers the direction of the return. We return right, left, and middle.

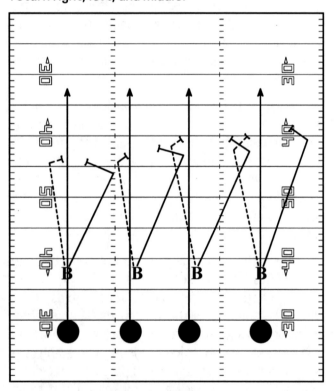

Diagram #5. 4-on-4

The coaching points for the returner are to know the return and set up the return by bombing the middle first. He wants to own the ball and think score. The blockers see the ball off the tee, snap to find the returner, and leverage the return. The coaching points for the coverage team are to stay onside, win with speed, attack leverage, and fight pressure.

The thing about snapping the head is to get the proper running lane to where the ball goes. The blockers may have to widen their running lanes to their landmarks depending on the kick. We tell them to run across three yard lines before they turn. If they stop running, the coverage runs past them. They have to adjust their paths according to the direction of the kick.

If we had only one drill for kickoff coverage players and return blockers, it would be this drill. We call this drill "lions and gazelles" (Diagram #6). This competitive drill pits the two blockers against two coverage defenders. They apply the rabbit drill and gauntlet drill skills. We tell the coverage team to win with speed. If contact is unavoidable, they attack and fight pressure. We set cones to represent the running lanes of the coverage players. We set up a five-yard box, which represents the contact zone. We set the drill up two different ways. We can give the advantage to the blockers or give it to the coverage team.

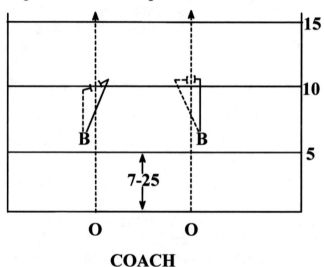

COACH

Diagram #6. Lions and Gazelles

When we start the drill, we start with the blocker and coverage player five yards apart. That advantage goes to the coverage because the blocker cannot set up in that amount of time. If we increase the distance to 7 to 10 yards, the advantage goes to the blocker. We run the coverage down the hash marks to give the blocker a landmark for leverage. He knows the running lane the coverage takes and can get leverage to the inside or outside of the hash mark depending on the direction of the return.

This should tell the return blockers they have no chance to block a defender if they do not run and get depth so they can establish leverage. As the distance puts the coverage farther from the blocker, the blocker has more time to get into a leverage position and use the momentum of the coverage to run them past the return and to the pylon of the end zone. From this drill, we evaluate the coverage personnel and blockers. If we find a player that can leverage a defender in a five-yard box, he will play.

When the defender is in the speed zone, he cannot slow down. If he does, they block him. He knifes or skins past the blocker and stacks him behind him. Coverage is all about speed and pressure. If the blocker establishes leverage on the coverage, the only thing left for the defender is to attack the blocker and go to the ballcarrier. The limit to the drill is 25 yards from the start to the contact zone. The speed zone is everywhere outside of four yards from the blocker. If the coverage gets within four yards of a blocker with leverage, that is the contact zone.

The punt is "the most *important* play in football." The punt can change the field position for your team. It is important that you protect the kick and cover the punt. A blocked punt is one of the biggest momentum changers in a football game.

We have a procedure we use with our punt alignment. We huddle on the sideline with the ability to:

- Sprint to alignment and call the direction of a punt
- Sprint to alignment and call a fake
- Sprint to alignment and shift formations
- Sprint to alignment and snap the ball on various tempos
- Sprint to a "sugar huddle" for a kwik call or a regular tempo

The personal protector calls the protection, front, and direction of the punt. An example of the call is "lucky, lucky, blue, blue, ready...set." We use lucky and ringo as the direction call for the protection. The color is the direction that we kick the ball. The colors are red for right, blue for left, and white for middle of the field. The "ready" command allows everyone to get in position so

he can handle his assignment. During this time the personal protector checks the sideline for any audible the coach may call. "Set" tells everyone, "Do not move, I am ready to snap the ball." Following are the two tempo calls we have for our punt team:

- Regular—Personal protector checks defense and makes a ringo or lucky call, and the rest of the normal calls we just talked about.
- Kwik silver—Sugar huddle. When the ball is marked ready by the official, break huddle like a fire alarm set—snap the ball.

PUNT ALIGNMENT

Center	Down on ball ready to snap eyes on punter
Left guard Right guard	Inside foot 1.5 yards from the near foot of center, toes on center's heels, eyes on the ball
Left tackle Right tackle	Inside foot 2.4 yards from near foot of guard, toes on guard, toes eyes on assignment
Bullets	Inside foot, 3 to 10 yards from near foot of tackle. Toes on toes of tackle, eyes on assignment.
Left shield	Helmet in A gap, toes at seven yards from LOS, eyes on assignment.
Right shield	Helmet in A gap, toes at seven yards from LOS, eyes on assignment.
Personal protector	Behind right shield shoulder square to the sideline, toes of right foot next to inside heel of the RS, as ball passes fill hole, eyes on assignment.
Punter	Toes at 14.5 yards ready to receive ball

On our blocking assignments, we count the defenders from the outside to the inside. In a 5-5 alignment, there are #1 to #5 on each side of the ball. The personal protector counts the front and calls the direction of the protection.

If we have an even number of rushers to each side of the ball, we call ringo because the punter is right-footed. When we get an unbalanced overload, we call the protection to the side of the overload. If they overload left, we call lucky.

Our blocking technique is to stop the charge and get downfield. The blocker wants to cage the rusher and leave. He does not want to step lateral, allow

RINGO PROTECTION—5X5

Left bullet	L4
Left tackle	L3
Left guard	L2
Center	Release to ball
Right guard	R3
Right tackle	R4
Right bullet	R5
Personal protector	R1
Left shield	L1
Right shield	R2

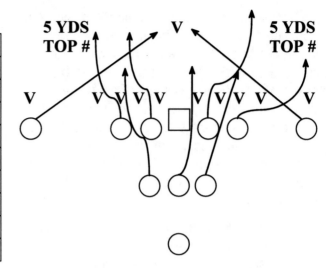

Diagram #8. Lanes and Leverage

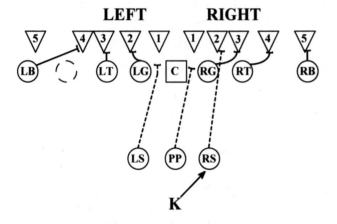

Diagram #7. Ringo Protection

penetration, and scramble to stop the rusher. All we are interested in doing is stopping the charge of the rusher. We want to attack and release through their blocking assignment. We destroy his charge, shed him, and cover. It does not matter whether the assignment is inside, head-up, or outside, the technique is the same. When we practice, we do not cover past five yards. We protect and get off. We want the reps on protection not the time spent running down the field.

While the inside blockers work on protection and get-off, the bullets work on coverage (Diagram #8). If a bullet gets a chance to take a shot at the returner, he does. He does not come to balance;

he goes for the return man. We tell the bullets to sweep the opposite leg. If the bullets arrive at the same time, they scissor the returner. We do not want the ball coming up the gut. We want the ball bounced outside because that is where the coverage will be. The snapper and bullets' job is to keep the ball from coming up the gut of the coverage. The tackles get a width of 10 yards and are the contain players.

The guards initially cover five yards outside their alignment and squeeze the ball. When they get to the initial coverage, they keep the ball inside and in front of them and squeeze it until they tackle it. The shield players are 10 yards behind the coverage and are the linebackers. The personal protector is the Mike linebacker. We want to play players at the shield areas that can run and run fakes. It has helped us.

Coaching is a great business and what you say has a tremendous affect on the players you coach. Whatever the coach says is what they believe. My coaches shaped me and you will shape your players. When you teach your players, make sure you do it correctly. Encourage your players and be patient with them. I hope you get a chance to come see us play next year. I appreciate your attention.

UPDATES ON THE WISHBONE OFFENSE

U.S. Air Force Academy

I want to congratulate you coaches for getting up this early and coming to this clinic. I do not know whether it was a late night or a short night or both. I want to show you a couple of things we do out of the shotgun. We are underneath the center about 70 percent of the time.

About four years ago, the U.S. Air Force Academy started doing some things differently. Everyone at the Academy each semester has to run a mile and a half in 11:30 minutes. That means our big players have to run the mile at a 7:45 pace. They do the running at 7,200 feet of altitude.

We are not big, but we have sharp players playing football. The players that come to the Air Force Academy must be a 3.5 GPA student with a 25 ACT or an 1150 SAT. Everyone that comes to the Air Force Academy goes through the same regiment. Before they ever get to the football field, they go through six weeks of basic training. They all graduate in four years and there is no such thing as a redshirt player. Their curriculum is very scary for the average student. They take two levels of calculus, two levels of chemistry, and two levels of physics, aeronautical engineering, and many other courses. In terms of academics, the load is rather sturdy.

Every one that comes to the Academy has the same major. It is character and leadership. Every player knows that when he graduates, he has a five-year service obligation on active duty. However, the opportunities they have are beyond special. The day they graduate, they have a job that pays exceptionally well. The school does an outstanding job of preparing these young men and women. I would recommend anyone to come see the Academy. If you vacation with your family and are in our area, make sure you stop and see the Academy. It is outstanding.

We play with undersized players in Division I football. This year, one of our offensive tackles was 245 pounds and the other was 250 pounds. These players fit what we do and they have an extra something inside of them that most other teams do not have. The bloodlines of all our players are good.

We have no two-a-day practices at the Academy. In the summer, our players go all over the world. Two years ago, I had a starting tackle and kicker that spent the summer in China. He was working on learning language with applications to their active duties. This past year, I had players in Japan and Morocco. We do not get to work with our players in the summers. You may wonder how we coach football in a situation like that.

On August 1st, all the players get back from wherever they spent the summer. School starts on August 5th. After school starts, we have 90 minutes of practice time each day in August and September. All our players take a full academic load with at least 18 semester hours. They take real stuff in those classes. It is not something for which you just show up. When October 1st comes along, the practice time is cut to 75 minutes a day. The coaches do not like it, but the players have a full load on their plate and need that extra time for study. You have to give the players a chance to take care of what they have to do academically.

Because of the makeup of our players, they are highly motivated and find ways to get things done. They find the weight rooms and do the workouts it takes to play at our school. The Air Force bases where they spend their summers are all well equipped with weight and training facilities. The thing they have to do is to find people to work with as far as the technical skills of throwing and catching.

I know that today's football is more spread and shotgun in fashion. That is 30 percent of our game. We have a few options we like to run out of the shotgun that are simple to run. They are simple to run but are a little different from what most people run.

The first thing we do is to run a true triple option out of the shotgun (Diagram #1). The quarterback aligns four and a half yards from the back tip of the ball. The running back aligns with his toes on the heels of the quarterback. His split from the quarterback is eight and a half feet from the quarterback's crotch. The reason for the eight and a half feet is what we do with our offensive line splits. The offensive line may be as tight as 18 inches and as wide as four to five feet. We constantly expand and tighten our splits in the offensive line. If the defense will split, it opens up the running lanes to the inside.

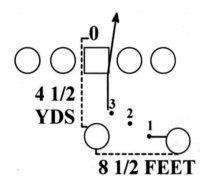

Diagram #1. Running Back Alignment /Steps

We train the running back with an old fire hose. It is marked with the C in the middle of the hose. At eight and a half feet on each side of the C is a red dot to mark his alignment. We cannot align him on the inside leg of the offensive tackle because the splits are not the same every time.

On the play, the running back takes a lateral step with his inside foot toward the quarterback. His second step puts him in line with the playside foot of the quarterback. On his third step, he meshes with the quarterback and directs his path toward the playside foot of the center. He stays on that track until he gets into the heels of the offensive line.

He cannot change his track and move around in the three steps movement as he goes to the line of scrimmage. The mesh between the quarterback and running back has to be the same every time.

In our formations, we have two split ends most of the time (Diagram #2). That gives us an outside blocker for this play. We bring a blocker from the inside to block on the outside of the option play. We align him in the backfield as a tight end or motion someone from the other side of the formation to that position. We can turn that blocker back inside on the support defender. He can switch with the outside blocker and kick out the defender over the wide receiver.

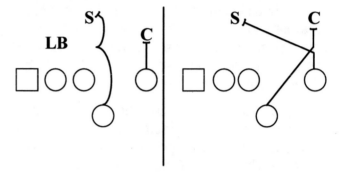

Diagram #2. Perimeter Blocking

The basics of the play are the same regardless of where the inside blocker comes from. We can run the play with 1-2 personnel (one back, two tight ends). One of the receivers will be the pitchback, the one back is the dive back, and the extra tight end runs the horn and blocks the alley player. We can run the play from a number of different formations, but the basics of the play remain the same.

The line blocking for this play is inside zone blocking scheme. If we run the inside zone to the left, we zone read the C-gap player to the right side of the defense. That usually is a 5-technique defensive end. Outside of him is a defender playing the D gap. He is generally a linebacker.

Our guards and tackles are always in a three-point stance. If the defense is a normal 3-4 defense, the center steps laterally with his left foot into the playside gap (Diagram #3). The backside guard does the same thing. If it is a standard 3-4, the noseguard has the backside A gap as his responsibility. We want the guards to take a three-foot split unless he has a player in the center's backside gap. The playside tackle steps to the inside of the 5-technique defensive end and gets inside leverage on him. If the defender goes outside, the tackle releases up the field. If the defender slants inside, the playside guard will block him.

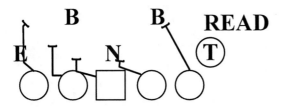

Diagram #3. Inside Zone Blocking

To the playside, if there is an overhanging outside defender, we let him go. We have never had a problem with an outside defender crashing from the edge. We do not block him. The playside guard works into his outside gap looking for the slant from the 5-technique defender. If there is not an inside move by that defender, he climbs to the second level for the linebacker.

If we play a team with a quick reading linebacker that can get over the nose and back to the backside, we block man-to-man. The offensive tackle locks onto the 5-technique defender and the guard goes up on the 30-technique linebacker. If the backside tackle does not have a threat to the B gap, he takes a free release at the linebacker. If there is a bubble in the B gap, the tackle steps with his inside foot and releases across the 5 technique to the linebacker. If the defense moves the 5 technique to a 4 technique, the tackle slams the tackle and comes tight off his butt to get up on the linebacker.

If we get the eight-man front look, we do something different (Diagram #4). If we have a 3-technique defender to the right and a shade nose to the left, we have to block the 3-technique defender. When we see the eight-man look, we want to load the play. The backside guard and tackle work a combination block on the 3-technique defender. The backside guard takes a step with his inside foot and comes up on the 3-technique. The

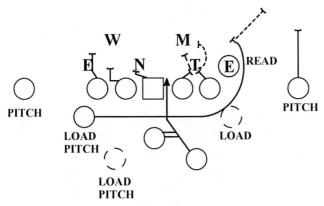

Diagram #4. Load Scheme

backside tackle comes inside on the 3-technique defender and the guard and tackle double-team, looking to get off on the backside linebacker.

The load blocker will align at the playside wing, backside wing, or in the backfield opposite the dive back. If he comes from the backfield, he comes tight to the offensive tackle. He turns up and looks for the Mike linebacker. If the guard and tackle consume the Mike linebacker, the load blocker turns outside and runs flat for the safety. The center reaches for the shade nose and the playside guard and tackle run their blocking scheme.

The quarterback zone reads the 5-technique defender on the backside of the play. We do not block him. We are going to read him and run the option off that read. If he steps up the field, the quarterback gives the ball to the dive back and runs his fake to the outside.

The pitchback, in the option scheme, has to maintain a relationship to the quarterback. The pitch relationship is two yards deep and four yards in front of the quarterback. The dive back can be a fullback or a running back and the pitchman can be a receiver or a running back. Sometimes the pitch is forward to the outside. That is legal behind the line of scrimmage.

When we use motion, there is timing involved with the option play. We have to get the motion back in the proper place to time up the pitch relationship. The motion back may have a blocking assignment and that requires him to be at a particular place to make the angles of the block work. When we motion, we want to go seconds before the snap. We want to make the communication on the defensive side of the ball difficult.

We want to use the motion as a confusion factor for the defense (Diagram #5). We may motion the slot receiver from any position. We like to use reverse motion and unique motions. We align in a wide slot position and bring the slot receiver in motion toward the opposite side. When he reaches the halfback alignment on the other side, he reverses his motion and runs behind the fullback to become the pitchback on the option. The advantage we have is looking different and running the same play repeatedly. That makes it simple for the offensive line.

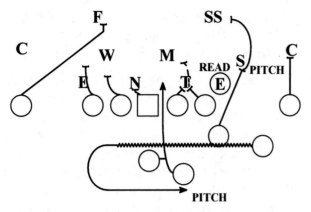

Diagram #5. Motion

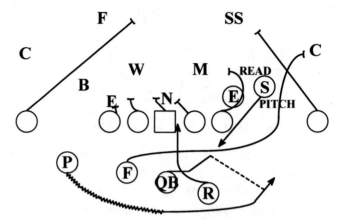

Diagram #6. Option 20 Personnel

The steps for the quarterback are simple. For the inside zone to the left, the quarterback takes a six-inch step at a 45-degree angle with his right foot. He swings his left foot into a balanced mesh facing the read key. The running back comes over the ball on the back leg of the quarterback. The quarterback reads from his back foot to his front foot. The running back takes a lateral step with his inside foot, a cross step with his outside foot, and gets the mesh on his third step. The coaching point for the running back is not to leave until he sees the ball in the quarterback's hand.

The variable in this play is the center's snap. We want the snap in the same place every time but it does not always happen. If the snap is less than perfect and the back leaves early, you have a bad play.

When we pitch the football, the quarterback grips the bottom half of the football. It is not the point of the ball but the bottom half of the ball. When he pitches the ball, it is a wrist flip as if shooting basketball. They do not need the laces of the ball to pitch it. It does not matter the size of the hands. We do not turn the thumb under. It is a simple wrist flip.

I want to show you the play with a two-back set and the three wide receivers look (Diagram #6). The slot receiver is the pitchback on this play. He comes in motion to get into position. The fullback aligns to the left side of the quarterback and is the load player to the playside. He cheats up so he does not run into the back running the zone play. He goes in front of the zone back and has to clear before the back gets there. The key to the play is the tackle's block on the Mike linebacker.

If there is a 4-technique defender on the tackle, he steps with his inside foot. If the defender slants inside, the tackle comes as close to the defender as he can. He goes behind the slanting tackle, comes off the defender's hip, and seals the Mike linebacker. If the outside linebacker crashes, the quarterback has to pitch quickly.

From the same look, we can run a simple lead play (Diagram #7). It is the same formation with the same motion and fullback cheated up. The play looks like the zone read. We turnback block with the offensive line. The center tries to get to the backside linebacker. He comes tight off the nose and works into the backside A gap. The backside guard fans out on the 5-technique defender.

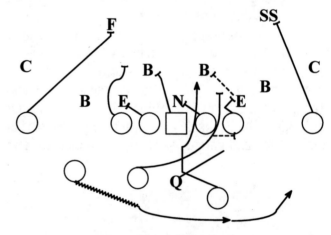

Diagram #7. Lead Play

The backside tackle has to come tight off the hip of the 5-technique defender and get up on the backside linebacker. He attacks the outside number of the 5-technique defender. If the defender goes inside, he has a tight line to the linebacker. If he tries to avoid the defender, he gets too wide and never gets to the linebacker. We use the fullback to block the playside C-gap defender.

The playside tackle takes his inside step on the 5-technique defender. If the 5-technique tries to slant inside, the tackle blocks out on him. The fullback reads his block and either traps the 5 technique or turns inside and blocks the linebacker. If the defender stays outside, the tackle blocks the linebacker and the fullback traps the 5 technique. The running back runs the same track to get the ball. He knows it is not a read and he will get the ball.

There are a number of ways to change the load blocker on the play (Diagram #8). We can bring the slot receiver in motion behind the quarterback. The quarterback receives the snaps and runs the zone play with the running back. The quarterback has the slotback in motion as the load blocker and the backside running back as the pitchman. The wide receiver blocks the corner and the slot receiver loads on the free safety.

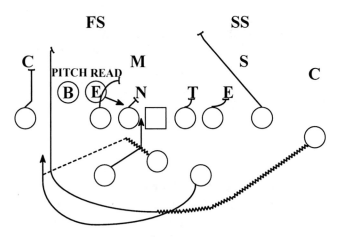

Diagram #8. Wide Receiver Load

The wide receivers must block in the option game. We have two ways the wide receiver and the inside load blocker can block the switch call. If the corner aligns with depth, the wide receiver can go directly to the strong safety without worrying about the corner on quick support from the outside. However, if the corner rolls down in a cover-2 look, the wide receiver drives off on the corner to keep him from attacking the pitch. He stays on the corner and releases after he walks him downfield. He comes off on the strong safety late and the inside load blocker kicks out the corner.

It is a good change-up to their blocking scheme and it secures the pitch. The problem rests with

communication of the switch. The load has to know he is coming outside and not sealing inside on the safety.

The good thing about these types of plays is it forces the defense to be gap and assignment sound to both sides. That forces them into a balanced defense.

In the zone option play, we want our blocking scheme to read the C-gap defender. The offensive line cuts their splits to two feet to bring the pitch keys closer to the quarterback. We are in the shotgun and this is a one-back play all the way. We read the C-gap defender and block him. We pitch off the D-gap defender. If the defense has a 5-technique defender and a 9-technique defender, we block the 5 technique and pitch off the 9 technique. The C-gap defender will be in two spots. He is a 5 techniuqe on the outside shoulder of the tackle or a 7 technique on the inside shoulder of the tight end or wing.

If we have a 5 technique, the tight end has a chip rule (Diagram #9). He bangs the 5 technique and goes up to the next level. The tackle's rule on this play is to hook or reach the 5 technique. The tight end has the first linebacker in the box. He blocks the Mike linebacker. When the tight end chips on the 5-technique defender, he pounds this inside hand into the outside hip of the defender. When he escapes off the block, he comes at an angle to the outside up to the second level.

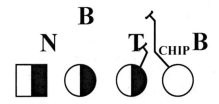

Diagram #9. 5-Technique Defender Rule

The inside linebacker runs immediately because there is no inside fake to hold him. To have a chance to block him, we have to go where he is going, not where he is. The tight end does not want to go inside; he wants to ricochet to the outside off the chip.

If there is a 7 technique, we have an overtake rule for the tackle (Diagram #10). The tight end comes off the ball and steps with his outside foot. He brings the inside foot into the 7 technique and punches with his inside hand into the armpit of the 7 technique. He keeps his outside hand out of the block. He wants that hand to remain free. The tackle takes a wider step and overtakes the 7-technique defender with a reach block.

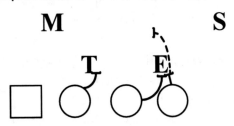

Diagram #10. 7-Technique Defender Rule

The tackle, as he comes off the line, loses about six inches on his first step. We have trouble thinking like that at the Air Force Academy. We do not like to lose ground on anything we do.

If the alignment of the defender is a 6 technique head-up the tight end, the tight end applies his 7-technique rule. He steps with his outside foot and brings the inside foot and hand into the defender. He works the inside hand through the armpit of the defender and pushes him up and inside so the tackle can overtake the block. Under no circumstance should the tight end use his outside hand on that technique. He has to use the outside hand to get off and bend back inside for the linebacker.

The tight end's responsibility is the first linebacker inside the box. It is the 10-technique linebacker in the 7-technique alignment or a 30-technique linebacker in the 5-technique look. The coaching point for the tight end is not to get in a hurry to block the linebacker. That is especially true with a 10-technique linebacker. He is an A-gap defender and will not get to the off-tackle as quickly as the B-gap linebacker.

On the perimeter, we pitch off the D-gap defender. It does not matter which defender that is. It could be the 9-technique linebacker, a strong safety, or a corner.

The guard and center work the same combination as the tackle and tight end (Diagram #11). With a shade nose, the guard chips the nose and the center reaches that defender. The center reaches the shade nose and the guard goes up on the backside linebacker. It is the same technique as the tackle and end on the 5-technique defender.

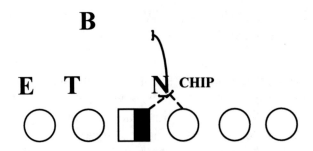

Diagram #11. Shade Nose Defender

If the defender to the playside aligns on the guard, the center uses a takeover technique as the tackle on the 7-technique defender. If the defender is a 1 technique or a 2i technique, the guard steps with his outside foot and brings the inside foot and hand into the defender. The center works for the overtake block on the defender, and the guard goes to the second level for the backside linebacker. If the defender is a 3 technique, the guard uses the same technique so the center can overtake the block. This gives us good angles on both combination blocks.

If the guard or tackle cannot see an inside box linebacker, they stay on their armpit technique until they need to come off. They could push on that defender as the quarterback pitches the ball. However, we like for them to get up the field to the third level and block on the safeties or corners pursuing.

The quarterback catches the ball and takes off immediately. He goes slightly downhill toward the C gap. Once he passes the C gap, he puts his foot in the ground and turns north and south down the field. That forces the D-gap defender to do something. If he attacks the quarterback, it allows us to pitch the ball sooner and gives us more time on the perimeter.

We can run this play from a variety of sets. We can use a 2x2 or a 3x1 formation (Diagram #12). On this particular play, the defense aligned in a 4-3 type of front. We align in a 3x1 tight end set. The defense plays press man coverage on the single receiver and walks the backside linebacker up on the line to the outside. The running back is set to his side in the original set. We move the back at the last minute in short motion.

The playside guard has no backside linebacker to block. He stays on the 3 technique with the center on the overtake block. If the center has secured the

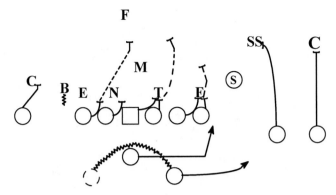

Diagram #12. Zone Option to 3x1

block, he goes downfield and cuts off the weakside safety. The double flanker set cracks on the strong safety and stalks the corner. We pitch the ball off the Sam linebacker.

The outside receiver on this formation has to stalk block on the corner. We want the receiver to attack the outside number of the corner and work to keep him inside. He wants his body on a slight tilt to the inside and working his outside foot up the field. He has to stay in contact and work him up the field. We do not want the receiver to get his shoulders parallel to the sideline. We want to pen the corner and work him to the middle of the field. Once the receiver gets leverage, he shoots his hands and works him to the inside. The trick is to keep the hands inside the framework of the body.

Every blocking scheme has to adapt to defensive adjustments. With the defensive end in a 9 technique on the tight end and the Sam linebacker in an inside stack position, we make a change call (Diagram #13). We pitch off the 9-technique defensive end and the tight end goes up and blocks the Sam linebacker.

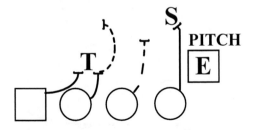

Diagram #13. Change Call

If the tackle can handle the 5 technique without the chip, he gives a free call to the tight end. The tight end takes the first linebacker in the box immediately. He should have good outside leverage

on the linebacker. The tackle hooks the outside half of the defender. When the tight end chips, he chips off the outside heel.

If we play I-formation football with the quarterback under the center, we use the same blocking rules (Diagram #14). The difference is that the stalk block comes from the fullback or that someone has motioned into that position. The line blocking is the same and has the same rules. The quarterback's read is the same. He pitches the ball off the D-gap defender. He comes down the line of scrimmage instead of from the shotgun set. The fullback becomes the load blocker on the corner. We crack the safety with the outside receiver.

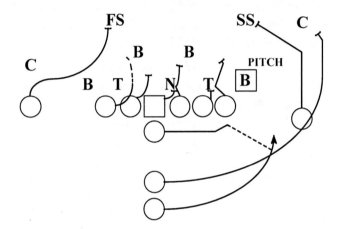

Diagram #14. Option Under Center

We can do the same thing from a 2x2 set by using motion to get the backside slot receiver into a playside load position. We bring him motion and snap the ball when he passes the playside guard. We always tell the load or arc blocker to take a path outside the D-gap player unless it becomes ridiculous. If the D-gap players get that wide, the quarterback will keep the ball inside.

This play is great against short yardage defenses (Diagram #15). With a two tight end alignment, the defense plays 1, 5, and 9 techniques to each side of our alignment. The inside linebackers align in 30 techniques crowding the line of scrimmage. The safeties and corners walk down and play man-to-man on all receivers in the set. We align the flanker to the shortside of the field and bring him in motion to the wideside.

The blocking rules for the offensive line are the same as before. The motion receiver turns

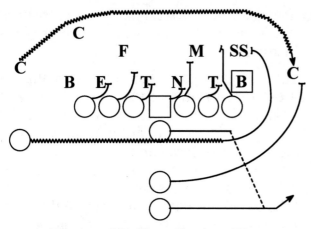

Diagram #15. Short Yardage Play

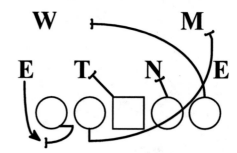

Diagram #16. Shovel Option Blocking

immediately back inside and cracks on the rolled up corner. The fullback loads the corner covering the motion. It is the same read for the quarterback and same blocking for the offensive line.

Our players have a tremendous amount of stamina. I do not think we condition any different from the teams we play, but we train at a high altitude. I think that makes a difference, especially when we play at home. Our situation is different from teams we play against. Everyone at the Air Force Academy is on scholarship. The players play for us because they want to play. The people that play for us could be doing many other things with their time. They really sacrifice to play football.

There are pluses to coaching in this kind of environment. We do not worry too much about the intangibles in football. We do not worry too much about leadership, chemistry, and grit. Usually people that are committed to this type of college life already possess those kinds of qualities. They are self-motivated and not self-absorbed.

The next thing we do is the shovel option (Diagram #16). We block the play like a power O play. The center blocks backside for the backside pulling guard. The backside tackle steps into the backside B gap and makes sure there is no threat in that gap. If there is no threat, he turns back and blocks aggressively on the C-gap defender.

The playside guard has an inside blocking assignment. If there is a nose or shade player to his side, he blocks him. The playside tackle comes inside and blocks the backside linebacker. He wants to stay up on him and not try to cut him. If there is a playside 3-technique defender, the playside guard

and tackle double-team him with the tackle coming off for the backside linebacker.

The backside guard pulls and keys the 5-technique defender. If the defender squeezes to the inside, the guard goes around him and blocks the Mike linebacker. If the defender goes up the field, the guard turns inside and blocks the playside linebacker.

The backside running back takes three steps forward, gets in the guard's hip pocket, and follows him to the hole (Diagram #17). He wants to be two yards in front of the quarterback and four yards behind him. The right running back is the pitchback on this play. He wants to be two yards behind the quarterback and four yards in front of him. If the 5 technique squeezes the play, the quarterback runs the zone option pitching off the D-gap defender. If the 5 technique comes up the field and attacks the quarterback, he pitches the ball back inside to the shovel back.

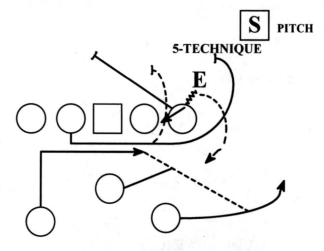

Diagram #17. Quarterback Action

The perimeter players block the zone option play. This is a good play for the playside tackle to take a three- to four-foot split. The alignment puts the 5 technique on an island and makes the read easier. The playside tackle has to make sure his angle to the backside linebacker is correct. If he goes too flat, the linebacker has no trouble getting over the top. If he is too deep up the field, the linebacker can come under his path. He wants to aim at the frontside shoulder.

The backside tackle can see if there is a threat of a B-gap run through by the linebacker. If the linebacker is at normal depth and he does not suspect a blitz, he takes a short jab-step inside and turns back aggressively on the backside C-gap player. That player generally chases the play off the backside edge. We want to secure the inside pitch and make sure he cannot catch the play from behind.

I want to thank you coaches for what you do with young people. The coaches have such a positive impact on young men. There is no way to overstate what you people do. The discipline, guidance, structure, and stability that you provide for those players is invaluable.

When that player is 16 years old, it may not seem worth it. However, 8 to 10 years later when he comes by to see you, that tells you the effort was worthwhile. You can provide something to the players they may not be able to get somewhere else. When players like the sport, they are willing to pay the price to play. They develop dedication and perseverance. They develop the social skills of teamwork, getting along with other people, and mutual respect. All those things help them become leaders.

It is awesome what you do. I know you do it for the love of the game. If you are ever in our area, make sure you stop by to see us. If you come during spring practice, we will treat you right. Thank you for your attention.

OFFENSIVE EVOLUTION AND PROGRESSION

Jacksonville State University

Good morning guys. Only people who get up this early on a Sunday morning would appreciate this title. The title of the lecture is "Evolution," which is a different approach. I have a chemistry degree. I did not play college football and I have always been from another place. When I was 41 years old, I became the head coach at the University of Arkansas. When the boosters found out they had a coach that did not play college football and who had a chemistry degree, that bothered them.

Our game of football is about tradition, but along the way, the game has changed. Gene Chizik and Larry Fedora were graduate assistants for me at one time. Watching coaches like those two who were thinkers and seeing their evolution into great coaches is something to strive for and you hope to achieve. Houston Nutt, who was here yesterday, belongs on that list also.

In my 40 years of experience in the coaching field, I have been there, done that, and seen many things. My peer group of coaches includes Bobby Bowden and Mack Brown. What I am going to talk about are the things we talk about in football. If you ever wondered what coaches of that status talk about when they are together, this will be an insight to that.

Thinking is what gets us to what we do and how we coach. The term *evolution* relates to a coaching career. If you coach long enough, you will experience that. You will go from season to season and evolve in your thinking and schemes. You will go from school to school, look back on what you have done, and evolve a bit more. For me, I went from level to level. I coached high school and went to college. I coached in the SEC, ACC, Southwest Conference, and even got out of coaching for a while. I got tired of being a mercenary. People hired me to come into their program and fix it.

I was hired at Auburn University to teach them how to run the wishbone. At the University of Arkansas, they wanted me to get them out of the wishbone so they could run something else. Thinkers can do both those jobs because there comes a point in time when you have to change. You must have a mental thought process where you anticipate change. There is a thin line between being committed to something and changing with the trends. If you change with the trends in football, all you do is create confusion in your program. You have to stand for something.

You try to keep what you are consistent with at a principle level. That gives you the ability to change. Modern day football is all about putting the responsibility for the offense on the quarterback. I disagree with that point of view.

I have a short story about that situation. Mike Shanahan and I go back a long way. He was at the University of Florida and I was at Auburn at the same time. He went to Denver and had a great quarterback in John Elway. They offered me an assistant's job at the same time. Dan Reeves drafted Elway and wanted a college coaching staff to handle him. Shanahan, Chan Gailey, and Alex Gibbs went to Denver to be on that staff. They offered me the same job but I had Bo Jackson at Auburn at the time and chose to stay there.

I did not go but I stayed in touch and attended some of their quarterback meetings. Shanahan said in 1984, "There are 28 teams in the league that were trying to win with their quarterback. There are only six teams that can do it and the rest of them are getting their butts beat trying." Shanahan is one of the smartest coaches in football today. That statement was a pearl of wisdom I have never forgotten.

I have often thought if I had a quarterback like Elway I might do that too. However, I had never had one like him until I got Ryan Perrilloux from Louisiana State University. When he transferred to Jacksonville State University, it changed many things in our program. Having a good quarterback tends to influence other quarterbacks to give you a look. The next quarterback beat The University of Mississippi in the first game of the year. He took us down the field on the last drive and scored. We made the two-point conversion, tied the game, and won it in overtime 49-48.

The evolution of our offense occurred when Perrilloux arrived but he was gone the next season. We had to think about some adjustments to what we did with Perrilloux. I think we finished this season paying the price for keeping a system. We started the season as ESPN's darlings of the season. At one time, we had the longest winning streak in the country. At the end of the season, we lost part of what we were with Ryan and we did not have him. That leads me at a point of evolution with my thinking about our offense. You have principles that you live by, and when you do not meet them, you have to evolve. At one time, we were third in the nation in scoring with the longest winning streak but some of the principles were not right.

I told my coaches we needed to reevolve into what we were. I gave them the example of Pat Sullivan. Pat Sullivan won the Heisman Trophy at Auburn. I was a new coach at the time and spent many hours studying Auburn. Pat Sullivan and Terry Beasley were the best passing duo in college football. The next year Sullivan and Beasley both graduated. The following season, Coach "Shug" Jordan did something you could not believe. Bear Bryant at The University of Alabama overshadowed coach Jordan so much that he did not get the credit for how great a coach he was.

However, the next year, Auburn lined up in the I formation with a player by the name of Terry Henley. He was not very fast. He ran 4.8. Auburn ran the football, kicked it, played great defense, and did not turn the ball over. They had a better record than the best passing duo in college football. In one season, they did a complete flip in their philosophy. They went from a passing team to a running team. That was a great coaching job and an example

of evolution of great magnitudes. That evolution showed the insight and understanding of Coach Jordan and his staff.

The fact that I was a chemist helps me in my thought process. I spent my entire college career doing research. You have to recognize productivity and value research. I am going to talk about some things that I feel are the drivers of evolution.

DRIVERS

• Better
• Different

The drivers of your thought process tell us we have to be better than the other team or you have to be different to be successful. There has to be a balance between those two factors. When you are a member of the FCS, you play one to two teams on your schedule each year that make money. Therefore, we play teams that are better than us and we do not have to defend ourselves for doing it. Next year, we are the homecoming game for the University of Kentucky Wildcats. You will see that Kentucky is better than we are but so was Ole Miss. The year before, we opened up with Georgia Tech followed by The Florida State University. They were the number one and two offensive teams in the ACC one year ago.

We learned a lesson in the Georgia Tech game, and the next week we almost upset Florida State. We probably got Coach Bowden fired because the game went down to the last play. Once the chatter started, it was hard to recover from those negative aspects of the game. We get a chance to approach the drivers very openly. People do not like to say that teams are better than they are. There are teams on our schedule that are better than we are and we do not defend ourselves over the fact that we say it.

If you play a schedule that has the same types of teams on it, you do not get to say things like that. When you play teams repeatedly that are better, coaches have a tendency to evolve into the offenses they run. I am glad that next season we do not open with a game against a team that is better than we are. We do not play Kentucky until late in October.

We get more practice in August than we do in the spring. It is an important development time for us. When you have to play an SEC or ACC opponent in the first game, you spend too much time trying to be different. We spend the time trying to be different instead of trying to make ourselves better.

Better

• Personnel

• Execution

• Organization

There is a way to approach being better. The first thing you have to do is assess your personnel. We get all the help we need from people in the stands with assessing the personnel we have. They always want you to play someone different. Against Ole Miss, the highlights on ESPN showed Coty Blanchard making the throw to the back of the end zone to score the touchdown and making the two-point conversion that tied the game up. He only played 12 plays the entire game. It disrupted the chemistry at that position.

However, he was "Mr. Football" in the state of Alabama and turned down a pro baseball contract to play college football. The contract was half a million dollars playing for the Baltimore Orioles. He wanted to go to a college where he could play both sports.

Player evaluation on your team is tremendously important. You have to find a way to make your players the best they can be. The starting place is in the staff meetings. You must have frank and open discussions about your players. Too many times, coaches get into an ego battle over which side of the ball a player should play. These battles are counterproductive and lead to ill feelings. The head coach will make that evaluation on that situation in the end. That is his role.

The major improvement comes with better personnel but you can get better with great execution. That is where the coaching takes over and improves the quality of your team. The last part of getting better comes from the head coach. He has to organize everything that happens within the program.

There is a book entitled *The Art of War*. I have always said that *deception* was the art of war. If you do not have this book, you need to look into acquiring it. I was in southern Mississippi recruiting and dropped in on Larry Fedora at The University of Southern Mississippi. They were preparing to play in a bowl game. I walked into his office and there on the desk was a copy of that book. I gave him the book many years ago and he still had it. I asked him if it was the same book that I gave him and he said it was.

The second driver is being different. That has to do with deployment and tactics. Being different has to do with getting an advantage. It is probably what the coach can manage. You cannot manage personnel. You can manage being different. However, you cannot allow being different to screw up your organization or your personnel. The personnel, execution, and organization must have continuity. All of the coaching staff has to teach the same things.

You cannot expect to throw something out in practice on Monday and see it Friday night. That is a worst-case scenario. You need a way to be different and not lose being better. That is the art of coaching. You try to create uncertainty in the minds of the teams you play and take all the uncertainty out of the minds of your team.

I have never been at a school where we did not win a championship. I have three from the Atlantic Coast Conference, two from the Southeastern Conference, two from the Southwest Conference, two from the Gulf South Conference, and two from the Ohio Valley Conference. That career required many changes and an evolution at all the different spots.

I want to introduce one last piece of philosophy before I get into some football. You must have flexibility and specificity. Those two items represent both sides of the coin. All the plays we draw up will fit against some templates. I listened to the national championship game this year. They had Urban Meyer as one of the coaches previewing the game. The ESPN announcer made a statement that the audience was about to see two spread offenses on the field. Urban took exception to that statement. He said there was one spread offense and one I formation team disguised as a spread team.

In the fourth quarter, we saw what Urban was saying. Auburn had a 220-pound running back and a 240-pound quarterback running downhill at the University of Oregon. They had a hard time trying to tackle them. We have seen the evolution of power, option, and the spread offense. Every coach in here will go through types of plays. You will constantly evaluate your offense and add more of the option and less of the power. You will add more of the spread and less of the option. You have to be flexible.

Auburn had the flexibility to become a power football team in a moment that they needed power to put the game away. I did not think Oregon had a choice in their package. They were what they were. When you play Jacksonville State, we may play many different types of backs. However, we always have one big back that no one wants to tackle in the late stages of a game.

You have to define your advantages. You must do that for your coaches, players, teaching, game planning, and your play calling. When you get away from it, you lose your ability to game plan and call plays. I believe as Bobby Bowden did—the offensive coordinator calls all the structured plays, but when it comes time to run the reverse, I call them. When Mark Richt was Bobby's offensive coordinator, he said that drove him crazy. I am sure I do the same thing to my coordinator.

ADVANTAGES IN FOOTBALL

- Grass
- Angle
- Numbers

When you call a play, you need to know why you called it. We call a play because the blockers outnumber the defenders. We call a play because we have superior blocking angles. We call a play because we have the wideside of the field or grass. If you run a play because you want to run it, that is bull crap.

I went to Florida State to watch a scrimmage. Florida State's linebackers coach used an unusual teaching tool with his linebackers (Diagram #1). At the end of the scrimmage, the coach had a piece of graph paper with the linebacker's name on it. On the graph paper was a circle for every place

the linebacker had a chance to make a play. For the linebacker to make a play, he had to break up a pass or make a tackle. We call this measuring productivity. If you cannot be productive, you cannot play. The circle may represent ripping a block and filling a gap or anchoring a gap. Every time the linebacker did that, the circle had an X in it. Every time he did not do it, the circle was void. Can you think of a better way to show a linebacker how he played? We insert the player's number on the graph. Here, we are measuring #55.

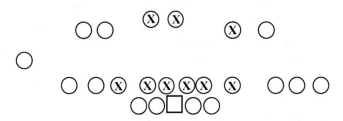

Diagram #1. Production Graph

In this case, the graph was filled in on the inside plays, but the farther the play went outside, the fewer the number of *X* circles there were. That is an example of the *grass* as an advantage. If you have an Oklahoma drill in practice, the offensive and defensive coaches seem to disagree on the space between the dummies in the drill. The offensive coach wants them farther apart, and the defensive coach wants them closer together. That is an example of *grass*.

The first thing the defensive coach sees is the size of the splits in the offensive line. That is what you see in spread offenses. They want the ball on the perimeter in the open field. They want the advantage of *grass*. I look for high school running backs to play linebacker. Against some football teams, you do not need to have angles or numbers. You need to get them in space and open grass. The thing you cannot forget about running wide is the conditioning factor. The big play may not occur the first time you run the ball wide, but if you do it enough, the defense has to be in shape. Some defenses slow down as their linebackers get tired.

There are psychological factors in every football game. One of the big factors is conditioning. In the fourth quarter, is the defense still running as hard as they can to the outside? Factor the grass into your game planning in any offense.

Angles are a simple principle you have to consider. It is easier for the offensive guard to block down on the 1-technique defender than to try to reach the 3-technique defender. I know we are in the world of zone blocking but, personally, I think it is dangerous. In the national championship game, I saw a zone looking offense with man blocking. They used many angles in their blocking scheme. The defense must play differently against angle blocks as opposed to zone blocking.

There are two specific plans of attack on defense. There is rush and cover or contain and pursue. If you look at the stance of a 5-technique defender, he tells you what he is doing. If a defender has weight on his hands, there is no way he can be protecting his linebacker. He cannot play man blocking schemes and keep the linebacker free to run to the grass, with weight overloaded on his hands. Zone blocking schemes have trouble with hard penetrating defenders.

Today's defenses have evolved into rush-and-cover defenses. If the defense gets a load of option football, this principle of defense does not work. If the wideout goes inside and cracks the safety, someone has to contain the ball coming down the line on a speed option.

Angles are a particular advantage in high school football. So many high school teams do not have the size to execute the zone scheme.

I have become almost an administrative head coach. We just built a new 64 million dollar stadium. The best FCS stadium in the country is at Jacksonville State.

This statistic was still true until just recently. The most successful and consistent offense was the wing-T. When Tubby Raymond had all his success with the wing-T, he had four quarterbacks in a row that had NFL careers. They took their blocking angles and it worked like a charm. Ara Parseghian used that offense to beat the hell out of Alabama for the national championship several years ago. The wing-T is all about angles in their blocking schemes.

Does your team block better using the man scheme or the zone scheme? You need to know why you use a zone scheme. Are you using it because that is the national trend or because you do a better job using it? That is the decision you have to make. Being different in this case may be better.

The next principle is *numbers*. With numbers, you must consider three areas (Diagram #2). We need to count the number of players in the box. We need to know the numbers to the right and left of the football. We need to know the number of defenders in the secondary defending the pass.

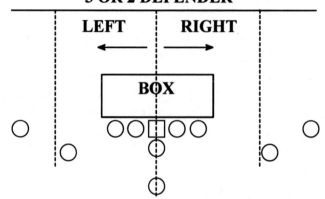

Diagram #2. Numbers

If you spread two receivers to the outside and the coverage is three deep, the curl/flat scheme will beat that every time. Steve Spurrier has many flat/curl patterns in his offense. If you play three deep on four vertical patterns, the numbers are bad for the defense. In each example, we talk about number of defenders against the number of receivers.

When I was 32 years old, I was a phenom football coach and offensive coordinator at Auburn. I took an invitation to speak at a football clinic in St. Angelo, Texas in 1982—it was a massive clinic. It was in Texas and they invited the best coaches in the country. I was full of myself being on the dais. When I showed up to speak, the entire University of Texas at Austin defensive staff was in the audience. We opened up with Texas the next year. I have not trusted Texans since then.

Coaches steal from each other. I got this from Chan Gailey. You have five offensive linemen in the offense and a quarterback. You have at least one running back in the offense. Most every offense has two receivers. All Chan wanted to know was what kind of players were the other two players. He wanted to know who your number 10 and 11 players were.

The box is the area from tackle to tackle and five yards deep. The defense wants to put at least seven defenders in that area. With 11 personnel (one tight end and one back) on the field and the eleventh player aligned as a slot receiver, the defense has to react. They have to reduce their front and take one defender out of the box. There is one problem with that thinking. The defense tells the offense when they can run or pass. I do not believe that.

The defense with seven or six in the box still has to tackle. If you ask an offensive lineman if he would rather run or pass block, he will tell you run block every time. If he tells me he wants to pass block, I want him to go to play for one of our opponents. The true offensive linemen want to run block and they want the ball run up the middle. They do not want it on the perimeter. If your linemen are not like that, you need to change the attitude of the linemen.

You need to have a base way you train the quarterback. He has to be able to count the numbers in the box. In the evolution of football, if you evolve out of being able to play power football, you are headed for trouble. There are programs all over the country that do not have a fullback in the offense. We have trouble recruiting tight ends and fullbacks at our school. When you base everything you do on offense with reducing the number of defenders in the box, you need a quarterback. If you do not have one, the quarterback you play will get you beat. Oregon's quarterback in the championship game had a hard time with Auburn's four pass rushers.

If you look at defensive linemen in the South at the big schools, they are different. Teams that throw the ball will have trouble outexecuting the defenses they face in the SEC.

The principle of grass, angles, and numbers are important, but do not get away from running power football. Make sure the numbers bring you to power, pass, and option. I was a wishbone coach at one time. Those coaches base that offense on grass, angles, and numbers.

In defensive football, there is a five-man side and a six-man side. Whatever you do offensively, you have to define your advantage. When I had Perrilloux, he defined my advantage. If I had Cam Newton, he would define my advantage.

Mike Shanahan was a graduate assistant at The University of Oklahoma when he started out. From there, he went into a run-and-shoot offense. The wishbone and the run-and-shoot offenses base off the premise of symmetry. If you go back to symmetry, you can use grass, angles, and numbers. I got people into the wishbone and got people out of the wishbone.

I thought Pat Dye was going to kill me one year at Auburn. He brought me to Auburn to run the wishbone and Bo Jackson showed up the next year. We had a frustrating year and I told Pat we needed to get out of the wishbone. We got out of the wishbone and Bo won the Heisman Trophy the next year.

Bo was not highly recruited. The only reason he came to Auburn was because Bear Bryant wanted him to play defense. Bo was a hard-to-handle dude. Pat never trusted him with the ball. He was not a bad actor but he was very eccentric. We told him he could play running back but I put him at fullback at the beginning. He impressed us in the scrimmages we had and Pat suggested we move him to running back. That is how Auburn left the wishbone and evolved to the I formation. Pat Dye was a defensive thinker. You cannot be a defensive thinker and evolve quickly enough on offense.

To have flexibility and specificity, you must have a good system. The system has to be bigger than the team you coach at the present. When Ryan Perrilloux arrived at Jacksonville State, the system was already in place. He wanted to know when he came if the system would fit what he could do. Incidentally, he is probably going to be the backup quarterback for the New York Giants next season.

Before I go any further, I want to talk about some principles. I call these the "13 principles" (Diagram #3). I walked into our offensive meeting room and asked the coaches if we were applying the 13 principles. Following are the 13 principles:

• Right: A gap, B gap, dive, quarterback, pitch, corner, safety

• Left: A gap, B gap, dive, quarterback, pitch, corner

We have to attack the defense in those principle areas and with different schemes. You have to

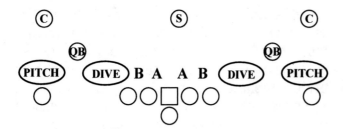

Diagram #3. 13 Principle

threaten the perimeter with option and power. Make the defense prepare and cover all the seams in the running game. Use the tenth and eleventh players to pressure the defense with the run and pass.

The 13 principles are about option, power, and pass. You have to know how to insert a blocker. The blocker may be the second back or an H-back. If the edge defenders are playing rush and cover, we run the zone read and run into the seam they cannot cover. You have to be able to attack the defense using the 13 principles. You have to understand what you are doing when you insert the tenth and eleventh players into the formation. They have to fit what you want to do. If you want to run power, they need to be tough players. If you want to pass, they must be receivers. If you want to run the option, they must have that mentality. Tie the productivity of the offense to the tenth and eleventh players.

One day, I had to explain to Pat how I wanted to reorganize everything he had always done under Coach Bryant. Pat Dye did not know me. I went to The University of Alabama at Birmingham and got a degree in chemistry. I did not play college football. I started my career as a high school coach and moved on to small college football and had success. He started calling me about a job after that success. When he hired me, he did not think anything like I thought. I had to tell him some things about how I organized practice.

These things have to do with practice organization.

PRACTICE ORGANIZATION

- Time
- Score
- Field position
- Alignment
- Personnel
- Psychological
- Field and weather

I work from the bottom instead of the top. I will talk to you about the fourth quarter and running downhill. This is what I explain to my coaches every year. We sit down in August and have many conversations about getting ready to play games during the season. We talk about all the situations that occur in a game or at some time during the season.

I want to tell you what is going to happen. There will be a game in November when we have to play a game at Martin, Tennessee. All the assistant coaches will be talking about how hard the wind is blowing and how the field is wet. That will be more important than anything else on their minds. To avoid those situations, we talk about that situation right now before the season starts.

The first two practice organization items of time and score are important. We were down 21 points to Ole Miss at halftime. The time and score was not in our favor. That is not a bad place to be sometimes. When you come in at halftime to talk to the team, you know what they are thinking. You do not need to talk about what they are thinking. When we were down 21 points at halftime, they were all thinking that was what was supposed to happen. We were not supposed to win.

It is hard to be down 21 points to a team that is as good as you are. If you are down 21 points to a team that is better than you are, that is worse. Ole Miss had just won the Cotton Bowl. They had lost some of their better players but they were not exactly the "Little Sisters of the Poor." When you speak, you have to bring a thought that thumps them in the head. Coach Bryant was in a similar situation in the early years at Alabama. He came into the locker room and told the team, "Boys, we got them right where we want them."

Time and score, have to do with the two- and four-minute offenses. If you can be good at those extreme times, you have the potential to be a great football team. A team that is good at the two-minute offense is not as good at the four-minute offense. When we had Ryan Perrilloux for two years, he was magic. In practice, those drills are the last things we do. It is a competitive drill but it is not live. The first time he did not score during one of those drills, he ran up to me and said we had to do the drill again. He could not quit until he had scored. He engrained the two-minute offense into our practice mentality.

We started a quarterback last year that played behind Ryan for two years. Against Ole Miss, we got the ball 75 yards away from a chance to tie up the score. It looked like we wanted to run out the game and get out of Dodge with our hides. Everyone thought it was going to be a moral victory and we were not going to get blown out.

The quarterback got in the huddle and brought the offense 75 yards as if it were a two-minute drill in practice. When we practice the two-minute drill, we always end up with a two-point play, whether we need it or not.

We spent all of August getting ready with the two-minute drill. We knew we had to open up with someone better than us and thought we would need the work. I always tell my players that in one of the first three games, we will have an opportunity. It will be the offense trying to score on the last drive or the defense trying to stop a drive to save the game. I dwell on and talk to them about their confidence level. I start talking to them in June and July while they are in summer school and practicing 7-on-7.

In that situation, their confidence level will step up or I will have some work to do because it did not. They have to know the two-minute drill like the back of their hand because we work on it all the time.

From the Ole Miss game, we went on to have the longest winning streak in the country. We will be much better next year than we were last year. The Ole Miss game made us into something we were not. We were a better team playing from behind than we were with the lead. We played games when at the end we were hanging on for dear life. I got after them hard and was dog cussing their butts. Finally, an assistant coach told me during week seven of the season that I needed to change my attitude. We were 7-0 and on a 13-game winning streak. He said if I did not tell them they played well,

they would quit playing. In five straight games, we had to score on the last drive to win the game.

I can tell you one thing I believe is true. If you do not have a power game, you are setting yourself up to lose. Try to run the spread formation coming off the two-yard line. In our defensive scheme, we will see if the offense can hit the 16-yard sideline cut having to protect from the end zone. The quarterback had better be really good.

That is the attitude that goes along with the power running game. If the scales of balance have grass, angles, and numbers on one side and attitude on the other side, they will balance (Diagram #4). I can program my players and coaches to have the attitude it takes to run the power game. You create attitude on a football team by being physical and having a tough mentality. You do that by hitting and by aggressive play.

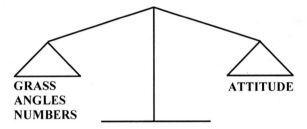

Diagram #4. Balanced Scale

It does not matter who you have running the ball, if you do not give them the ball and develop an attitude, you will not have a running game. I have had good running games with a Heisman Trophy winner and I have had good running games without one of those players.

There comes a time in a game when the running back knows he has to work. During the four-minute offense, he knows he will get the ball eight straight times. If he does not pick up two first downs and run the clock out, the four-minute drill will last longer than four minutes—it will last until we learn the importance of it. You can get a bunch of attitudes working by doing that.

When Bo ran the ball eight straight times, I thought he was going to knock the crap out of me. When you talked to him, it was like talking to a 30-year-old man. He was a sharp dude but he did not like anyone imposing an attitude on him. He is my friend today.

We work with quality control within our program. When you break down the plays of a game, 12 to 14 possessions in a game do not vary much. Eight of those possessions will start on the negative side of the 50-yard line inside the 35-yard line. Three of the possessions will be between the two 35-yard lines. One of those 12 plays will start going into the end zone. There is an average of 66 plays in a game. Twelve of the 66 plays are possession starts. There are 16 other first downs made by the offense during a game. There are 22 second-down plays during a game. There are 16 third-down plays. The distribution is equal among short-, medium-, and long-yardage plays.

One of my pet peeves is a long list of long-yardage plays. If you have a long list of third-and-long plays, that means we will be in that situation many times. Do not waste your time practicing 5 to 10 plays for a situation we will be in five times during a game.

If you organize the plays into coming out and going in, the players should be able to call the plays. They know from this place on the field, this is what we run. That is how we should practice. You cannot stand on the sideline and create uncertainty by doing something that you do not practice. On occasion, I have the coaches take our script, put it up beside the down-and-distance calls, and see what we did. If the coach cannot justify the differences between the script and the situation play calling, you will confuse the players. The biggest plays are the ones we practice.

What I talked about today is what I do. This is one head coach talking to another head coach. This is the thinker's time in football. Jacksonville State University is the only university to have won a national championship in football, basketball, and baseball. Florida, the University of Michigan, the University of Southern California, and Texas have won two but no one has won all three. That tells you about a culture in Division II. We lost our culture because we did not know how to make the next step. I am the second coach to come in at the FCS level, and in two years, we will be at the FBS level. We will be in the Sun Belt Conference. That is what they brought me to Jacksonville State to do.

We have the highest winning percentage of any team in its league in the FCS. We are in the OVC with a winning percentage of .762. We play in Kentucky twice next year. We play Kentucky and Murray State University. I can tell you Chris Hatcher is a great coach. He runs the spread and I respect what he does with his players. He scares the hell out of me.

I am honored to address you today. I appreciate your time and attention. Thank you very much.

TRAINING QUARTERBACKS AND TEAM CORE VALUES

Duke University

I am excited to be in Charlotte. First, I want to congratulate the Butler High School staff and head coach Mike Newsome for winning the State Championship again this year. In addition, I want to congratulate all of you that had outstanding years including Jimmy Wallace of Northwestern High School of South Carolina. We have coaches here from several states, including North Carolina, South Carolina, Tennessee, Georgia, West Virginia, and Virginia. Do we have anyone from another state here today? Alaska! I love that.

As coaches, we should not label players. Coach Paul "Bear" Bryant was the best I was ever around who could make people believe they were better than they really were. All of those hopes and dreams those kids carry around with them through middle school, they bring to you at the high school level. You may say you do not have a big-time program. It does not matter who you are or where you are, the kids bring their hopes and dreams to you.

What coaches do to instill discipline, academic integrity, and integrity as a human being is a big deal in what we do. Remind me at the end of this lecture to tell you a story about Todd Helton. I will tell you that story because that is what sums up coaching.

I am going to talk about quarterback play. I am going to talk about the mechanics. I am going to talk about some things we feel make quarterbacks good football players. I am also going to talk about things I think make others good players. I will show you tapes of different eras on offense. I want to show things on the consistency of the offense, and teaching habits, from place to place and era to era, that we continue to have success over the years. Many coaches have success because they believe in what they teach.

I will start with some footage from 1994 and 1995 tapes. The tape is of Peyton Manning when he was a very young player at Tennessee. A lot of coaches will look at him as a skinny kid, which he was. Most coaches look at his hands, which we do look at the hands as he takes the snaps. A lot of teams today do not teach their kids how to take the snap from under the center. Don't fail to teach your kids how to do that. There may be a time and place where they will need to know how to take the snap from under the center. They need to know this, and you need to know how to teach it as well.

What I am looking at are his feet. What do you see that is unique about his feet? Can you see how narrow based he is? This keeps him from taking false steps and from stepping on his own feet. His stance is a little too tight here, but it is an exaggeration. We talk about this so you will be aware of the feet of the quarterback. You cannot play quarterback without great feet. You cannot develop great feet unless you start early awareness of this with the quarterback.

There are two ways to train the quarterbacks. First is from the neck up. Second is from the neck down. You can give them a ton of information to work with in their brain and in their eyes. From the neck up, it is critical.

Footwork is very important to all positions in football. The offensive line coaches in here can tell you they spend a lot of time on footwork with their linemen. They will tell you that you must do the drills repeatedly to get the footwork down. The same is true with the quarterback.

As you watch Peyton's footwork, see how low his feet are to the ground. That is an important factor for a quarterback. The quarterback does not want to pick his feet up very high. If you go look at tapes from the Indianapolis Colts, you will see he still has his feet close to the turf when he moves. The quicker he gets his foot back on the ground, the quicker he can make things happen. If they do not do something in 1.2 seconds, they are going to be on the ground with the defenses they face today.

We do not pretend to coach quarterbacks. We coach quarterbacks! That is the difference. The reason the good quarterbacks are successful is because of the good habits they develop. How do they develop those good habits? By running plays over and over again the correct way.

To be the greatest handoff quarterback in the NFL and the greatest faking quarterback in the NFL requires no special skills other than the most important skill in football, and that is discipline. It is the discipline and willingness to do it time after time.

How do you train kids? You do it every minute you are with them. If I am a position coach, and I come into the room for a meeting or on the field, I have their attention. They are sitting where I want them to sit, they are doing what I want them to do, and their eyes are on me. There is energy about my mood because our day has begun. At that point, we are getting better. I am talking about pre-practice and pre-snap periods before practice. We watch the quarterbacks as they go through the drills. We coach them in the drills every day. It is just a matter of developing good habits.

One of the keys for a quarterback is to keep the front shoulder flared a little so he has command of the field. He uses his eyes on the defenders as soon as possible. Peripheral vision is phenomenal. If the quarterback can use it to his advantage, read to the goalpost, and get good at reading the defense, it really helps. He will know what the secondary players are doing. He can see linebackers moving sideways or moving with depth. This gives the quarterback a lot of information on the first two steps.

The game is fast, and we must coach it fast. We want them prepared to run out of the pocket when we call run. When the pocket collapses, we want them to have two hands on the football. When he comes out of the pocket, we want both hands on the football. When the quarterback is out of the pocket on a scramble, we want him to maintain the ability to throw the ball.

He must keep his eyes downfield while he is on the move. That will make a defender hesitate one second. If the defender hesitates, the quarterback has a chance to get back to the line of scrimmage and to make some plus yards on the play. Once he crosses the line of scrimmage and becomes a runner, he is the same as any other offensive back or receiver. He must tuck the football away.

We want the quarterbacks to have core strength. It does not take a lot of strength to throw the football. One of the ways to teach a player to throw the football is to get him in a room and have him throw the ball to the ceiling. If he releases the ball properly, the ball will come right back to him. Did any of you do this when you were a kid? I used to do it all the time. I would lie in the bed and throw the ball to the ceiling, and it would come straight back to me. If the release is right, it comes straight back to you. There is not much wind up to the throw. If you do it proper, it becomes a habit.

In the old house I grew up in, unless the ceiling has been painted since, there is a brown dot on that ceiling where I threw the ball time after time. My daddy spanked me a couple of times over this. Nevertheless, it was worth it to me. This is what I told him. "Daddy, there is no one at school who can throw the football like I can throw it."

It is a matter of developing good habits. It is like letting kids shoot a basketball that is too big for their hands. They develop bad habits, and they never get out of it. They never become great shooters. Therefore, it is important at the beginning to develop good techniques. You may have to throw the shorter passes. Do what you have to do to develop the good habits in the quarterbacks.

You should come to watch us practice to see what I mean by good habits. People say, "Perfect practice make perfect." I do not buy into perfection. I do not think there is such a thing. What practice does is to make permanent. What you do over and over is what you become. The players you see on Sunday may not be the best athletes in football. However, those that play on Sunday are willing to commit to doing things the right way, over and over. Again, practice makes permanent. Your personal habits will make you who you are. There are no ifs, ands, or buts about it. It is not an accident. It is a habit.

We want to make practice like a game. When I walk into a meeting, we are in a learning session.

"It is who you are! They become who you are." Success is not an accident. There is a great book by Tommy Newberry with that title: *Success Is Not an Accident*. People want to say, "Man, you are lucky." I have never been lucky. I am fortunate. Luck is totally random. You cannot measure luck. No one on this earth has found a way to measure luck.

You can be fortunate. That is what I do. I have been around some phenomenal people. I have tried to study the good points from every one of them. I have taken the opportunity to grow. I am here preaching to the choir, and you guys are here on Sunday morning. Where are all of the other coaches? Again, it is not luck. You can be fortunate. Good fortunate is a great thing. Take advantage of it.

I love to check the quarterback's ability to focus, look back to see how accurate the ball is. I throw challenges to the quarterback anytime I want to. This is a taste of what we do with our quarterbacks.

If we want to talk about labeling kids and labeling a program, this is what we hear often: Duke? Football? When I travel through the airports, I have some smart-asses ask me if Duke University plays football.

I want to talk about our core values. This is the same information I gave to our quarterbacks when I was an assistant coach. As a team, we believe in these core values as a position and as a program.

DUKE FOOTBALL CORE VALUES

- We are a team that is unselfish and unified to accomplish our collective goals. Individual rights and agendas are set aside because the good of the team is much more important than the agenda of any individual.
- We are a team that has respect for each individual on the team, knowing that each member is essential to our collective success.
- We are all about hard work. No one will outwork us in the weight room, on the practice field, or on the playing field.
- We are a team of utmost integrity. Our words and our deeds are the same. We are who we are in class, at home, and in the community.
- We are mentally and physically the toughest team in the country. No one outhits us, and we do not let adversity affect us negatively. Surge!
- We can count on loyalty with each member of the team. We are loyal to each other, to the coaches, and to the core values of the team.
- We thrive on discipline because we recognize that discipline is the key to our success.
- We thrive on conditioning. This is our path to always being the best we can be.
- Winning is our destiny. We play to win every drill, every practice, and every game. This means that each player is consistently striving to reach his potential.
- We always play with our heart. This means that we are passionate on the playing field. Every part of every second of every play.

Those values are things we believe in, and this is where I start in evaluating a quarterback. Certainly, he must have command of the ball. I like the skilled athletes playing quarterback. I like to see the quarterback how he uses his hands with the ball. The next thing I want to see in the quarterback is this: does he make everyone around him better? That is the greatest gift the quarterback can have outside of having command of the football. We have all played with those type quarterbacks, we have coached them, or we have seen them. They make everyone around them better. This is where it all starts, and we truly believe in the first core value.

All of the core values are important. We believe in hard work. In the weight room, the preparation is the prize. I met with a group of walk-on candidates recently. That is a big deal with us at Duke. I told them all of the things needed to get to become a walk-on at Duke. Walking on at Duke is the greatest deal on earth. Number one, you get to enroll at Duke. They are getting one of 1,700 slots where 27,000 apply at our school. That is a good start for the walk-ons.

I tell them the walk-ons will get a personal trainer. They can change the player's habits for a lifetime. They get a physical therapist and trainers. I finally wrote on the chalkboard: "Hard Work = ?" I told them it was going to be hard work, and after I wrote it on the board, I had no idea what the answer was going to be. I did not talk about receiving a scholarship later, or playing time, or anything else. I asked them this question: "What is the most valuable part of that equation?" I did not get a single response. I replied, "The most valuable part of the equation is the hard work itself." What a gift you can give to young people to work their rear ends off. This is an unbelievable gift.

The time in practice and training becomes who you are later. I had the meanest high school coach who has ever walked the face of this earth. We practiced football often without a football. It was a joy for the quarterbacks to get to use a football in practice. Can you imagine practicing without a ball? However, I kiss him on the cheek every time I see him now.

I lost my father early in my life. All of the hard work my high school coach put me through and what my mother did for me is who I became. Hard work is the greatest gift you can give a youngster. You work them with the right spirit and attitude.

I had to dismiss some players from Duke, unfortunately. I do not like to do that. One of the things we will dismiss a player for is for him to lie to us. If he looks at one of the coaches in the eye and then he lies to us, we will get rid of them. We let three of them go. They only get one chance to tell the truth. We will fight for the players behalf, but not if they lie to us. If they lie to us, we are going to dismiss them. There is nothing worse than to tell us a lie.

If you believe those core values, you have to back them up. We thrive on discipline. It is the key to our success. Discipline is a big word. You may have to work that out yourself as to how you want to build discipline in your program. You must decide where you are going to draw the line on discipline.

One of my great beliefs is this: the start and finish of a drill, the start and finish of a play, the start and finish of a practice, the start and finish of a game, can often be broken down. If I am watching a drill that Peyton Manning does, I can watch in a meaningful manner. Our rule is to break it down to the first, second, third, and fourth quarters.

We all want to be better in the fourth quarter. Games are won or lost in the fourth quarter. How did you do that? The only way to develop a habit

of winning is to finish strong. We always want to start good. If we are working with players in a drill, we want them in a good stance, we want them alert, and we want them ready, but they must be better at the end. If you are an offensive lineman, you must be surging at the end of the play. If I am a defensive football player, I have to be better at the end of the play. If that becomes a habit in each of our coaches' drills, then guess what? "We are going to become a good fourth-quarter football team." It is a learned habit like everything else. That is what winning happens when winning becomes a destiny. It is playing with heart and passion, and playing every second of every play.

I want to go over our mission statement. This is something I think everyone should have. Even the position coaches should have a mission statement for the position they coach.

DUKE FOOTBALL MISSION STATEMENT

Our duty is to compete in everything we do at a level to win the Atlantic Coast Conference Football Championship. Our standards of excellence ask, "Is this good enough to win the Atlantic Coast Conference Championship?" We value discipline, conditioning, and integrity. We are unified in faith, family, future, and football. As a Duke Football family, we believe that every person who is a part of our program will be a better person for the experience. We strive to leave people and places better than we found them. We will be champions in all that we do. Win the Atlantic Coast Conference Championship!

This is something I wrote, and it is exactly what it says. If you write it in a mission statement, then you should value it. I have more championship rings than I have fingers. I am thankful for that. I have been in a bunch of championships. I have never compromised in putting the three Fs in front of football. It is faith, family, future, and football, in that order. I have run into administrators who did not see the game the same way as I see it. However, our players lose faith in us if we do it any differently in our dealing with them.

I feel our team believes the coaches allow them to put faith, family, future, and then football in their lives. They can celebrate their family values amongst each other. Their future is filled with a lot of things including academics. They are disciplined, and they have opportunities in life, and then it is football.

What Coach Bryant used to tell the players about the football helping them in the future was interesting: "What football is all about is this: Football is going to help you in the future. You are going to be 45 years of age. You go in to pick up your paycheck, and the boss tells you that you no longer have your job. You have a 16-year-old, a 14-year-old, and a 12-year-old kid at home. When you get home, you find out your wife has left you for someone else. You must decide if you are going to give up on life, or if you are going to continue with your life. This is how important the game of football is to you."

Academics is not the only thing we are concerned with here. We go back to the hard work we went through. It goes back to bowing the back when it gets tough. Not enough of us are teaching those lessons.

All members of our total staff are better for being a part of our program. In addition, we are better for having them as a part of our program. Moreover, our equipment people are awesome. They will do anything to help the kids in our program. This makes it special. This changes what we do in that it makes things a lot more important. We strive to leave people and places better than when we found them.

I am going to insert a personal reference here. This point is what we are really talking about. This is the same story I have told every freshman I have ever coached. My father died when I was young. We did not have much, but we had everything we needed. We had one car in our possession: a 1952 Chevrolet. My dad had to work seven days a week. On occasions, he would get a Sunday off. I can remember the first time he took us to the park. He had six kids in the Chevrolet, but my mother did not go with us. She did not like riding in a car, and she had never driven a car. When we arrived at the park, we came rolling out of that Chevrolet like gangbusters. We took over that park. My dad sat under a tree and smoked his cigarettes while we ran around the park. We had a great time. This was heaven to us.

My dad could whistle. With him, it was like the red light, green light game. When he gave the first whistle, everyone stopped dead in his or her tracks, right there. On the second whistle, you better come running like a pack of dogs to my daddy. My dad gave the second whistle, and we went running over to him.

It was nearly dark at the time. One of my sisters outran me and got into the car. My dad yelled out, "Oh no, you don't." He told us all to come over and join him. He got us all up on a big concrete picnic table. He asked us this question over and over: "What do you see?" We all were yelling to go home and telling my dad that we were hungry. We did not see anything other than all of the other people leaving the park. It was time to go home.

My dad started telling us what he saw. He said, "I have been sitting over here watching things all day. There is litter and trash all over this part of the park. I want every piece of paper picked up before we leave." Our reply was, "Daddy, we did not throw the paper on the ground. "Hush your mouth, and get busy picking up the trash."

All of a sudden there were six Cutcliffes running around picking up the trash and garbage. You have seen those big 55-gallon oil drums they used in World War II surplus. We filled up three of those drums in less than an hour. The streetlights were coming on in the park by then. He sat us back down on the big concrete table again.

Again, he asked us what did we see? Before we could answer, this is what he said: "Now, this is what a park should look like. The grass is green, and it looks like a carpet." He told us how good the park looked after we had picked up the trash. Then he told us something that I have never forgotten.

"I want you to remember something important. When a Cutcliffe goes somewhere, you leave the place better than what you found it. Do you understand this? It does not matter what the circumstances are; you leave the place better than what you found it."

That is a great lesson. If every Duke freshman could make this commitment, how good could we be in four or five years? It should be very special. They should not be at Duke unless they are special people. We should not recruit them if they are not special. That is how you build championships. It is a start for football. That football is not worth a damn if you do not have some substance behind it.

I have some slides of the back of the new press box at Duke. We are taking out the track and filling in the end zone. Behind the end zone is the area where our new indoor practice facility is being built. It will be a full-length, 120-yard football field inside the facility. We will have a full-length turf field behind the scoreboard. We are taking the track out, and we are going to lower the playing field five feet from where it currently is located. We are going to maintain grass on the field. We are going to bring the stands down closer to the field. This will give us a seating capacity of 44,000, which is about perfect for what we want. We want the highest quality stadium in the country. I am real proud of what we are doing with the stadium. Our field house should be finished by August 1, 2011.

Let me get back to some of the things I wanted to tell you about the quarterback. These are points we start with for quarterbacks. We make this presentation very intense, and it is critical to our success.

Be the Leader of the Offense and the Team

- Earn, command, and keep the respect of your teammates and coaches through:
  ✓ Your attitude
  ✓ Your commitment to the team
  ✓ Your plan, in practice and in games
  ✓ The habits you form on and off the field
  ✓ Your desire to be a champion
- Set an example off the field
  ✓ Preparation for the opponent (mental and physical)
  ✓ Attitude and demeanor in the meeting room
- Own the huddle
  ✓ Command the attention, respect, and confidence of your teammates with your presence.
  ✓ They must believe in you and the play you are calling.
  ✓ Be loud and clear. Make sure everyone has the call. Show them with your eyes and your actions that you believe it will work.

Practice Hard and Compete Every Day

- We have no days off (mentally, physically, or emotionally).
- Our performance affects the performance of others dramatically; make your teammates better each day. Be fundamentally sound.
  ✓ Take care of the football.
  ✓ Quarterback-center exchange
  ✓ Run game transfers (handoffs and tosses)
  ✓ Front-hand pressure in the pocket (two hands on the ball)
  ✓ Break the habit of "patting" the ball.
  ✓ High percentage throws
  ✓ Eliminate "poor decision" turnovers (bad reads, bad throws, bad choices).
  ✓ Know the "silent alarm" (the time when you know something must be done with the ball—tuck, throw away, run, find a receiver).
  ✓ Make a profit every snap.
  ✓ Lead the country in least number of turnovers.
  ✓ Be coachable in trying to correct mistakes.
  ✓ Work hard to correct mistakes that we make.
  ✓ Work hard to not repeat those mistakes.
  ✓ Improve every day at something.
- Footwork—everything a quarterback does is affected in one way of the other by his footwork.
  ✓ A quarterback must get to the proper depth on all of his drops in the passing game.
  ✓ Make proper angles from center to ensure safe exchanges and good tosses in the running game.
  ✓ Start on balance in the pocket, step and throw on the same line, and finish on balance to give the best chance to throw accurately. No falling away!
  ✓ Run and throw on the same line when you are throwing on the run or moving the pocket.
  ✓ Redirect your feet with your eyes when you are going through your progressions in the passing game; do not throw across your body.
  ✓ The subtle movements in the pocket that keep plays alive require an ability to move short distances with quick feet, keep your balance,

help your linemen and backs maintain their blocks, and understand how to handle the rush that is presented without giving up on the play.

- Throwing mechanics
- Processing information
  - ✓ Pre-snap
  - ✓ Anticipate possibilities.
  - ✓ Use your drops to gather information.
- Be a great faker with and without the football.

Pass Progression

- Know how to read pass play.
- Be disciplined in your progression.
- Know the difference between a progression read and a coverage read:
  - ✓ Progression read: A pass play where three or more receivers are looked to in a 1-2-3 progression. "Is he open, is he open, is he open?" Read blitz answer 1-2-3.
  - ✓ Coverage read: A pass play in which the coverage played by the defense will help determine which side of the field you will be reading. (*Coaching point:* On progression read plays, the coverage could help to determine where to begin your progression by taking away one or more of the options you would normally start with.)
- Improvise only when things break down.

Once the quarterback learns coverages, it enables them to move on in the teaching progression. Coverages include quarters, half, and thirds if it is zone defense. Coverage is man, man underneath, combination, or up. Once they learn this as a quarterback, it makes it a lot easier to teach them.

The other thing I do with quarterbacks is that I will not talk about passing routes with them for one month. All we do is to teach them defense for a month. We teach them the history of defense. We teach them the history of the zone blitz. We teach them what it is, and what is happening in the defense. On progression read plays, coverage could help us where we would begin our progression. What I am telling you is to have a plan to teach the quarterbacks what they are doing.

I said I would share one story with you today. We signed Todd Helton at Tennessee as a quarterback, but he was also a great baseball player. I knew his first love was baseball. He is now a star with the Colorado Rockies. His lifetime batting average is .330. He is going to be a Hall of Famer. He has had a great career.

When I was coaching Todd, he loved the fact he was a backup quarterback. He had the best seat in the house. When it was cold, we gave him a jacket. If it was hot, he was under the mist fans.

We were playing Florida, and I always gave the quarterbacks a test on a list of some reminders and tips the night before the game. At the end of that session, I always included a section called the bonus round. I would write down some things I had read that reminded me of an important issue about life. They had nothing to do with the game. Players still ask me to give them the bonus session. Tee Martin told me still had every bonus I gave him.

After the Florida game, Todd came into my office the next day, fussing. He said, "Coach, you gave me a lot of stupid questions on the test, and in the bonus section, you included something I will never use." I told him to get out of my office and get to work. He yelled back, "But you made me miss my batting practice."

Someday when Todd retires from baseball and is 45 years old, he is going to be driving down the road around 3:00 p.m. and he is going to pull up next to a school bus stopped at a red light. It will finally hit him. What I told him before the Florida game was this: "Be sure to smile at the kids when you pull up next to a school bus. You will never know how much that means to kids."

He is going to look up at that school bus and see a second-grade student looking out the window, and he is going to smile. Then, he will know how important the little things are in life.

It is the same in coaching. You never know how important things are to a young kid. It is awesome the amount of influence coaches have on the lives of young kids, still today.

Thanks for your attention. Good luck next season.

DEFENSIVE CONCEPTS AND LINEBACKER PLAY

The Ohio State University

I want this to be as informal as you want. If you have questions, ask them. I came to Ohio State as a defensive end. Through the evolution of things, I slowly moved to the inside at tackle. If I had gone one step further, I would be in the offensive line.

I am going to start by talking about some concepts we think are important. The first thing is what we refer to as a "time step." When I talk to our players, I talk in theory. Some of the young players we bring in do not understand that, and I have to break it down for them. I am going to give you a little theory and reality. You have to know the difference between theory and reality.

There is a theory behind what we teach, but there is a reality in what we get. We want to get the players into a position where they can relate. I call this a time step. We are a 4-3 defense, but we are not traditional in any way. We put our players into position where they can be successful.

We are a base 4-3 defense, and we try to teach our players that we are a gap-control defense. We align in a three-man front and a four-man front. However, the concepts of what we try to do behind it still remain the same. When we have movements in the fronts, we call that a concept. The things we do in the base defense hold true in our zone pressure games. The concepts of being a gap-control defense remain constant regardless of the movement.

A time step means we, as coaches, can stand behind a player, watch his footwork, and know whether he knows what he is supposed to do. The linebacker has to know that if the line moves in one direction, he has a reaction to that movement. If the line movement goes to the right, he knows his movement has to be in a left direction. He has to understand what he is doing. He plays fast if the play-action is away from the movement of the front. He can slow down if the play-action goes in the direction of the front.

If the ball moves in the direction of the front movement, it will be a cutback play. If the ball moves away from the movement of the front, it will stay to that side. The linebacker plays fast away and slows toward the movement. That is a theory of the concept. People talk all the time about the speed of players. The speed of a player does not matter if he runs the wrong way.

We talk to our linebackers about being patient and under control. The eyes see the ball go in one direction, and it tells the feet to chase it. In theory, if the ball goes in the direction of the front's angle, it will come back to him. That is what the mind tells him.

In theory, we are not a big run-through-the-gaps team. We allow our front to beat up the offensive line and the linebacker scrape and run. Sometimes, we will play coverage where we end up a gap short on our scheme. By changing the gaps, we can force the football to go where we want it to go. We stunt the front to change the bubble of the defense. That is where offenses like to run the ball. They want to run the ball to the bubble areas. That is why we move the defensive line. We want to change the bubble and make the offense run where we want them to run. When we move the front, we force the football to where we expect it to go. That allows the defensive front to be aggressive and penetrate the gaps even though we are a gap-control team.

When we play defense, it is not going to be about the scheme. We are going to play with great technique and make sure they understand what they can do. We put them in a situation in which they can play, in order to be successful. That is why we spend so much time on drill work.

Everything with us starts with vision. We work hard in the summer on conditioning and in the weight room. The number-one thing you can say about a great running back is that he has great vision. We need to know how to train the vision of an athlete.

Whenever we do a drill, we start with vision. If you work 7-on-7, individual work, or with the team, you have to know what you see.

When I played the defensive line, I could play better with my eyes closed. If I could get my hands on the offensive blocker, I had a better idea of where I was going.

We are going to be a body-control team. I do not care if the linebacker does not have blazing speed. One of the best linebackers I have ever worked with would run a 4.7 on a good day, but was closer to 4.9 on a normal day. He had great vision and played with great body control. That goes back to the conceptual attitude. I do not want players with great speed who just take off and run. I want players with great position. I want their feet underneath them and shoulder-width apart. I want power. Playing square is power.

In every drill we do, I want to overemphasize those points. When we make a tackle, we drive the ball back five yards. That does not happen in a game. In every drill, we want overemphasis on every technique. In drill work, we want the linebackers to have a 90-degree bend in their stance. It does not happen that way in the games, but we want overemphasis. However, everyone knows the way you drill it is not the way it really works in a game. In practice, we take the ballcarrier back five yards on a tackle. In a game, we hope it is a stalemate.

We train the body to play. We train the eyes to see. However, when it gets fourth-and-goal from the one-yard line, it is not going to be about the call. It is going to be man-on-man. As long as you play fundamentally sound and with confidence, all you can do is bend your knees, buckle it up, and go.

The drills we do train the eyes and feet to work together. We want to stay as square as possible so we can read the number of the offensive player all the way across the line. The linebacker changes his pace off the running back. If we can open our hips and run while keeping the shoulders square, that is the best we can do. If the linebacker feels he is going to be outrun, he opens his hips and runs. When we pursue, we want to be slow and stay on the back hip of the back. We do not want to be in front of him. The sideline is the friend of the defensive football player.

The tackler has to stay square, be patient, stay on the back hip, and he will make the tackle. Players know when it is time to run. What they do not know is when to be slow. We want to train the eyes to see the change of pace. I want to see a change of speed and still be under control.

We do a simple mirror drill. The linebacker mirrors the action of the back. The points of emphasis in the drill are:
• Be square.
• Open the hips if needed.
• Keep the ball hip and back.
• Be slow.
• Be patient.
• Go lateral downhill.
• Change speed and body control.
• When you feel a need to open and run, do it.
• Be able to read numbers.

When we work a bag drill, we work on getting downhill (Diagram #1). We work on stepping downhill over bags. We stagger the bags going toward the line of scrimmage. We work on eyes, being fast down the bags, and body control. They attack the line of scrimmage over the bags as fast as they can. When they get over the last bag, they plant the outside foot, change directions, and run down the line of scrimmage with their shoulders square.

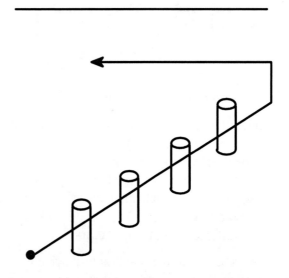

Diagram #1. Downhill Bag Drill

When we do these bag drills, I do not want the eyes down. They have to see the ballcarrier. They cannot look down at people on the ground. They have to step over or shuffle around objects on a football field. The players have to build confidence that they can keep their eyes up and still run. We want to train the peripheral vision. We all drive cars, and most of the time all we see is the bumper in front of us. I miss my exit half the time because I am in a trance, watching the car in front of me. Get your eyes up, and look through the car in front of you. If he breaks, you will see it. If the road turns, you will see that, also.

It takes much more concentration to do that. If I do not think about it, I am back, focusing on the car in front of me. Try to find ways to train your player's eyes. If the linebacker locks in on one key, he is not nearly as quick. The linebacker has to look through the guard and see the back with the quarterback in his peripheral vision.

We do a simple bag drill to teach different foot movement (Diagram #2). We step over the bags and shuffle through them, staying square. I am sure everyone in this room has done the drill at one time or another. We teach the same things. We teach eyes, body position, good stance, and footwork.

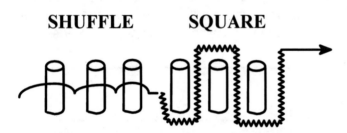

Diagram #2. Shuffle and Square Drill

Ninety percent of the work we do is under the chute. You can work the bag and shuffle drills under the chute. There is nothing special about working under the chute, but the entire idea is about being fundamental. In the fundamental stance, we are in a low stance with good knee bend. We want to maintain that stance in the drill work.

The thing the chute teaches is staying low and taking small steps. When you get under the chute, you cannot take big steps without rising out of the fundamental position. When you take short steps, they make you stay in a good football position.

They develop muscles in those positions, which allow them to play better. We want to develop the muscle memory to stay in that position when we play in a game. If I do the same drill without the chute, they are eight inches higher.

I know they are not going to play with a 90-degree bend in their knee. We do not expect them to play that low, but it trains the body to keep the feet underneath the player. In the game, if we have a 120-degree bend, it is good.

The next drill we teach under the chute is a zone fit drill (Diagram #3). We work the linebacker under the chute, moving to a fit point in the zone scheme. The linebacker moves under the chute, and the back runs to a cone. The linebacker uses good tackling techniques and drives the ballcarrier back five yards. He does not take him to the ground.

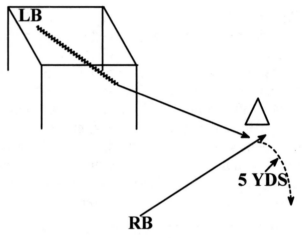

Diagram #3. Chute Zone Fit

In the drill, the linebacker works on staying on the inside hip and behind the ball. He wants to be slow and patient with his pursuit. The thing you want to watch for is the linebacker that starts hopping under the chute to get through it. They are not going to hop on the field during the game, and they will not do it in practice. We do this drill in the tenth week of the season. We may do it only one time, but we still work on fundamentals every week. When things go wrong with the way players play, go back to fundamentals.

When the linebacker tackles, he has to have his feet on the ground. He wants to keep the feet close to the ground and run through the tackles. Power generates from the ground up. The more foot you have on the ground, the more traction and power you can generate.

When a linebacker turns his shoulder and runs, he is out of control. If he keeps the shoulders square and the back still outruns him, he learns a better pursuit angle. If the linebacker is not fast enough to intercept the running, he has to adjust his pursuit angle. He cannot call on more speed. The results of working under the chute will pay dividends.

We work on goal line tackling under the chute (Diagram #4). We also work the same drill without the chute. We want the tackler with a good base. When we make contact with the ballcarrier, we want both feet on the ground. We use the expression "to bite the football." We want to put the head right on the ball. In the tackle, we want the outside foot down for the power produced in the tackle. The tackler starts under the chute and shuffles out of the chute and attacks square on the ballcarrier. The ballcarrier aligns with the tackle and takes an angle to line up slightly outside the chute.

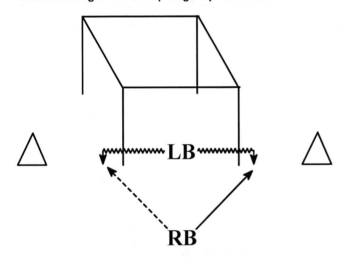

Diagram #4. Goal Line Tackling

When we run the drill outside the chute, we align a back behind a dummy played on the ground (Diagram #5). We have two cones three yards apart at the goal line. The running back attacks from one side of the dummy. The linebacker shuffles to the side of the ball and attacks the ballcarrier. He performs the same techniques as he did under the chute. When he attacks, he must have a good base. We want to bite the ball and have both feet on the ground when we make contact. The outside foot provides the power for the hit. We have to tackle with our eyes. You must see what you hit.

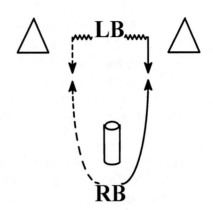

Diagram #5. Goal Line Tackling Cones

We have to be low and play with good body angles. We have to get the outside foot in the ground and get square on the ballcarrier. We must have good drive with the feet and follow through with the tackle. If you do not do those types of things, you have no chance of stopping a 250-pound fullback at the goal line. I want the eyes going across the body to the football.

We have to prevent the ballcarrier from spinning off the hit. You do that with leg drive and wrapping up. The tackle goes back to the great vision and feet. You have a fighting chance if you strike with the feet in the ground, are square, and drive with the legs. If we do not have all those elements in place, we may be able to get the ballcarrier out-of-bounds, but we may not be able to stop him. When we run this drill, it is always a quick whistle.

The next drill we run puts two linebackers under the chute (Diagram #6). This drill is similar to the goal line tackling drill. This drill generally associates with a two-back offense. The first linebacker in the chute is the frontside linebacker, and the second

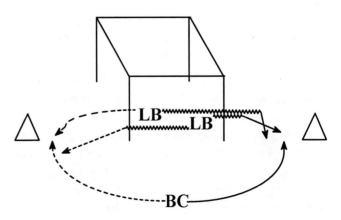

Diagram #6. Two Linebackers Chute

linebacker is the backside linebacker. We align a back and give him a cone to run at. He can run to the cone and turn up at any point. The first linebacker out of the chute attacks downhill at the running back. The second linebacker works laterally out of the chute and fills downhill outside the first linebacker.

This is a leverage-type drill. The first linebacker tackles the ballcarrier or forces him outside into the second linebacker. The first linebacker leverages the fullback from the inside out. The backside linebacker plays laterally in his flow and fits over the top of the frontside linebacker.

If we take the linebacker out of the chute, they both want to fill downhill on the back. We have to train their eyes to read whether the back is toward them or away from them. If he is toward the linebacker, he plays downhill. If he is away, he plays laterally in his initial footwork. All these drills start with eyes and footwork.

We are not worried about someone hitting a big lick. All we are working on is the eyes, feet, and body position. We work off the angles of the backs. I amuse myself sometimes when I talk to young players about what they read in high school. If they tell me they read the guards, I wonder if they knew there were backs in the backfield. Some players tell me they read the ball. I tell them that maybe we can work them in on special teams.

Playing linebacker is all about vision. You have to play on what you see. We mirror the action of backs, and we work our butts off trying to perfect those reads. I have been to places that read the guards when the quarterback is in the shotgun and the back when he is under center. You cannot argue with coaches about the system they want to use. We mirror the path of the backs and make it as simple as possible. We coach the linebackers hard to get the fits of the linebackers in the proper place.

I do not believe you can switch up from week to week with your keys. You cannot read the guards one week and the backs the next week. We want to coach up what we do and be good at it. We want the first linebacker to come downhill working inside-out and the second linebacker to come laterally. He works on a different angle with his flow over the top of the first linebacker. That is what you have to train in their eyes.

We do not do every one of these drills in practice every day. We want to give the players more repetitions in the drill rather than have a bunch of drills with few repetitions. We want to overemphasize everything in practice and engrain in them the techniques. We want to become good at what we do. That may mean we do not do as many techniques, but we are good at what we do. We do everything we can to play good technique and finish everything we do.

We work on a cut drill from under the chute (Diagram #7). I am not sure what the rules are in high school on cutting defenders, but we must work on it in practice. This is a hard technique to train because we do not want to cut each other in practice. We use dummies at the feet to get the players to play with their hands and eyes. Body position is the key in this drill. Two years ago, we had a linebacker get his knee blown out in the first game with a cut block. The linebackers have a better chance of not getting hurt if they play downhill. As soon as they get lazy and do not get into position, they take the chance of the cut block.

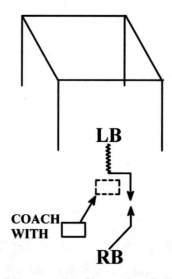

Diagram #7. Chute Cut Drill

The key to doing the drill is eyes, good body position, quick feet, and quick hands. He has to keep his eyes on the ballcarrier and see the bag with his peripheral vision. By working under the chute in all these drills, we want the players to become more comfortable in that body position. We train the body position by using repetition on bending the knees and staying low.

The vulnerability of our linebackers is how fast they see pulling guards. We try to train their vision of the triangle. We do not talk to them so much about reading the triangle. We talk about any target that crosses his face. It does not matter who it is. It could be the backside tight end or fullback. They know the triangle they have to see and any color crossing their face.

In our base, we talk about three things. We talk step and shed (Diagram #8). We know that step and shed is about the inside zone. It is an isolation play. The shoulders of the back we mirror are square and heading in a downhill movement. The linebacker takes on a blocker, sheds, and makes a tackle with the play coming straight at him.

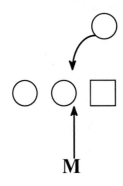

Diagram #8. Step and Shed

We talk rip and run (Diagram #9). That is an outside zone type of play. We have to understand the difference in the technique. We base the read off the angle and shoulders of the back we mirror. In the rip-and-run read, the shoulders of the back angle to the outside. We need to know and understand in his first two steps which way he is going. If the frontside linebacker gets that read, he rips and runs over the top of the edge blocker.

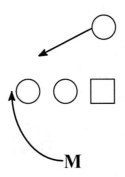

Diagram #9. Rip and Run

The backside linebacker knows he has to rip and run, but he has to go much farther before he gets to the rip part of his technique. He has to move laterally before he can get downhill.

The last thing we talk about is rock back (Diagram #10). That is a counter play or a bend isolation play. It is a play with a color crossing the linebacker's face that brings him back away from the original action of the back.

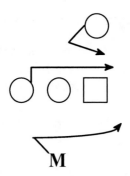

Diagram #10. Rock Back

These are the three things we communicate and teach to the linebacker. The important things are how they play their techniques and what they see rather than the specifics of the play. When we read the triangle, the linebacker sees the counter step of the back and the color of a puller going across his face. He may not know who the puller is, but he sees him. That is his rock back key. We want him in control and patient in his reads.

The linebacker knows who the possible pullers are by the alignment of the formation. If there is a tight end in a tight slot, he is a possible puller as well as the tackle or guard. It could be a fullback or H-back in that position.

There is another concept to this type of thinking. We play our defensive ends so heavy that we get many fold techniques by the playside guard. The guard pulls around the tackle and up on the linebacker instead of coming straight out on him. They block the tackle down and fold the guard behind him for the linebacker. The linebacker gets the rip-and-run read by the back. However, he sees the frontside pull by the guard (Diagram #11). He knows he has to get downhill on the guard before he gets his shoulders square and heads up the field.

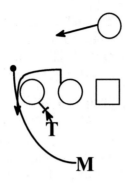

Diagram #11. Frontside Pull

He cannot wait on the puller. He has to be inside-out on the puller, but we have to hit him before he gets his shoulder square and turned upfield. The rip-and-run technique turned into a step-and-shed technique when the guard stepped around the 3-technique defender.

The difference between spill and leverage is about two inches. We tell the linebacker to run through the contact. If you are a spill player, you strike the blocker on the inside eye. If you are a leverage player, you strike the blocker on the outside eye. That difference is about two inches. If he was supposed to spill the play but ends up leveraging, it is not a big deal. However, we want him to attack on the play two yards across the line of scrimmage.

That is the same concept on the edge with attacking a puller. It is not important as to spill or leverage if the contact is deep in the backfield. The offense has to do something with the ball, which requires an adjustment for their designed path. The key to playing these techniques is to hit deep and fast. The backside linebacker plays rip and run, but the frontside linebacker has to attack downhill on a frontside pull.

The frontside linebacker coming downhill on the frontside puller has a chance to make something happen if he attacks the guard on his side of the line of scrimmage. If he lets the 320-pound guard get his foot in the ground and turn upfield, his chance of success is not very good. If the guard gets in a square position, he will overpower the linebacker. As the guard folds around the tackle, his momentum is going sideways. If we hit him while he is going sideways, the laws of inertia take over. We can drive him deeper and completely disrupt the play.

The technique we want to play is step and shed. We hit the guard, but we want to get off him and make a play.

We want the football going east and west. That means the linebacker pursues the back using the same techniques for making a tackle. He pursues from the inside out and stays on his backside hip, using all the techniques I talked about before. Eight out of 10 of the long runs we gave up came outside the edge of the tackle. We have to rip and run to prevent that from happening. When we attack blocks on their side of the line of scrimmage, we have a chance of making the ball bubble to the outside.

BLOCK DESTROY DRILLS

- Hands above the eyes
- Butt back, not under
- Bent knees
- Quick feet
- Hands, hands, hands
- Both feet on the ground
- Power, quick hands, pop

These are the key elements to this technique. We use a simple eye-opener drill to teach a simple technique (Diagram #12). We call the drill a block-destroying drill. When we attack a blocker or make a tackle, we want the hands to make contact above the eyes. If the hands are below the eyes, the defender is straight up in the air. If the defender can get his hands above his eyes, he has power. He has to keep his butt back and get the hands up. It does not matter if it is a defensive lineman, linebacker, or a defensive back playing a stalk block, they must have the hands above the eyes.

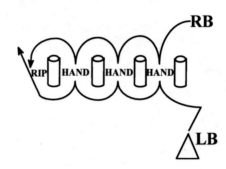

Diagram #12. Eye Opener

That is what we teach and work on. It is the theory, but the reality is in the games the eyes and hands are probably on the same level. Two weeks into pre-season camp, I ask the linebackers if their hands are sore. If their hands do not hurt, they are not using them right. Linebackers must have heavy hands. You have to train them to use the hand until it becomes second nature or a habit to them.

When we do the hands-above-the-eyes drill, we are more concerned with the hands above the eyes. We are not so concerned about hand placement into the breastplate. Linebackers are not going to be stronger than most of the guards they face. We must generate power to offset the strength. The linebacker is not going to hit the guard and bench-press him. It is a quick power stroke to stun him and create an advantage situation for quickness. We deliver the power stroke with both feet in the ground. We do drills with repeating movement to make sure the hands, feet, and eyes are working together at the same time. They stay square in the drill and do it repeatedly.

This year's linebackers were not as good as the ones in the past at blocking destruction. They did a better job of ripping and running away from blocks. That may hold them back somewhat at the next level. It is something we have to work on. Every linebacker has to work on his weaknesses to play.

If the hands of the linebacker are on the offensive blocker for more than a second, we are in trouble. If we keep the hands on him, he will hold the linebacker. We have to hit him with power and get off him. If we cannot do that, we will not win.

The biggest practice periods of our day we spend under the chute. The next biggest block of time we spend tackling. We build most of our tackling into the chute drills with what I call "in-the-box tackling." Most of the tackling a linebacker does is in the box. However, he has to walk out in space and tackle. We spend most of our individual time on open-field tackling. I felt good about what the Arkansas coaches said about our open-field tackling. They said they did not expect us to be so good in that area.

When we get in the open field, we must have pursuit from everyone. The thing we stress is to attack the ballcarrier. We want to take good angles

and challenge the runners with good leverage. We are not going to wait on the ballcarrier. We want to attack it and take some chances. That is what we drill every day.

TACKLING FUNDAMENTALS

- Buzz the feet five yards away.
- Accelerate to the ball.
- Maintain control.
- Take good angles.
- Eliminate the two-way go.
- Do not hop.

We want to challenge the ballcarrier and make a hit. Five yards from the ballcarrier, we want to buzz the feet and get the chest up. We accelerate to the ball and close the distance as quickly as we can. When the first tackler shoots at the ballcarrier, he wants to tackle with leverage because the pursuit is coming. If he misses the tackle, he wants the ball to come back inside and not go outside. The pursuit is coming from the inside.

If the back gets square on the tackler, we give him a two-way go. We do not want to do that. We want to cut off the angle and give him only one outlet. If he cuts back, he cuts into the tackle. If the back moves outside, we will make the tackle. If the back wants to get back inside the tackle, he has to make a drastic cut. That means he comes to a stop or slows down severely.

We teach open-field tackling in a simple angle tackling drill (Diagram #13). We work with the linebacker on the numbers of the field. The running back is between the numbers and the sideline. The linebacker drops in a pass drop and accelerates out

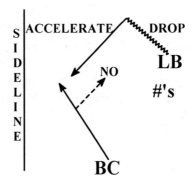

Diagram #13. Angle Tackle

of the drop back toward the ballcarrier, coming up the sideline. The linebacker cuts off the angle, accelerates, and drives through the ballcarrier, taking him out-of-bounds. We do not want to give the running back one way to go.

The coaching point is: "Do not hop." If the tackler hops, he has both feet off the ground and cannot change direction. He wants to come to balance and always have a foot in the ground. The more reps the tackler gets, the more confidence he gains. He begins to feel comfortable with his technique. The tackler must be aggressive and come hard and fast. He cannot slow down or stop when he approaches the tackle. He comes to balance, which does not mean he breaks down and chops his feet. He maintains his speed, gets his feet in the ground and under him, and attacks the ball.

At the end of practice, we condition by doing a strip drill (Diagram #14). We put the linebackers in a trail position on the running back. If the running back has the ball in the inside arm, we want to tomahawk, rip down on the ball, and take it away. If the ball is in the outside arm, we want to punch from behind at the ball. Turnovers and fumbles are not things that just happen. You must work on them so you can create fumbles and turnovers.

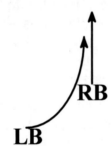

Diagram #14. Strip Drill

We do not do a lot of conditioning after practice. We work them hard during practice and spend time at the end of practice doing some teaching that has a conditioning factor with it. When the linebackers run to overtake a running back, they must work and run hard. This is a five-minute drill of running and chasing a ball.

The last drill I am going to show you is the option drill (Diagram #15). This is a competitive drill between the linebackers and the quarterback and running back. This is a quarterback and the pitchback on the linebacker. When we play the option, we squeeze the quarterback, and slow play the option. If the quarterback turns up with the ball and gets past the linebacker, it is two points for the offense. If he pitches the ball and gets 10 yards, it is one point for the offense.

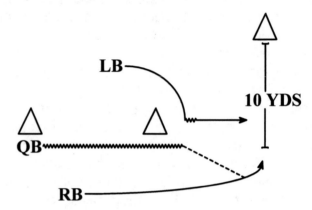

Diagram #15. Option Drill

The primary responsible of the linebacker is the quarterback. We do not expect the linebacker to make the play on the pitchback, but we want to reward effort.

If the linebacker gets the quarterback, it is two points. If he tackles the back, it is two points. If the linebacker causes a fumble and recovers it, that is seven points for the linebackers. The linebacker wants to be patient and make the quarterback pitch the football. If the pitch comes out, the linebacker turns and pursues down the line and tries to catch the running back. If the linebacker hits the quarterback, he throws out his outside arm and tries to hit the pitch. It is a competitive drill, but the linebackers do not usually win this drill unless they cause a fumble.

Thank you very much for your attention.

SPREAD PUNT FORMATIONS AND COVERAGES

Purdue University

I started coaching at Eastern Kentucky University a few years ago. Today I do see some familiar faces here. You are going to see some things today on the punting game with multiple formations. We do everything I am going to show you today and I will show you some things other schools use against us.

I have a ton of stuff to show you. I hope I do not go too fast. The biggest thing I want to talk about is *operation time*. The cardinal rule in kicking is not to have a punt blocked. If you do, there is a great chance you will lose the game. A team does not lose the game because it got the punt blocked, but statistics show when it does happen, the team generally loses.

MULTIPLE PUNT FORMATION

- Operation times
- Spread punt formation
- Traditional punt formation
- Double twins punt formation
- Trio punt formation
- Rugby punt
- Personnel selection

At Purdue University, we run a spread punt formation. Many teams in the major conferences run this type of formation. I want to compare the traditional punt formation with the double twins punt formation. We name the formation from a defensive standpoint. The formation is a double slot look. We have a trio look with three players split one way and a single player the other way. I will also show you the rugby punt games and a couple of different ways to block it. I will talk about a couple of different ways to punt the rugby punt. I will talk about the personnel selection for the punt team.

The spread punt is a trend in college football today. It is not popular in the NFL because of their rules. They only allow three players down the field before they kick the ball. I think every team in the NFL would use it if they could.

THE SPREAD PUNT VS. TRADITIONAL PUNT

- Long snapper does not have a blocking responsibility
- Better personnel on the field
- Attack defenders at the line of scrimmage instead of four to five yards deep with a kick-slide technique
- Attack with momentum moving forward or sideways versus backward
- Teaching time is cut in half (if you can count, you can do it/no kick-slide)
- Already in your cover lanes
- Fake possibilities are unlimited

The biggest thing is that the snapper does not have to block. Everyone in this room knows that is an advantage. It takes the pressure off the center to snap the ball and block someone. That is invaluable for the punt team. With this formation, we can get better personnel on the field. You can get six gunners on the field as compared to two on the traditional punt. That allows us to have six of our best cover defenders on the field. The defensive team does not have six corners that are better than the six cover defenders.

You can attack the defender on the line of scrimmage instead of trying to block them four to five yards behind the line of scrimmage. The technique for the traditional punt is a kick-slide technique used by the offensive line. In that movement, the protector goes backward as opposed to forward. In the spread punt, the blocker attacks the defender at the line of scrimmage going forward or sideways.

It takes half the teaching time when you use the spread punt. You have to teach the kick-slide technique to players that do not use it at any other time. You spend 90 percent of your time in the traditional punt teaching the kick-slide. Late in the regular season, we spend about five minutes a week teaching the punt team. If you coach special teams, you know that time is valuable. You never get enough time coaching those teams. The fact that we do not spend time on the punt formation teaching allows us to devote more time to the other aspects of the kicking game.

When you think about statistics with the punting game, it is not about the length of the kick that matters. Do not be fooled into thinking that the punting average is what is important. It is the net yardage in the punting game. You can kick it 60 yards, but if they return it 50 yards, your net is 10 yards. The net yards in the punting game gives the offense a starting position or the defense a place they can defend.

The spread punt put the coverage in their coverage lanes through alignment. You may not be exactly in the lanes, but you are three-quarters of the way there. In the traditional punt, the coverage team has to fan the field and spread their coverage.

The fake possibilities in the spread punt are unlimited. You have more athletes on the field and your chances of creating big plays increase. The formations make the defense spend time preparing for this formation.

Optimum Operation Times

Level of Completion	Snap	Punter Hand to Foot	Total Operation
High school	.8 or better at 12 yards	1.4 or better	2.2 or better
College	.75 or better	1.35 or better	2.0 or better

This chart is not set in stone or a perfect analysis of every team. This gives your snapper the best chance to throw a great ball. It gives the punter the best chance to get a great kick. Too many times, the coach rushes the punter to the point he cannot get off a great kick. These times give the punter time to get a good grip on the ball, spin it properly, and drop it correctly so he can get the great kick. The times of the snaps for college and high school are close to the same because of the distance of the snap. The high school depth is around 12 yards and 15 yards for the college game.

Teach your specialists early so they have the time to mature before the season starts. That keeps you from getting a punt blocked in the season. Get the optimum times where they need to be before the season starts. If the coach teaches the punter to shorten his steps, he can decrease the operation time immediately. You do not need to take long strides to punt the ball long.

The next part of this is personnel identification (Diagram #1). This is how we identify our players. I am going through our alignment, assignment, and our techniques. In our alignment, we have two guards, two tackles, and two tight ends. We play a right back, middle back, and left back in our shield formation in front of the punter. This is not rocket science and it is the simplest thing you will teach. If you can count, you can play on the punt team.

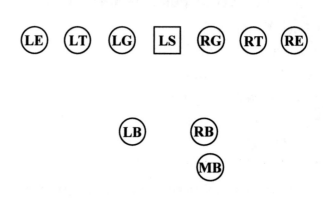

Diagram #1. Personnel Identification

There are different split rules from team to team. These are the rules we use (Diagram #2). We think the splits we teach are the soundest blocking principles there are. In the A gap, we split two yards between the guards and the center. The B and C gaps are three-yard splits. The toes of the shield blockers are eight and a half yards from the line of scrimmage. The right back aligns his outside foot on the inside foot of the right guard. The left back aligns with his outside foot on the inside foot of the left guard. It is a symmetrical alignment.

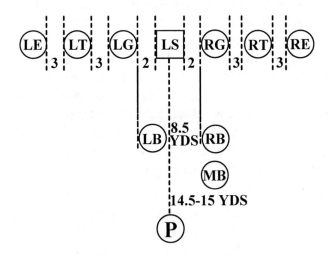

**Diagram #2. Personnel Alignment—
Shield/Punter**

The middle back stands behind the right back, splitting his inside foot in his alignment. He stands in a hinged position like a door. When the ball goes through the gap between the left and right backs, he swings back, closing the door into the gap. There is only a six-inch split between the shoulder pads of the shield blockers. They cannot allow anyone to split them. They protect the block spot two and a half yards behind them. They must hold their ground and not back up or be knocked backward.

The punter aligns at 14.5 to 15 yards deep. The distance depends on the length of his steps. The block spot is two and a half yards behind the shield. That is the magic number. If it takes the punter four yards to get it off, he aligns at 14 yards. If he takes five yards to get the ball off, he aligns at 14.5 or 15 yards. Eight and a half yards for the shield blockers is the best geometry to ensure that we protect the block spot.

The front linemen align with their toes aligned even with the heels of the center. That keeps the line in a legal position on the line of scrimmage. As the season goes on, we work back off the ball, making sure the helmet breaks the belt line of the center. We do not want a penalty for being in the backfield. We start with our toes on the heels of the center and work back so the helmet breaks the belt line of the center.

The personnel selection is critical to the coverage team. The right and left tight ends are the best cover men. They are the gunners to the ball. They are the fastest personnel on the team. We want defensive backs, running backs, and wide receivers in these spots. That position should be the leading tacklers on the team.

The tackles are the second best cover men. They are safeties, running backs, or big wide receivers. They have to run but be quick enough to block a defender in a stack position. The guards need to be bigger people that can run. These might be linebacker personnel, strong safeties, running backs, or big wide receivers. The guards must be more physical because they have to take on bigger defenders in the middle.

The shield protectors have to be the meatheads on the team. The defensive end that has no fear and loves contact can be in this position. The pulling guard that can run fast can be in this position. Any big lineman with exceptional speed can fill this position. The big tight end is another choice. They must be courageous and give themselves up for the team. Big defensive linemen run from the line of scrimmage with the intention of a big collision with the shield backs. However, the middle back has to be intelligent. He makes all the checks and calls for everyone on the punt team.

I want to go over some general assignments for the blocker (Diagram #3). The diagram shows an eight-man defensive front with a balanced alignment. There are two linebackers off the ball over the offensive guard. We count the blocking assignments from the outside to the inside. We only count defenders on the line of scrimmage. The last man outside on the line of scrimmage is #1 in our count system. The second man in on the line of scrimmage is #2. We count from the outside to the inside to the center on both sides. If the linebacker walks up to the line of scrimmage and breaks the heel line of the down defender, we count him. The linebacker at depth is not a threat to block the kick. He becomes a threat when he breaks the heel line of the defensive down personnel.

The middle back calls the alignment of the front. He counts the front from left to right. In the diagram, there are four defenders on the left and four defenders on the right. The call is 44.

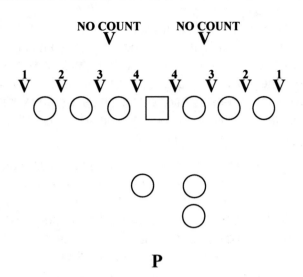

NO COUNT   NO COUNT

Diagram #3. Assignment Count

The blocking assignments for the guards, tackles, and ends are #1, #2, and #3 defenders (Diagram #4). The #4 defenders come through and the shields block them. We never want more than three defenders on the shield blockers. If we have four defenders attacking the shield, we have problems.

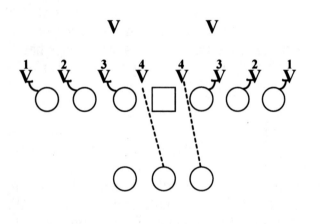

Diagram #4. 44 Front Right Kick

I want to cover the techniques we use. We are in a square stance on the line of scrimmage. We bend the knees to get the power angles in the ankles and knees. The feet are underneath the armpits. We get the elbows in, make circles with the index finger and thumb, and place the hands on our knees. The eyes are up so we can see the defense. They see the ball and the defender using peripheral vision. It is critical to have a great get-off.

The front line uses a bucket step off the line of scrimmage with their outside foot. If the defender touches any part of the blocker inside, head-up, or outside, we consider that as on the blocker. We use a stab technique to attack the defender. With the defender inside the end, he steps with his inside foot using a short six-inch step. He pushes off the back foot and at the same time delivers the stab blow into the sternum of the defender. It is a one-handed blow to knock him off an undisturbed charge. We hit with the heel of the hand right through the numbers of the defender.

If the defender is extremely wide, we use the bucket step like a zone step. We get depth and width in the step, make up the ground, use the stab punch, and get downfield. With a wide defender, it is critical to have a quick get-off. If we take the bucket step and the defender redirects his charge, we do not worry about it. If he redirects, he cannot block the punt. If you can stop his feet with the stab, he cannot block the punt. If the defender does not rush, we get downfield as fast as we can.

The shield blocking is zone protection. They are like the wings on a field goal. The shields protect from the inside out. If there is no threat inside, the outside shields can step to the outside. If there is a threat inside, we need to be heavy inside. The right and left shields can never get their outside hand involved in any blocking. If the outside shield involves his outside hand, he loses his ability to get a punch on an outside rusher. He closes inside to the inside threat but must get a punch on anyone coming outside of him.

The 55 front we count the same way (Diagram #5). The blocking scheme on a 55 front changes. We directional kick the ball. To the kick side, we always block the #1, #2, and #3 defenders. If we kick the ball right, the right guard, tackle, and end block #1, #2, and #3. We release the outside defender away from the kick. The kick side bucket steps and attacks the defender. If the defender is wide, the bucket steps need to be deep and wide. If the defender is close, he steps at him and stabs through his numbers.

The shield backs are responsible for the #5 defenders. They must also block the #4 defender to the side of the kick. The middle and right backs block the #4 and #5 defenders to the kick side, and

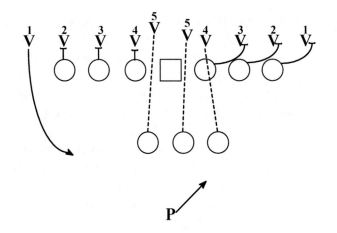

Diagram #5. 55 Front, Right Kick

the left back blocks the #5 defender away from the kick. The end man on the line of scrimmage belongs to the kicker. He steps right and avoids him completely. He knows the defender comes unblocked and makes sure he gets the ball off.

It does not matter where the right guard, tackle, and end align on the field; their blocking assignment is #1, #2, and #3. The right back always has #4 to the kick side and the middle back has #5. If you want to bring him in motion from the outside, you can.

We must protect the next blocking scheme from this formation. We cannot use another formation (Diagram #6). In this scheme, we turn both the outside defenders loose. We block #2, #3, and #4 with the guards, tackles, and ends. We turn both #5 defenders loose up the middle. This does not break the rule of four defenders on three shields because we directional kick. We block the #5 defenders with the middle and left shield. The right shield has the outside rusher coming from

the kick side. It is 3-on-3 and the outside rusher away from the kick cannot block the kick. The right shield does not leave and attack the outside rusher. He stays in position and knocks him off. He has to protect middle threat to outside.

This is a simple blocking scheme and you can teach the players you have on the team to bucket step in no time. The players are athletes and have no trouble with the footwork.

The next thing is a rugby punt. This is a great scheme when you know the defense is coming after the block. Use this type of punt at the end of a game to let the clock run down and prevent a run back. You kick the ball low and end over end. It hits the ground, rolls, and the referees blow the ball dead. We use full zone blocking scheme on the rugby punt. You can zone all the blocks down or outside. At Purdue, we block everyone down. We have a right-footed punter and always roll the protection to the right.

The guards, tackles, and ends block down on their inside gaps (Diagram #7). The right shield goes to the #1 defender coming off the edge of the defense. It does not matter if there are four or five defenders to that side; he blocks the #1 defender off the edge. He attacks him downhill immediately. The middle shield blocks the #2 defender coming from the kick side. If there is no #2 rusher coming, he scans the frontside looking for leakage. The left shield is responsible for the frontside A gap to the backside A gap. The punter does a three-step rugby punt. He rolls to the right and gets the ball off.

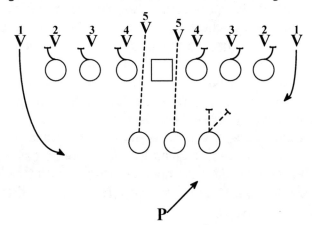

Diagram #6. 55 Adjusted Scheme

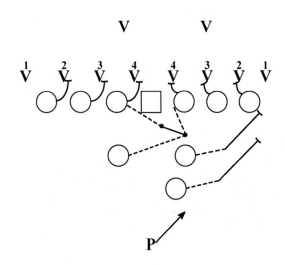

Diagram #7. Zone Blocking Inside

When the line blocks down, they block the defender in the inside gap. If there are two defenders in the gap, the player wants to try to get to the far defender. That means he crosses the first defender and tries to block the far defender. If the blocker tries to get to the far defender, he disrupts the path of the defender closest to him. He can block both defenders by disrupting the paths of both defenders. This type of punt can take 13 to 15 seconds off the clock.

The down side to this blocking scheme is the limitations we have in the coverage of the punt. However, the left side coverage people have momentum inside and can release to the ball quickly. By angling the kick to the sideline, we lessen the chance of a long return or any return at all. We pen the receiver into the sideline with the punt. Anything rolling on the ground is dangerous to try and pick up.

We can use another zone protection moving to the right (Diagram #8). Instead of the guards, tackles, and ends zone protecting inside, they protect to the right. The right side bucket steps to the defender to their outside. The backside bucket steps inside or to the right. It is the same bucket step and the stab we used before. The rule with two defenders in the gap is the same. The blocker goes for the farthest defender and disrupts the nearest defender's path. The rules change for the shields. The right shield, instead of attacking the outside, rolls to the right and looks for any defender coming from the outside first to the inside. The middle shield looks to the right A gap and the left shield takes the backside A gap.

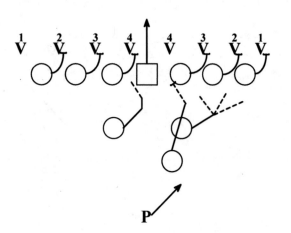

Diagram #8. Zone Blocking Right

When we go to the double twins set, we go back to a traditional blocking scheme (Diagram #9). We have a call for the center and personal protector to designate the gap they block. If we call ringo, the center blocks the right A gap and the personal protector blocks the left A gap. We substitute for the left and right shield players and they become the outside coverage people on each side. The left and right wing or slot players are the left and right ends in the original punt formation. The tackles become the shields and the middle shield is the personal protector.

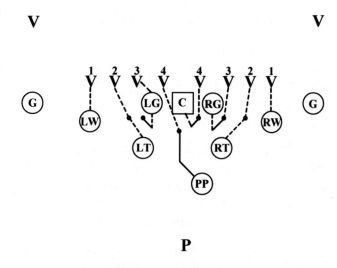

Diagram #9. Double Twins Formation

This gives us four gunners covering and a traditional blocking scheme to the inside. The technique uses the kick-slide by the guards and center. If you have time invested in a traditional punt scheme, this allows you to keep that scheme.

The rules are the same for the trio formation (Diagram #10). Instead of having a double twins, we have three gunners to the same side. The inside wing player has to know that his responsibility is the #1 defender to that side. If he splits and is uncovered, he has to come back inside to block the #1 defender. If the defense does not cover your gunners with three defenders, they run the risk of a tunnel screen. The inside rules are the same. The personal protector gives a lucky or ringo call to the center and blocks opposite that call. All these schemes are simple. If the players can count, they can protect.

There are different ways to cover the punt. We base the cover lanes on our personnel. You can

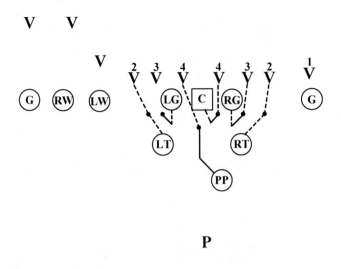

Diagram #10. Trio Formation

turn the tight ends loose to the ball or you can use them as contain players. We do it both ways. The advantage of turning the tight ends loose is the chance they can make a big play on the returner. The disadvantage is the loss of containment if the tight end misses the tackle on the return player. If you send the tight end to the ball, the tackles have to contain.

When we set up the cones in our coverage drills, we want five-yard spacing between the coverage team at 10 yards down the field. The initial split almost puts the coverage team in position. That is the advantage of using a spread punt over the traditional punt formation.

We use directional punting (Diagram #11). The center works down the hash mark to the side that we punt the ball. The guard is five yards outside the center and the tackle is five yards outside the guard. The tight end is five yards outside the tackles. The shield blockers become the safeties on the left, middle, and right. If we kick the ball left, the coverage reverses. The center sets the lanes down the hash mark. He does not have a blocking assignment and can leave immediately.

PUNTING TEAM THOUGHT PROCESS

- Alignment
- Assignment
- Block execution—pre-snap read to determine if defender is rushing or trying to hold me up
- Release—rip, arm over, etc.

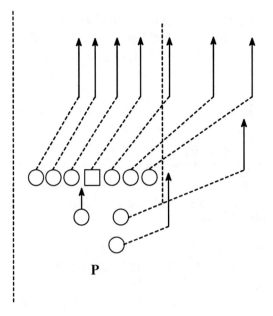

Diagram #11. Coverage Lanes

- Acceleration—stack my defender
- Leverage inside and in front
- Squeeze, come to balance, make the tackle

When we come on the field, the first thing we do is align correctly. After we align, we have an assignment. We know the techniques we use. We assess the defender as to his width and speed. We know where we need to go to block him. Before we snap the ball, we think about the release from the defender. We accelerate and stack the defender. We want our hips and shoulders in front of the defender. If we get in front of him, he can never block us. We leverage the football on the inside shoulder. We keep it inside and in front of us. We want to squeeze the ball and come to balance. That does not mean break down and stop. We want to continue to move on the returner and come to balance to make the tackle. That is the most important aspect of the coverage team.

When we practice the punting game, we do it with a circuit. We are fortunate to have the time to work on the special teams. We work half line in the circuit. We have the left tight end, tackle, and guard working with three coaches. The manager runs the stickball for us. We have a football on a stick to assimilate the snap. To get the great get-off, you must use something to start them. We work off movement and not cadence. The right side and the shield blockers work together.

We are not trying to run the legs off anyone. We work on footwork and hand placement during this time. The shield players work on coming together and working from the inside out. The middle shield gives the signal to the center when everyone sets at the line of scrimmage. He stacks behind the right shield, splitting his inside leg in his stance. When everyone is ready, he flicks his hand and the center snaps the ball some time after that. He can also use a cadence if the team can hear him. The middle shield moves into the gap as the ball passes and executes his block.

In the individual drills, we work on the left and right shields keeping their outside hand freed up. As the ball passes the shields, they step up to eight yards to greet the rushers. We work the individual work for four minutes every three days. We do the drills just enough to brush up the techniques.

The coaches align the scout team in different alignments with different splits. They widen the defenders and stack them. The different looks come during this period, not during the team period. When the blockers stab, they stab through the near number to the far number. We redirect their feet and stop their feet with the hands. In this period, we work on the kick-slide technique.

We do not worry about teams running stunts in their front. If the defenders run sideways at the line of scrimmage, they cannot get to the ball. A looping defender will not get home. Unless there is a bad or a mishandled snap by the punter, any defender that runs lateral or stops his feet at the line of scrimmage will not block the punt. As long as the line takes their proper split, the edge rusher cannot get to the punt if left unblocked.

The general rule for out protection is simple. If we have a four-man side, we block #1, #2, and #3. If we have a five-man side, we block #2, #3, and #4—it does not matter how many defenders the defense puts on a side.

If the defense comes with a maximum rush, we apply our rules (Diagram #12). If the rush is a 64 alignment, we block #1, #2, and #3 to the right and #2, #3, and #4, to the left. That leaves #4 to the right and #1, #5 and #6 to the left unblocked at the line of scrimmage. We do not block #1 coming off the edge in any of the five-man schemes. We block

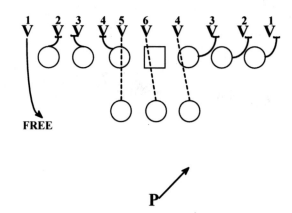

Diagram #12. Spread vs. 64

#4 to the right with the right shield. We block #6 and #5 with the middle and left shields. That is 3-on-3 in the middle of the scheme.

In practice, we go with the punt team against the punt return team. We go best on best and use the JUGS® machine so we get a great kick every time. This allows us to get our punt and punt return work done at the same time. This is a live drill. We work on punt coverage. We work on our footwork, stab, and coverage lanes. The JUGS machine assures that we get the kind of punt we want. It does not happen that way in a game, but time is important. We do not want everyone running and then the punter shanks the ball. When we get to the tackle at the end of the coverage, it is not live for us. The blocking at the line by the punt team and the blocking downfield by the return team is live. However, we do not tackle backs after the catch.

To make the drill complete, you can include a block punt drill. Put a punter in the drill and let the punt return team practice on taking the ball off his foot. We snap the ball to the punter, the defenders rush, one of them blocks the punt. We fire the JUGS machine and the drill goes on. This all occurs in the same drill. The JUGS machine punts the ball, the coverage team covers, the return team runs the ball back, and someone blocks a punt.

This is a great opportunity for your return teams to get live reps in practice. That does not happen often. When the coverage man comes off the line, he assesses what the defender does. If he does not rush, the coverage man sprints, gets in a stack position on the defender, and gets to the ball.

Question: Which zone scheme do you like with the rugby punt?

The inside zone scheme gives you limited coverage down the field. With all the blockers going inside, everyone gets jammed up inside. It is hard to get out and cover from there. The advantage is you will get the punt off. It is very secure and the defense will not block the punt using this scheme.

The zone scheme where everyone zones in the same direction allows good coverage. However, by zoning everyone the same way, the defense can load up one of the A gaps and make it tough on the A-gap blockers. You could get a punt blocker with this type of coverage.

Question: What do you do if you cannot snap the ball 15 yards?

You must have the block spot two and a half yards behind the shield. If you set the punter at 12 yards, the shield has to move forward in the right relationship to the block spot. The defender trying to block the punt cannot get to the block spot unless he runs around the shield blockers. His alignment and movement keep him from getting to that spot. He could hit the punter but he will not hit the ball. The angle is too great for that to happen. It is the block spot and not the depth of the punter that is important.

Thank you and enjoy the rest of the clinic.

A NO-HUDDLE FOOTBALL TEAM

University of Pittsburgh

It is an honor to be here. I never pass up an opportunity to speak to high school coaches, especially in western Pennsylvania. I am going to give you a few things that I believe will help your football program.

I consider myself a fundamentalist. I believe it is all about coaching kids. I am very blessed at the University of Pittsburgh because of the quality of kids that I coach every day. We are very open with the high school coaches that we speak with. During spring practice, we have chalk talk days to explain some of the things that we are doing. You are welcome to come to our place. When you watch us, you are going to see our coaches coaching with a lot of passion. You are going to see coaches treating kids with respect. We are going to strain them and train them. We are going to make a difference in their lives.

I want to talk about my philosophy on how to set up our program. This is my plan and the plan I have used everywhere I have been. We are not just a no-huddle offense. We are a *no-huddle football team*. If you come to Pittsburgh and ask the secretaries, they are going to tell you they believe in the no-huddle philosophy. I want you to understand what we mean by the no-huddle philosophy. I am not the type of coach that will hire an offensive coordinator and let him do what he wants to do. I will not hire a defensive coordinator and have him do what he wants to do. I am going to dictate the vision and the philosophy of our program and how we interact and build relationships. I am going to dictate what the principles are that those relationships are built upon. I am old school. If we line up on Saturday and get our tails kicked, it is going to be by doing the things that I believe in.

What the no-huddle represents to us is that we want to physically wear the opponent out. We want to be more physical than the other team. What is different for us is that we do not have to be a spread team and throw the ball every down in order to be a no-huddle team. People always talk about how we were the number one offensive football team in two of the last four years. What they do not talk about is how we rush the football. What we try to do with our philosophy is to run the football and then we want to stop the run of our opponents. That is how you win football games.

There are certain factors that go into playing winning football. Number one is explosive plays. In the last four or five years, whether it be at Rice, The University of Tulsa, and hopefully here at Pittsburgh, we want to lead the country in explosive plays. What I mean by that is one-play touchdowns. I do not mean just explosive plays on offense; I also mean explosive plays on defense. We want explosive plays in the kicking game. We coach our guys with a great deal of passion, and we also believe that being smart and having great character is also a talent. When people talk about talent, they usually talk about how fast or how big a player is. I believe having great character is a talent. How do you win football games? You get players to do what you coach them to do right—the first time you ask them to do it. I do not think players are different today than what they were 20 or 30 years ago. I believe we have lowered the standard on how we go about doing things.

When I talk about how we do things with character, the number one goal is this. We are going to win every day with great character and integrity, and we are going to build championship citizens, fathers, and husbands, and we are going to develop men with giving hearts.

When I grew up, I did not have a dad. My mother raised five kids by herself with an eighth-grade education. Coaches made a difference in my life. That is why I am standing up here in front of you. That is why I am a coach today. I see myself as a teacher. What we have been doing the last few months is first, assessing and evaluating our players and secondly, we have been building relationships. We want to get to know those kids, not just as football players, but in every aspect of their lives.

We want to build trust. For the first time in the history of our country, there are more kids in nontraditional families than in traditional families. A coach becomes pretty darn important to these kids. Our job is to teach players to win every day, not just on Saturday during a football game.

When I talk about integrity and in doing things the right way, it starts with our staff. When I begin to work on my staff, I try to get better men and women than what I am. They make me a better person by the type of person that they are. They are great fathers and husbands, and they have a passion for young people. If we accomplish our number one goal, then all the other goals will fall into place, whether it is to graduate 100 percent of our kids or to win a championship. If you come out and watch us coach, I am not just a cheerleader. We are going to get after their butts. We are going to coach them hard. We are also going to love them and we are going to treat them with respect.

What I like to look at when I first get to a program is how people respond to adversity. When we first get there, everybody has a positive attitude until something bad happens. How do you respond to that is what I want to know. We coach body language. I want to put them in uncomfortable situations and see how they respond. This is where I am going to coach them.

People ask me all the time if I really started as a seventh grade football coach. They want to know how I got to become a Division I coach. I can tell you this, every coaching job I have had, I have coached with passion. Every single player that I have worked with, I have tried to make a difference in his life. I have never focused on my resume. I have not had a resume in 15 years. The only thing I want to do is go out there and coach those players and develop a relationship with those men, and make a difference in their lives. We teach, teach, and teach. If we're not teaching, we are listening and learning, learning, learning. We are going to adapt what we are doing to the skills and talents of the players we have and the players that we recruit—year in and year out.

We have principles that we go by. I want to elaborate on those principles so you can see where we are coming from.

Faith is believing in something without knowing. We talk to our players about that. The players will meet every expectation that you set for them. It is like my stepfather taught me about discipline. "The pain of me whipping your butt is going to overwhelm your desire to screw up." We do not have time during a game to get everyone's opinion. We have to have faith in everything that we are doing.

A couple of weeks ago, I drove 80 miles an hour to get to a clinic where Joe Paterno was speaking. I just wanted to be in the same room with Joe Paterno. I was jacked up as I was listening to him. One of the things that he said was, "At Penn State, we do not wear earrings." I thought, wow, that is great. We are going to do that at Pittsburgh. I did not go in there on the first day and say, "There are no earrings." I do not really care if they wear earrings or not. I walked into our first meeting and said, "Guys, I want us to be the most unique program in the country. I want you to understand that when you walk in that door, I am going to ask you to do something for me. I want you to take your earrings off as a symbolic gesture to say that it is not about me, it is about the team." I do not know if we are going to win any more games because of that or not. I think we will. It is a physical gesture that they do every day to remind themselves of the importance of the team. I think that is a big deal. At our place, there are no earrings, no bandannas, and no filthy language. I believe what you visualize in your mind, what you work at with a passion in your heart, and what you speak out of your mouth has great power. We are going to have faith, belief, integrity, and character.

What does it mean when I talk about *integrity*? I was recruiting a player this off-season and he was interested in coming to the University of Pittsburgh. One of the things that he said to me was that one of our opponents told him that they were going to make him a first-round draft player. I said, "Really?" I said, "I am not really interested in that." I told him that I would make him the best defensive back in the country, not only on the field, but off the field, in the classroom, and in dealing with people socially. I told him that I was going to work him harder than he had ever been worked before. I would make him the very best that he could be. I told him, "Son, when you get married, I will be sitting there. When you have kids, you are going to pick up the phone and call me to tell me about them. That is what I am going to offer you. If you get your eyes off of all that me, me, me crap, all the good stuff takes care of itself." What I want to do is to bring out the best from every one of my players every day and not accept the worst. That is what we are talking about when we are talking about integrity.

We want to have an *attitude of gratitude*. We are not entitled to anything. We are not guaranteed anything. We want to be givers and not takers. I want people with passion and a work ethic. I am jacked up every day. One of my idols in coaching is Tom Landry. The reason Tom Landry is an idol of mine is because of what he stands for as a person. He has great faith, great character, and great integrity. I am going to be genuinely who I am. When you come over and watch us practice, you are going to see players and coaches hustling. I do not know what is going to happen next fall, but I can tell you this, we are going to run to the ball like our hair is on fire. We are going to be passionate about what we are doing and we are going to make something happen.

This is not nanotechnology. I do not think many people have a plan. It is really simple. It goes back to this, I believe in old-school traditional values. *Work ethic* is important. You do not get anything in life for free. You reap what you sow; you get what you work for. Everything that we do is based on our training and it starts with our mental aspect. I truly believe this. We have a passion about it. I want my coaches to be confident and I want my players to be confident. I do not want them to get down when something goes wrong.

I am going to *speak victory* over them, and I am going to train them mentally. We do not believe in the "Fellowship of the Miserable." Some people are miserable every day. We go into a game, and we expect to win. We do not talk about what we cannot do; we talk about what we can do. I can tell you that our expectation of ourselves is a lot higher than what anybody else's is. In our building, there are signs all over the place that say, "Nine Time National Champion." Everywhere in our building

where those signs are, I have put another sign under them that says, "Expect Number 10." We have not won a game yet so it is not something to boast or brag about. This is just our mentality.

It goes back to our training, our mental training, our physical training, and training our guys emotionally. Training is especially important when you are facing adversity. Everything that we do with our no-huddle or that we do schematically goes back to our training. We operate fast and faster. We are going to go fast and efficient. No one in the country has run more plays than we have run in the last four years. Last year, we were sixth in the country in penalties. That measures your discipline. Everything that we do is going be based on training, speaking victory, and being positive. Strain them and train them. If you can get that kid's heart, you can work them hard. You can train them harder than they have ever been trained in their lives and they will go places that they never even thought of going. I really believe that.

We want to be unique. We have 20 special plays that we run on offense. They are not trick plays because we run them all of the time. We run them in our offense, and certain ones are designed for cover 4, and some are designed for certain areas on the field. We are complex in our organization. Our players know that when we are on the 41-yard line and on the right hash mark that we are going to run a particular special play for that area of the field. Complexity in organization makes for simplicity in our operation. We do not have any trick plays in our offense. We have 20 special plays, including at least two reverses we use per game. I would like to run two reverses per half. We are going to take 10 vertical shots in a game. That is throwing the ball vertically, deep over 42 yards and outside the hash marks.

We believe that being *smart* and having character is a talent. We are able to do more schematically because if we are smart, we should be able to do more schematically. When I ask a player what separates him from everyone else, I want him to say, "I'm smarter. Coach, I have character." I do not want him to say that it is his skill. I am not looking for any superstars. It is old school. I want 11 guys on the field working as a group. We want to be that one program that wins the BIG EAST championship.

We want to be the one program that wins a national championship. In order to do that, you have to be unique. We want to be one of a kind in everything we do. No one in the country will run what we run on offense. We need to adapt everything we do based on the skills of who we have to work with. The first person we look at in order to do that is obviously the quarterback.

We are going to eliminate penalties as a result of our *discipline*. Do it right the first time. We talk about being blue-collar and having a hard edge. You have to have a fullback and a tight end in order to be blue-collar and hard edged. Almost 70 percent of the time, we are a two-back offense. Nobody really notices that because of how we package it. Everybody thinks that we are a spread no-huddle team, but we are really not. We are going to run inside zone, power, and we are going to run our isolation plays. We are going to run our play-action passing game.

We are going to be the *toughest*, hardest working, most disciplined, and prepared team in the country. Our no-huddle philosophy represents how physical we are going to be. We are going to create a fifth quarter by going fast and efficient. We are not going to get penalties. We are going to run the football and stop the run. Our players are going to play with unbelievable passion. We are unwavering in our belief about what we are doing. You have to have a plan for diversity. This is big.

We are going to make it fun. We are going to be innovative. No one really runs what we run on defense. No one really runs what we run on offense. That is good for us. No one really does what we do on special teams. We want to be unique and one of a kind and innovative about what we are doing. We do that because it makes it fun for our players. The design of everything that we are doing is designed to take care of the football on offense and get takeaways on defense. We were number one or two in the country this year in turnover ratio. It is not because we do a strip drill, it is all about the passion and focus of what we do, and we get what we emphasize.

We are designing explosive plays on offense, defense, and in the kicking game. That is the key to what makes it fun. If you watch a 17-14 game, you will find that everyone is bored. We operate our defense out of basically a 3-3-5 defense. We will rush four guys most of the time. You are not going to know which four guys that will be. We are going to bring them from all over the place. We focus on attacking protections and impacting the quarterback and making things happen. We are not going to try to defend every pass play; we are going to, first and foremost, impact the quarterback.

We have accountability on our coaching staff. I have accountability. We are accountable for being who we say we are every single day. We are accountable for doing the things that we say we are going to do.

Following are the six things we are going to do at Pittsburgh. First, we are going to physically dominate. That means that we are going to outhit and outhustle every single team that we play. That means we have to be the best-conditioned team in the country, both mentally and physically. We practice with high tempo and high repetitions. I think the key to winning big football games and winning as a program is the retention of your quality personnel—both your players and your coaches. My coordinators have five-year contracts. Our organization is built on trust. We are going to be a team that physically dominates.

What we run on offense, and everything else that we do, is based on being efficient at running the football. We were 15th in the country in running the football this year. First, we are going to run the football. We are going to be physical. We are going to have a tight end and a fullback. We are going to have a two-back attack and we are going to be known for running the inside zone, the power, and the isolation. We are a run and a play-action pass football team. We are going to run the football 65 to 68 percent of the time.

Secondly, tempo is important. We are going to be fast tempo and going 100 miles per hour. We want to snap the ball every 15 seconds. We make sure that, in practice and in everything that we do, we are going fast. We want to teach our players to go fast and to go efficient. We have three tempos— fast, faster, and fastest. This is how we operate our no-huddle on offense, our no-huddle on defense, and our no-huddle in the kicking game. The whole idea is to wear the opponent out mentally. We want to play every single snap with a passion. We coach this in practice. We talk about straining and that every single play counts, because you only get so many snaps. I believe that our players are going to play like we coach them.

Thirdly, we want to lengthen the game and wear our opponent out both mentally and physically. Gus Malzahn and I would argue all of the time about whether time of possession is important. I am old school. I think time of possession is important. Gus did not believe that. We compromised in believing that snaps are important. If you are coaching defense in college football and we snap the ball 75 to 78 times on offense, you are going to give up 35 plus points. I do not care how good of a coach you are. You cannot play that many snaps and be efficient on defense. We are big on the number of snaps. We want to run 80 plays on offense and about 65 on defense.

I believe vertical passes are important. I started charting every time the ball was thrown 42 yards deep and outside the hash marks. About 70 percent were complete, about 29 percent were incomplete, with one percent intercepted with an average of a three-yard return.

Next, we started looking at where on the field we can get these opportunities. So many opportunities are missed during a game. If our offense has you in a first-and-five situation, buckle up because we are getting ready to take a shot. When we cross the 50-yard line, I think that second down is now first down, third down is second down, and fourth down is third down. We are going to go for it. We are going to get aggressive.

If we are on third down and have five yards to go and we are past our landmark going in, we are going to take a shot. Everybody else is throwing the ball to the first down marker. We are not going to pass up those opportunities. At halftime, I go in and I ask our offensive coordinator, "How many vertical shots did we have in the first half? How many reverses did we run? How many specials did we run?" We want to make sure we are getting the opportunity for explosive plays. Our offense really has a lot of wing-T principles in it. We are all old high school coaches and we have coached on both sides of the ball. I like to contribute to the offense by thinking as a defensive coach.

Fourth, we like to run a lot of misdirection. The base design of what we do offensively is designed to slow the defense down. We create misdirection in the run and misdirection in the passing game. We will run reverses. We cannot run enough naked bootlegs. We will run to the field, we will run to the boundary, we will run to the left side, and we will run to the right. We will be efficient at running misdirection plays.

Fifth, we run a lot of multiple formations. We have about eight running schemes along with the triple option. We have about 10 to 12 pass concepts. We also have all of the motions, shifts, unbalanced, and in-and-out of structure formations.

As a defensive coach, we would base everything off the offensive formation. We will come out in an empty set and end up in a two-back formation. We may come out in a two-back formation and end up in an empty backfield. We want the defense to know that we are multifaceted. We are not just going to run the option; we are going to run the triple option. We do that a lot of different ways. If we want to be the BIG EAST champion, then we are going to have to beat the best teams in the BIG EAST. Sometimes we may not have the better talent. The triple option is the great equalizer. Our offense has to have the triple option incorporated within it.

Sixth, we have been one of the best teams in the country at taking care of the football. We really have to emphasize it. We do everything possible to try to reward our kids and have a focus in taking care of the football. That is big for us and in getting takeaways on defense. We have to be disciplined and with no penalties and no turnovers. At Tulsa, we went two years with only one penalty in the kicking game. You are going to get what you emphasize.

Complex organization is important for us. We have a call sheet for every type of situation that we may face. We are not going to just script a bunch of plays. We are going to have every series scripted. It is based on landmarks. Every time we hit a landmark, we have scripted plays for it. If it is first down and nine yards to go down on the goal line, we are going to have a scripted play for that situation. That takes in a lot of complexity and organization. As a staff, we want to have talked about those things before we get into those particular situations. We do not want to be reactive to everything that happens in the game, we want to have a pre-scripted plan for anything that can happen in a game.

We play in the left lane and we put the hammer down. There are two types of people out there. There are players out there trying not to mess up. There are players out there trying to make something happen. We want people out there that are trying to make something happen with speed and explosive power. Part of our philosophy is about taking shots and in getting the right look. Because we go fast, the defense starts to tip their hand by lining up fast. We can plan if they get into a certain type of coverage, and then we can take a shot. We plan for that type of coverage based on how they have lined up, and we can read their coverage because we play fast. We are looking to get defenses out of position. When they get tired, they will be going all over the place. It gives us a chance for big plays.

Smaller but faster guys can play in our system. Our system is about speed. Last year, the guy in our offense that had more all-purpose yardage than anyone else in the history of college football was 5'6" tall. He weighs about 165 pounds. Our players were phenomenal this year. I think it goes back to this. We work with our kids every day. In all three phases of the game, we are emphasizing playing with speed and being high-octane and explosive. Our guys expect good things will happen. We talk about good things happening all the time.

We talk about not having stupid penalties. We talk about pulling off of a block if it is going to cause a penalty. We coach to compete with a passion. It is about getting players to buy in and getting players to play with passion. You are not going to step onto our field unless you are going to do it "the Pitt way" and how we teach you to do it.

When I was a defensive coordinator at both West Virginia University and at Tulsa, we had one of the best defenses in the country. When I became a head coach, I said I wanted to develop the most prolific offense in the country. When we did that, we did it at the expense of our defense. I learned from that. Defensively, the number one thing we are going to do is to stop the run. We are going to be a physical defense. We practice being physical every day. I have learned that you have to have a definitive plan on how you are going to attack the quarterback. We spend a lot of time on it.

We practice very hard on competing until we hear the whistle. An idea I took from a high school coach in Jacksonville, Florida has helped us. We have someone dressed in a referee's shirt to throw a flag down during our scrimmages when the whistle blows. That way I can see on film who is letting up and who is running to the whistle. It is a big emphasis that we have on both sides of the ball. If you are going to say you are going to pursue the ball, you must have a way to measure that.

If you are going to emphasize tackling and you are going to emphasize takeaways, then those things have to be perfected in your individual drills. Every single day that we are in practice, we run 25 to 30 minutes of individual drills. This helps us to be good fundamentally. Every day, before we go on the field, we have 35 to 40 minutes of class session. We are going to teach them hard and then we are going to have them teach it back to us.

As far as the kicking game goes, our defensive staff works with the kickoff coverage, the punt, and punt returns. The offensive staff takes the kickoff returns. By doing this, our coaches and players take more pride in the kicking game. If our offensive coordinator wants to have good field position, then he'd better coach up the kickoff return team because it is going to predicate his field position. Once we started doing this, we became one of the top teams in kickoff coverage and one of the top kickoff return teams in the country. We were number one in the country last year in punt coverage.

One of the things we take pride in as a coaching staff is working with high school coaches. If you want to come watch us practice or want to hear us talk football, you will find us very open. We do not really think it is about X's and O's, we think it is about how you teach it. When you come watch us practice, you will know that we do it a little bit different from others.

I am probably the luckiest guy in the world to come from where I came from and to get to where I am today. I hope I have said some things that might help you. I want to thank you for making a difference in young people's lives. I was one of those kids, and it made a big difference for me. My seventh grade coach made the greatest difference of anyone in my life. That is why I am a coach today. Thank you.

LINEBACKER TECHNIQUES AND DRILLS

Wake Forest University

I want to tell you how happy I am to be here. I want to thank Nike® for all their support. They not only give to college football, but also all the other sports and the athletes that participate in college programs. Nike is great to us and I cannot thank them enough for all they do for Wake Forest University.

During my career, I have had some tough jobs. I went to the University of Virginia and was a graduate assistant for a year. I coached high school football at Liberty High School in Bedford, Virginia. I coached at Emory & Henry College, a Division III school in southwest Virginia. I coached at Marshall University. I had the opportunity to coach the linebackers for Fisher DeBerry at the U.S. Air Force Academy for 11 years. From there, I took the head coaching position at Ohio University. I was there six years. Following that, I moved to Wake Forest as head coach and have been there for 10 seasons.

The one thing we try not to do is to be a gimmicky football team. We try to teach blocking and tackling. It is tremendously important to have *teamwork*.

One of the first things I want to emphasize is that *character counts*. At the Air Force Academy, Coach DeBerry told our players every day "you are who you associate with." I tell my players the same thing today. It is important to remind our players every day that it is more important to be a good person than to be a good football player. They are not getting that message from many places. Make sure they surround themselves with good people.

The second thing he has to be is a *college bound player*. He does not have to be the number one student in his class but he must want to go to college and get a degree. The third thing is he must be the type of football player that can help us win games and compete for championships. You have to approach players in that order. You recruit them with character, academics, and football ability. Your job depends on you doing that.

The thing we were able to do at Ohio University and Wake Forest is *not to dwell on negatives*. You spend too much time worrying about what you do not have and too little time looking at the things that are in front of you.

At Wake Forest, we have gone through many changes in our schemes. When we recruit, we try to sign the best players we can find. Other programs may recruit players to fit their offense or defense. If they are an option team, they find an option quarterback. We take the best players we can find and mold them into a scheme that fits them.

When we came to Wake Forest, we began playing a slant and angle defense out of a 3-4 look. The problem was we did not have many linebackers. Our two outside linebackers coming off the edges and dropping into the flats were not making any plays. We played The Florida State University and they exploited our weaknesses. We could not make plays when we came off the edge with the outside linebacker and we were late getting into our pass coverages. We were three games into the season and changed our defensive scheme. We went to a 3-5-3 scheme because we had more defensive backs than we had linebackers.

We put a corner in at safety and kicked the safety out to the outside. We played a 3-3 alignment inside and had more skilled players playing on the perimeter, which made us a better team. However, as we recruited, we ended up with more four-man-front type players. We had defensive ends and big inside tackles. We stayed with the 3-3-5 concept but began to kick the front one way or the other and used four down linemen.

This past season, we graduated our two good inside players and had to play younger people. Out of our top six inside players, five of them were freshmen. They were redshirt freshmen but they were inexperienced and not strong enough to play the way they needed to play. However, they were quick and agile. We changed our thinking and went back to the 3-4 defense with the slant-and-angle scheme. We took advantage of what they could do. We moved the front by using slant-and-angle stunts in our scheme.

The good thing about playing a slant-and-angle defense is it gives you many playmakers on the field. That allows the defensive linemen to slant and hold offensive blockers and keep them off the linebackers. If you can get athletic players on the move, that will give you many playmakers.

Our base scheme this year was a 50 look or what coaches call a "3-4 defense" (Diagram #1). We have a left and right outside linebacker. We ask both of these players to do the same thing. Therefore, we do not flip them from side to side. If you drew a line down the middle of your defense, it would not matter on which side these players were. They both have to pressure and drop in the scheme. The safeties and corners are mirror players. However, you might want to play the most talented corner into the field and the more physical corner into the boundary.

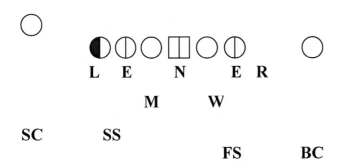

Diagram #1. Base Defense

In our scheme, we will play quarter-quarter-half and roll the coverage into the boundary. That means the boundary corner will be involved with more support and blitz types of play. The safeties have to be good run support players as well as play coverage. The inside linebackers have to be physical players. The outside linebackers are more safety type players than the inside linebackers are.

We play with two defensive ends aligned in 4 techniques head-up the offensive tackles. We play

with a noseguard head-up the offensive center. The inside linebackers align in outside shoulder positions on the offensive guards and the outside linebacker's alignment will depend on the offensive front he sees.

We play our safeties and corners at a depth of seven yards straight across the field. The key to what we do is disguise. We cannot tip our coverage until the offense snaps the ball. If the offense can read the secondary, they have a good idea where the front will go.

I am going to concentrate most of my talk on the inside linebackers. To talk about linebacker techniques, you must start with the stance. I do not think there is anything more important than the way you start. The stance becomes more important when you stunt and blitz your linebackers. Because we want to disguise what we do, the linebackers constantly walk in and out of the line of scrimmage and move before the offense snaps the ball.

When they move before the snap of the ball, they have to set, reload, and get ready to go. That leads to a big problem of false stepping in their technique because they are not ready to play football. There are different sized linebackers.

The thing we do not want them to do is get too wide in their stance. I do not care if their feet are square or in a stagger. Once they get a flow key, we want them to step without wasting any time. If they are too wide, they false step in their movement. In a wide stance, the linebackers gather their feet before they take their first step. If their stance is too narrow, it causes them to hop before they go.

You want the linebackers to have good angles in their knees and hips. If he gets his feet too wide, he cannot move laterally. The only thing he can do in a wide stance is take on a block coming straight for him. You want them to be able to start downhill at a 45-degree angle to the line of scrimmage without wasting any kind of motion.

If the linebacker is standing too tall in his stance, the first thing he will do is drop-step. The important thing about playing linebacker is not to waste time. They have to get where they are going and get there in a hurry. When the linebackers see full flow, we want them downhill and being aggressive.

The linebacker looks through the guard to the backs. We refer to it as feeling the guard and seeing the flow of the backs. The typical fullback will take the linebacker where he wants to go. The simplest way to talk to the linebackers is whether a play is full flow or not. If the play is full flow, they need to get on their horse and move. If it is not full flow, they need to redirect and stay at home.

When the linebacker reads flow toward him, he has to flow into a stacked position behind his defensive end or the C-gap defender (Diagram #2). He does not sit behind the defensive end and wait for the play. We want him full speed in his pursuit by the time he gets to the tail of the defensive end. We want him to pitchfork off the defensive end. If he has read his keys, we want him to get penetration and try to make a play on or behind the line of scrimmage. He wants to penetrate, slip blocks, get through the line, and make a play.

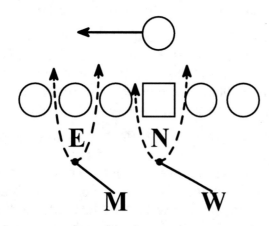

Diagram #2. Flow Toward

He gets downhill and must decide whether to continue to get downhill and penetrate or get wider as the ball moves. That is what we call the "pitchfork technique." He has to decide whether to keep going outside or plant and get back inside. The linebacker's fit off the defensive end depends on where the end charges. The defensive end aligns in a head-up position on the offensive tackle and moves to the inside on a spike stunt or the outside on a loop stunt. The linebacker runs his fit off the defensive end's play. His landmark is where the defensive end originally aligned. We want to push the ball inside out.

The backside linebacker, on flow away from him, does a mirror image of the frontside linebacker. His

fit technique is the same as the frontside linebacker, except he moves into a stack position on the noseguard. He reads and reacts like the frontside linebacker. He reads his keys and pitchforks off the play of the noseguard.

If the linebackers get a fast flow read down the line of scrimmage, they must use a crossover run to get into the play. At other times, the linebackers get what we call a "gray read," where they are not sure what is happening. In that case, they use short, choppy steps to get into their proper pursuit flow.

The good thing about the stacked position in the full flow is you can adjust quickly to the counter (Diagram #3). If the linebacker starts his flow to the stack position but realizes the play is going the other way, he can adjust quickly. If the frontside linebacker starts toward the defensive end but realizes the play is going the other way, he restacks his pursuit angle over the noseguard. He redirects his charge and pitchforks off the noseguard as if the flow had gone the other way.

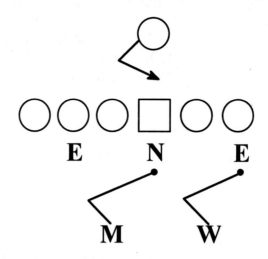

Diagram #3. Counter Flow

It makes it easy for aggressive linebackers playing inside as to their reads and getting to the football. I have different kinds of linebackers. I had a linebacker that was a great hitter and would knock you out, but he could not find the football. I worked with him before, during, and after practice on his keys. He was getting frustrated because he was not making plays. I finally told him, "When they snap the ball, go knock somebody off his feet." I told him I did not care who it was. I told him not to be afraid to make a mistake. When he stopped worrying about it and started playing at full speed, he started to find the football.

The important thing in linebacker play is to get the linebackers running and playing at full speed. The key is to make sure they stay behind the football and pursue from the inside out. We want to press the ball to the sideline because we have help outside. When the linebackers start to run to the outside, it is important for them to keep their shoulders as square to the line of scrimmage as possible. If they turn their shoulders parallel to the sideline and run, it is easy to overrun the ball. If they keep the shoulders square and feel themselves overrunning the football, they have a chance to go into a shuffle mode to slow it down.

The outside linebacker has a different technique he has to play on an option. If his responsibility is the quarterback on the option, he has to play with his outside foot back and slow play. However, when the quarterback pitches the ball, he has to roll over the top of his outside foot, turn his shoulders to the sideline, and pursue down the line of scrimmage as fast as he can. He has to make himself a bonus player on the pitch. He will probably not get to the pitch unless he is an exceptional player.

One of the things you have to do is teach your linebackers how to defend themselves against a blocker. Our linebackers coach, Steve Russ, played for me at the Air Force Academy and for the Denver Broncos for four years. He was a big linebacker but got bigger when he went to the NFL. He likes to teach the three-point explosion. He wants to get the hands and face mask into the blocker. That is a good technique for the inside linebacker who is big and physical. He can get downhill, strike with his hands, get the arms extended, and get off the block. A linebacker with short arms has no chance using that technique. The blocker consumes him.

A good technique to use with the inside linebacker is a forearm shiver. We want to use the inside forearm shiver, get the pads under the blocker's pads, and use the outside hand to get off the blocker. The risk of using a forearm is the offensive blocker holding the defender. That is why the off hand is important to free the linebacker from the blocker. He wants to use the same foot and forearm as he takes on the blocker. He steps with his inside foot and delivers the inside forearm.

The off hand pushes inside to disengage from the blocker. The smaller linebacker must get his pad under the pads of the offensive blocker and maintain leverage.

This is simple stuff, but it was good for us at the Air Force Academy and I think it will be good to us at Wake Forest. The big thing to know about this technique is the guard cannot cut off the linebacker. The advantage the linebacker has is he has outside leverage on the guard by alignment. The gap responsibility of the linebacker could be an inside or an outside gap. If the guard tries to cut off the linebacker, his angle will tell the linebacker where the ball is going. That is one of the rules we have for the inside linebacker. He cannot let the guard cut him off from the ball.

In this defense, we depend on the noseguard making tackles from offensive tackle to offensive tackle. If the offensive tackle tries to zone the noseguard, we expect him to make the play coming down the line of scrimmage (Diagram #4). If the noseguard slants left and the play goes to the right, we expect him to come back down the line of scrimmage. With the noseguard slanting away from the flow, it leaves a gap for the linebacker to cover. However, if the noseguard pursues down the line and the backside linebacker fills, there is no gap.

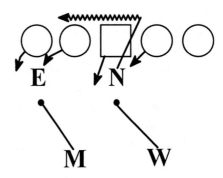

Diagram #4. Noseguard Fill

The other thing that is important to tell your linebackers is to play by their instincts. If they sense something happening and a hole opens, they needs to fill it. If the offense guesses right and catches you in the wrong defense, they have to adapt. When the guard blocks out on the 5-technique defensive end, instead of doubling on the noseguard, the linebacker has to adapt to that. When the angle of the guard's charge takes him toward his defensive end, he has to sense the gap created inside. When he sees the gap, he has to plant and fill his way back into the seam.

This is not rocket science. We want the linebacker to run and make plays. You do not want him to be a robot working on nothing but footwork. He has to know where the ball is going and go make the play. He has to be aggressive and take a chance occasionally.

Another thing we have to teach the linebacker is how to defend low blocks from the offensive linemen. This is primarily a skill for the outside linebackers, but all our linebackers work on this skill.

At the Air Force Academy, we did something that became great for us as a defensive unit. We viewed the percentage grade for our players as if it was the gospel. If one linebacker graded 90 percent and the other graded 80 percent, the 90 percent linebacker played in front of the 80 percent player. That was how we ranked all our players.

When we started studying how our players were playing, we found something else. I had a sophomore linebacker playing for me. At that time, it was unusual for a young linebacker to play. We played mostly juniors and seniors. When we graded the scrimmage films, he graded out at 75 percent. The older linebackers graded out at 90 percent. What we started noticing after each scrimmage was the linebackers with the best grades were not making any plays. The sophomore linebacker was racking up bonus points and making plays all over the field. We stopped posting percentage grades and started posting bonus points to evaluate our players. We stopped looking at the percentages and started looking at how many tackles, forced fumbles, interceptions, tackles for loss, and things of that nature they had.

The point is we want the linebacker to take the 45-degree angle step toward his defensive end as he flows, but that is not the important thing. If he does not take the 45-degree angle but ends up in the same place and makes the tackle, that is the important thing. Make sure you play productive players that execute and make plays.

Do not force your inside linebackers to take on every block. You want them to run and make plays. If they can avoid the blocker entirely and make the play, that is what we want. The blocking scheme

we see today is the zone scheme. If the defensive end reduces to the inside, the offensive guard is working for him with the offensive tackle climbing to the linebacker.

The linebacker has two ways to play the tackle (Diagram #5). He can take him on with the three-point punch and try to fight over the top. However, if the offensive tackle gets too far up the field, the linebacker wants to use his speed and come under the block of the offensive tackle. He does not need to take him on. He avoids the contact and gets the penetration that kills most zone plays.

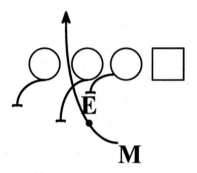

Diagram #5. Run Under the Block

That does not mean we want the linebacker running around blocks. I do not want the linebacker avoiding a blocker because he does not like contact. What I am talking about is undercutting a block and making the play. If they can make the play and not play the block, that is what we want them to do. We teach linebackers to take on blocks, defeat blocks, and defend blocks, but what we want is a linebacker making a play. If they can make a play, we are happy with that.

To help our linebackers with avoiding the blocks of offensive blockers, we run stunts (Diagram #6).

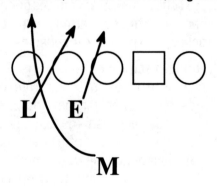

Diagram #6. Slant Stunt

We take the defensive end and slant him hard off the hip of the offensive guard. We bring the outside linebacker off the tail of the offensive tackle. The inside linebacker scrapes and presses hard underneath the zone scheme with flow coming to him.

We have a similar stunt that involves a long stick stunt from the defensive end and outside linebacker (Diagram #7). This is like the angle stunt, except the aiming point for the defensive end and outside linebacker becomes the neck of the offensive guard and tackle. The defensive end goes all the way into the A gap, and the outside linebacker ends up in the B gap. The inside linebacker's path is flatter to get over the top of the inside zone block.

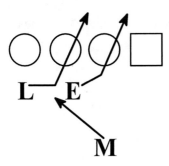

Diagram #7. Long Stick Stunt

When you run this stunt, we try to confuse the offensive tackle. He sees the linebacker inside and sets tighter to the line of scrimmage. The outside linebacker fill the B gap, and the inside linebacker fills over the top of the offensive tackle's block. The linebacker has to understand that he cannot avoid playing blocks. There are times he has to get physical and knock someone out of the hole.

One skill the linebacker has to possess is the ability to tackle. It has never been as important as it is today. Concussions are going crazy. We have always done a good job in college football of dealing with concussions. There has been so much publicity coming from the NFL that it is important for us to see to it that our players do not get a concussion. When a player receives a blow to the head, there are a battery of questions the player must respond to within a time limit to reenter a game. If he cannot answer those questions in a satisfactory matter, he will miss some game time.

We need to be proactive as coaches to make sure we teach the right fundamentals with our players. When concussions happen, we have to know we are teaching the right methods. I learned the lesson the hard way. When I was coaching at Marshall, I had a linebacker named Jim Devine. He was a physical, tough, hard-nosed player. He was a thumper. His problem was he was a contact player with his helmet. He was my best linebacker but he was hurt all the time. He had burners in his neck and got concussions. He dropped his head when he made contact.

My problem was how to get him on the field. I started talking to him about chest tackling people. I tried to get him to keep his helmet out of the tackles. We worked on it in practice and as a result, he became a better tackler. Those techniques made him lead with his chest and hands. He kept his head up and saw what he was tackling.

The thing you need to work on in tackling is keeping the head up and buzzing the feet. The feet are tremendously important in making a tackle. You have to run through the tackle. The momentum of the tackle stops when the feet stop.

The next thing that we work on does not happen so much with the inside linebackers as it does with the outside linebackers. We work on openfield tackling. The key thing in making a tackle in the openfield is to close separation as quickly as we can. They have to keep their feet hot and close the distance on the ballcarrier.

The thing we work on is forming the V in the openfield (Diagram #8). When the defenders know

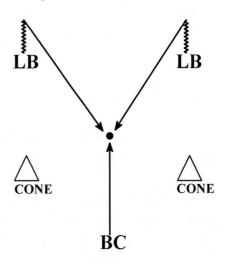

Diagram #8. Form the V

they have help in the openfield, they want to squeeze the ballcarrier. If you have a rolled up corner and outside linebacker bracketing a ballcarrier, their pursuit angles form a V to the target. We drill this with two linebackers. They drop into a pass responsibility. When the ballcarrier starts upfield, the linebackers converge on him in a V formation with one keeping the ball on the inside shoulder and the other keeping it on the outside shoulder.

In this drill, you can work on stripping the ball. If one tackler arrives before the other, the first player makes the tackle and the second tackler attempts to make the strip. The thing that cannot happen is the ballcarrier splits the tacklers.

We teach route reading with our linebackers. However, this spring we are going to work extremely hard on seeing the ball. We have linebackers in position to make plays but they never see the ball in flight. If we do not knock the ball out with the hit, it is a completed pass. This spring we will work on knowing where the landmarks and drop areas are in our zones. If they have a middle, hash, or numbers drop, they must get there. After we understand where our drop areas are, we can start seeing what the receivers are doing.

This spring, I want to see the linebackers get their hands on more balls thrown downfield. I want them to make more plays on balls and be active in seeing what the quarterback does. Right now, we concentrate too much on reading the routes; we never see the ball coming to the receivers.

Another adjustment I have made in my coaching involves the drop of the Sam linebacker. He is our middle zone dropper on most passes. I used to teach him to flip his hips and run to his responsibility. That area was directly behind him. Now, I let him backpedal to his area. It makes more sense. If you do that, they have a better chance at breaking on the ball. However, always start the teaching by getting them where they belong in their zone. After you teach that, you can refine the techniques you want to use.

I want to show you some drills and how they apply to the game situation. Initially, we want our linebackers—as they read their keys—to think short, choppy steps. That allows them to work their way downhill in a controlled fashion. Using the short, choppy steps gives them the opportunity to redirect their charge if they recognize a counter. They must keep their shoulders square to the line of scrimmage. The short, choppy steps give them the chance to redirect over the top without getting too far up the field.

The steps are short, six-inch steps at a 45-degree angle (Diagram #9). We align them in lines five yards apart with five yards between the players in each line. We work right going downhill and repeat the drill going left. The coaching points are the footwork. We do not want them to false step as they work right and left. This drill is all about time. We want them to get to a place on the football field as quickly as they can. The short, choppy steps allow the linebacker to slow down so he can adjust to a counter or pass responsibility.

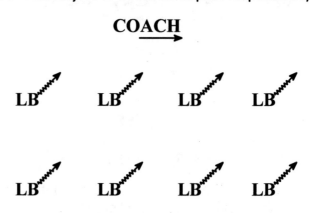

Diagram #9. Short, Choppy Steps

The next thing we do is work them under the chute (Diagram #10). We adapt the drill and incorporate a second skill in the drill. We work through the chute with short, choppy steps. When they come out of the chute, we give them a redirect movement. After coming out of the chute, they redirect and use a crossover run in the direction given by the coach.

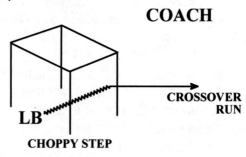

Diagram #10. Chute and Redirection

Anytime you can get your players in the chute, it is good for them. It teaches them to stay down and maintain a good stance and movement. The last thing you want a player to do is get in a good stance and stand up when the offense snaps the ball. We want them at the same level doing the drills as they were in their stance.

The next drill is a simple crossover run drill. The crossover run is running toward the sideline but keeping the shoulders square to the line. We start with short, choppy steps and convert into a crossover run on the coach's direction. The emphasis in this drill is to keep the shoulders square to the line of scrimmage and the pad level down. We take this drill to the chute and do the same thing. They use short, choppy steps to get into the chute. Once they flip their hips, they have to stay under the chute and use the crossover run to the end of the chute.

If we have a fast flow key with no threat to the inside, the linebacker gets into the crossover run immediately. An example of that type of play is a toss sweep or speed option to the outside. If the linebacker feels he is overrunning the ball, he gets back to his short, choppy steps. That slows him down and keeps him inside.

We call the next drill "block destruction" (Diagram #11). We work the drill on a one-man sled. It is a three-point punch drill. The linebacker aligns to the right or left of the sled. He takes two choppy steps to get square on the dummy. He delivers a hand shiver into the sled, locks out, and rips off to the outside. This skill depends on the size of your linebackers. The emphasis is to keep the head up and shoot the hands from a good position. We want the punch with the hands inside the hands of the offensive blocker. When the linebacker punches, he wants to lift the sled, lock out, and rip through to the outside.

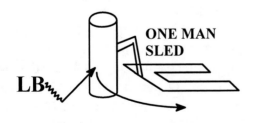

Diagram #11. Block Destruction

The points we want to make are to use the punch and get rid of the blocker. We do not want to stay on a blocker. We want the linebacker to go make a play. We want our players to be physical with blockers, but we do not want them to seek out the contact with them. If they can get under the block and not make contact, that is the technique we want to use.

The next drill is a cut drill (Diagram #12). We use the big rubber ball for this drill. We align the linebacker in his position. The coach stands with the ball outside the off-tackle box marked with a cone. The linebacker shuffles with the short, choppy steps and begins his crossover run to the outside. The coach throws the ball at his feet. The linebacker has to see the ball. We want him to push out at the ball and not down on it. The emphasis is to keep the outside leg free. We get the cut blocks on perimeter run plays. We also get offensive linemen trying to cut the linebackers on inside run plays.

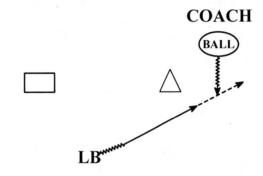

Diagram #12. Cut Block

We do not spend too much time working with the inside linebacker on openfield tackling. They usually have help from the inside or outside. When we work on openfield tackling in practice, we use a redirect drill (Diagram #13). We place two cones five yards apart with a ballcarrier behind the cones. We align the linebacker at a five-yard depth. The linebacker—on movement—flips his hip and retreats five yards. The linebacker squares up at five yards and continues to chop his feet. When the running back starts toward the cones, the linebacker reacts up and makes the tackle. The running back can move right or left through the cones.

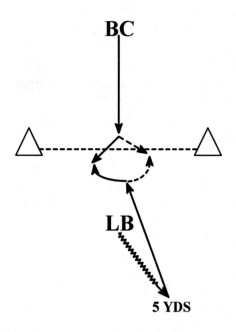

Diagram #13. Openfield Head Up

You can use this drill as a live tackling drill or a form positioning drill. In this drill, we do not want to be a thug. We want the linebacker to get the ballcarrier on the ground, not try to knock him out. He has to keep his head up and keep his feet active. Our basic coaching point is to get the ballcarrier down. It does not matter how much form or how pretty the tackle is. We want them on the ground. If the linebacker ends up by himself in the openfield, he has to be athletic and keep his head up. The most important thing is to close as much ground on the ballcarrier as quickly as you can.

We call this drill the "Gator roll" (Diagram #14). This drill teaches desperation tackling. This is a diving tackle. When the angle is wrong or the back is about to outrun the linebacker, this is what he does. Speed can outleverage linebackers. We set the drill with four flat dummies on the ground. A manager or coach has a tube dummy at the end of the dummies

three yards deep. The linebacker uses a crossover run and runs across the dummies on the ground. The manager starts to run dragging the dummy behind him. The linebacker comes over the last dummy and attacks the dummy as it moves away from him. He tries to get his head across the dummy and roll. As he grabs, the dummy goes to the ground.

An alligator that attacks his prey will roll the prey in the water. That is the object of this drill. Make the contact and roll the ballcarrier. This is the type of tackle made on a dead sprint. We want to grab the ballcarrier and aggressively roll him to the ground.

I learned one thing about incorporating different skills into one drill. If you have a drill where the linebacker drops, breaks on the ball, and intercepts it, make sure you teach each of those skills individually. Teach him to drop. Teach him to break on the ball. Teach him to catch the ball. After you teach him all three things, you can put them together. Too many times, we try to think of how many things we can put into one drill. The thing you have to remember is stepping stones. You have to go one step at a time.

We practice tackling into a Port-a-Pit® (high jump pit). That allows the tackler to attack the ballcarrier and drive him into the pit. It encourages the tackler to keep his head up and feet moving all the way through the tackle, and it avoids injuries to the ballcarrier. We align the ballcarrier one yard in front of the pit. The tackler is one yard from the ballcarrier. The tackler attacks the ballcarrier and drives him into the pit on his back. We incorporate this tackling drill with the three-punch drill. The tackler executes the three-punch drill on the one-man sled, rips off the sled, and tackles the ballcarrier into the pit.

The last thing I want to talk about is pursuit. We work on that every day. You have to swarm people to the football. If you can get three or four players to the ball hitting people, by the fourth quarter that starts to wear on the ballcarriers. Every day, we try to do some kind of pursuit drill, tackling circuit, or turnover circuit. You have to get four or five players to the point of attack so it is easier to tackle people.

It has been my pleasure to visit with you today. Thank you.

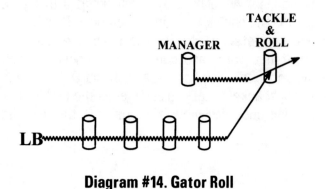

Diagram #14. Gator Roll

DISGUISING THE NICKEL AND DIME PACKAGES

Western Kentucky University

I want to tell you a little bit about myself. I grew up in Louisiana in a small town. It has 3,000 people, one traffic light, and a bunch of stop signs. From high school, I walked on at McNeese State University. I went on scholarship my second year and started four years. It was a great move for me. I learned the 4-2-5 defense while I was there. The other strong safety and I were the guinea pigs of that defense. I cut my teeth on the defense. After I finished playing, I became a graduate assistant and coached the strong safeties.

When you start coaching the defense, you begin to learn what you were doing while you played. I figured out that I was not a very good player. After my wife got pregnant, I gave up the graduate assistant job and I had to go make some money. I took a job in Leesville, Louisiana. We had the best running back that has ever come out of Louisiana. His name was Cecil Collins. He is in jail now. However, he was a special player. I coached at other high schools in Louisiana and ended up back at McNeese State.

After the third year, I became the defensive coordinator. We played for the national championship that year. We had a very good team but Western Kentucky University beat us in the national championship game. Things go full circle in this business. I was in and out of high school football and back to McNeese State until 2009 when I went to Miami University with Mike Haywood. We were 1-11 my first year. The second year, we turned the season around, went 10-4, and beat Middle Tennessee State University in the bowl game. Mike got the head job at Pittsburgh and I was set to go with him. That all changed. I became the interim head coach at Miami of Ohio. I coached the GoDaddy.com Bowl, which we won. When they named a head coach at Miami, I came to Western.

I am so happy to be at Western Kentucky. We have a great staff and we signed a good recruiting class this year. I am excited. My topic is about some of the blitzes we ran at McNeese and Miami and how we disguise those blitzes.

COACHING PHILOSOPHY ON DEFENSE

- I believe that we must coach with great *passion* and *enthusiasm*. Our players must feel both *energy* and *compassion* when being *praised* and *corrected*.

- If we are going to be demanding and coach our players hard when correcting them, then we must show equal if not more juice when our players are successful on a play (e.g. do not be like most media).

Too many times when coaches coach a player hard, they do not bring the same enthusiasm in praising them when they do something good. I tell the coaches that this is like the media. If someone does something wrong, it is on ESPN and repeated every other minute. When the problem is resolved, the results come out on the crawler at the bottom of the screen. Sometimes that is the way parents feel. If you get on the players constantly when they do something wrong, you had better come out of your shoes with praise when they do something right. You have to show the same excitement because that is what they are looking for. The temperament you show has to be the same for the mistakes as for the positive things.

The first thing I want to talk about is a pursuit drill we do (Diagram #1). I am not a big pursuit drill coach. We always had a rabbit in the drill. The drill depended on his performance. If he did not run or somebody stopped him, the drill was no good. My graduate assistant got this drill from Youngstown State University and it is a good drill. This drill is the only one I like.

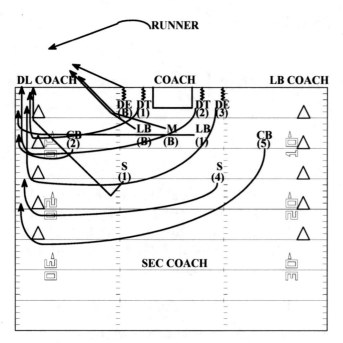

RUNNER

DL COACH   COACH   LB COACH

SEC COACH

Diagram #1. Pursuit Drill

We are a 4-3 defense. We align in our base defense. We have four coaches involved with the drill. The coordinator stands in the middle of the defense as if he were the center. The defensive line coach aligns on the numbers five yards behind the line of scrimmage. The linebackers coach is in the same place on the opposite side. The secondary coach is 30 yards deep in the middle of the field opposite the coordinator. We have five cones starting at the line of scrimmage set five yards apart on the numbers. They are on both sides of the field. We use the kickers as rabbits in the drill.

The coach tells the rabbit which way to run and calls the snap. The defensive line hits the ground on their stomachs. The playside defensive end scrambles off the ground and pursues the running back headed for the coach to that side. The playside linebacker is the first support player and pursues as soon as he sees the toss. The Mike linebacker works downfield and arrives at the coach in between the defensive end and outside linebacker. The playside defensive tackle gets off the ground and takes an angle to the first cone. He rounds the first cone and runs to the coach on that side. The backside tackle gets off the ground, pursues around cone two, and gets to the coach. The backside end gets off the ground, goes around cone three, and gets to the coach. If the ball is his way, he goes to the coach on the outside. If the ball is away, he goes around cone three to the coach.

The off linebacker takes a shuffle step in the direction of the ball and pursues around cone number one to the coach. The playside corner takes a read step and goes around cone two and to the coach. The safety to that side takes a read step and is the secondary support player. He pursues around cone one. The backside safety goes around cone four, and the backside corner goes around cone five to the coach.

We place a rabbit behind the coordinator and one in the middle toward each sideline coach. We use those players to run reverses in the drill. That makes the players start one way and react in the opposite direction.

The playside defensive end, the Mike linebacker, and the playside outside linebacker are the only ones looking at the ball. Everyone else runs looking at his cone. If the ball reverses, they must communicate that to the rest of the defense. They yell, "Reverse, reverse," and everyone goes around the corresponding cone going in the other direction. The playside defensive tackle starts to cone one but as the ball reverses, he has to retreat and go around cone two on the opposite side. We change things up from day to day, so they do not know what is coming.

SIX DEFENSIVE BACKS PACKAGE

• Dime
  ✓ Four down linemen
  ✓ One linebacker
  ✓ Six defensive backs
• Dime/money
  ✓ Two down linemen
  ✓ Three linebackers
  ✓ Six defensive backs

The money package has six defensive backs in the scheme. We can change the upfront personnel by using dime or money as key words. In the dime package, we have four defensive linemen in the game and one linebacker. In the dime/money package, we have two defensive linemen and three linebackers. The two down linemen are our best pass rushers. We run the money package when we know the offense has to throw the ball.

We play this defense before the half or at the end of the game, when we know the situation. The alignments to the front may vary. We can play the two down linemen at defensive ends or tackles. If they align at the end positions, the linebackers walk up, down, in, and out of the line of scrimmage. If we put them inside, the linebackers align on the outsides.

The scheme I will show you today is the money scheme (Diagram #2). We call the first alignment "smoke cover zero." On this scheme, two defensive backs will blitz. The blitzing backs depend on the formation. Smoke means we come from the outside. I tell them they have to smoke outside the house but they can light a flame inside the house. If they rush from the outside, they have to control the flare pattern run by the backs in the backfield. We play straight man-to-man coverage in the secondary.

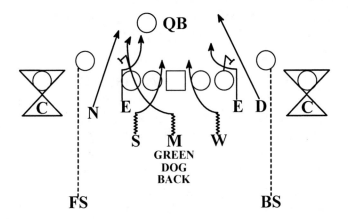

Diagram #2. Smoke vs. 2x2

The Mike linebacker adds on to the coverage and green-dogs the running back. If the running back flares, the Mike linebacker knows he does not have to take the flare pattern. One of the defensive backs has the flare and the Mike linebacker adds himself to the rush where the defensive back dropped off. We want to bring one more rusher than they can block. If the running back blocks one of the defensive backs, the Mike linebacker adds to the rush at that point. If the running back runs inside, the Mike linebacker runs through him to take care of the screen.

If the defensive ends align on the edges, they come hard up the field for the first three steps. They want the offensive tackle to get into their pass set. When that happens, they come underneath the tackle. We do not take the inside immediately. We want to come up the field and come across their

face after they set. The Sam and Will linebackers jump around and fake the gaps they will blitz. They run a double A-gap blitz. If the guards get any depth off the line of scrimmage, they want to do the same thing the ends did. They start up the field and come underneath the guards.

The Mike linebacker blitzes to the side of the back. If the back flares or blocks, the Mike linebacker is the outside blitzer from that side. In a 2x2 set, the nickel and dime defenders are the outside rushers. The corners lock onto the wide receivers and the safeties have the slot receivers.

We had a problem at Miami because our two safeties could not run. Our safeties were slower than any safety I coached in high school. They were both around 4.7 in the 40-yard dash. We could not ask them to play man coverage on the slot receivers. We called "flip," put the safeties into the box, and dropped the nickel and dime into the safeties' slots. We do not blitz every time from this alignment but I will talk about that later. That is an example of letting cover players play coverage and rushers do the blitzing. This builds some flexibility into the package.

If the offensive set was a 3x1 set, we made an adjustment (Diagram #3). The dime player goes to the trips side of the formation and plays over the #3 receiver. He still comes on the blitz from that position. The corners match the wide receivers, the nickel matches the slot receiver, and the field safety has the #3 receiver in the trips set. The boundary safety wiggles down and blitzes off the single receiver side. Everything else is the same.

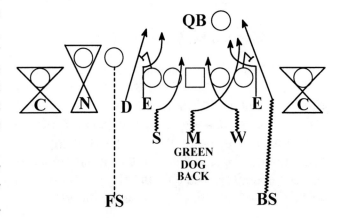

Diagram #3. Smoke vs. 3x1

We can flip the field safety and the dime defender if we need to. The Mike linebacker runs the green-dog on the running back. If the running back goes across the formation, the Mike linebacker has to redirect his charge. Teams began to slide the protection the other way and bring the back across the set because they knew what we were doing. However, we had an answer to that. We switched up with the Sam or Will linebackers. We let the Mike linebacker blitz the A gap and the Sam or Will linebacker became the replacement blitzer to the side the back blocked or released.

The next formation is the empty set (Diagram #4). In the empty, the Mike linebacker walks out and covers the #3 receiver to the trips side. He runs the green-dog blitz from that position. Since there is no back in the backfield, he adds on from that point. The corners take the outside receivers. The nickel takes the slot receiver to the trips side. The field and boundary safeties take the #3 receiver to the trips side and the slot receiver to the twins side of the formation. The dime blitzes off the two-receiver side.

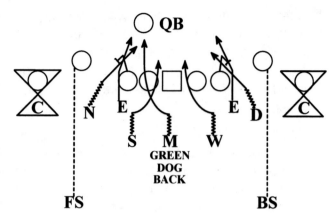

Diagram #5. Flame vs. 2x2

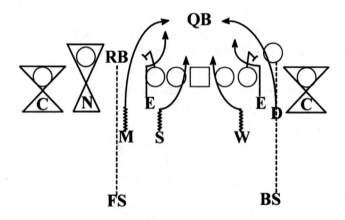

Diagram #4. Smoke vs. Empty

The dime back has a simple rule. If there are two receivers into the boundary, the dime back aligns into the boundary. If there is one receiver into the boundary, the dime aligns to the fieldside of the formation. It does not matter if there is a trips set into the boundary. In that case, the dime back is into the boundary. The only time he is not into the boundary is when a single receiver is that way.

The next package is flame cover zero (Diagram #5). In this package, we bring two defensive backs into the B gaps. That means the defensive ends

have flare control on the backs in the backfield. The ends come off the line of scrimmage and stay up the field, keying the backs. The nickel and dime backs blitz inside the defensive ends. The Mike linebacker adds on to the blitz to the side of the running back's release or block.

The corners take the wide receivers and the safeties have the slot receivers. The coaching point to the nickel and dime backs is not to come under the defensive ends immediately. They stay up the field as if they were taking flare control on the backs. At the last second, they come inside the charge of the defensive end. The running back usually sets up to block the blitz back coming off the edge. If the back comes underneath the defensive end, the back does not see him. If the back sets up to block the edge blitzer, the Mike linebacker wants to come under the blitzer. The blitz runner stays on the running back's outside shoulder and draws his block. The Mike linebacker comes under the blitzer and straight to the quarterback.

We tell the blitzer to run through the block of the running back and take him to the quarterback. We do not want the blitzer to avoid the running back. That serves two purposes. If there is a screen, we want to collision the back and hold him in. The second thing is to occupy the back's block and allow the Mike linebacker to come clean to the quarterback. Once the Mike linebacker sees the running back take on the blitzer, he knows there is no screen play and rushes.

In the 3x1 formation, we have the same concept (Diagram #6). The dime back applies his rule for receivers and comes to the trips side of the

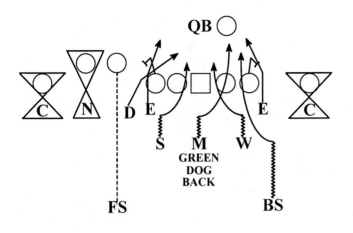

Diagram #6. Flame vs. 3x1

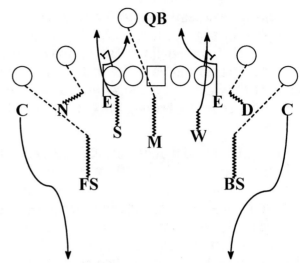

Diagram #7. Sticky Cat vs. 2x2

formation. He aligns over the #3 receiver and runs his blitz from that position. The boundary safety wiggles down and runs the B-gap blitz off the boundary side. It is important for the blitzer to have some knowledge of the cadence so he can time his blitz. He cannot come down too quickly or too late. If he moves too early, he tips the blitz. If he gets there too late, he cannot get home with the blitz.

We need to read the quarterback or the center to time up the movement. If the quarterback gives a hand signal or lifts his leg to signal the snap, the blitzer needs to know that. If he times off the center, watch to see his routine on the shotgun snap. Does the center look once and snap when he lifts his head? Does he look down and up before he snaps the ball—we need to know the routine. When you run this scheme, you have to do your homework and know the cadence or the signals. We are playing man coverage with no free safety. That means we are vulnerable to the big play. We have to do something to keep the offense honest.

You cannot align like this every time and expect the offense not to devise some counter scheme to beat the blitz. We change up with a "sticky cat." This disguises the flame or smoke blitz by showing no safety-level player. We invert the corners to become the half-field players and play man under with a cover 2 scheme.

This comes from Coach Bull Reese, who coached at Louisiana State University and The University of Texas at Austin (Diagram #7). We walk the safeties down over the slot receivers. The quarterbacks coach teaches the quarterbacks to look at the

middle of the field and to see whether it is open or closed. The safeties are showing that there is no roof on the coverage. When there is no one in the middle of the field, the coverage is cover zero, which is straight man with no free safety.

The nickel and dime receivers come in as if they are going to blitz. The safeties walk down as if they are man-to-man on the slot receivers. The disguise is important. When they get to six yards, they widen their alignment slightly. At the snap of the ball, they immediately go after the #1 receivers and play man-to-man to each side. The nickel and dime backs widen and take the slot receivers man-to-man. The corners bail out and play the half-field zones behind the man underneath coverage. We invert the corners and safeties and play a man under cover 2.

The Mike linebacker runs the green-dog blitz but must take the back man-to-man if he releases. If your Mike linebacker is not a good cover linebacker, you may want to use the Will or Sam linebacker to cover the back. You can easily switch the responsibilities of the linebackers to fit your personnel.

The Sam and Will linebackers are free to devise any stunt with the defensive end they want. You can put the end inside and the linebacker outside or the opposite. You do not have to do the same thing on both sides. One side may cross charge and the other side may play straight.

We tell the field and boundary safeties to take away all inside routes from the #1 receivers. We want them underneath his hip. The nickel and dime backs play the same technique. We do not want to open up to the receiver. If we do that, the receiver will break behind the defender and get into the middle of the field. The defender has to get in his backside hip and make him come over the top of the defender.

The corners read the quarterback as they break back into their zones. I want them in their regular alignment. I want them at seven yards. I want the inside foot up and the outside foot back because that is our alignment when we play man coverage. I want the corners, on the snap of the ball, to drive into their half-fields getting as much depth as they can. When the quarterback settles, I want them to go into an easy backpedal and read the quarterback's actions.

This works well for us with the quarterback reads of the secondary. On third-and-five, the offense likes to throw the slants and skinny posts. When the quarterbacks see the safeties coming down, they oftentimes check to go routes. That is exactly what we want. That allows our corners that are better cover players than the safeties to play the deep ball.

The quarterback cannot read what the defense does until they snap the ball. If he sees the corners on the retreat, he is a good quarterback. I think it is a tough read for him. The weak point of the coverage is the slot receiver running to the flat. If he runs to the flat, he runs away from the coverage. We have an answer for that but it requires you to make the right call in the right situation. The offense likes to run the flat route into the boundary and the double slant into the field.

The next set is the triple set against the sticky cat (Diagram #8). The alignment is the same as the smoke or flame. The Sam and Will linebackers and defensive ends run any game they want. The dime back shows blitz but covers the #3 receiver. The nickel aligns over the slot receiver but he covers the #1 receiver. It is too far for the field safety to go to get to the #1 receiver. The field safety matches the slot receiver. The nickel wants to get even with the slot on his alignment because he has to get to the outside receiver with the proper leverage.

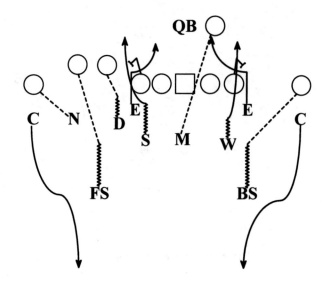

Diagram #8. Sticky Cat vs. 3x1

The boundary safety has the single receiver. He uses the same technique as he did before. The boundary corner has the same technique as he did before. However, the field corner has to make an adjustment in his technique. He cannot drive and stay deep to his half. He has to midpoint the area between the #1 receiver and the #3 receiver if they both come deep. He has to see the quarterback and react to what he sees. We want the corner to get over the slot receiver so he has a play on the #3 receiver going deep. If there is a chance of the #3 receiver going up the seam, both corners have to be aware of that situation.

The next scheme we talk about is sticky Tampa 2 (Diagram #9). We disguise flame or smoke blitz

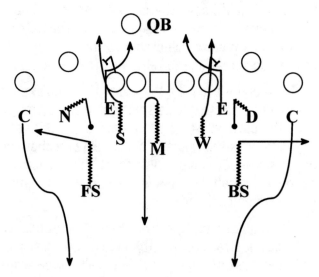

Diagram #9. Sticky Tampa 2 vs. 2x2

by showing no safety-level player. We invert the corners to become the half-field players. The difference is we play zone underneath instead of man under. The appearance of the alignment is no different from the other defenses. We want to show blitz from this alignment. The nickel and dime backs show blitz and, on the snap, get into a position on the slot receivers. We want them to collision them from the inside out. They drop into a hook/curl zone at 12 yards.

The field and boundary safeties start to creep down as they did on the other blitzes. On the snap of the ball, they buzz to the flat zones. If the wide receivers are trying to get vertical, the safeties collision him from the inside and try to knock him out of bounds. If we knock him out of bounds, that is what we want. If the receiver is working back inside, the safety passes him up and plays the flat. If the situation is third-and-five yards for the first down, the safety has to think flat zone. He has to see the slot receiver going to the flat. If the slot goes to the flat, the safety has to get all over the receiver.

If the slot receiver runs a slant pattern, the safety does not go to the flat. He finds the wide receiver because he probably will run the slant pattern also. He wants to stay inside and play that pattern. The Mike linebacker shows blitz, and on the snap, he gets into the middle zone and carries patterns up to 18 yards.

Question: How do you play the bubble screen into the trips formation from the sticky cat?

We work the nickel and the field safety in practice on the bubble screen. The field safety comes down on the #3 receiver. When they snap the ball and the #3 receiver bubbles, the field safety turns and runs through the slot receiver's outside shoulder immediately. We still have the corner over the top, which gives you the safety net. We have two free players. Once the dime back sees the receiver bubble, he turns and finds the slot receiver. He wants to know if the slot is blocking the safety or running.

If he is running, the dime wheels and gets under him and plays in his hip pocket. The safety switches to the #3 receiver and plays him inside out. The corner cannot play the bubble at all. The corner has to get out and into the deep half.

If the safety reads the slot receiver going out, he finds the wide receiver. If the wide receiver is coming in, we switch that between the safety and the nickel back. That play is the jailbreak screen.

The key to playing the bubble is to work it in practice so you know what to do. You have to know what they do on third-and-five. You cannot play the scheme unless you work hard on it in practice.

The sticky Tampa 2 gives you a better chance because you are zone instead of man. You have to mix up what you are doing. You have to disguise what defense you are playing. You cannot ever do the same thing every time. If the offense knows what you are doing, they can scheme for certain things. The offense cannot know if you are running a straight blitz with a man scheme underneath or a zone. They do not know who covers the back. You have enough flexibility in the scheme to keep them off-balanced. If you play an offense that runs many screens, you want to play more Tampa 2 than the sticky cat.

Anything you can draw up, we have an answer for it. It is who has the pen last. Everyone has an answer for every situation. The problem is that you have to play those situations. The advantage we can have is the disguise so the offense is not sure what they see. The offense versus the defense is a cat-and-mouse game.

When we play the sticky Tampa against the 3x1 set, we let the dime back run through the middle (Diagram #10). Everything stays almost the same

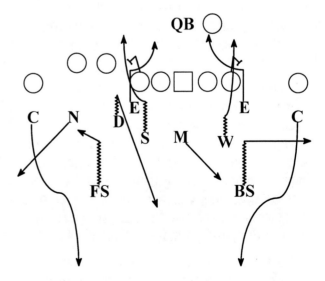

Diagram #10. Sticky Tampa 2 vs. 3x1

as it was in the 2x2 set. The nickel back flashes to the flat. The field safety comes down as if he were working for the #3 receiver. He wants to collision the curl area. The dime is responsible for the #3 receiver. The Mike linebacker becomes a curl dropper away from the three-receiver side.

The boundary safety works under the wide receiver to the single receiver side. The corner runs to the deep half-field. The two defensive ends and the Sam and Will linebackers run their scheme like the other schemes.

If the #3 receiver runs up the pipe deep and the slot receiver comes underneath, the dime stays on the #3. The boundary safety's job is to collision the wide receiver going vertical. If he can knock him over the sideline, that is the technique we want to use.

We do not play with a field and boundary concept when we call defenses. We do not set the front according to the field and boundary definitions. If the ball is in the middle of the field, we declare to the formation. We declare the nickel by passing strength of the formation. If the ball is on the hash mark and we call a field blitz, we bring the nickel on the blitz if we are in a five defensive back package. The nickel back always aligns to the side with the most receivers.

In one-back offenses, we always set the front to the tight end. If we are on the hash mark, we do not set the front to the field. We set the front to the tight end, if there is one on the field. We align our 5-technique defender to the tight end side and the shade defender to that side. If there is no tight end in the game, it does not matter where we set the 3-technique defender.

When we play cover 3, we spin the coverage to the weakside of the formation. We do not spin the coverage to the strongside. If you spin the coverage to the strongside, the boundary safety has a hard time getting through the middle and stopping verticals coming from the strongside. To play that coverage, you must depend on someone getting a collision on the #2 receiver and rerouting him. I am not confident that will happen all the time.

We are an under front defense. If the offense aligns with 21 personnel, we align to the formation strength (Diagram #11). The tight end is to the field

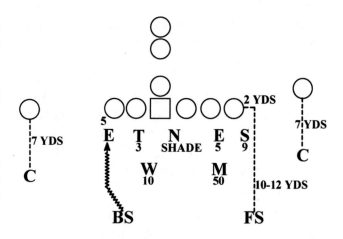

Diagram #11. Under Push 3 Weak

and we align with a 5 technique and a shade nose to the tight end side. To the weakside, we align in a 3 technique and a 5 technique.

We align the corners at seven yards. We want a field safety that can run and ideally is corner-like. I want a field safety that can match up on the slot receiver and play the middle of the field. The boundary safety needs to be a good tackler.

On this defense, the boundary safety makes a call depending on whether there is a slot receiver into the boundary. If there is no slot receiver into the boundary, he gives a push call. If there is a slot receiver into the boundary, he calls box. When he gives the box call, he tells the Will linebacker who has the flat area. In this situation, there is no slot receiver and he gives the push call.

With a push call, we move the Will linebacker into a 10 technique to the weakside. He aligns in the weakside A gap. We move the Mike linebacker to a 50 technique on the outside shoulder of the tackle to the strongside. He stacks behind the defensive end. The Sam linebacker aligns in a 9 technique on the tight end.

On the snap of the ball, we want to spin the boundary safety down into a linebacker position. He puts his foot in the butt of the defensive tackle. He is a weakside B–gap player. If the wide receiver cuts his split, the boundary safety comes down early and shows what he is doing. We cannot let the receiver block the safety out of that position.

If we get pass read, the corners play deep thirds on the outside. The field safety runs through the middle of the field and plays the middle third. The

Sam linebacker drops to the strong flat. The Mike linebacker plays the strong curl zone. He works to the #3 receiver if there is one. The Will linebacker is the curl player weak.

If the play is a power run to the tight end side, we ask the Sam linebacker to spill the football (Diagram #12). The Mike linebacker becomes a leverage player and comes to the outside, keeping his outside arm free. The Will linebacker fits underneath the 5-technique defensive end to the strongside. He fills the B gap strong. We coach the Sam linebacker to get underneath the fullback and get to the second level. If he can do that, he picks off the pulling guard. The boundary safety fills off the backside and is the cutback player. The Will linebacker is an extra player and is always behind the running back. He is not over the top or way behind him.

This puts pressure for the boundary safety to make that type of play. If the offense runs this play, many times we use a tag call for the 3-technique tackle. When we tag the tackle, he comes inside into the A gap. If the center blocks back on the A gap, the 3-technique tackle wipes across the

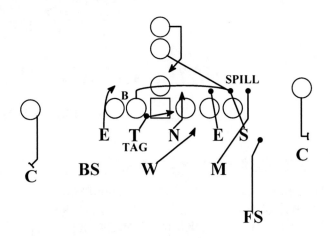

Diagram #12. Power Run Strong

center into the strongside. What we are trying to do is force the ball to cut back into the unblocked boundary safety in the B gap.

Coaches, I appreciate your time but I have used mine. That is all I have. If you want to talk about anything, I will be here for a while. I enjoyed talking to you. If you have any questions, I will try to help you the best I can. I have seen it all over the years. I appreciate it.

HATCH ATTACK: ALL-OUT PASSING GAME

Murray State University

I appreciate that welcome guys. It has been 12 years since I last spoke at this Nike Clinic. That was when I was fortunate enough to be at the University of Kentucky. We are going to talk a little passing game today. If you have questions, please ask them. I am going to talk a short time on some of the beliefs we have in the passing game. I want to talk about some quick screens, quick game, and mesh game with you today.

You always get nervous any time you get up to speak. It does not matter how many times you have done it. Today is different because I have some young whippersnappers that take care of me. They take care of my audio-visual material.

One of the things we pride ourselves on is throwing the ball short and treating it like a running game. That allows us to get by with lesser offensive linemen. I have always coached at a smaller school and have not been able to get the huge pass blocking linemen that the bigger programs have. Our linemen are smaller and probably more suited to running an option than throwing a drop-back pass. That is how our system is built.

We run the Mike Leach and Hal Mumme system of throwing the football. I will show some of the basic things we have done and, over time, we tweaked the system to fit what we do. I want to show you some things we added that have been good for us.

What I want to show you first are some of the things we believe in on offense. You must have a belief system to define what you want to do.

OFFENSIVE BELIEFS

- Have a belief system—know what to teach and how to implement it.
- What is a coach? He is a teacher/motivator.

We believe you must have a belief system. You have to know what it is and how to teach it. Our belief is we want to throw the football as much as we can throughout the course of the game. We want to identify what a coach is. I think the coach is a teacher and a motivator. It is the coach's job to teach them what you want them to know. It is just as important to motivate the players to get them to do what you teach them.

HATCH ATTACK PHILOSOPHY

- Get the ball in space to people who know how to score
- Well-coached backyard team
- KISS method
- Put players in position to succeed
- History tells us about simplicity
- Talent and preparation are keys

We have some basic philosophy we try to follow. We want to get the ball to people who know how to score. Throwing the ball is what I prefer to do. Because of that, we are fortunate enough in our system to have a good running game. We had a running back this year that only played seven games but had 904 yards rushing. He had two games with 200 yards rushing. I like to think of us as a well-coached backyard team. We do not have landmarks on which our receivers align. We feel like that is too much for them. We give those clues and tips about alignments. On a particular play, we may tell them to get wider or cut down their split. We give our players ownership in the system that allows them to go out and have fun.

We try to run precise routes but we give them leeway with their routes. If the tight end is supposed to run a middle curl at 10 yards, he can alter his pattern and run it at eight yards. If he runs it to

10 yards, the linebacker covers him. Instead of running the pattern into coverage, we tell him to break off the route and the quarterback will find him.

One other thing that we did worked well for us. We had no illegal procedure calls this year for not having enough men on the line of scrimmage. We let our wide receivers determine who is on or off the ball. The outside receiver makes sure that the inside receivers know whether they belong on or off the line. If the outside receiver has a deep route, he gets on the line and pulls the other receiver off the line. That cut out all the terminology and helped our communication.

We have a very simple system. We have a couple of five-step and quick games and only four running plays. We have a multitude of screens but the players' actions are all the same. We use only one protection scheme per game. We keep it simple and use numerous tags on our plays to give us the diversity we want. If you look at all the great, high-scoring offenses, they are all simple.

You may have a guru come in one year with many fancy ideas. They may light up the scoreboard, but history tells us that the simpler you are, the better you will be in the end. Talent and preparation are the keys to any successful program. Good players make you a better coach. However, good players have to prepare over the course of the week to be ready to go on Saturday.

HATCH ATTACK

- Success geared toward the quarterback's strength
- Only run what the quarterback can comprehend
- Room full of plays must have a package
- 3-day installation
- Reps
- Can't practice it, we don't run it
- Game on the line, run the best plays

We gear the success of our program toward the quarterback's strengths. You can only run what your quarterback can comprehend. Our offense changes a bit every year because we only run what the quarterback can do. If the entire team understands 100 percent of your offense but the

quarterback understands 70 percent of it, 30 percent of the offense is a waste. You are wasting time trying to run that 30 percent because the quarterback is the trigger player on your team.

I have a board in my office covered with ideas. I carry a laptop computer everywhere I go. I am constantly making notes and drawing up plays. I may see something on TV and get an idea for a play. I have enough plays to fill this room. However, you have to package the plays that make sense to your team. We use the three-day installation period. That means, if you have more offense than you can install in three-days, you have too much offense. During the course of a week, we have only three workdays. In some weeks, we have only two days. If you cannot get the reps you need to fit within those three days, you have too many plays. If it takes too long to get the plays installed, we must cut them down.

If we cannot get the reps in practice on a particular play, we do not run it in the game. I have a simple question for my coaches. I ask them if they would call a particular play if the game was on the line and the situation dictated it. I want to know if we have practiced the play enough to use it. Ninety percent of the time, the coaches tell me to go with the plays we run well.

ADDITIONAL HATCH ATTACK PHILOSOPHY

- Revolves around two things
  ✓ Playmakers/scripting
  ✓ Tempo—control it
- Main objective is to score one more point than the opponent

Our philosophy revolves around two things. It revolves around playmakers and scripting. We want all our playmakers on the field at any given time. We like a bigger tight end that can block a little. We want him to get his hands on defenders on the zone play or at least be able to cut off the backside on a running play. We want him to catch the ball over the middle and run well. We had one of those types this year.

However, we do not have one coming back for next year. We moved a 5'7", 165-pound player, who you could not catch in a telephone booth, into the Y-receiver position. He is our next best playmaker and we will adjust our play calling to fit his ability. You have to do that.

Scripting is very important. Early in the game, we want to make sure every one of our playmakers touches the ball. It may go for zero yards but everyone that we feel is a playmaker has a chance with the ball. We try to get the ball to all of them during the first two series.

Great players that do not get the ball early have a tendency to fade out late. Players who are not very good, like me, can get it late and they are happy to get it. They still play hard even if they do not get the ball. The egos of the good players affect them if they do not get the ball early. That keeps them in the game and playing hard.

Tempo is important in the flow of the game. We want to speed up the tempo or slow it down, depending on our needs. With all the blitzing game you see in today's football, it is important to control the tempo. You must have those tempo packages so you can dictate and control the speed of the game. Our main objective is to score one more point than the opponent does. That is the philosophy we have in our program.

The first play I want to show you is the quick screen to the Z-receiver (Diagram #1). We used to get our interior linemen out in front of the receiver. I studied the play last year and found out that 85 percent of the time, the linemen coming out into the play were making the tackle on the receiver. They got in his way and in some cases actually knocked him down. We ran the play 84 times this year and averaged eight yards a catch.

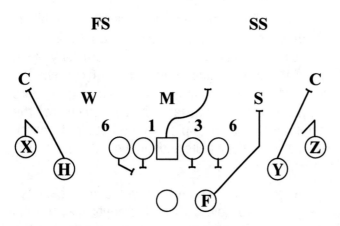

Diagram #1. Quick Screen Z

The Z-receiver aligns on the ball with his inside foot forward. We want him to take a big step coming off the ball with his arms moving as if he were going deep. He retraces his steps and stands, waiting for the football. The coaching point is to make sure he does not back up from his original alignment. We do not want him to catch the ball five yards behind the line and have to run five yards to get back to the line of scrimmage.

The inside receiver on the play, kicks out the MDM (most dangerous man) on the play. The coaching point for him is to get his head between the defender and the ball. After he makes contact, he takes the defender where he wants to go. We do not cut the defender. We stay up on him and take him where he wants to go. If the corner bails out into three-deep coverage, he is not the MDM anymore. The Sam linebacker becomes the MDM. The wide receiver blocks him and the fullback works around for the corner. The key coaching point is once the blocker makes a decision on the blocks, he has to go right now. Even if he makes a mistake, he cannot try to recover and block the right man. He has to go and get out of the way.

If we are in a 2x2 set, the fullback free releases and blocks the flat defender. He blocks the alley in the screen. The coaching point to the fullback is to stay flat originally and work up the field once he sees his role. The fullback's normal alignment is toes at five yards from the line of scrimmage. He aligns shoe to shoe on the offensive tackle. His outside foot is aligned on the inside foot of the tackle. To help him get out, we cheat him out to splitting the crotch of the tackle. At some times, he gets his inside foot on the outside leg of the tackle.

We number the defensive techniques in sequential order from the inside. Head-up the center is a 0 technique. We have a shade technique on the shoulders of the center. From there, we number starting with the inside shoulder of the guard going to the outside shoulder of the tackle. The inside shoulder of the guard is 1 and the outside shoulder of the tackle is 6. The head-up positions of the guard and tackle are a 2 technique and a 5 technique.

The playside tackle takes a two-step quick set. We ask him to do whatever he has to do to get the hands of the 6-technique defender down. If the 6-technique defender drops in a zone blitz or recognizes the screen, the offensive tackle chases him. He has to block the 6-technique defender regardless of whether rushes or not.

We assign the uncovered lineman to the playside to the inside linebacker. It could be the center or the guard. One of them chases the inside linebacker. He comes out flat and chases like the fullback. He does not always get there, but that is his assignment. The remaining linemen use our 60-set blocking drops and secure the pocket. We want to secure the inside gaps first. The backside tackle sets inside to take care of the B gap, checking for blitz, and then kicks back outside for the rush. The backside receivers mirror the frontside screen.

The quarterback aligns with his toes at five yards. He catches the snap and gets the ball out of his hands as quickly as he can. His target is the upfield shoulder of the Z-receiver.

We tell our blockers that if they whiff on the block to do it away from the ball. The blockers do not have to be the best athletes in the world. They need to get in the play and make the defenders adjust and move to avoid the blocks. We tell the linemen to cut in the openfield. We teach them to tackle the defender in the openfield. Very seldom do we get a holding penalty in that situation. The playmaker makes the play go. We tell the linemen to never break down on a defender. They are not athletic enough. We want them to run and maybe one of the defenders will run into them. The objective of the play is to get five yards. We use this play against blitzing teams. I used to tell the receivers to get back outside, but now I tell them to get five yards. Anything over five yards is a bonus on the play.

I have been a head coach for 12 years. The first play of every game in those 12 years has been a screen. Everyone knows it, but I figure out a way to run one. The thing about the screen is it slows the defensive linemen and it allows us to throw the ball downfield.

I like to run the same screen into the triple set (Diagram #2). The fullback aligns opposite the screen, runs out the backside, and blocks the flat defender to that side. The alignment in this triple set is X-, Z-, and H-receivers. The Y-receiver splits to the single receiver side. We do not tell the blocker anything about the MDM. The Z-receiver

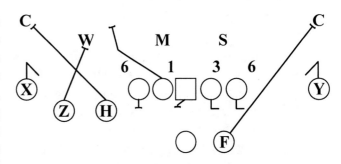

Diagram #2. Quick Screen to Trips

blocks the man over him and the H-receiver kicks out the corner. Everything else is the same.

If we get press coverage in this situation, we use an automatic call to get out of the play. We try not to run the play against a rolled up corner or a press man-to-man corner. If the Z-receiver had trouble blocking, we aligned in a 2x2 formation and motioned him into his position. That gave him a running start at his blocking assignment and helped him out. Using the motion opens plays on the backside of the triple set.

When you run the screen into the triple side effectively, it opens the backside screen (Diagram #3). We see the secondary rotate to the trips side, and the Will linebacker begins to creep back into the box. When that happens, we throw the quick screen to the single receiver side and use the fullback as the kick-out blocker on the corner. The uncovered lineman goes to the backside and tries to block the Will linebacker. The frontside of the formation runs the quick screen fake to draw the defense.

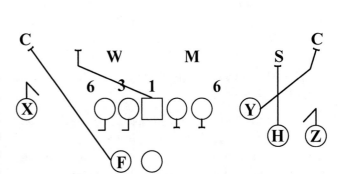

Diagram #3. Quick Screen to X

As the fullback goes out, we tell our fullback not to block a blitz defender. We pass them up and get to the blocking assignment. If the blitz defender is his blocking assignment, he goes to the next threat.

Our number one play this year was a simple pass out of the quick game (Diagram #4). We call it "64." This is our quick out pattern to the slot receiver. The backside patterns are quick in routes for both receivers. To the frontside, the Z-receiver runs vertical. We have a term to describe what he does. The term is "MOR" (mandatory outside release).

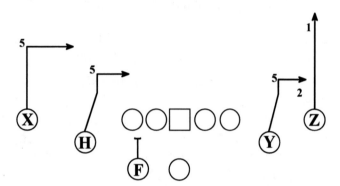

Diagram #4. 64

If the receiver does not think he will get the ball, he collisions the outside shoulder of the corner. That makes the corner turn his shoulders and cleans the read for the quarterback. If the receiver reads cover 2, he is thinking to get in the hole on the sideline before the safety gets over. The inside receiver runs a three-step out cut. It is a speed cut. That gets him to a depth of five yards. He does not fake, plant, or square off the pattern. On the third step, he breaks out and looks for the ball immediately.

The quarterback takes a quick drop and looks initially for the wide receiver on the vertical. If the ball does not go deep, the quarterback delivers it to the out route. The fullback stays in and blocks. The pattern hits too quick for him to get into a pattern. He checks his assignment and helps on any leakage from the offensive line.

On our standard protection, we are man blocking with the offensive line. The fullback has the inside linebacker not taken by the offensive line. If he does not come, he looks outside and then to the safety. If he has a release, he has to check his way out of the backfield. If any one of his responsibilities comes, he stays in and blocks.

The backside patterns are important. The H-receiver has to run his pattern inside the flat defender. He has to stem his release to get across the face of the flat defender at a depth of five yards. If the Will linebacker aligns on the H-receiver, we tell the receiver to get a ghost man inside the defender before he breaks his pattern. A ghost man is a defender that is not there. He works to a position one man inside the defender.

The outside receiver runs his pattern off the inside shoulder of the corner at a depth of five yards. He trails the H-receiver across the field. The inside patterns on the backside can settle against zone coverage. However, they have to stay flat and run their pattern in a hurry because the ball will come quickly. This is how we teach the play, but we do not run it from this formation too many times. The coaching point we use is to not run through the window in the zone. If they read zone, they gear down their patterns.

If we want to run the play to the other side, the play is 65. We can also add tags to the play to give us an adapted pattern (Diagram #5). If we call 65 Z post, we look for the post route. Everyone runs 65 except the Z-receiver who runs through the post. When we tag a play, we hope the quarterback knows we think the pattern will be there. It does not mean he has to throw the ball if he reads something else.

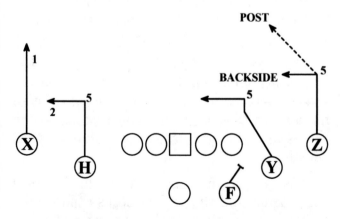

Diagram #5. 65 Z Post

On 64, the quarterback looks to the right first. We want the quarterback to take some peek-time in his pre-snap read. That means he peeks at the coverage on the wide receiver. If he thinks he might get the deep ball, he takes more time on his first read. If it is not a kill shot, he forgets it.

If we run 64 with the trips set, the slot receivers run out cuts at five yards and an in route to the single receiver side (Diagram #6). The H-receiver comes to the right side of the formation and aligns as the middle receiver in the trips set. The Z-receiver runs the vertical. The H- and Y-receivers both run five-yard out cuts. The X-receiver is the single receiver and runs the in route off the inside shoulder of the corner. When the receiver catches the ball, a coaching point is to have the receiver turn in the direction of the target. If the quarterback throws to the right shoulder, that means the defender is on his left side.

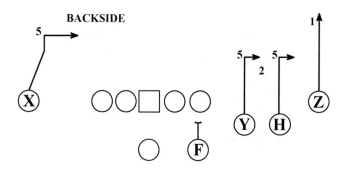

Diagram #6. 64 Trips Side

We do such a good job of throwing the ball that the defense begins to move defenders out of the box. When we read a true five-defenders-in-the-box, we run the ball. A true five-box means the outside linebackers are out of the box playing pass. They are not half in and half out. We do it backward from most people. We use the pass to set up the run.

If we find people loading up to the trips side to play the out breaking cuts (Diagram #7), we run the entire group of receivers in the trips side on in routes at five yards. The X-receiver to the single receiver will have single coverage. We send him on a vertical and let the quarterback peek in his direction. This is where you take advantage of a mismatch with the X-receiver.

The mesh package is a big part of our offense. I used to be in a two-back set. We do not run the smash play as much anymore. We run the smash and mesh concept in the same play. That gives us more reps on the play since you do not run the

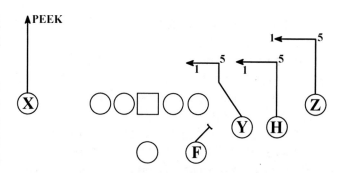

Diagram #7. Quick Game Peek

patterns separately. We run the mesh package about 95 percent of the time out of the empty set.

The empty mesh form puts the fullback and H-receivers as the wide receivers to each side off the line of scrimmage (Diagram #8). The X- and Z-receivers are on the line of scrimmage. The Y-receiver is off the line and is the inside slot. The fullback and Z-receiver run the smash concept. The Z-receiver runs a 10-yard corner route. He moves down the field and sticks his toe in the ground at 10 yards. We tell him to run to grass away from the defender. If the quarterback reads the corner up and grass behind him, he throws to the Z-receiver. The fullback runs up the field three yards and stops.

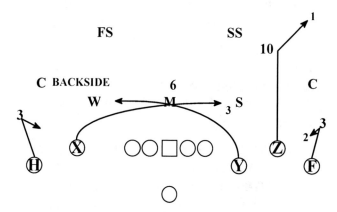

Diagram #8. Empty Mesh

The Y-receiver is the inside slot to the three-receiver side and responsible for setting the depth of the mesh at six yards. The Y-receiver sets the depth and the X-receiver makes the pattern happen. The Y-receiver is always over the top with the X-receiver underneath. Once the two receivers mesh and cross, they find the first open hole in the zone and pull up their patterns. They throttle down and settle in an open window for the quarterback to find them.

If the coverage is man-to-man, the receivers continue to run. When they cross, they continue to run and bow their patterns up the field. It is only a slight bow. The coaching point to help the receivers identify the coverage is to look at the mesh receiver coming from the other side. If there is a defender following him, it is man-to-man. The Y-receiver does not look to settle but continues to run across the field gaining a bit of depth as he goes.

We have some rules for the receivers in zone coverage. When the receivers mesh and start to settle, they must settle into an open area. Never sit down in front of a coverage linebacker. Once they catch the ball, they turn and get up the field. They turn up the field to the side that the quarterback throws the ball. The defender is on the other side. The receiver turns away from the defender and gets straight up the field. Turning straight up the field causes the defensive back and linebacker to miss tackles and often avoid big collisions.

When we read man-to-man coverage, the receivers want to stay tight to one another as they cross. We do not pick defenders, but they might find themselves in a rub situation. When you have two receivers with two defenders chasing the receivers, they sometime run into one another. As the receivers cross, they want to bend up the field and lead the defender into the traffic.

The outside receiver to the two-receiver side is the H-receiver. He runs the same pattern the fullback runs on the three-receiver side. He runs a three-yard hitch pattern.

We align the quarterback at five yards from the line of scrimmage in the shotgun. On the snap, he takes a three-step drop. He had a base rule when we ran this from a two-back set. His first read is the corner pattern going deep. The second read is the mesh with the third going to the back. When we are in the empty shotgun set, we read the corner, back, and mesh. With the back in a split position, we read him as the second progression of the read. The third read comes off the Sam linebacker. If he starts to expand to cover the fullback, we have the mesh.

If the quarterback reads man-to-man coverage, his read changes slightly. His first read is to the

corner route. If he does not like that read, he goes to the backside mesh receiver immediately. He is the receiver that will come open on the backside.

The reason we have the back as the second read is because he is a playmaker. It puts the ball in the running back's hands in the openfield. The running back in our offense does not care how many carries he gets. The thing we want to do is get him touches. He may carry the ball 10 times but catch 10 passes, which gives him 20 touches or carries. The fullback in a spread offense has to catch the ball. He is part of the passing scheme.

We had the smash route on the outside with the Z-receiver and the fullback and the crossing mesh route with the Y-receiver and X-receiver. We had the mesh and the smash concepts in the same pattern. We like the way we do it now.

If the quarterback reads the blitz with a pressed up secondary, we get out of the play. If they press your hitch receivers, we have no hot route to throw. If he does not read the blitz or cannot get out of the play, he has to throw the ball away or extend the play with his feet.

Defenses that try to read your personnel to figure out what package you will run do not get a clue from us. We run the empty formation with the same personnel we have on the field. If the defense wants to blitz your empty set, it will come in the form of an automatic called on the field. The quarterback can pick up those communications and has an idea if the blitz is coming.

When we have success throwing the quick screen, the defense gets leery about blitzing the quarterback. If we can burn the defense a couple of times, it changes their thinking. If they start playing a soft zone against you, it opens up the middle of the field.

We can add a tag to the empty mesh that gives us a good change-up (Diagram #9). We call empty mesh Z post. Instead of running the corner with the Z-receiver, we change his pattern and he runs the post. The cover-2 corner has to hustle to get on top of the smash corner. The Z-receiver comes down and works the middle of the field against the safety instead of taking the corner.

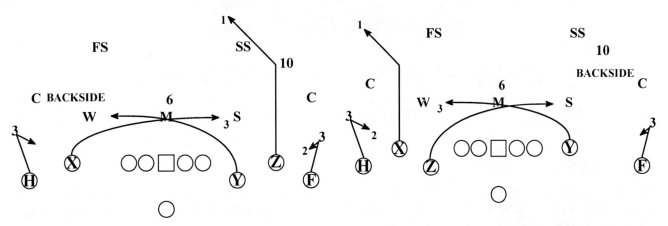

Diagram #9. Empty Mesh Z Post

Diagram #10. Empty Mesh Switch

We can switch patterns with our receivers (Diagram #10). We call empty mesh switch. If we want the X-receiver to run the smash concept, we bring the Z-receiver in motion to his side or align him there. The two outside receivers run the smash concept and the mesh receivers run the mesh. The H-receiver runs the three-yard hitch route and the X-receiver runs the corner route. To the backside, we have the Y-receiver and fullback. The fullback runs the same pattern he did in the smash route and the Y-receiver sets the mesh. We have a different receiver running the corner and mesh routes.

I think it is imperative to get the ball to your receivers in space. My main goal today was to show you some of the things we do to change up the spread game. This offense has been good to us. We came to Murray State University last year. We went into a program that had won 13 games in the last five years. We were fortunate to go 6-5 this year. I have a young staff and they do a great job. Our offices are always open. Anytime you want to come by and talk ball, we are happy to do that.

I wish all of you the best and I hope something I gave you today makes you a better football coach in the fall. Thanks and I hope you enjoy the rest of the clinic. I appreciate it.

DEFENSIVE GAME-WEEK PREPARATIONS

The Ohio State University

It is a pleasure to be with you today. I really love this time of year. This is the time of year where I have a chance to meet with other coaches and learn new things. This is a great clinic and I will share some ideas with you that I hope will help you in your program.

I have coached at all levels. I started as a high school coach and then I moved on to a Division III school in Ohio. I was a graduate assistant for Don Nehlen at Bowling Green State University and was an assistant coach there with Denny Stolz. From there, I went on to the University of Washington with Don James and coached the defensive line. I left Washington and went to coach a Division I-AA school as a head coach. In 1996, I went to The Ohio State University and have been there ever since. I have been the defensive coordinator for the last six years. It has been a great time for me and a lot of fun.

I want to start with something special that we do at Ohio State. This is something Coach Jim Tressel puts a lot of emphasis on. We do a lot of teambuilding. Two weeks ago, we met with all of our seniors and presented them with the statistics of how our teams have done over the past six years. I asked them what they would like to accomplish as a group. They will meet five or six times before spring ball to discuss what they want to accomplish in their senior year. I tell them that this is their baby, and I do not care what format they use, or what they put down, or even really what their goals are.

After spring football, they will all get together and finalize their goals. Then, they present them to the coaching staff. The seniors present what they want to accomplish, what they want to be known for, and how they want to get it done. This is their idea and we do not restrict them on anything. Last year, they had, as one of their goals, to have swag.

I am not sure what swag is, but we did not stop them. I figure that if you win, you can have swag.

After the presentation for the coaches, the seniors will present their ideas to the entire team. We, as coaches, will use this to get points across to our players throughout the year. As an example, "They want to compete with relentless effort." If we have a practice where we do not get good effort, I can bring them in as a group and tell them that one of their goals was to compete with relentless effort and that they did not give it on that day. Now, it is their idea and it becomes important. Before, if I said to a player that we did not get great effort, it was not as important to him.

This has worked really well for us. Our seniors will get up before every game and talk about it. Our team has really embraced it. I feel that our defense has a real sense of ownership in what we are trying to accomplish.

Last week, we had a basketball tournament with the team. We were at our arena at midnight. That is the only time that we can get some time in the arena. We have a 3-on-3 and a 5-on-5 tournament. We will put a freshman, sophomore, and a junior together as a team. We will put players together that would not normally hang out with each other. This forces them to get to know their teammates a little better. We try to make it fun and we have pizza for them at the end of the night.

We will have a softball tournament outdoors underneath the lights. We get some of the Ohio State girls softball team pitchers to pitch. It is kind of silly, but it is amazing how embarrassed our players are when they cannot hit the pitch. They get a good laugh out of it. They take pride in winning, though.

We will have a track meet where we get to the track at 6 a.m. Our players talk all the time about how fast they are and how great they are. Now, we give them the chance to prove it against each other. We will do fun things and run some relays. It really is nothing more than building up our team and the camaraderie that goes with it.

Defensively, we want to have 11 guys flying around the football. We want our guys playing extremely hard every play. We think that this type of teambuilding helps with that. We like to do nonfootball related things together as a group. Our regular football training is crazy. Sometimes I worry that we spend too much time training. We think that it is helpful to do things outside of football together.

Another thing that we do is we give a test to our guys on the last day before fall camp is over. We have them write down the name, number, high school that he went to, and hometown of every player on our team. They only have so much time to complete the form. In the end, the player that has the most correct answers will only have to run one sprint or conditioning drill for that day. The ones that have the fewest correct answers will stay out on the field until the end. We feel that we get our players to know each other a little better with this activity. This way, our freshmen will know what our seniors are about, and our seniors will know a little about our freshmen. Our guys will do a good job with it because they would rather do this than run.

Let me tell you about our practice schedule for the week. Sunday, for us, is a practice day. We want to try to get some things accomplished. We want to see our players on Sunday and find out how they are feeling after the game. We want to see what kind of movement they have. If they have an injury, we want to address it then, not on Tuesday. We will run them a little and get a light cardiovascular activity in them. We want to go over yesterday's game and get that out of the way. We will try to plant a seed about next week's opponent as well. Sunday is a big day for us.

Something that Coach Tressel does on Sunday that has been big for us is to emphasize game situations in a team meeting. Following is a list of some of the things that we go over:
• First-and-ten
• Third-and-medium
• Third-and-long
• Turnovers
• Explosive gains
• Red zone
• Short yardage
• Sudden change
• Two-minute defense

We call this our "blueprint." The situations are critical with us. We evaluate them every day in practice. I believe this really helps us zero in on the process rather than the just the outcome.

If we win the majority of these situations, we feel we have a great chance of winning the game. Coach Tressel stands up front and goes over every one of those situations, both offensively and defensively and then as a team. As an example, the opponent may have had 33 opportunities at first-and-ten, and we held them under three yards 17 times. Offensively, we may have had 30 opportunities at first-and-ten, and we had gains of three or more yards 13 times. As a team, we were 30 of 63, which is not very good. We can coach tougher in that we have to work harder during the next week of practice in order to fix the problem.

"Coming out" is where we tell our defense that if the opponent starts inside the 10, we have to make them punt without getting a first down. Our punt return team has to get the ball across the 50-yard line. That is the only way we can accomplish our coming out goal. Both criteria have to be met for us to be successful.

The two items that we emphasize the most and that we feel are the most important throughout the year are turnovers and explosive gains. An explosive gain for us is 15 yards or more on a running play and 20 yards or more on a pass play. We feel like, and statistics prove it out, if we win those two items, we will win the game.

Our guys have bought into this. On the field, we talk about pre-snap preparation. What is the situation? This helps us slow the game down a little. Sometimes the game goes so fast that players do not even know what is going on. If we have them think, pre-snap, what the situation is, they can be better prepared. If it is a first-and-ten situation, through our preparation we know what plays the opponent likes to run. One of the things that we always emphasize is *the next play is always the most important*. This is something that is very critical, and we have ingrained it into their brains. No matter what happened, good or bad, on the previous play, our next play is the most important.

One of our defensive goals for each game is to hold the opponent to 14 points or less. To me, that is low. I have tried to argue it with Coach Tressel. That was our goal years ago when everybody was running the isolation play. Now, with all of the spread offenses and no-huddle, I think that goal is a little low, but I have been unsuccessful in getting it changed.

We want to try to keep their rushing average below 3.3 yards per carry. We want their passing average to be below five yards. We are going to try to get three turnovers. If we can get five three-and-outs, we will count that as one turnover. We do not want to allow any 15-plus-yard runs. We cannot allow any 20-plus-yard passes. For the red zone, we do not want to allow a touchdown in the red zone.

These are all of the situations. After Coach Tressel has his team meeting, we will have our own defensive meeting and go over the same defensive situations again. It is just repetition over and over again to emphasize our points. We do all of these things on Sunday. We get all those things out of the way on Sunday, and then yesterday's game is in the past.

To plant the seed for our next opponent, we will put a picture of the opponent's quarterback in the locker of every defensive player. Our defensive players will see that the very first thing when they come in on Sunday. We want them to know that we must affect that quarterback. We are going to really emphasize the quarterback.

It has been my experience through the years that if we can get after the quarterback, we have a chance to win the game. If the quarterback is successful, we probably are not going to win the game. From day one, we talk about the opposing quarterback. We have to give him different looks, contain, sack him, pressure him, and flush him out of the pocket—all those things. That is the first thing we do on Sunday. This is the guy. If we have a quarterback that is successful against us, we will meet right after the game to talk about it. We want to know what happened. We want to know why we did not get after their quarterback.

We will also go through all of the opponent's personnel. We make our guys memorize some of the things about each one of their players. On Friday, our seniors are going to stand up and talk about each one of the opponent's offensive players and tell us something about each one of them.

Monday is an off day for us. The NCAA makes us give players one day off a week during the season. We tell our guys that it is an academic day. If they have any schoolwork, special tutoring, or they need to see a professor, they are to do it on Monday. As a defensive staff, we develop and finalize our game plan. At the end of Monday night, our game plan is going to be completed.

We are a 4-3 defensive team. However, we will play a lot of 3-4 as well. We are either going to play a base defense, a nickel defense, where we will take a backer out and put in a safety, or a dime defense, where we take the linebacker out and put a corner in. When we are talking about game planning, we are going to look at the opponent to see what their personnel groupings are.

We just recently played the University of Arkansas. Arkansas had eight personnel groupings that they worked like crazy. Each one of them was a big part of their offense. They did a great job of disguising their personnel groupings. They might have three backs on the field at one time and come out in a no-back offense. It is just getting more difficult all the time to figure out what the offense is doing.

We look at their personnel groupings and try to figure out who we will want to have on the field at that time. Then, we will come up with two or three things that we would like to do in that situation. We will take each one of our packages and come up with three or four different coverages, three or four different zone pressures, and maybe four or five different blitzes.

We will do this with our 4-3 defense, our 3-4 defense, and our nickel and dime packages. What we are trying to do is just like what the offenses are trying to do to us. We are going to try to give them a lot of different looks and make them prepare for different fronts and schemes. Monday is a big day for us as far as coaches.

We have four coaches on defense. The first thing we do on Monday is break down our opponent's situations. Defensively, each one of us has a few different situations that we are responsible for in getting the information and statistics together. Once we have that done, we come together as a group and start to work on our game planning. The other thing that we will try to do on Monday is to start working on third-down situations. We believe third-down situations are critical.

Tuesday is our first day of heavy practice. Tuesday, we try to really concentrate on first down. We spend a lot of time on first-down-pass and play-action-pass situations. In the earlier part of the year, we will spend more time on individual drills than we do as the season goes on.

We do two things that I think are good. First, we have a 10-minute run-through. This is a change from when we had a 10-minute walk-through, when we would have guys just messing around. We have an offense from the scout team. We do not have helmets on. It is slow motion and technique sound, and they better have their knees bent and in a good football position.

Secondly, the other thing that we can do here is to work on the tempo of the no-huddle offense. We have the defense turn their backs. When I blow my whistle, the offense is in their stances and ready to go. At the same time, when I blow my whistle, the defense gets their signal and turns around. We are trying to simulate the hurry-up offense. It is not a crazy racing type of drill. We want to emphasize getting lined up and being ready to play in a hurry-up situation. We are getting a run-through look and the players learn a lot.

In every practice, we will have ones versus ones for at least five minutes. This is something a little different from what most coaches will do but Coach Tressel wants to get this done. We will have the number one offense run against the number one defense for three offensive plays. One will be on the left hash mark, one will be in the middle of the field, and one will be on the right hash mark. On Tuesday, we concentrate on first-and-ten, and we will run it

from the three positions on the field. After that is over, we will break up and have our normal scout teams that we will go against. We might work on third-and-medium for a while. We will then go back and compete against our first team, again working on third-and-medium. This way, we are working on some good physical play, but also getting in the repetitions.

A long time ago, I learned the four rules of learning:

- *Explanation.* We are going to explain the drill, explain the situation, and explain what we are trying to do.

- *Demonstration.* We are going to demonstrate or have somebody demonstrate the correct execution.

- *Imitation.* We will have each player imitate the correct execution.

- *Repetition.* Everything that we do is high-speed and high-paced in order to get as many repetitions as we can.

On Wednesday, we run a similar practice. We will run our red zone defense against our number one offense and we will run the two-minute drill against our number one offense.

On Thursday, we go through our checklist. This is similar to what everyone else does. Coach Tressel has his own checklist that we go through. This checklist will have every possible situation we may be confronted with during that game. As a coach, we need to know what our call is in any situation such as first-and-short yardage. What does the opponent like to do on the first play of the game? Over the past five games, what does the opponent like to do after a turnover? What is the opponent likely to do after they complete a pass on first down?

Those are our checklist items we monitor to make up our call sheet. On Thursday, we will have a 30-script practice where we script 30 plays and run them from different parts of the field. We make sure that we call all of our defenses at least once during those 30 plays. We want to make sure that we are on all hash marks and on all ends of the field. We also make the last play on Thursday the last play of the game.

Friday is a big day for us. Our seniors take over our practice on Friday. The seniors get up and talk about their opponent. We make sure that they are sincere and respect their opponent. If you have a player that does not respect a lesser opponent, this is where you can get into trouble.

Next, the seniors will go over our blueprint. They will go over all the things we need to do in order to win the game. We go over what we have done in the past for each one of those situations. After that, we will do the same thing, but this time by position. Here is what we need to do as an offensive line in order to be successful. Here is what we need to do as linebackers in order to be successful. This again, is for all the seniors.

On game day, we always start with team. Everything has to be team oriented. We talk about one of 11. This game is one of the 11 games that we will play during the season. We emphasize that this is an important game, but it is just one part of the season.

Next, we talk about tackling. We talk about fanatical effort. We focus on the process. We have to play the first play first. After that play is over, we will play the second play.

We will never have a practice where we do not give great effort and then let it go. If we have a practice where we do not feel we are getting our best effort, we will make them stay and watch the film of practice and then ask them about their goals for the year. We do not really call anybody out or call anybody's name, but we ask them as a group if this is the type of effort that they feel will allow them to reach their goals. We really got our point across when we did that.

My time is up. Thank you.

ZONE PRESSURE OUT OF MULTIPLE FRONTS

Marshall University

We have some great ideas, and I want to tell you why we think we will win at Marshall University. I grew up in Hurricane, West Virginia. That is about 20 minutes from the Marshall campus. I grew up on a farm. I still have that farm and live on it. I knew Marshall was a great job. I watched Bob Pruett and Jim Donnan as they coached here. People do not realize that Marshall University had the winningest program in the country in the late 1990s and early 2000s. During that time, Marshall won over 10 games a year and competed for conference championships every year.

Deep down I knew it was a great job, but I turned it down six years ago. I did not think it was the right time for me. I had just taken a job at the University of Florida with Urban Meyer. I have been very fortunate in this business for 30 years. The schools I worked for never fired me, and I was able to stay ahead of the wolves. I had three great jobs. I was at West Virginia for 25 years and got to play for a couple of national championships there. I went to North Carolina State and won more games in five years than they had won in a while. Those were the Philip Rivers years. I went with Urban at the University of Florida and won a national championship there.

I remember going to the first meeting with the team at Marshall. Marshall had gone six or seven years without winning a championship. That meeting lasted about 30 seconds. Someone came in late, and I threw them all out of the meeting and told them we would have another meeting when they were ready for it. We came back two days later and had the first team meeting.

I asked them a question that day. I asked how many players sitting in the room had ever won a championship. Not one hand went up. I introduced my staff to them. I have nine coaches on my staff who had won a national championship in some capacity. I told them we had people on the staff that can help you win championships.

I told them that what they had been doing for the last five years has not worked. We have to change. If you do not like what is happening, you have to change and go in a different direction. You must have a change of heart. The players had not won. They had not done what they had been coached to do. The players were uncomfortable, it did not feel good, and it was hard being in the program.

We made it extremely hard on them in the weight room and the classroom. When I got to Marshall, we had the worst GPA in the history of Marshall Football. Last semester, we had the highest GPA in the history of Marshall Football. We had six missed classes for the entire semester. I know you want to know what that has to do with winning. There is a direct correlation between doing the right things on the field and doing the right things off the field.

When I went to the University of Florida, the one thing we tried to do was change the attitude. It was our job as football coaches to go into a program and work with the players that are in the program. It was not our job to fire players and weed out the bad actors in the program. Our job is to get the players to live right, work hard, and changes their attitudes.

With that being said, there were eight players at Marshall I could not change. They were into some things that could not be overlooked. The fact that I dismissed them from the team probably cost us a bowl appearance this year. In the end, the foundation we built this year is in place and is solid. We will win championships in the future because of what we had to do.

At the first meeting, I told the players how we were going to win. I told them the plan was in place, and it was infallible and tested. There was a reason the teams at Florida won more games than any other school for the four years we were all there.

ELIMINATE THE HUMAN ELEMENT

- Failure is not an option.
- Forgo rights, choices, and entitlements.
- Embrace responsibility, assignment, and duty.
- The team is the focal point.
- Selfishness is not tolerated.
- Success is favored.
- Adherence to the team standard will be rewarded, revered, and honored.

The first thing you have to do is eliminate the human element in your program. The human element is anything that gets into your program that keeps you from winning championships. I told them that failure is not an option. If you can eliminate the human element, you can eliminate failure.

Players and coaches forgo their rights, choices, and entitlements for the betterment of the team. They had to embrace responsibilities, assignments, and duties both in and out of the program. The team must become the focal point. The team cannot allow or tolerate individual selfishness and attention. We will favor success within the program. Individuals who excel and perform to our standards within the team concept will reap reward, reverence, and honor.

How many times have you heard, "We are going to treat everyone equal" as a player or coach. I hated that as a player when the coach did not follow through with that claim. If you do the right thing in our program, we treat you as if you are gold. If they go to class, live right, practice their butt off, and do the right thing, we give them everything we can. If I have a player who does not do the right thing, it becomes a bad deal for us.

I had to dismiss a player the other day. We had a team meeting. I had the player stand up, and I told the team he was dismissed and why. We have a program based on truth, and there is nowhere to hide in our program. If you are not tough and do not like football, you have a hard time making it in our program. You must eliminate the human element. When we left the University of Florida,

the human element was sport agents. That element permeated the players' minds and kept them from being great players.

BE INVESTED

- Prepare
- Physical superiority
- Attention to details
- Conditioning
- Mentally prepared
- Actions are taught or allowed
- Highest level plays

The second thing I always tell our players and coaches is the most invested team always wins. Invested and prepared teams always win. It is our job, and my commitment as the head coach at Marshall, to make sure our team is the most prepared and invested. I told them they will be the hardest working and best prepared team in America. Attention to detail will eliminate the margin for error. We leave nothing to chance, and we will prepare the team to overcome every challenge they face.

The physical superiority of our team will be evident. We want to outhit and be more physical than our opponent. We condition the players so they can play at full throttle the entire game. Mentally, we will coach the players in a clear, clean, and concise manner to eliminate confusion. Players who know what to do can play fast.

If we watch the tape of a game, we see what we coach. If it is not what you want, you are teaching it or allowing it to happen. If you do not see on the tape what you coach, you need to try a new method. The players are not getting what you are coaching, or you are allowing them to make mistakes.

The players who perform at the highest level will get the playing time at Marshall. If the players work harder than they have ever worked, they will be the most invested team. I constantly tell our players there is no harder working team in the country. I just hired a new strength coach from the University of Southern Mississippi. We played Southern Miss last year, and they kicked our butts physically. It was an embarrassment. That game was early in the season.

TRUST

- Build trust between coaches and players.
- Do your job.
- No trust, no play.
- Emphasize special teams.

The third thing to building winning in your program is trust. They must have trust to do the job. I hate logos and slogans. I have one thing on my wall in my office. It is a sign that says, "Do your job." That statement goes for coaches, trainers, secretaries, and players. If everyone connected with your program does their job, you have no issues.

If you hand a player a T-shirt that says, "Beat somebody," it does not help get the job done. If we invest, outwork the opponent, and eliminate the human element, we will win. It is not a T-shirt. We win the games on how the team works on Monday through Thursday.

When players do the job and take care of business, it builds trust between the players and coaches. Only players that we trust will play. Therefore, players who do their job on every play will be trusted. One thing Urban did well with player development at Florida was his use of players on the special teams. At Florida, the players did not get on the field on offense or defense if they did not perform well on special teams. If he could trust the player on special team, he could use him on offense or defense. Last year at Marshall, we had trouble doing that because of our depth.

In the West Virginia University game, we had a freshman fumble a kickoff that lead to us losing the game. People ask me why I played him. I told them because I trusted him. He performed well on special teams and deserved trust.

LEADERSHIP

- Set the example.
- Set standards.
- Only trust players that become leaders.

You create leadership within a team by setting a good example for the players to follow. You have to set standard and make sure everyone lives up to those standards. Every championship football team I ever coached had a great leader. At West Virginia,

we had Oliver Luck, Jeff Hostetler, and Major Harris, who played on those great teams. I coached Philip Rivers at North Carolina State. At Florida, we had Tim Tebow and Chris Leak guiding those championship teams. They were great leaders. They set standards and made sure everyone lived up to those standards. It is imperative to have great leadership.

PLAN TO WIN

- Play great defense.
- Keep the turnover margin low.
- Score in the red zone.
- Have great special teams play.

To be successful, you must develop a plan to win. The plan starts with playing great defense. That was one of our problems this year. The teams that played for the league championship this year were the first- and third-rated teams in team defense. Central Florida was number one and Southern Methodist University was number three in the league. As bad as we were, we ended up the season fourth in the league in total defense. When we started the season, we could not stop anyone. By the end of the year, we played good defense, and we're bringing 10 of the 11 players back on defense.

The second thing you have to do is take care of the ball. If we could have done that, we would have won eight games this year. The West Virginia and Bowling Green State University games would not have been close, and we could be celebrating a bowl victory.

The third thing you have to do is score in the red zone. When you get into the red zone, you must score points. We want to score touchdowns and not just kick field goals. However you score, you have to come away with points when you get into the scoring areas.

The last thing in the plan is special teams play. To win football games, you must have great special teams play. You have to win the special teams battle because that leads directly to field position. If you win that battle, you have a chance to win.

If you do those four things, you win every game. I did not say one thing about scoring points on offense. The special teams take care of the field position. Taking care of the football gives the defense a better chance. You do not put them in bad positions. If they cannot score, they will not beat you.

I coached with many great defensive coaches at Florida. They went on to other jobs and are doing great. Charlie Strong is here at the University of Louisville. Chuck Heater is the defensive coordinator at Temple University. Gregg Mattison is the defensive coordinator at the University of Michigan. It was not what we did defensively that was important. We all felt we had to be a great tackling team. We played an over and under front at Florida, and we play it at Marshall. We had a goal at Florida to go into the games and hold the opponent to single digits with tackling. We won the national championship in 2006. The one game we lost that year was to Auburn. In the game, we had 19 missed tackles.

I bring that up because I want to show you some of the tackling drills we do at Marshall. Every practice, the players wear pads; we begin with a tackling drill. This first drill is an angle tackling drill (Diagram #1). It is an open field type of drill in a 10-yard area. We put the tackler on the numbers of the field and the ballcarrier splitting the different between the numbers and the sidelines. The tackler has to use an angle to tackle the ballcarrier.

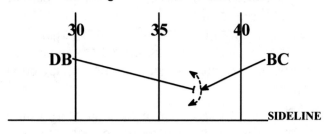

Diagram #1. Angle Tackling Drill

The mistake tacklers make in the open field is giving the ballcarrier a three-way go. The object of this drill is for the tackler to take away the ballcarrier's ability to cut back. The tackler wants to give the ballcarrier only two ways to go. The ballcarrier has to run out-of-bounds or cutback into the tackler. The back either cuts into his tackle or breaks into the sideline. The emphasis in the drill is to take away the cutback run by the back. When the back breaks to the sideline, that is what the tackler wants. It is easy to get him out-of-bounds or make the tackle. It is important to work in both directions so you work with both shoulders and angles.

We do the same thing working from the sidelines instead of from the numbers. The ballcarrier is running in the same direction and doing the same things. The tackle comes from a different angle and has to adjust to the ballcarrier to give him only a two-way go. The back breaks into the tackler or out-of-bounds. The key for the tackler is to never get in a head position on the ballcarrier. He has to maintain leverage on the inside hip of the ballcarrier. He has to take away the cutback run, force the ball through him, or force him to run something else.

The important thing in this drill is the angle of the tackler, but you still have to coach tackling techniques. We want their heads up so they can tackle with their eyes. When we make contact, the feet have to come alive and finish the tackle. We want to grab cloth and wrap up on the ballcarrier. In any open-field tackle, it is important to close the distance on the ballcarrier as fast as you can. We call it "taking the grass."

In every drill we do, there is a winner and a loser. Two times a week we put our players in position where they will win or lose. The winners get everything. The winners go in, get the Gatorade, or whatever we give them. The losers get nothing. They need to understand it is a bad thing to lose. In our competitive agilities on Wednesday, the teams that win go to the locker room. The teams that lose have eight-timed gasser. On Friday, we have agilities and wrestling at the end. The wrestling is more of a fight than wrestling. It is not a wrestling match. We take two players and give them nine yards they have to cover. The first player there is the winner. It is not a race. The winner goes over and watches the other matches, and the loser does 150 up-downs.

We constantly put our players in situations where they have to win. They need to understand that losing is a bad deal for them. You can make these tackling drills a win-or-lose situation.

During the season, we do a low angle tackling drill on Tuesday (Diagram #2). We wear the pants on Tuesday. We do it every day in the spring that we wear pants. This live full-speed drill puts the safeties in a game situation. We align the tackler and safety 20 yards apart. They both start from the middle of the field. On a middle yard line, two yards inside the numbers are two cones placed five yards apart. The ballcarrier starts running to the two cones from his position in the middle of the field. When he reaches the two cones, he can break the ball back inside or continue to the sidelines. He cannot cut back until he reaches the cones.

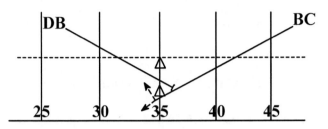

Diagram #2. Low Angle Tackling

The defensive back aligns on the ballcarrier and attacks at full speed to the cones. He wants to execute a low tackle on the ballcarrier. He wants to go through the knees of the ballcarrier with his shoulder and his head across the tackle. The same rules for tackling still apply. He has to tackle with his eyes. He gives him only two ways to take the ball. He takes up the grass as quickly as he can. He keeps his feet moving all the way through to the ground.

There are several things at work in this drill. The running back learns to protect the ball and protect his knees by staying low. The tackle learns to tackle with his eyes. The position of the coach in this drill is important. The coach wants to be in a position near the cones so he can see the eyes of the tackler. The coach must continually remind the tackler to keep his head up. That is such a big concern today with all the neck injuries. Do not let them drop their heads. The head coach has to get his coaches to coach their butts off about keeping the eyes up, whether it is tackling or running the ball.

When you first start to do the drill, the tackler throws his body and does not wrap up the ballcarrier. They must wrap up with the hands and arms. Make sure you work both ways.

I want to get into our defensive scheme. This particular defense is not something new. When we put this defense in at Marshall, we did not practice against each other enough live. As a result, we were not a good blitzing team early in the year. During the season, we started working our blitz scheme against our offense live one time a week. We did not hit the quarterback, but we work full speed against the first offense. The offense worked on blitz pick-up, and the defense worked on blitzing. The safeties and linebackers worked on their blitz and pass rush techniques and forced the ball.

The key to blitzing is bringing the player that can get home in a game. Some players are better at that than others are. Do not blitz players who cannot make a play if they come free. Change personnel if you have to, but send someone who can have an effect on the quarterback. When we drilled the blitz package against trashcans, we set a cone nine yards behind the cans. The blitzing linebackers sprint to that cone.

FIRE ZONE PHILOSOPHY

- Extra man concept versus the run, 8 defenders versus 21 personnel, 7 defenders versus 12 personnel
- Front line pressure movement gives outside pressure and inside linebacker pressure creates confusion for line blocking schemes
- The offense can block the pressure versus pass, the speed and intensity of the pressure is what makes it successful

The thing I like is not having to play cover zero and giving up big plays. You have an eraser with the middle safety. The blocking scheme can block the blitz on paper, but we can create some issues with backs trying to block defensive ends or linebackers.

The blitz I want to talk about is the Sam scrape. We can run it from our field defense, which is our base front. We can run it from the Okie or odd front defense. We can run it from the Bear front, which is a double Eagle front. We can run it with our nickel package. The opponent has to prepare for six different looks. Our players run the same techniques and have the same responsibilities from all those looks. They get repetitions running the blitz because they use the same techniques on each look.

2010 Sam Scrape Statistics

- Run: 29 attempts = 35%
- Pass: 52 attempts = 64%
- 29 runs = 1.34 yards/carry
- 52 pass 53/22 = 42.3 complete percentage (12 yards per completion, 3.15 yards per attempt)
- Zero passes over 20 yards
- Three sacks
- One interception
- Two quarterback hurries for 3 yards (no touchdowns)

Our base defense is our field defense (Diagram #3). We play the Sam linebacker in a 9 technique to the fieldside of the formation. The defensive tackle to the field aligns in a 5 technique on the outside shoulder of the offensive tackle. The nose tackle aligns in a shade to the field on the center. On the boundary side, the defensive tackle aligns in a 3 technique on the offensive guard. The boundary side defensive end aligns in a 5 technique with no tight end or a 9 technique with a second tight end. The linebacker Mike linebacker is to the field and aligns in a 30 technique. The Will linebacker aligns into the boundary in a 10 technique.

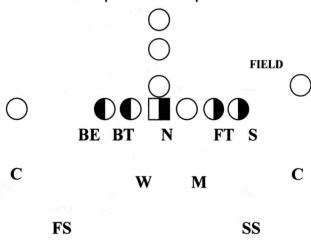

Diagram #3. Field Defense

When we run the Sam scrape blitz, the 5-technique tackle runs a long stick (Diagram #4). We coach him to take a lateral step with an aiming point for the inside earhole of the offensive guard. He is responsible for the fieldside A gap. When he gets to his gap, we want penetration up the field. The nose tackle lateral steps across the center into the boundary side A gap and penetrates. He

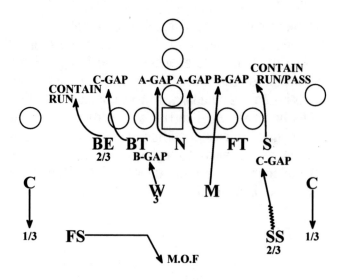

Diagram #4. Sam Scrape Blitz

uses a jump technique to get to the other side. The Sam linebacker comes off the edge of the defense.

The 3-technique tackle takes a loop step, which is a jump step, and gets into the C gap to the boundary side. He penetrates and gets vertical up the field. If the play is a pass, he has to contain the pass into the boundary. The 5-technique end contains the running play and drops if the play is a pass play. His pass responsibility is to match and carry the #2 receiver. The field linebacker blitzes the B gap behind the long stick of the 5 technique. It is important to come tight off the stick stunt. If he comes tight, he can make a play on the other side. The Will linebacker has the B gap against the run and drops to match the #3 receiver in his pass coverage. The strong safety aligns to the field and is a C-gap player against the run. If it is a pass, he matches and carries the #2 receiver to his side.

FIELD ZONE COVERAGE PRINCIPLE

- Three-deep zone
- Match, carry, and deliver
  - ✓ Match your receiver to the flat; run with him.
  - ✓ Carry your receiver vertical to the next deep coverage defender.
  - ✓ Deliver your receiver to the next underneath defender.

In the first diagram, the boundary 9 technique and the strong safety play the same techniques on a pass. They match the pattern of the #2 receiver to their side. If the #2 receiver runs to the flat, the defender runs with him. If the #2 receiver runs up the field, the defender carries him up the field and gives him to the three-deep coverage at 12 yards. If the #2 receiver runs across the formation shallow, he delivers the receiver to the next underneath defender.

The corners align in a press technique on the wide receivers and bail out into three-deep zone coverage. We want to give the appearance of a cover-2 shell. The corners bail, and the strong safety comes down on the #2 receiver into the field. When we drop the strong safety down, we load the box with defenders.

The thing we do not want to happen is to have a player with their hand on the ground, trying to cover a detached receiver in space. If that occurs, we make a "hook-it" call. That switches the responsible of the inside Will linebacker with the drop end. The Will linebacker widens his alignment and takes the #2 receiver, and the drop end takes the #3 receiver in the backfield.

We play man-free defense. The alignment looks like the cover-2 shell. The corner can press or bail and play man-to-man on the wide receivers. The underneath defender match their receiver and run all over the field with them. We have the free safety free in the middle as the eraser on mistakes that get deep.

When we match up in zone coverage, we do not spot drop. If the drop end matches the #2 receiver, he jumps him and runs with him. In the match-carry-deliver scheme, it allows defender to exchange responsibilities with other defenders in the scheme. The reason we match cover is to make the quarterback hold the ball. We do not want to play soft and let the quarterback dump the ball quickly. We want him to hold the ball and give the blitz time to get to him.

If the #2 receiver runs to the inside, the defender delivers him to the #3 defender. If the #3 receiver crosses to the outside, the #2 defender has a new #2 coming from the inside. He releases the old #2 defender to the inside linebacker and pick up the new #2 receiver coming outside. When the receiver crossed, the receiver going inside is #3, and the receiver coming outside is #2.

When we change the front, the responsibilities do not change. In the Okie front, the field end aligns in a 5 technique and long-sticks to the A gap from that position (Diagram #5). The nose tackle aligns head-up the center and angles into the boundary A gap. The 3-technique tackle moves into a 5-technique alignment on the offensive tackle and comes up the field to play the C gap and contain on the pass. The Sam linebacker crashes the edge from the field, and the Mike linebacker blitzes the B gap off the butt of the long stick. We run the stunt from the alignment of the defense.

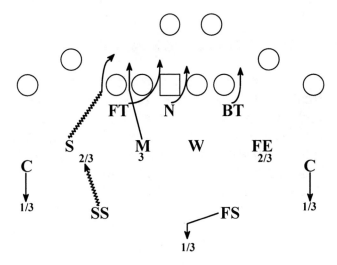

Diagram #5. Okie Front Sam Scrape

If we have the nickel back on the field for the Sam linebacker, he runs the edge stunt. Nothing changes in the execution of the blitz or the coverage in the secondary. Everyone has his rules in coverage.

From our base and the Okie front, we can run a swap call with our inside linebackers (Diagram #6). This situation occurs with a trips set to the blitzing linebacker side. The Will linebacker has coverage on the #3 receiver. The #3 receiver in the trips set is opposite the Will linebacker. If we move the Will linebacker across the set to cover the receiver, we give up the disguise of the defense. To avoid that, we give a switch call, and the Will linebacker runs the blitz into the B gap off the long stick. The Mike linebacker steps out and has the #3 receiver to that side. Nothing else changes in the responsibilities, except the Mike and Will linebacker sway their responsibility.

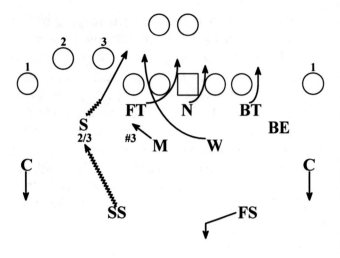

Diagram #6. Swap Call

The third front we run the blitz from is the Bear front (Diagram #7). The nose tackle aligns in the zero technique head-up the center. The field defensive end and 3-technique tackle align in 3 techniques on the offensive guards. We run the stunt from those alignments. The field defensive end sticks into the A gap. The nose tackle slants into the boundary side A gap. The 3-technique tackle uses the loop or jump movement into the C gap. He contains on pass and plays the C gap on running plays. The Mike linebacker blitzes the B gap off the butt of the stick stunt. The Sam linebacker or nickel back runs the blitz from their edge position, depending on where they align. Their position depends on the formation. If there is a tight end, they run the blitz from the 9-technique position. If there is no tight end, they could be in a walked off or stacked position.

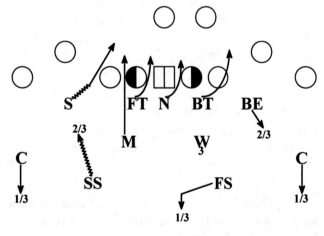

Diagram #7. Bear Front

Mike Cassity, who coaches our secondary, is with me today. If you have any questions for Mike or me, we will try to answer them. We do not have any secrets. I drove here today from Hurricane, West Virginia, in about three hours. You can be at the university in two-and-a-half hours. If you have a desire to come up and watch practice, we would be proud to have you.

The key to winning is not what you do in your scheme; it is getting your players to play extremely hard and tackle well. If you do that, you have a chance to win every game. I keep emphasizing the plan to winning. I have a chaplain who works with our team. He has helped me with the players. One hundred percent of our players go to his service before our games. He is the reason they go. He is good with his message. He knows when I need to talk to someone. He put this big sign on my office door, which read: "Don't flinch." That means, "If you are doing the right thing, keep on doing it."

That will eventually win games for us. We are going to recruit great players. We will maximize them as people. We will maximize them as players in the weight room and on the field. We will win championships because of it. We lost a couple of game this year because I had to dismiss my two starting corners. We went into the season with no corners.

We won five games. However, we won four out of the last five games we played. The foundation is now set, and the players understand they have to do the right thing or they will not be part of our team. Our strength program has taken off. Strength coaches are like football coaches. They all talk to one another and exchange ideas about their programs. I think that most of them do the same things. I know that work on the neck is very important in today's game. I am pleased with the way our program is going.

If there is one thing you get from this lecture today, I hope it is about tackling. Teach them to tackle with their eyes open and to keep their heads up. It is a bad deal when you have an injury because they used the head as a weapon. Many of the correct techniques of tackling are not taught today. Coaches have to be more responsible and teach the skill better today.

Whatever you are doing, believe in it, and do not flinch. I appreciate you coaches being here. Louisville is a great town.

COACHING THE OFFENSIVE LINE

Tampa Bay Buccaneers

Thank you. It is a pleasure to be representing the Tampa Bay Buccaneers. Coaching the offensive line is a challenge but a very worthwhile endeavor. There are some offensive line core beliefs I want to talk about before I get to the offensive line. The players can control three things. They are important to the development of any unit. They can control the attitude, effort, and preparation. None of those things has anything to do with the talent a person has, but all of them have to do with the success of an individual.

To play in the offensive line you must be smart. The linemen must be accountable to each other. We had a catch phrase we used this year. The phrase was "Don't be satisfied." We tell the team that what you did today will not be good enough tomorrow. We were such a young team; we wanted to make sure they understood that, so we told them every day.

The offensive line has to establish the tempo of the game and enforce its will on the opponent. That falls back into the things the players can control. They can prepare, have a good attitude, and put forth the effort to make those things happen. The offensive line plays together and protects one another.

The stance for the offensive linemen we use is no different from what you use. We align in both three-point and two-point stances. We want the feet at shoulder width. We want to be comfortable in the stance. We want good flex in the body with a good knee bend. We want to maintain all the power angles in the ankles, knees, and hips. We want the down hand in the three-point stance in front of the eye in its alignment. The stagger will vary according to the body type and style of the athlete.

Pre-practice is a big time for the offensive linemen. Everyone knows about stealing time. We have limited individual time and need to create time slots to work on essential techniques that are vital to offensive line play. The head coach allots about 10 minutes a day for individual time. There is too much to cover in 10 minutes. We have to steal some time before practice actually starts to work on as much body positioning as we can. We want them winded before they get to the stretch period. We do not want them gassed but we want the systems working.

During this period, we want to set the tempo for practice. We want to be the hardest working group on the field. We want to work on eye work during this time. We work blitz pick-up drills and twist stunts. One of the drills we do during the pre-practice is a mirror drill. I am sure most of you do this drill. The thing we do that is different is we put one hand behind the back. The mirror drill becomes a total footwork drill. In the drill, we want them to maintain their posture and balance at all times.

Another thing we do is the cone drill (Diagram #1). I am sure most of you do some form of this drill. We set the cones in a square-shaped area 10 yards apart. We start at the corner cone and go vertical to the second cone doing a duck walk. We do the duck walk with the toes turned out as if you were into a drive block. The feet are slightly wider than the shoulders. We use short, choppy steps. The

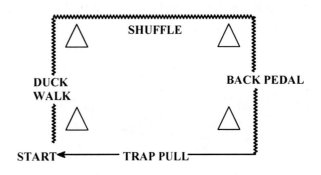

Diagram #1. Cone Drill

steps are about six inches in length and done very rapidly. On each step, we want the entire foot on the ground. We do not want to see anyone on his toes. When they do the duck step, their arms are in time with their foot movement. We want them to pump the arms in coordination with the feet.

When the player reaches the second cone, he redirects his movement and shuffles to the third cone. In the shuffle, we want the feet close to the ground and the lineman in a low body position. We want the shuffle steps done rapidly. Everything we do keeps the feet as close to the ground as possible. We do not want a crossover step in this part of the drill.

When the player reaches the third cone, he redirects again going backward. We duck walk backward or backpedal to the next cone. The technique he used on the duck walk going forward is the same as he uses going backward. When he reaches the fourth cone, he shuffles back to the start. We can change the drill at this point and have the lineman execute a pulling technique. The lineman backpedals from the third to the fourth cone. As he reaches the fourth cone, he plants his foot and executes a pull technique back to the starting cone.

In the pre-practice drills, we work on the twist game. You must attack the twist game (Diagram #2). We get many twists in third-down situations. Some of them are run twists but the vast majority are pass twists. The key to handling the twist game is how you pass off the penetrator. We get the twist from both the defensive tackle and the defensive end. The looping defender is easier to pick up in both stunts. If the defensive tackle is the penetrator, he charges into the B gap working outside. The guard has to pass the penetrator off to the offensive tackle, settle, and come back inside on the looping end coming inside.

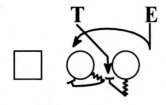

Diagram #2. Tight End Twist

The penetrator wants to split the block of the offensive guard and offensive tackle and get under the offensive tackle's block. This gives him a straight line to the quarterback. The problem is the offensive tackle getting to an inside leverage position on the penetrator. The offensive guard has to flatten the charge of the penetrator and shove him onto the block of the offensive tackle. After he does, he has to settle and get back inside on the looping defensive end coming inside. We have to coach the path and the eyes of the offensive guard. He has to find the looping defensive end coming inside after he makes the pass of the penetrator.

His footwork is vitally important. He has to move the inside foot quickly to get an inside-out leverage point on the defensive end. Both defenders want to penetrate straight up the field. The biggest problem the offensive guard has is staying on the penetrator too long. You have to coach their eyes to see the defensive end. He has the same problem as the tackle if he cannot get inside leverage on the defensive end. If he attacks him on an angle, the defensive end runs through his block to the quarterback.

The same thing is true of the defensive end as the penetrator. The tackle must flatten his charge, pass him to the guard, and get back outside on the looping tackle coming from the inside.

Everything in blocking starts with a step progression. The guards and tackles start working with a six-inch step. The center is different because he has to snap the ball. If he takes a six-inch step, he takes the ball with him. We want to shorten his step to half of the guards' and tackles' step. He steps with a three-inch step to secure the ball exchange with the quarterback.

The second step is the contact step. We want to make contact with the face and hands at the same time. We want to concentrate on the arms and elbows in the punch. If the lineman brings his arms and elbows back before he strikes, it takes a longer time to hit the target. The longer it takes the lineman to get his hands into the chest of the defender, the less chance he has of hitting the target. He wants to bring the arms and hands straight from the ground into the defender. If he winds up with his elbows, his face hits the defender first and the hands may never get to the chest.

We like to think of the hand movement as an explosion of a bench press repetition. If he gets into that position, it gives him a more violent and quicker punch. We want him to punch through the defender with his hands. The movement of the hands is up and through the defender to get maximum leverage.

The drills for offensive linemen do not change much. We do the punch progression drill. We do many hit-and-drive drills. Those drills incorporate the first and second steps with the punch. We work the punch progression on the boards. In this drill, we want to take a short, six-inch step with the back foot and roll off the up foot into the contact area. The force of the third step generates off the second step.

The feet have to stay close to the ground. We have no force with the foot in the air. The success of the block depends on how quickly we can get the second step on the ground. The second step is where the hips begin to roll into the block and the hands start to extend on the punch. The second step is the foundation for the rest of the block. We work the board drill straight ahead from the three-point as well as the two-point stance.

The next drill in the progression is to attack with the board right of the blocker (Diagram #3). The step progression is the same except we have to take a lateral step to get into position on the board. An adaption to the drill gives the linemen a direction to move when they reach the end of the board. A coach stands at the end of the board and gives the linemen a direction to move when they come off the board.

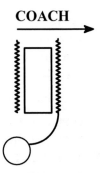

COACH

Diagram #3. Lateral Board

The coaching points to the drill are to watch for false stepping. We do not want a wasted movement in their charge. We also watch for the loading of the arms and hands. We do not want a windup that brings the elbows behind the body. Shoot the hands directly from the ground into the chest. It is a short, quick, and concise punch. Emphasize keeping the elbows tight to the rib cage. If he elbows get away from the body, the lineman loses power and control. When we work the lateral board, we go right and left with our footwork.

The next drill is a bucket step drill (Diagram #4). We use this drill in blocking a linebacker. We put the board on an angle with the linebacker at the end of the board. We work on two things in this drill. We work on targeting the numbers of the linebacker and taking the angle to where the linebacker ends up playing. If the play goes outside and the linebacker plays slow, the lineman targets the outside number of the linebacker. If the linebacker is fast flowing, the blocker targets the backside shoulder of the linebacker. He uses his backside hand to wash the linebacker past the hole.

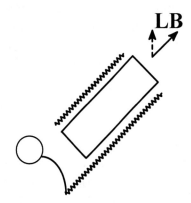

LB

Diagram #4. Bucket Step Drill

We work the drill with three linemen going at a time. You do not have the time to do one individual at a time. I also want to work and condition in these drills. By the time we get to practice, I want them a little fatigued. This makes them concentrate and focus on what is going on in practice. We have to think when we are tired.

The next thing we do with the linemen is work on bag drills. We have small stepover bags that we use. We teach basic running mechanics. We run them through the bags teaching forward lean with one foot between the bags and then two feet between the bags. Two feet makes them chop down their steps to get to both feet in between the bags. We work on shuffling through the bags.

The next part of the practice gets into individual blocks. We run the zone play many times in our offensive scheme. I want to talk about the playside guard on the inside zone to the right with a 3 technique aligned on him. His first step is a lateral step to the right with his outside foot. He keys the left foot of the 3-technique defender. If it steps outside, his aiming point is the outside number of the defender. However, he wants to keep a strong inside hand. His second step with his inside foot is important. We want the second step to the near foot of the defender on the inside number. The key to the inside zone play is a strong inside hand on the defender. That allows the blocker to lock out with the inside hand when the defender tries to react back inside.

If we run the outside zone play, the guard has to get wider in his technique. He takes a deeper lateral step and tries to shoot his hand to the outside. The backside hand works to the frontside number of the defender. The backside foot works to the crotch of the defender. The second step is in the crotch of the defender, but the third step has to be up the field. When we have problems, it is the third step of the linemen. They make the mistake of not getting the step up the field. They tend to flatten out on the line.

We play many teams that run a 3-4 defense. This is true on the frontside or the backside of a play (Diagram #5). If we run an inside isolation play or a sprint draw, the playside guard and tackle read the defensive end's inside foot. The guard and tackle both drop-step and key the inside foot of the defensive end. If the charge is an inside charge by the 5-technique defender, the guard and tackle use an angle drive block on the defensive end and

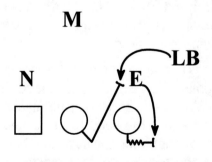

Diagram #5. Twist Stunt

outside linebacker. However, what we see many times is the defensive end up the field and the outside linebacker folding inside on a twist stunt.

If the defensive end goes up the field, the guard drop-steps and keys the inside foot of the defender. When the guard sees the foot going up field, he pushes the defensive end outside and climbs, looking to get inside leverage on the linebacker coming inside.

When we run the inside zone play, the scheme has to do with the linebacker. We want to know where he is playing (Diagram #6). If he is stacked, the double-team on the 3 technique is heavy. The linemen have to communicate that to all the linemen involved with that block. The backside trail blocker has to take more of the double-team. An example is a shade nose on the center with a Mike linebacker stacked behind him. We call this a "bounce" technique. We want to generate movement on the noseguard and, at the same time, get him cut off. We want the center to overreach the noseguard. The guard opens so the center can come under the nose. The guard knocks the nose onto the block of the center and bounces up the field for the Mike linebackers.

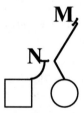

Diagram #6. Bounce Technique

If the Mike linebacker is not stacked and is to the playside, the center knows he gets no help from the guard. He uses a hands technique. He gets his hands into the nose and flattens him to the line of scrimmage.

The other technique is force (Diagram #7). We use this against 3-4 teams. If the defensive tackle is a 4-technique tackle head-up the offensive tackle, the playside guard keys him. If the defender does not come inside, the guard sees the linebacker. If the linebacker hangs behind the play, we use the force technique on the tackle. The guard punches the defender from a 4-technique alignment into a

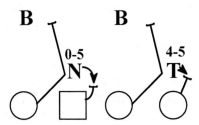

Diagram #7. Force Technique

5-technique alignment on the offensive tackle. He punches him on that block and comes up inside on the linebacker. The backside guard punches the 0-technique nose into a shade nose and gets up on the backside linebacker.

This allows everyone to push the defenders to the playside and lets the back cut behind the noseguard. As with any zone play that is successful, someone has to cut off the backside pursuit.

We run many three-man zone combinations. The first man in the combination sets the edge for the play (Diagram #8). If the first blocker is the offensive tackle with a 5 technique on his outside shoulder, he has to reach that defender. He can sell out on the reach block because he has inside help. If he reaches and the 5-technique defender goes inside, he punches him with his inside hand and climbs upfield. He punches with his inside hand and slows down as he goes upfield. If he does not slow down, he gets too far up the field. The linebacker will not play over the top. When the linebacker sees the gap open, he comes under the blocker and makes the tackle.

Diagram #8. Three-Man Zone Combo

The big coaching emphasis goes on the second man in the scheme. He is generally the lineman that is uncovered. With a 5-technique defender, the offensive guard is the second man in the scheme. He keys the inside foot of the 5-technique defender. His first step is a bucket step to the outside. He comes off the line of scrimmage and keys. It is hard to see the near foot. We tell him that if the color comes to him, he overtakes the block. He works to get his backside hand to the playside number of the 5-technique defender. When he gets to that position, he executes the block progression on the defender. His third step has to be up the field.

If the defender goes outside, the reach blocker takes him and the guard focuses back inside for the next color. It is generally the linebacker. The third man in the scheme reaches the playside gap.

The three-man scheme becomes more important when you have defensive line movement, when teams align in a standard 4-3 look and use a pirate stunt to bring both the defensive end and tackle into the A and B gaps. The tackle reaches for the 7-technqiue defensive end. When the color comes inside, he blocks it. The guard reaches for the 3 technique. When the 3 technique slants inside, the center overtakes that block and the guard slow climbs to the second level. The tight end takes the frontside linebacker in the scheme.

I want to get into our pass protection fundamentals. Our inside foot is our post foot and the outside foot is the set foot. We want to make the aiming point for the offensive blocker as small as possible. That is especially true with the tackle. You cannot have a tackle aiming at the number of a defender. We want the focus on the inside shoulder of the defender.

In our set, we carry our hands high. If the lineman carries his hands low, he can deliver a more powerful punch but it takes a long time for the punch to hit the target. We want the hands high and the punch short, accurate, and quick.

The offensive tackles have two kinds of sets. They use a jump set, which is a quick two-handed punch delivered at or near the line of scrimmage. We want to get on the defender quickly. We do not want to jump set a wide upfield rusher.

If we have a primary pass rusher, we vertical set on him. We want the inside hand as the strong hand with the outside hand free. We want to keep the outside hand free to combat the swim or rip moves by the defender. The tackle's pass protection set establishes the width of the pocket.

We do a couple of different things inside with our center and guards. They determine the depth of the pocket. We want to keep the depth of the pocket as close to the line of scrimmage as possible. If the guard has a 3-technique defender aligned on him, he never sets back off the line. He sets in a direction toward the defender. He attacks the defender and stays lateral and flat to the line of scrimmage. If he sets back, the defender has momentum and pushes the depth of the pocket back into the quarterback. The guard must protect the tackle's hip with his set. The center has to protect the guard's hip. They must slide inside and out to protect. When we do that, it is a basic shuffle and not a turn.

That is the biggest coaching point for the guards and center. They must make sure they slide and not turn. Once they turn, they open up the hips and expose the protection. The players that are the biggest culprits of giving up the hips are the centers. You have to work with the center extremely hard at staying flat to the line of scrimmage. They have a tendency to open up and give up the hip quicker than the other two positions. If the center turns, he can never recover his position.

We use the same kind of stepping that everyone else uses. We have a power step, jump step, and kick-slide. They have to move their weight from one foot to the other in transference of the weight. They have to redirect their direction and we drill all those movements. When you work footwork, you cannot let the linemen get their feet too wide. They have to maintain a width slightly wider than the stance. If they get their feet outside the armpits, the weight transfer is difficult. The weight distribution on the feet has to remain on the inside of the feet with the knees inside the ankles.

Another situation we work with the guard and tackle on is in their blitz pickup in our slide protection. If the guard is covered and a mug linebacker walks up in the gap, the tackle and guard take an inside drop-step. If the linebacker does not come, the tackle has to get back to the outside rusher. He cannot kick-slide out. He has to use a vertical set at that point to reestablish leverage on the defender coming off the edge. If he tries to kick out, he gives up the sack.

We do a drill called "inside control drill." It is about defeating the bull rush. When the hands of

the defender come up together, the blocker should read that as a bull rush. If defenders are going to swim, rip, or club, they start the movement with an inside or outside hand. The blocker has to get inside the hands of the defender. He wants to get inside position and, at some point, he has to drop the hips and anchor the back foot. If he does not, the rusher walks him directly into the quarterback.

We can base protect from a seven-man base or a six-man base (Diagram #9). In both cases, we are blocking the four down linemen and the Mike linebacker with the five offensive linemen. In a seven-man base protection, we assign the backs to the outside linebackers. It is a maximum protection scheme.

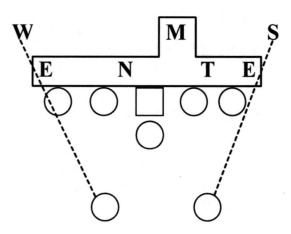

Diagram #9. Seven-Man Base Protection

The first thing we have to do is define the protections. We have a base, slide, and turn protection. If the protection is a seven-man base protection, we block the four down linemen and the Mike linebacker. We also block the two outside linebackers in that scheme.

The next thing I want to cover is our protection schemes. We call our dual protection "drag." It is really a slide protection. The difference is the slide protection includes the outside linebacker. A drag protection includes the outside and inside linebacker.

If it is a six-man drag protection, we have a direction in the protection. If we run a 76 drag, it goes to the right (Diagram #10). The 77 drag protection goes to the left. In a 76 drag, the center, guard, and tackle in that direction have the two defensive linemen and the Mike linebacker. In the drag protection, we have

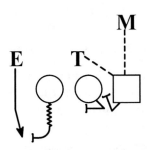

Diagram #10. 76 Drag Protection

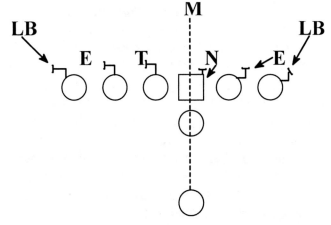

Diagram #11. Seven-Man Slide Protection

three players and sometimes four players working together. The tackle sets to the widest rusher to that side. If the tackle has a slot formation to his side, the widest possible rusher is the defender over the slot. He sets vertical off the ball and takes the widest rusher, whoever it may be.

The tackle vertical sets and looks for the outside pressure. If the defensive end charges outside, he blocks him because that is the edge rusher. If the defensive end charges inside, the tackle gets his inside hand on him and looks for someone else coming from the outside. If there is no one coming, he does not sit and block air. He pushes the defensive end inside.

The center and guard are responsible for the remaining down lineman and the Mike linebacker. The guard can set heavy outside on the 3-technique defender because he has help from the center should the 3 technique angle inside. If the Mike linebacker blitzes, the guard or center blocks him. If he blitzes the A gap, the center steps into that gap and blocks him. If he blitzes the B gap, the 3-technique defender comes inside, and the center blocks him. The guard steps out and takes the Mike linebacker. In a six-man protection scheme, we have a running back in the protection scheme. The difference between the drag and slide is the slide pushes to the outside linebacker and the drag makes sure the Mike linebacker is blocked.

The seven-man slide protection is the next one we use (Diagram #11). We use this protection many times with our play-action passing game. In this protection, we slide the center, guard, and tackle to the direction call and the backside has a man scheme. If we have two backs in the backfield and a tight end, one of the backs has a free release. We slide the protections away from the tight end

and the remaining back scans for any leakage. Slide protection is good against a zone blitzing team. The offensive line in a slide scheme blocks the outside linebacker, defensive end and tackle, and Mike linebacker to the direction side of the slide. The tight end or running back has the outside linebacker away from the call.

On the six-man slide protection, we block the slide the same way. The difference is we have to dual read with the back going away from the slide. He reads inside to outside on his scan.

In our turnback protection, we turn the entire offensive line in the direction of the call. The running back blocks away from the call. He has the first threat coming off the edge.

We teach the quarterback the same schemes we teach the offensive line. The quarterback can override the call of the center or change the protection depending on his pre-snap read. He may be able to see things in the secondary that lead him to think the protection is wrong.

We have a general rule we follow. In a 2x2 set, the linebacker designated as the Mike linebacker is usually to the weakside of the formation. In a 3x1 formation, we designate the Mike linebacker to the strongside. We want to balance the protection by putting three offensive players to the right and three offensive players to the left. The running back is the third blocker to the right or left depending on the protection. If we find an overload in the defense where they have a four-defender side, the back works to that side.

If we have a 2x2 formation and it is a right formation call, the slide will be to the left. The back blocks away from the slide and makes the third blocker to the formationside. We are sound in this protection as long as the secondary is two deep and there is a defender over the slot receiver. However, if the defense has a single high safety and there is a defender over the slot receiver, we have to go to a base protection. The defender over the slot receiver is the rolled down strong safety. The Sam linebacker is a threat to blitz from the formationside. The running back can pick up the Sam linebacker if he blitzes and the base protection takes care of the Mike linebacker.

If we align in a 2x2 formation with the back offset to the side of the Mike linebacker, we drag protect toward the running back (Diagram #12). The determining factor is the number of defenders to the running back side. If there are three defenders to the #2 receiver and running back side, the center drags to that side. The center, guard, and tackle block their drag rules. When we count defenders, we never count the far defender to the field. In the diagram, we do not count the field corner. He is too far to the outside and not a threat to get to the quarterback. We count the Sam linebacker, Mike linebacker, and strong safety.

If we are in a 3x1 formation, we always work to the three-receiver side with our drag protection. This may sound confusing but it is not.

When we use the slide protection, we slide and do not turn. If the center turns, he exposes the guard's hips. The offensive linemen have to protect each other's hips. They cannot allow defenders to get to the hips of adjacent linemen.

Whenever the offensive lineman becomes free, something generally is coming to him late. He stays active and goes to find work. If the guard frees up on his pass blocking assignments, he helps the center.

When we slide or drag the protection scheme, there are situations that break the slide (Diagram #13). If the scheme is a slide protection to the right and the 1-technique defender in the right A gap goes to the left, whose man is he? The center has to break the slide and stay with the 1 technique. That is a rule we struggle with in this scheme. The center cannot turn or open up to the tackle. He has to slide back with the defender to protect the hips of the guard. It does not have to be a physical block. However, the center has to stay with him.

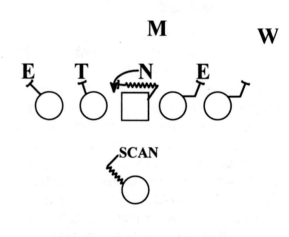

Diagram #13. Slide Breaker

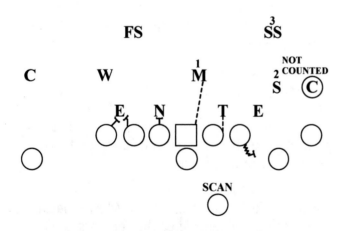

Diagram #12. Drag to Three Defenders

If there are two defenders to the slot defender and the running back, the center works the drag away from the running back. The offensive line can read safeties and corners cheating to cover receivers. They roll down so someone can blitz. We know that and see it coming. Very few blitzes are complete surprises to offensive linemen.

Another situation is what to do on the zone blitz. If the guard sets on the 3-technique defender and he leaves the line of scrimmage in a pass drop, the guard has to redirect to the inside in his slide and look for the blitzing linebacker.

The last thing is a Mike, Mike call (Diagram #14). In the drag protection, the tackle vertical sets for the outside rusher. If the Mike linebacker blitzes the edge, the tackle will not see him. He looks outside and the Mike linebacker comes from the

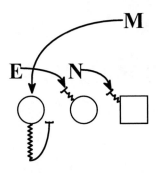

Diagram #14. Mike Call

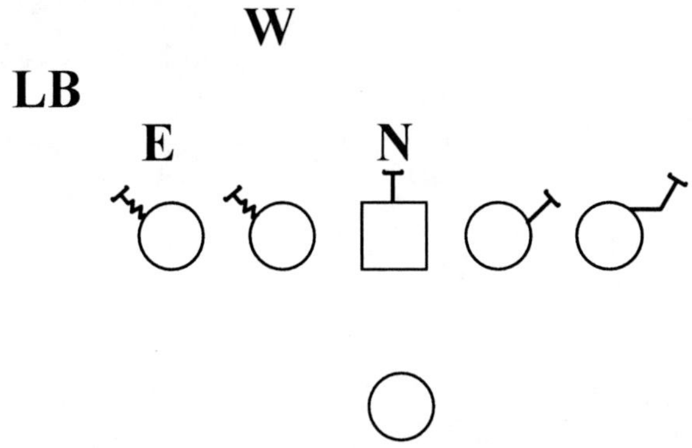

Diagram #15. Gillie

inside. When the center sees the Mike linebacker going to the outside edge stunt, he yells, "Mike, Mike, and Mike." When the tackle hears the call, he puts on the brakes and comes back inside to block the Mike linebacker.

In the odd front when the center has a nose head-up him, we adapt a protection called "Gillie." That is short for Gilligan's Island (Diagram #15). This is a three-down protection scheme. The center is on the island and has the nose alone. The guards and tackles perform a double fan drag to the outside. When they do the fan, they do not turn and aggressively fan to the outside. They observe the

rules—they drop and stay on the line of scrimmage. The tackle on the dragside vertical sets and takes the edge rusher. If the outside linebacker comes, the tackle has the outside rusher. The guard fans for the next defender. If either guard finds he is free, he helps the center who is on Gilligan's Island.

Coaches, I know there was more detail than you can write down. I have a second session where I can go into some of the particular techniques of the protection scheme for you. If you have questions about anything that we do, I will be around for a while. Thank you very much for your attention.

DEVELOPING SECONDARY FUNDAMENTALS

Georgia Tech

Thanks to the Nike Staff for having me at the clinic. On behalf of our staff, we appreciate the opportunity to get out of the office to visit with coaches. I would not be standing here if it were not for Coach Jack Hines. He gave me my first college job. Actually, he talked me into taking my first college job. At that time, I was coaching high school football at Central High School in Phoenix City, Alabama. He was the secondary coach at Auburn, and Wayne Hall was the defensive coordinator. That was Terry Bowden's first year at Auburn.

Coach Hines asked me if I wanted to come to Auburn as a graduate assistant. I told him there was no way. I saw what GAs had to go through when I played college ball, and I did not want any part of that. He talked me into coming up to visit the school. Coach Hines told me if I came on the staff with him, he would let me coach. He did what he said he would do. We went undefeated that season. Four or five players who started for us that year ended up playing in the NFL.

Many of the things I will show you today came from things I learned from several coaches over the years. I thought the thing I could offer the coaches today is how we coach our defensive backs. Several coaches have asked me want we do to develop our players in the off-season and during the season.

The things I am going to cover today can be beneficial to whatever scheme you may run. What we try to do is develop defensive backs. Before I get into my lecture, I want to tell you something that took me 18 years to learn. I am the secondary coach at Georgia Tech. I coach the defensive backs, and that is my job. Al Groh is our defensive coordinator. He is the architect of our defense, and I am the contractor. It is my job to build the secondary and make it look like he wants it to look.

I know as a young coach, you have many ideas about how to do things. It all comes down to understanding that you work for the coordinator, and you have to make the product look the way he wants it to look.

I say the same things repeatedly. People who have heard me speak say the same thing. I keep saying the same things because that is what we believe. We do not change every six months because we go to a new clinic. We believe in building defensive backs from the ground up. We start at the bottom and work our way up to the top. I have a quote that I believe in very much: "As time goes by, fundamentals apply." There is a difference between techniques and fundamentals.

Techniques change from time to time. For example, if I am a cornerback, some teams play a press technique and some teams play off man-to-man techniques. Those techniques change, but the fundamentals of being a defensive back do not change. That is where we are going to concentrate.

When we talk about building from the ground up, I want to talk about that from an evaluation standpoint. It does not matter if you are evaluating recruits or your players on a daily basis. We are doing the same thing. We are looking at them and evaluating what they do. It does not matter what level you coach on; it is the same process. Everybody is going to have a weakness. You will not find a player who can do it all.

PLAYER DEVELOPMENT

- Feet
- Hips
- Hands
- Eyes
- Hearing

In player development, the first things we look at are the feet. When we turn on the film to evaluate the player, that is the first thing, we see. If he is inadequate with his footwork, we can stop the film right there. If they struggle with any portion of their game, we take it all back to the basics. We go back to stance and work up.

The second thing we concentrate on is the player's hips. Once he masters his feet, we go to the hips. That is something you can train and work with. I have coached players who were extremely fast, but they did not have the hips to be an exceptional defensive back. They could not turn the hips.

When you work with defensive backs in their hip movement, you can tell if they are stiff. If the defensive back is stiff, you will never work him out of not being stiff. You can play defensive backs who are stiff, and they will make plays. However, you have to understand what you are working with. Do not ask them to do things they cannot do.

The next fundamentals involve the hands. There are two ways a defensive back uses his hands. In college, we have an advantage because the defensive back can get his hands on the receiver. The thing we talk about all the time is to deny vertical entry. If the offensive has a good quarterback and receiver, they will complete passes all day if you give the receiver a free release into the field.

That is why they put the rule into the NFL. If the defensive backs in the NFL could get their hands on the receiver past five yards, there would not be too many passes completed.

We use the hands to deny vertical entry, but we also use them to make a plays on the football. We want defensive backs who can make plays on the ball and intercept them. The hands lead us into the next fundamental. The eyes are tremendously important in playing defensive back. The defensive back must play with his hands and eyes. We have to know if they can play the ball in the air.

We do a drill every year in camp and in practice called "go ball" drill. We run deep on a go route and throw the ball up in the air. The defensive back has to jump into the air and catch the ball with only his hands. We do not want the ball trapped against the body. If the defensive back cannot do that, he will be a detriment to your defense at some point during the year. That is something we stress.

The defensive back has to put his eyes where they are supposed to be. Many coaches run drills for feet and hips but forget about the eyes. We train the eyes just like your feet. You have to work repeatedly putting the eyes in the right place.

I have made comments about players playing well with their eyes. People ask me what I mean by that. That means he sees everything. He has a feel for what is happening. He can find the ball in the air. He sees the route.

Another factor in playing defensive back is hearing. In today's game, we see a tremendous amount of spread formations and no-huddle offenses. Communication is a big part of the defensive game. The secondary has to be able to communicate at a high level. You cannot do that unless you hear and listen to what the communication on the field is.

I went to an Arkansas practice when Houston Nutt was the head coach there. He assembled the players in a group and talked to them about something that was going on in practice. One of the players was not paying much attention. He pulled the player up in front of the group and explained to the group that listening was a skill. He said it was just like running and tackling. He said you have to listen and hear things to be successful.

DEFENSIVE BACK SUCCESS

- Communicate the call.
- Tackle in the open field.
- Play the ball in the air.

In the secondary, that is an essential. You must be able to communicate with each other. We want our player to know what it takes to play. A defensive back has to do three things to play in our secondary. The number-one job of our safeties is to get the defense lined up and communicate the call. If they cannot do that, it does not matter what else they can do. They cannot play in our defense. The second thing you must do is tackle in the open field. The third thing is to play the deep ball. If you are not good with your eyes and ears, you cannot do that.

We want to develop habits. It takes 360 perfect repetitions for something to become a habit. The example I want to use is the golf swing. For something to become muscle memory, you have to do roughly 360 perfect repetitions. If you do the new exercise 100 times and revert to the old way, you must start all over to create muscle memory. You base everything you do on perfect repetition. What you reinforce is what you will get. That brings us back to fundamentals. Habits are what the defensive backs play with on Saturday afternoons.

I never talk to a defensive back about his stance or backpedal during a game. He cannot be thinking about those things. They should be habits. The thinking about stance and backpedal has to be done in the spring, summer, and pre-season camp. We have to make adjustments in the scheme, and he has to play with a habit. That is the same thinking with technique. If you try to do five different techniques, you will not be very good at any of them.

Another thing you have to remember, and we have this posted in our locker room: "Practice does not make perfect." What you do in practice makes permanent what you do in games. What you do in practice is how you will play in the games. The truth is: "Perfect practice makes perfect."

You must have a practice tempo. This goes hand-in-hand with teaching fundamentals. I am the world's worst at coming to practice and wanting everything to be wide open and done with a high tempo. You cannot teach at that tempo and expect them to learn. You cannot teach something and ask them to do it full speed on the first rep. He may be able to do it fast, but he will do it wrong, and that reinforces a bad habit. We have a teaching speed, learning speed, and full speed. Learn how to walk before you run. Learn how to run before you sprint. As a defensive back, we do the same thing as other players, except we do it going backward.

I have a drill sheet that I use in the spring and summer workouts. We break our drills into three categories. The first category is what we call "first things first." That is what I am going to concentrate on today. We do these fundamental drills every day. We do not do all of them every day, but we do some type of the drills.

This set of drills is feet and hip drills. The drills develop the things we talk about as building from the ground up. The next set of drills relates to releases from our zone and man technique coverages. For example, our dog technique is our press coverage. We work the dog technique against an inside and outside release by the receiver. We also work

the dog technique with a speed turn and a trail technique with a safety over the top.

The next category is how we attack blockers. I hope that we will get to some of that today. We do not talk about taking on blockers. We talk about attacking blockers. The last category is tackling, ball drills, turnover drills, and blitz drills.

I do not have anything in the lecture about the blitz drills today, but coaches talk about it all the time. We bring the zone blitz all the time. At one time or another, we blitz every member of our secondary. I started doing this when I was defensive coordinator at Nicholls State; we used the fire zone blitz with the weakside corner. I got very frustrated with our corner because he got picked up or missed coverage from the blitz. I remember bringing a corner on a blitz, and the running back picked him up. The running back was little and not very physical, but he blocked him.

In the spring, I began to think that we worked our defensive line and linebackers on a pass rush drill, but we never worked the defensive back on a pass rush drill. How were they supposed to know how to pass rush if we never drilled them on the skill? At some time or other, we bring everyone from the secondary on a pass rush. We needed to work on those skills. Those skills are in the third category of drills.

We went back and worked on the angles of the blitz coming from the boundary or through the B gap. If you expect a player to do something in a game that you do not work on, it is pure luck if it happens. The blitz does not have to sack the quarterback, but we want to pressure the quarterback to create the bad throw. Pressure is one thing the defenders have to understand. When they blitz, they do not have to sack the quarterback, but they must affect the throw. If they do not, the secondary is at a disadvantage.

I want to go through the drills we use in the first category. We call the first category "first things first." We call the first drill "pedal out." This is a simple backpedal drill. Defensive backs have to be good at moving backward. If you have an athlete who possesses good feet, hips, hands, and eyes, he may not move naturally going backward. I learned this a long time ago about evaluating defensive backs. He does not have to move backward well to begin with to be a good defensive back. You can teach a player how to backpedal if he has the other assets.

In these drills, I like to work two players at a time. When you show the defensive backs the film, you can compare what they are doing. One of them will always be better. That way, you can point out to the one who needs to improve what he should be doing. In backpedaling, I do not want too long of a stride as they reach back with their feet. I do not want too short a stride. Their steps should be even as they reach back.

The stance to me is not that important. I want them in a stance that is not too wide and they are comfortable. What I want to see is the pad level. Whatever level they start is where they should be throughout the pedal. I do not want their hips moving up and down as the move back.

The hands tell the feet what to do. If you have long hand movement, you will have long foot movement. Remember what I said about practice tempo. You cannot start teaching the movement at full tempo. You have to teach and learn before you can go full speed. The hand movement is like pulling a piece of wet spaghetti. You do not want to pull hard enough to break it. You want to pull hard enough to keep it in your hands. If you tighten the hands, it tightens every muscle in the arm. That has a tendency to make you tight all the way down to the feet. Try to stay as smooth as you can.

In the weight program during the off-season, we took our defensive backs and put them on a treadmill. We ran the treadmill slowly to start and made them backpedal. As we increased the speed, we wanted to see if they could maintain a smooth hip and foot movement.

When teaching defensive backs, it is essential that you work down yard lines. When we do the backpedal drills we generally work from the sidelines to the hash marks on a yard line.

The second drill is a hip weave (Diagram #1). This is a simple drill. The defensive back starts in the basic backpedal, and the coach moves him from one side of the line to the other by hand motions. The reason we do the hip weave is to make

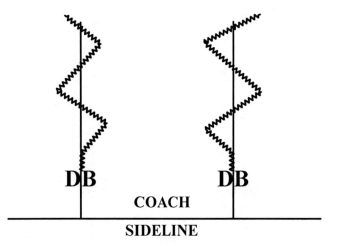

Diagram #1. Hip Weave

the defensive back move from side to side in his backpedal without turning his hips. We do not want the defensive back in the hip weave to open his hips to change direction. He has to maintain a square hip position to the line of scrimmage. The important thing is to work down the line. The hip weave allows the defensive back to maintain his leverage position on a receiver as he backpedals.

If he has an inside leverage position on the receiver, he wants to maintain that position. If the receiver releases to the inside of the defensive back, the defensive back has to be able to hip-weave to the inside to maintain his leverage. He cannot open his hips to the inside. He has to stay square in his backpedal. When they do the weave, their feet should stay at the same width apart. We do not want them to get wider in their foot position.

We film all our drills and teach from them. We have our players working to improve their technique and skill. They see these same tapes.

From the hip weave, we go to the hip flop (Diagram #2). The defensive back works down the line, beginning in his backpedal. On the coach's movement, he rotates his hips to the direction of the coach's movement. He opens to that side and rotates his hips running as fast as he can and runs down the line. On the next movement of the coach, he rotates his hips in the other direction and runs as fast as he can. The emphasis of the drill is to stay on the line and low in the rotation of the hips. We do not want him to drift off the line or stand up as he rotates his hips.

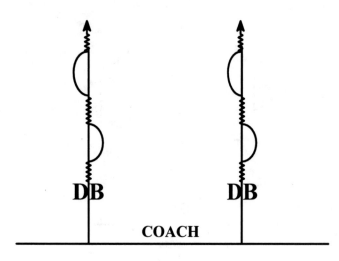

Diagram #2. Hip Flop

We want to see if the defensive back can run as fast as he can go, rotate his hips, and go in the other direction without slowing down. You can tell if the back is running hard by the movement of his hands and arms. We want to see the movement as if they were running a 40-yard dash. In the hip flop drill, four of the five assets are used. He uses his feet, hips, hands, and eyes. We want his eyes on the coach even though he is running away from him.

The next drill is open and drive (Diagram #3). On this drill, the coach gives the backs a direction with movement of a ball. The defensive back opens his hips and drives in that direction at a 45-degree angle. On the next movement, the back plants the outside foot in the ground and rotates the hips, running in the opposite direction at a 45-degree angle. It is using the hip flip technique but moving off the line at 45-degree angles. We want to see if the

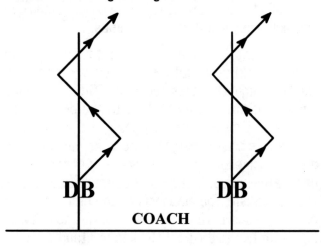

Diagram #3. Open and Drive

back can run as fast as he can, stick his foot in the ground, and go the other way.

From this drill, we graduate to the speed turn and go (Diagram #4). This drill starts out like the open and drive drill. The backs start backpedaling on the coach's movement. When the coach gives a directional movement, he opens his hips and runs in a 45-degree angle as fast as he can go. On the coach's next movement, the defensive back snaps his head around and runs in the other direction. He does not rotate the hips. He snaps his head and shoulder, turning his back to the quarterback, and runs in the opposite direction. He must get his head around once he has changed direction and locate the ball.

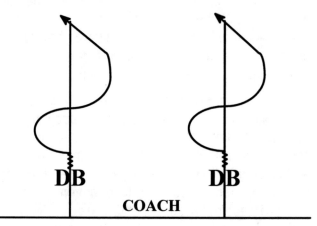

Diagram #4. Speed Turn and Go

The skill is exactly what it says it is. The speed turn is quicker than opening the hips and driving in the opposite direction. It does not matter what level you play; a defensive back will get in a position where he has to recover and make up ground on a receiver. If the receiver gets the defensive back into an opened hip run and breaks behind him, the defensive back has to adjust his run and get back to the receiver. This skill is the quickest way to do it. The defensive back has to get his head around quickly to relocate the quarterback or ball.

We coach receivers to break opposite the tilt of the defensive back. When the receiver forces the defensive back to open his hips and run, they break the opposite way from the hip tilt. This is when you use the speed turn.

The 45-degree drill is a drill we got from Mickey Andrews at Florida State years ago. (Diagram #5). We still use it. In this drill we incorporate the click

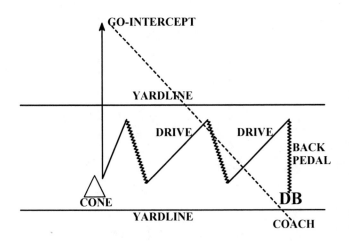

Diagram #5. 45-Degree Drill

step, which we teach, along with the plant and drive movement. We work the drill between two five-yard lines. The back starts on one yard line and backpedals. On the coach's movement, the defensive back uses a click step, which is a plant step, and reactions back to the line at a 45-degree angle. The coach gives a second movement, and the back breaks back in an open hip and drive movement. The coach gives the back a third movement, which puts him in another click step toward the line. On the last movement, the back uses a speed turn and runs deep. On the last movement, the coaches throws the ball, and the back intercepts.

We use the laundry bag drill to train the hands of the defensive back (Diagram #6). We use a laundry bag with four or five towels in it. The defensive back aligns on the sideline, facing the coach. The coach has the laundry bag. The coach throws the bag to the defensive back. He catches the bag in his

hands and shuffles down the sideline for five yards. In those five yards, he punches the bag forward and back assimilating a punch on a receiver. When he reaches the next yard line, he throws the bag down, opens his hips to the coach, and drives down the yard line, running deep.

If you want to make the drill more of a challenge for the defensive backs, soak the bag in a bucket of water. That weighs down the towels and makes it tougher on the defensive backs. This works on the hand strength of the backs. This trains the defensive back to be strong in the hands so he can play receivers with his hands. We work the drill going right and left.

In the off-season program, I have our defensive back work on a boxer speed punching bag. I do not want slow hands. Slow hands mean slow feet. In this drill, I want to see how quick the defensive back can get down the line, punching out with the bag. This is a good drill to work if you play cover 2 in your secondary. In cover 2, the corner has to reroute the receivers and carry them to an extent.

The next drill is quick out and go (Diagram #7). This is a drill to evaluate a defensive back when the receiver breaks his cushion. The defensive back aligns at seven yards off the receiver. We want to find out how far the defensive back can go before the receiver forces him to open his hips and run. We want to find out how long he can stay in a backpedal position. We put cones down at 6, 12, and 18 yards. By NFL standards, if a defensive back can maintain

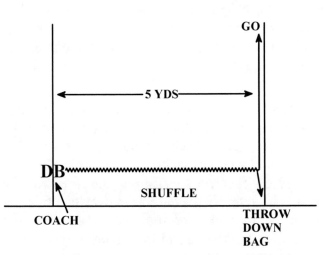

Diagram #6. Laundry Bag Drill

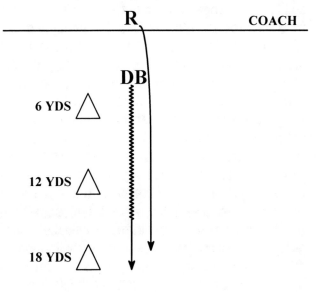

Diagram #7. Quick Out and Go

his backpedal through 18 yards, he can play at that level. It does not matter how fast he runs the 40-yard dash.

In 1993, we had a back who could stay in backpedal for 18 yards and ran the 40-yard dash in 4.7. He was as good as anybody was at finding the ball. He played in the NFL for 11 or 12 years. The cushion will vary from coach to coach and player to player. The cushion will vary from three to five yards. However, you do not want to play too many players that have a five-yard cushion. A general rule for us is four yards. If the receiver runs at full speed, the defensive back has to transition from his backpedal at four yards. It does not matter whether the technique is shuffle or pedal.

In a shuffle technique, the defensive back opens to the quarterback and shuffle as the receiver comes off the line. In the pedal, the defensive back is square to the receiver. One advantage of the shuffle technique has over backpedaling is it eliminates one step in the transition stage when the cushion breaks. The hips are already opened to the quarterback in the shuffle. In the pedal, the defensive back has to open his hips after the cushion breaks.

However, backpedaling allows quicker transition to the outside but we can break out of both techniques. There are advantages to each movement. The use of the shuffle or pedal depends on what coverage we play.

We do a drill to develop the defensive back's ability to change direction from a backward to forward motion. We call this drill pedal and click (Diagram #8). This is a drill to get us from a backward motion. It does not matter if we are shuffling back or backpedaling. We want them to come out of the backward movement the same. I want the cleats in the ground so he can get off that foot quickly. If the defensive back breaks inside, he plants his outside foot. If he breaks to the outside, he plants his inside foot. As we plant with the opposite foot, I want the pressure on the inside of the ball of the foot. I do not want the pressure on the toe. However, sometimes the heel of that foot gets in the ground, but that is all right. In this drill, we backpedal on the movement of the coach. When the coach gives the defensive backs a direction, they plant the back foot and attack forward at a 45-degree angle.

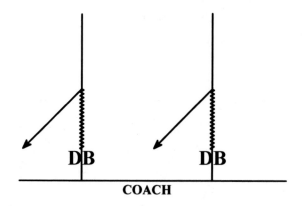

Diagram #8. Pedal and Click

In the first drill, I showed the break forward at a 45-degree angle. We also do the drill breaking outside at a 90-degree angle. We work off both feet moving in opposite directions. To add to the drill, we stand dummy players on the sideline in the direction of defensive backs' click step. The dummy receivers throw out their hands to the outside when the coach gives the signal. When the coach gives the movement to call the backs forward, they break to the hands of the players standing on the sidelines. This drill also trains the eyes of the defensive backs.

The go ball drill relates to our cover 2 and cover 3 (Diagram #9). The defensive back aligns in a 7- to 10-yard alignment. On the movement of the coach, the defensive back breaks deep into their deep zone. He shuffles or backpedals, then opens his hips and sprints deep. The coach throws the ball as a deep ball, and the defensive back goes to wherever the coach throws the ball and intercepts it.

We incorporate the speed turn into this drill. The back shuffles or backpedals, opens his hips, and runs deep. The coach throws the ball behind him, and he must speed turn, locate the ball, and intercept it.

The last thing I want to talk about is in-phase and out-of-phase. We tell our defensive backs to look for the ball when they are in-phase. That means if the defensive back can get his elbow on top of the receiver's inside arm, he looks for the ball right away. If the defensive back can feel the receiver, he looks for the ball. However, if the defensive back is behind the receiver and cannot feel him, his focus is on the hands of the receiver. If the receiver's hands go up, the defensive back

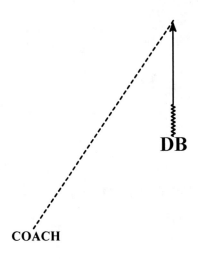

Diagram #9. Go Ball Drill

plays through his hands. If he can recover and feel the receiver, he looks for the ball.

On any vertical route, the defensive back works to get in-phase with the receiver. If the receiver beats the defensive back, the defensive back does not look back to the quarterback. He is out-of-phase and has to catch up. He gets his head down and sprints to recover the ground. If he can get in-phase, he can look back to the quarterback.

The mistake so many defensive backs make when they turn to look for the ball is looking in the wrong place. When the quarterback throws the ball, he throws it into the air with an arc on it. He wants the ball to drop over the defensive back into the receiver's hands. The defensive back has to look up to find the ball. He does not want to look back to the quarterback. If he looks back, he will not find the ball.

I am about to run over on my time. However, if anyone has any questions, shout them out. Our number-one goal on defense is to turn the ball over. When it is in the air, we want to intercept it. We are not worried about knocking it down. We want the interception.

I appreciate your time, and I am sorry we did not get further into the topic. I will stay around and answer all the questions you may have. I appreciate your attention, and thank you for coming.

EFFICIENT USE OF PRACTICE TIME

University of Oregon

Two short years ago, I was an assistant coach. When I was an assistant coach, I was the smartest coach in the country. I was always the smartest coach in our meeting room. I was not the head coach, and I said things like, "I would not do it like that way" or "I would do it this way." When I became a head coach, I realized I was not very smart. When I became a head coach and got the chance to do what I wanted to do, it became scary. I was the coach sitting at the end of the table, making those final decisions, and it became a bit tougher.

Statistically, 33 percent of the assistant coaches become head coaches during their career. When I took over at the University of Oregon, the first thing we had to find out was "What do we stand for?" You have to answer that in your offensive, defensive, and special team philosophies. If you are going to stand for something, it is not what you say it is. It is what people see in your actions. People should be able to come, observe you, and in five minutes know what you stand for.

That is the great thing about this game. There are so many choices of philosophies in this game. You have to decide what it is you want to do, and then do it. Do not be the coach who runs a play offense. That coach constantly adds plays that he likes and sees on TV or at a pro football game. Before he knows it, his offense is a mile wide of nothing but plays. He has nothing in that mass of plays to hang his hat on. Your players cannot say, "This is what we are." I suggest you take a long look at your program and identify what you want to be. If a coach tells me respect is an important part of his program, I should see it in practice. If I go to practice and I see a player who takes a cheap shot at another player and no one corrects him, that program has no respect in it.

WHAT WE STAND FOR

- Fast
- Play hard
- Finish

You need to sit down with your team collectively and ask them, "What are we all about?" If you watch the University of Oregon on the field, off the field, at practice, and in the classroom, you should know if we stand for something. When you watch us, the first thing that sticks out is the speed at which we play. When we talk to our team about fast, we have a simple concept. All they have to do as individuals is be as fast as they are.

We all have players who can run. If you have a 4.5 player in high school football, he had better score four touchdowns a game, and they should never catch him from behind. There are not that many 4.5 football players out there today. I do not care what state you come from. I have seen players run 4.5, but they do not run 4.5 in the games. I want the 5.0 player who runs 5.0 on every single play.

If a player is a 5.0 player and plays at 5.0, that is what we want. Do not be the 4.6 player who plays at 5.2 in the games. That is our concept about speed.

The second thing you should see from our team is we play hard. The ultimate compliment you can get from the opposing coach is "Your team really plays hard." It does not matter what the score was, if we play hard, that is all we can ask. There will be a time that you play a team who has more talent than you do. That is life. The reason you play the games is the team who plays the hardest wins the game.

That brings up another concept you should see from our team. The team who plays the hardest for the longest time is the one who usually wins. If you play against a good team, they will play hard.

The next concept is finish. If you come to our practice, you will hear that term all the time: "finish stretching, finish the drill, finish the run, finish the block." That is what you hear at our practice. Everything they do, they must finish. We engrain that concept in our players' heads.

What you decide is up to you, but find something to be. Our coaches got together as a group and talked about what we wanted to be. We wanted to know what the team was going to look like. What was our vision of what our team was supposed to be?

When you go to the practice field, you prepare against the vision of what you want to be. Every single game on your schedule is a rivalry game. If the cross-town rival is game six on your schedule, and you circle it in red, you have told your team the first five games do not count. It will be okay to lose a couple of games during that stretch.

Every game we play is the most important game of the season. We approach every game as if it was the Super Bowl. When we walk off the field after the game, we have to ask ourselves three questions: "Did we play fast?" "Did we play hard?" and "Did we finish?" If we can answer yes to all those questions, we have won the game.

TEACHING PHILOSOPHY

- I see, and I forget.
- I see, and I remember.
- I do, and I understand.

Within our staff, we talk about our teaching philosophy. It is a simple philosophy, and I will tell you about it very quickly. The first one is "I see, and I forget." How many times have you watched a tape and ask the question, "What is he doing?" The coach's answer is "I told him ...." If you catch yourself saying that many times, you have not put the player in a position to be successful.

Every coach in this room has a ton of knowledge. That does not matter. What matters is what the players know. Education is the transference of knowledge. You may know more than anyone in this room, but if you cannot communicate it to a player so he can go out and execute, it does not matter.

The alternative to that is "I see, and I remember." How do you learn to coach "I see, and I remember?"

How do you coach a player to step at a 45-degree angle? I can give you an entire clinic on a 45-degree step, but is that coaching? If you have a player who can do the technique, that is the best method. The player that can take what you say and perform the skill, becoming the example for the others. The coach told them how to do it, and then he showed them how to do it. The players heard what the coach said and saw what he wanted. They heard it, saw it, and remember it.

The next concept is "I do, and I understand." When we teach, we implement it in the classroom. We talk about what we are putting in that day. We show them what it is. After that, we go to the practice field and do it. The practice field is not where we talk. It is where we do the skills. We want to keep words on the field to a minimum. The words you use must have a meaning. When the players hear the word, you get immediate feedback.

When we go to practice, we want to use punch, hat, hands, footwork, and terms that have meanings to the players. They do not want to hear you give a 10-minute clinic in the middle of the field. Do not stop what you are doing so you can tell one player something. If you do that, there are 10 other players standing around doing nothing. If you want to talk to a player about something he did, take him out of the drill. Our coaches do a heck of a job of coaching players who are not in the drill or scrimmage.

A perfect example is the offensive line coach, Steve Greatwood. He watches the players in the scrimmage and coaches the group of players who are standing and watching. He gets constant feedback from the players watching, and that is his goal. When they are in the drill, they play. When they are not in the drills, he coaches them up by watching the mistakes of the players in the drill.

If the coach needs to talk to the player, he substitutes for him. Do not stop the drill and let everyone else stand around. That is not fair because there is only a certain amount of time we can practice. If you can make your practices more efficient, you will be more successful.

PRE-SEASON CAMP

You have to organize your pre-practice. I do not care what it is, but when they get to the practice field, they should be doing something. That bothers me. When the players get to the practice field, it is practice time. That period is not a walk-through period that we can teach in a classroom. I do not care what the group does, but the coach needs a routine that the players know. That way the players get into a rhythm and habit of doing something.

When we go out to practice early, they know what they are going to do, and they do it. The timetable for all positions is specific. The wide receivers work on the JUGS machine. The quarterbacks and centers work on snaps and footwork. The inside linebackers are doing a read drill. We are in teaching mode, but we are doing things. We are active and moving.

The first period in our practice is a drill period. That is a three-minute period when we concentrate on fundamentals. The defense works in a turnover circuit or on a pursuit drill. The offensive line works pass sets and steps. The quarterback, receivers, and backs have a "county fair." We work on the deep ball at one station. We have a curl station and a one-step 45-degree cut station. Everybody knows where to go.

The next drill is a five-minute core drill to work on formations and shifts in those formations. One day in practice while this was going on, I looked down at the other end of the field. That was where the defense did the same thing, working on their checks and adjustments to formations and motion. The defensive coaches were mad at number 97 because he could not go in motion the way he was supposed to go in motion.

He should not know how to go in motion because he was a defensive lineman. They yelled at him because he did not know what D-cross motion was. They coached the heck out of the player who was supposed to be going in motion. However, they were supposed to be coaching the defense. They were coaching a player who does not know what motion is, and if he did, he would not be playing in the defensive line.

To have both units working on the same thing at different areas of the field is not very efficient. We needed to bring the groups together and work on formations and defensive adjustment to those formations. The defense and offense both get

work, and the defense does not have to coach up the scouts. It maximizes our practice time. Instead of trying to coach a defensive tackle to go in motion, they coach him to play a defensive technique.

We have a great pre-season camp drill. We work the offense and defense in the same drill. It is a teaching mentality, but the offense goes through its formations and motion, and the defense goes through their checks and adjustments. We snap the ball, but we do not run a play. It is the best thing to do for your younger players because they do not know what to do. We get all those things done, and we do not run a play.

At first, we took a five-minute period for the drill. Later we got it down to a three-minute period. However, we create an opportunity for both sides of the line to learn. When you look at the drills you do, you need to find out how to make the drills more efficient.

That is your job as a coach. Coaching is one thing and one thing only: it is creating an environment so the player has an opportunity to be successful. When you teach him to do that, get out of his way. The coach is not playing the game. All we can do at the end of the game is to evaluate what happened in the game. Was there a situation that we did not cover in practice? The coach needs to know if he gave the player all the tools he needed to be successful in that situation. We have to continually analysis the situation and try to make it better.

When we have a team walk-through, we set a limit to the time we allot for it. When we do a walk-through, we do not spend time getting the defense aligned. They are ready so we do not spend time aligning the defense or getting personnel to stand in place. Our offensive line has the four down linemen and the Mike linebacker in our pass protection scheme. The tight end has the Sam linebacker, the running back has the Will linebacker, and the slot receiver has the strong safety. Everyone has an assignment in a walk-through drill.

We want them coached during this time. The offensive guard had better know what a 3 technique is. If the offensive guard does not know what defense they are in, you are in trouble. When you do the walk-through, you can find out what they know.

When we do stretching in practice, we do a dynamic stretch. We emphasize what it is, and we coach it. That bothers me when I go to a high school practice. The entire team is stretching, and the coaches are standing around talking to one another or throwing the ball around. A coach should not worry about spending time in stretching if they do not care about stretching. They show how they care about coaching by their actions during the period, not their words. If you do not think stretching is important, do not do it. If you think it is important, you have to show your team it is important.

The coach teaches everything the player does. If he does not do the stretch drill correctly or he does the wrong technique, he learned it from his coach. He did it because the coach did not think it was important enough to coach it. Every drill we do, our coaches coach for success. If the coach thinks what we do is important and shows it, the players buy into it, and they do it.

The conditioning coach thinks stretching is important. If he thinks it is important, we do it, and the players will buy into it. When practice starts until practice ends, we practice as hard as we can. Whenever we practice, we practice fast, and we finish everything. We emphasize the finishing part in stretching.

If you accept it, expect it. If you accept a player going eight yards when he is suppose to go 10, it will happen Friday night. If it is third-and-10 and you get eight, whose fault is that? Did you accept the fact that they went eight yards in practice instead of 10? Did you emphasize it in practice? If you are getting a huge amount of holding penalties in the game, you are allowing the players to hold in practice. If you allow the player to hold in practice and do not correct him, you should expect that on Friday night.

If that is your mentality, never yell at an official over a call. You have already told your players it is all right to cheat. When the player is caught holding, you get mad at him. You cannot have it both ways. You teach him to cheat, or you teach him how to do the skill. You accepted the player not finishing the drill, now you must accept the fact he gets caught holding. If the coach does not hold the player to a high standard, he is not going to do it. That is your job as a coach. You have to push them to places

they do not believe they can go because you see things they do not see.

How you run a drill is important because that is how your team is going to look on game night. Teaching has two speeds. You have a speed at which you teach, and there is game speed. There is no such thing as half speed. When we are in practice, we go hard. When you teach, there is teaching speed, but do not let them go half speed in practice. If the quarterback has a problem setting up, we walk him through it. We talk about the first drive step or the second crossover step and the balance step. However, we walk them through it at a teaching speed. After he works out his steps, he goes full speed. There is no speed between teaching speed and full speed.

Make sure when you teach something to your players that you identify it so they know what you want from them. The more you communicate with your players, the better they are. When you can explain it like Coach Paul Brown, the father of football coaching, explained the "whys" of football to your players, the better off you are. The players today do not do it "because I told you so." We do not live in that society anymore. Some of us grew up in it, but it does not work anymore. Players today want to know why. Tell them why. If you do not have a good reason why we do things, we probably should not be doing them.

I want to show you some statistic on some things that actually occurred in a game. Your practices should reflect what happens in a game. The first situation is the goal line offense. If you use the goal line offense when you get inside the five-yard line, how many times did you get inside the five-yard line? Do not spend time on something that does not happen in a game.

People worry about and practice third down all the time. The reality is we are not in third down that much. For the season, our statistic told us we had 49 snaps in third or fourth down with long yardage. In the third- or fourth-and-short situations, we had 31 snaps in the season. On our first- or second-down plays, we had 398 snaps for the season. You had better practice the first- and second-down situations.

The point I am making is to go through every scenario that happens in a game and practice it. You should not just put the ball down and run a play. That never happens in a game. Football is a game of situations. You have to practice those situations. When the game is on the line, your players better be able to call the play before you call the play. The only play that will work is the one they have confidence in running. Everybody at the end of a game knows the play we are going to call.

You have to practice it. We know what to do on the last play of the half. We know what to do on the last play of the game. We know what to do if we have no time-outs. We practice all those situations. I know at the end of the game with no time-outs and we have to snap the ball, we know what to do.

I want to take you through one of our practices. This a Tuesday morning practice for us. We start at 9:05 in the morning, and we finish at 10:52. We dress out in full pads.

Agilities are from 9:05 to 9:08 and walk-through from 9:08 to 9:13. Then I began to think. When you go to Coaching 101, they tell you if you have five-minute blocks that is 12 periods per hour or 24 periods for two hours. If you go with six-minute periods, you can get 10 practice periods an hour. As I watch our 3-on-2 period, I figured out that five minutes was too short but 10 minutes were too long. We made that period a seven-minute period. We want to run team offense by using two offenses against the third defense. We can get 14 plays in a six-minute period.

If you work too long in a drill, the players get bored. We like to keep the players fresh. We run a 10-minute special teams period. We have a 12-minute block period for team run. We work on first- and second-down plays. We work a 7-on-7 passing drill against the scout team. Ten minutes is too long and seven minutes is too short, so we work eight minutes in this period.

The point I am making with this practice schedule is you can make the time blocks as long as you want. Do not box yourself in to a period that you cannot use. Do not spend more time in the drill than is necessary. You have to figure out what you want to do. When a drill runs too long, adjust the time and get off the field. Be efficient on the field and get off the field.

WHY RUN THE SPREAD?

• Makes the defense cover the entire field
• Faster scoring
• Gets speed in space
• The defense cannot disguise
• Simple reads for quarterback

I want to talk about the fundamentals of being a shotgun quarterback. The fundamentals are different from being a quarterback under the center. The reason we are in this offense is we think we can score faster, and it makes the defense cover the entire field. If you stretch players from sideline to sideline, the defense has to cover them.

The offense gets speed in space and creates opportunities for your player to get bigger gains. The defense has to tip their hand and let you know what they are doing. If they do not, they will not cover some people. We are a spread team, but we run the ball. We averaged 300 yards rushing last year. We run the ball better than we throw the ball. We are effective running the ball because we have bigger lanes through which to run the ball. The reason for that is the number of people we have to run through.

If there are seven defenders in the box, there are only four defenders to play the pass. It is difficult to play man-to-man without help all day long. It lets you define the defense. For a quarterback, it is simple. There is one high safety, two high safeties, or no high safety.

If there are two high safeties, mathematically there can only be five defenders in the box. With one high safety, there can be six in the box. If there is no high safety, there can be seven in the box.

With two high safeties, we should run the ball most of the time. We have five blockers, and they have five defenders. We feel if we can get a hat on all five defenders, our running back should make yards. If the defense has one high safety and six defenders in the box, the quarterback has to be involved in the play. He has to read one of the defenders, in effect blocking him. We can block five defenders and read the sixth one.

If they have no high safety and seven defenders in the box, they have something going on. They are going to blitz or run some movement scheme. You must have a concept to handle that situation. It could be a screen, option, quick game, or a deep pass. It is what your plan is against that scheme.

It is hard for the blitz to get to the quarterback because of the gap. If the defense is good at disguising what they do, they will not get to the quarterback. That means the linebacker has to blitz from his linebacker depth if he wants to disguise what he is going to do. The quarterback is five yards off the line of scrimmage, and the linebacker is five yards off the line of scrimmage. That is 10 yards. The fastest time run at the NFL Scouting Combine for a 10-yard dash is between 1.5 to 1.7 seconds. That is without pads. My quarterback can get rid of the ball in that amount of time and complete a pass.

In a quarterback, I look for a quarterback who can run and not a running back who can throw. I want the quarterback who can beat you with his arm. If the defense forces him to run, he can do it effectively. We are not a Tim Tebow type of quarterback team. I am not going to run the quarterback 20 times on power runs. If I had a Tim Tebow, I might change my mind. You do not find the 6'4", 240-pound, 4.6 quarterbacks too many times.

If the quarterback is not tall, look at his hands. That is the biggest coaching point to finding a quarterback. How big are his hands, and how well can he control the football? The height of the quarterback is not the important thing. No one playing quarterback throws over the line. They throw through lanes in the linemen. The important thing is the size of their hands.

The quarterback's stance in the shotgun is a base stance. I tell them to think about a shortstop in baseball. He is in an athletic stance with his eyes in what we call "split attention." He sees the snap from the center and the defense. He cannot concentrate 100 percent on the ball coming back, and he cannot be 100 percent looking at the defense. We want the quarterback stance balanced so he can move and catch the bad snap. I do not want him to lean forward.

We have a good quarterback drill we use called "rapid fire." We snap five balls at the quarterback as fast as we can. On each ball, the quarterback has to catch the ball and reset to accept the next ball. He works on catching the ball.

We run a read drill every day. We run a ton of zone reads (Diagram #1). We do not run the zone read option much, but we practice it all the time. When we run the zone play, the quarterback reads the backside defensive end. He extends the ball into the mesh area, but his eyes are on the key. The read key may be a manager or another player. After the back comes into the mesh area, the read key flashes the quarterback a number. The quarterback verbally calls the number. That way, we know he is looking at the key.

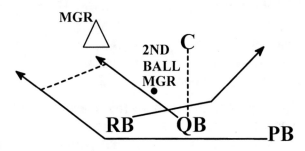

Diagram #1. Zone Read Key

This is a two-ball drill. After the quarterback hands the ball on the zone play, we hand him another ball, and he continues to run the option out from the backside and pitches the ball to a trail back. This allows us to work on the zone play, the read, and the option pitch in the same drill. It does not occur in a game because you do not play with two balls, but it saves practice time. This is an everyday drill for us. We work multiple skills in the same drill.

If you are a shotgun team, you still need to practice under-the-center snaps many times. At the end of a game when protecting a lead, you need to pass the ball from hand to hand with no air in the mist. Mistakes can happen under the center, but it is not as risky as the shotgun snap. In practice, you can get anyone to snap the ball. What is important is the quarterback must get accustomed to the snap.

The first fundamental is the grip of the ball. The grip should be with the fingertips. He has to have fingertip control. The top knuckle of his hand should be white from the grip on the ball. He should be able to pass his finger through the space between the ball and the palm of the hand. The smaller the hand of the quarterback, the further back on the ball he grips. The bigger the hand, the more of the ball the quarterback can grasp.

The quarterback wants to form an "L" with the index finger and thumb on the back of the ball. The index finger is the last finger to leave the ball. The elbow has to be perpendicular with the shoulder. If the elbow is below the shoulder, three things happen. The first thing is the ball comes out flat. The second thing is the ball sails. The third thing is the free safety becomes an all-state player because he intercepts the ball.

The coach is the quarterback's eyes. If he sees the ball sail, he knows the quarterback's elbow is too low. He draws the quarterback a picture he can envision. He tells him to hammer his all-state plaque into the wall. That means he put the plaque up high on the wall, and the motion he hammers the nail into the wall is the same one he uses to throw the ball.

The difference between a thrower and a passer is the fingertip control. That leads to the flick of the finger and wrist on the throw. That puts velocity on the ball. A good passer does not get sore in his shoulder. He gets sore in the middle of his forearm from flicking his finger and wrist as he throws the ball.

The fundamentals of throwing the ball do not change. He forms the "L" in his grip, hammers the nail, and flicks in the throw. We engrain the fundamentals so they become habit. When it is third-and-10 with the pressure on, he is not thinking about hammering nails and flicking footballs. The motion has to be a habit, which he learned. Make sure the player gets the answer. When you ask a player a question, and he says, "I don't know," if you go on to the next player, you have lost the first player. Do not give up on players.

When the player carries the ball, we want his elbows down and not out. His front shoulder is his lead shoulder. When he throws the ball, his eyes are on the target and stay on the target. If he follows the flight of the ball with his eyes, the ball will sail, and he is inconsistent to the target.

When he throws the ball, he wants the motion to be short and compact. The follow-through comes across the body to the opposite hip. He wants to throw with the entire body. It is all connected, and he has to use it all. When we target the receiver running to the sidelines, we want to throw to his left or right outside shoulder. If he hits the target,

he will hit the receiver in the face. We want the quarterback throwing to small targets so he can focus on them. The smaller the target, the more accurate he is.

When he throws with his shoulder, he has to keep the throw within the framework of his body. The next thing he throws with is his feet. We align the feet at the target. That means the lead step aligns to the left of the target so his hips and shoulder can come through at the target. He throws with his eyes. If he wants to throw the ball to the left, when he looks in that direction, he does not have to think about turning his hips. His eyes bring the body in that direction. All he needs to do is open his hips, hammer, and flick.

It does not matter what position you play, the eyes are the most important thing you can play with. The defensive lineman has to use his eyes. His hands go wherever his eyes go. The same thing is true of the offensive linemen.

If the quarterback walks down the street and passes a good-looking girl, his eyes turn his body to look at her. His body turns to look at her because the eyes look in that direction. That is what happens when he throws the football.

When the quarterback throws from the shotgun, he has already taken two steps. On the three-step drop, he takes one step back and throws the ball. If he throws a five-step pattern, he takes a drive step, a crossover step, and a balance step. His second step is his break step. He breaks, comes to balance, and moves forward with the delivery.

From the shotgun drop, the patterns have to be shorter or the quarterback has to hold the ball longer. He reaches the three-step depth in one step, and if he throws the ball with that timing, the receiver cannot get as deep. We adjust the delivery of the quarterback with a hitch before he delivers the ball. If he throws the ball at 10 yards, he takes three steps and a hitch to time out the pattern. He uses a three-plus-one step to the curl pattern and a three-plus-two step to the checkdown to the backs.

The rule is hard and fast for the quarterback. He goes three-plus-one to the curl route. He goes three-plus-two to the checkdown. He goes three-plus-three steps and leaves the pocket. If he has to hitch three times, he needs to get out of the pocket, get rid of the ball, or buy some time.

In our attitude, every sack is the quarterback's fault. It is not a sack if the quarterback throws the ball away. Nobody ever lost a game on an incomplete pass. Throw the ball away, and give us another opportunity to make a first down. If you throw it away, it is second-and-10 for the first down. If you take the sack, it is second-and-16 for the down. If you can stay away from negative yardage plays, you will be successful.

We base the success formula for offense on the total number of plays. Take those plays minus the dropped balls, offensive penalties, and negative yardage plays, and divide by the total number of plays. If the answer is 80 percent or better, you win the game. The total number of good plays is what you want to consider.

The job of a quarterback is simple. He has to "let it happen, and not make it happen." We want to move forward. That is a concept you have to make your team understand. The cardinal sin at our place is the quarterback sack. We want the ball out of the quarterback's hands in 1.5 seconds. That does not mean holding the ball until 2.5, waiting for someone to get open.

We teach the quarterback a base footwork in a bag drill (Diagram #2). The quarterback carries the ball in the carriage position. He shuffles through the bags. This teaches movement in the pocket. He goes forward, sideways, and backward with the shuffle movement. He has to have good ball carriage skills because he does not know when he

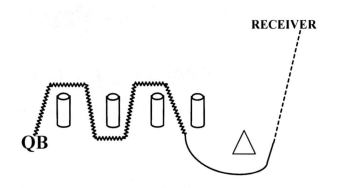

Diagram #2. Shuffle Drill

will have to throw the ball. He must be ready to set his feet and throw. He is not on his toes, and he is not flat-footed. He is on the balls of his feet with a little bounce in his steps. He is "keeping his feet alive."

To finish the drill, the quarterback comes out of the last bag, rolls out, and throws the ball on the run. When he throws the ball, he needs to hammer, flick, and follow his target with his eyes. If he does not follow the target, he will be off target.

Our players have a passion for playing football. We have a team that is all in, no matter what it is. If it helps our football team, they are for it. They do not care about personal interests. It is all about our team. We use 25 players on defense, and they all play. They all get excited about playing football.

People ask me how many different helmets we have. The answer is four. I do not have anything to do with the design of the uniforms, but the players do love them. Anyone have a question? Thank you very much for your attention.

PRACTICE AND PASSING GAME CONCEPTS

University of Southern California

Today, I want to get into to some things that will come from a practice prospective. However, we are going to look at our offense that we started working on 10 years ago when we first came to the University of Southern California. We will look at different core beliefs and philosophy within our offense.

I want to talk about practice in general. A lot of you do not have great numbers, so I may be able to talk in a unique perspective. Prior to this past fall, I would not have been able to talk much about having small numbers to work with. When we had the great years at USC, it was because of the way that we practiced. We practiced extremely fast, and we practiced ones versus ones. We practiced at a high level that made us competitive as could be.

We started each day with the previous day's 1-on-1 cut-up films of our pass rush. We watched our tight ends against the linebackers. Whatever the players did in practice, they knew their peers would see it on film the next day. No matter what the level of practice, we were going to practice as fast as we could.

I looked back to this past season, and one of the reasons we were not as good this year was because we changed that part of practice. We had some scholarship reductions, and our numbers were lower. I know some of you get into that situation toward the end of the season, and your numbers are down. It may be you are just going into the season and your numbers are down. Don't change what you are doing. If I could go back, I would want to practice the way we always did. We did not tackle at all during camp, and it showed up in games. I would recommend that you not change what you are doing based on your number of players.

I'm going to touch on the points we talk to our team about in the first meeting of the year.

The number-one thing we talk to our offense specifically about is to protect the football. That is the first thing they hear on offense. They hear this all of the time. It does not matter what level you are coaching at; you hear this.

We go over a list with them so they understand what our expectations are before we go into any plays. I am going to go over that first meeting with you today.

USC FOOTBALL

• Protect the football
• Be physical
• Protect the quarterback
• Red zone execution
• Move with urgency
• Do your job
• Play fast

The first year I was with the Oakland Raiders, I looked at the draft. Of the top four teams in the NFL, they were 32, 31, 30, and 29 in turnover margin. They were the four best in the turnover margin.

At the end of the season, if you will look at the turnover margin, you will see it is the most important of anything. If you look at the championship game last year in college football, the top two teams were first and second in the turnover margin. On the way to this clinic, I looked at our final PAC 10 stats, and Stanford University and the University of Oregon were the top two teams in terms of turnover margins. They both went to BCS games.

The first thing we talk about in that first meeting is protecting the football, and they hear it all of the time. Our coaches are yelling all of the time about being high and tight with the ball. Our defensive coaches are on their players all of the time about stripping the ball out of the hands of the ballcarriers. We explain to our offensive team that this is going to make our team better.

Our GAs keep a chart of the number of stripping chances we have for each practice. In our defensive meeting, the first thing posted from the practice the previous day is the number of strip attempts we had in that practice. We are rewarding the players who get the ball out. Our offensive players know how important the ball is. Our offensive players know the ball has to be high and tight all the way back to the line of scrimmage. They run all the way past the last defender and back to the huddle. That ball can come out at any time.

It may sound childish, but if the ball ever hits the ground, or the ball comes out of the arms of the ballcarrier, he has to run a lap. This may remind players of the days when they were in junior high school, but the important thing about this is the fact we are staying consistent with this rule.

When a player does have to run a lap, he may miss a turn at receiving the ball on the next down. If he is a receiver, he may miss the next opportunity to catch a pass. We want them to understand the number-one thing in our program is to protect the football.

The number-two thing we say to everyone, but especially the offense; we talk to them about being physical. "Be physical!" We want to make sure we are talking about it all of the time. This is not just for the offensive linemen. It is about everyone on our team. It is about the way receivers finish the block. It is about our backs not running out-of-bounds. We want them to finish through the defender, staying inbounds. We stress being physical to everyone on our offense.

The third point we make is to protect the quarterback. You say that is obvious for all teams. You can look at stats at the end of the year and find out the teams that do not give up sacks. On offense, it is everyone's job to protect the quarterback. Our offense hears this all of the time. When they sack the quarterback and he has to leave the game, you have to bring in the backup quarterback. We all know the difference that makes.

We challenge our guys all of the time to do things right, down after down. Players get so excited when they make a big play. Then what happens on the next play? This is during a 10-12 play drive. Great teams and great players finish drives by doing things correctly, down after down.

We talk to our players about this all of the time. In high school coaching, in talking to players about going to the next level, remind them of how much film college coaches watch. It is not just a highlight film college coaches watch. College coaches look at the films from high school, and they want to see players who do things right all of the time, and not just when the big play comes up.

Next, we talk about red zone execution. We talk about finishing the drives off. We all know the big difference in seven points and three points coming from the red zone. We know how huge that is throughout the game and throughout the season.

We want to make sure the play caller is giving us the opportunities to be aggressive in the red zone. We want to make sure we continue to talk to the quarterback about being aggressive as a play caller. That does not necessarily mean being aggressive as a quarterback. The quarterback must understand that he does not need to force the ball. "We are going to give you another ball."

If it's first down, he can check it down, and we will give him another shot. Even though we want to score a touchdown on the pass, he can check the play, and we will give him another shot. We want to make sure the quarterback has confidence in you as a play caller. He has to understand that you are going to give him another chance. They want to throw the touchdown pass, and they will force the ball on a pass if they do not believe you are going to give them another shot on the second or third down after that first play.

We talk to our players about moving with urgency. This goes back to the practice tempo and knowing what to do. We shift a great deal of the time on offense because we know this slows the defense down. The faster we can move, the slower the defense can play. We go back to practice to make sure we are moving fast. If we do not have a play clock in practice, we have someone behind the huddle calling out an imaginary play clock. Make sure the players are practicing as fast as they will be playing on game day. We want to break the huddle, sprint to the line, and get ready to go. The faster we can do that, the more time we give the quarterback to read the defense.

Do your job! We talk to the players all of the time about "doing your job." When players ask why they did not get the ball, or why the quarterback did not throw them the ball, we tell them the same thing repeatedly: "Don't worry about that. Do your job." We tell them not to waste time on anyone else on the team. "Do your job right on every single play, and do not worry about the other guys."

The next point is to play fast. This is critical to instill into your players. Your players would do anything in the world for you if you would tell them you can go from a 4.8 40-yard dash to a 4.6, or from a 4.7 to a 4.5. They would go out in practice and do any drill that you can make up. They believe the 40-yard dash is so critical to their football career.

If you can instill this point to them, they will understand how important it is to study in the football classroom. That is how they are going to play fast. It is because they will know what they are doing. That is how they can play faster. If they study the opponents, when a play comes up, they know what to do and what to expect from the opponents.

Players want to run fast times for the 40-yard dash. They want to look fast. They must realize that being fast is not about training to run the 40-yard dash in the off-season, is not nearly as much as knowing what you are doing.

We have all seen players who are slower than other players are, but they are more productive because they know what they are doing. They spend the time in the classroom and in the film room.

Our next point is to finish. We stress: "Finish everything you do." This starts with the strength coach in the off-season. We stress for them to finish in every single drill. We have a cone on every single drill we run, no matter what it is. We have this in the off-season, and in the indoor drills. We want them to finish past the cone. If one man pulls up before they pass the cone, we send the entire group back to do it over. We never send only one player back on any drill. We want the whole group to go back and do it over, because football is a team sport. This carries over to the two-minute drill and

to the drives before the end of each half. This is all a part of finishing everything they do.

When we started working on this offensive system 10 years ago, we wanted to recruit great football players. We wanted them to be able to play very fast. As we put together our formations, it was always about the players. It is not about the coaches. Coaches get involved in this because our staff is smarter than the players are. It does not matter what the coaches know; it matters what the players know and can execute.

We try to simplify things as much as possible all of the time. When teams go into their two-minute offense, why does the ball move up and down the field so much? Most people will say the reason is because the defense is very basic. That is not the reason why the ball moves up and down the field so much. The reason the ball moves up and down the field is because the offense is better prepared when they get into those situations. They are only running five or six different plays, and the players know those so well.

The offense is only running one or two formations. We are going from the no-huddle. We are running the same plays we have practiced over and over. It goes back to doing things that the players do really, really well. They are running slant routes and hook patterns. They are running plays that have practiced a million times. The more basic we can be, the better we will be.

As we put our formations together, we wanted to make sure we kept things basic. I grew up seeing a lot of football systems, and I saw a lot of extremely difficult and complicated offensive systems based on the personnel available to run the offense. We decided we would not make our offensive formation complicated.

Our offensive formation remains the same, regardless of the personnel in the game. It does not matter if I am the second tight end, the fullback, or I am the third wide receiver, I am the F-back no matter what.

Just to give you an idea of our formations, they are all simple. We do not use any code words in the formations. We do not use any animals in our formation calls. We call our formations like this. All formations that start with the letter D are 2x2 formations (Diagram #1). Our players know this the first day. It does not matter if we call dot right, deuce right, dual right, or double right. All that happened is the F-back moves.

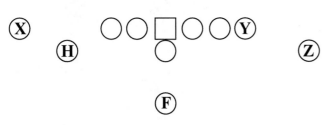

Diagram #1. D Formations

This helps the quarterback as well. The most important person in the calling of formations is the quarterback. You may have 22 personnel in the game, or you may have four wide receivers in the formation. The formation is exactly the same. I encourage you to go back and look at what you are doing formation-wise. Make sure the formations allow your team to play faster, especially the quarterback. You have been around some systems where the offense changed depending on the personnel that came into the game.

For instance, our double right 82, stay, Sluggo, X-win is the picture in the head of the quarterback no matter what personnel came into the game on offense. The stay tells the tight end he is to stay in and block on the play.

We can run all receivers on specific routes regardless of the personnel in the game. I know many of you have been in systems where the formations changed, depending on the personnel in the game.

Next, we go to "T" words. Trips, trey, trouble, and trio are all 3x1 formations. Our players know this right away. They know the Z receiver goes strong, and then the F-back takes his position. I am not going to go over all of the formations with you, but you get the idea. You can draw up your own formations to see how simple it is.

The first concept we are going to talk about here is our 81-91 (Diagram #2). It does not matter what you call the play. We run a slant and an arrow on the strongside, and double slant on the weakside. It is a great play in the no-huddle, a great audible, and a great call any time because it puts the quarterback in an easy situation.

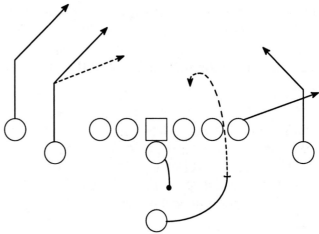

Diagram #2. 81-91

The quarterback's first rule on the play is on the slant/arrow side for a single high safety. On any single safety look or blitz look, he is going to work the slant/arrow routes. On all of our routes, except for special routes, the outside foot is back for our receivers. This makes it easy for them when they line up. They do not have to try to figure out which foot they should have back.

All slant routes are three steps. The outside foot is back, and they run three steps. The arrow route inside is getting to the three-yard spot from the line of scrimmage on the sideline. That is where the arrow route goes. The slant/arrow is for a single high safety.

We use the double slant routes against two high safeties. This gives the quarterback an easy audible to go to when he is in some spread out runs, or when we are in a downhill passing route and he sees pressure looks.

It is a three-step drop by the quarterback. This is quick smack protection. The line is four down to the Will. The tailback reads Mike to Sam to hook over the ball.

Up front for the linemen, anytime the center or openside tackle feels four-way pressure, and the tailback does not have to check backside, the quarterback can make a call and slide the line in a three-step move so the back can stay to the frontside. Most of the time, that frontside defensive end is dropping into coverage.

I want to show you some shots of play 81. We are running it from a 2x2 formation. We run a slant by the wide receiver, an arrow by the tight end, and double slants on the opposite side. The tailback is going to the strongside. If the defense gaps to the outside, it puts the tailback blocking the defensive end.

When the quarterback sees that the defense has moved to a single high look, he knows right away he is looking for the slant/arrow routes. It is not too complicated. Don't give the quarterback too much offense to think about on one play. This is true regardless of how good the quarterback happens to be.

Against single high, we are reading the flat defender. If he takes the arrow route, we run the slant in behind the arrow route.

One of the difficult things to do is to prevent your receivers from taking a false step with the front foot. We try to make the first step square so they do not waste half of a step.

One of the best things the play caller can do is to continue to throw the three-step drop passing game. We do not want to get complicated with all of these down-the-field patterns, 15-yard in routes, or 14-yard corner routes. If you run those deep routes, you are getting away from your core philosophy. We said we wanted to stress protecting the quarterback. The line does their job to protect the quarterback, and the play caller's job is to protect the quarterback by the way he calls plays. The more ways you can get the easy completions, the harder it is for the defense.

We see a lot of teams that want to be like the Pittsburgh Steelers and run all of the different blitzes they run. None of this matters if we can get the ball out on the three-step drop. Most of the time, we can find a way to get the ball out in three steps.

When we make a change on an audible, we want to make sure we practice the timing on the play. We can change the play in three seconds. The only way we can do that is to practice changing the play in our scrimmages. That can be the difference in making the play and a delay-of-game penalty.

Once we start running the slants, defenses will start jumping the routes. We run a Sluggo route (Diagram #3). It is still a pass to the receiver on his third outside step. This time, the receiver

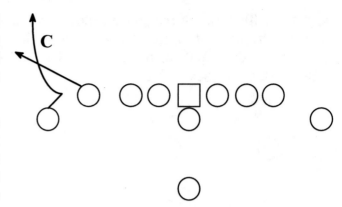

Diagram #3. Sluggo Route

pushes vertical, trying to stay back outside of the corner. If the corner is up tight from 8 to 10 yards on the Sluggo, he may only take one step inside. The quarterback has the ability to look at the cornerback and signal to Sluggo if the corner is sitting flatfooted. The quarterback can make the signal and run the Sluggo route or the slant route. We still have the arrow route to the inside receiver, which is the X-end here.

I want to move to the two high safeties look (Diagram #4). Now, we are going to work to the double slant side of the play. The quarterback is reading the first inside defender. If the defense takes away the inside slant, he goes to the outside slant route. It is the same footwork. It is three steps on the route.

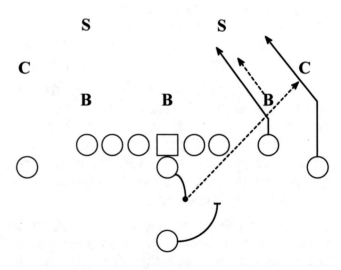

Diagram #4. Two High Safeties

The inside receiver wants to make sure he goes inside the first defender, and he does not want to be covered by the second defender. After he gets inside the first defender, he starts to skinny up on his route so he does not get too close to the second defender.

Our next concept is another three-step concept. In our 80-90 protection, it is our stem protection. This is a part of the West Coast offense called "spacing." It is an easy concept for the quarterback.

We put our best receiver to the weakside. In our system, it is the X-receiver. The X-receiver is our bigger and more physical receiver. The Z usually is our flanker, and he is a quicker moving player. He has to be in motion, and he has to be able to line up in the slot.

We want to get our X-receiver matched up 1-on-1 on the backside. You can have him run different routes from this position. You want to make sure the quarterback can get him the ball on any of his patterns. Several things can happen as you teach the quarterback this concept.

The slant route is the called route to the X-receiver. If a corner is sitting inside the X-receiver on press coverage, the quarterback can look outside to the X-receiver and give him a "hang loose" signal. This tells the X-receiver to be patient, but he has to win at the line of scrimmage.

We do not want the X-receiver to run outside on a fade route. We want him to be patient and to win at the line of scrimmage so he can run his route. He does not have to run outside right away. He can start outside and step back inside. He can start inside and then go back outside. Nevertheless, he must win at the line of scrimmage. This is not a touchdown throw on most occasions. This is a pass that you hit the receiver at the line of scrimmage and the ball could end up 19 to 20 yards down the field on a hang-loose pass.

The second thing that can happen on the play is this. You have the slant called. The quarterback signals the X-receiver on the hang-loose. On this occasion, the cornerback is playing off and to the inside. This happens to the backside formations often. The reason is because the defense is looking for the slant route on the backside. The quarterback can give the X-receiver a signal to change the pass route.

He could call a Sluggo route. It is three steps down, then three steps inside, and then back outside to the corner. Now, what happens is this. Regardless of what the defense does, your best player is on the backside, and it is hard for the defense to take him away from the offense. Your best player may be a tailback. We can move the tailback out to the X position, split wide.

Regardless of the player you put in the X position, you want one or two players who have practiced with the quarterback most of the time. It is a simple scheme, but it is difficult to defend once we put all of the things into what can happen with the concept.

The last route we have the quarterback signal to the X-receiver is the hitch route. Now, the cornerback is playing deep. He is 13 to 14 yards off the X-receiver. The quarterback can give the signal for the hitch route. All of these routes are three-step routes. Instead of trying to call the right play all of the time, as a play caller, you build into the system a play that is going to be a good play to call regardless of the defense you face. Against cloud coverage, we leave the slant route on. Against cover 2, leave the slant call on.

On the frontside, the first man inside, regardless of what it is, is going to be on a sit (Diagram #5). A sit is four to six yards over the ball, and it does not move no matter what. He sits down there no matter what the defense does.

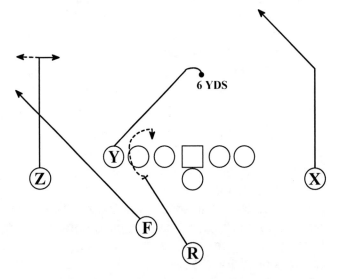

Diagram #5. Sit, Arrow, Pivot

The next receiver is on an arrow route. It is similar to what the tight end ran before. It is to the sideline three yards deep. It can be the slot or the fullback who runs the arrow route. Once again, we are teaching a simple scheme you can run from several different formations. You can motion the backs, or you can move them inside and move them outside, any way that you can create a 3x1 formation. You can bunch them in a simple alignment.

The outside man is on a pivot route. The pivot is six yards. Once the pivot is made and the receiver turns and looks at the quarterback, he can slide either way to get to the open area. The sit receiver does not move, but the pivot receiver can move. The tailback, because it is three-step protection, he is Mike-to-Sam, or straight up the edge once the line turns the play into gap protection.

We move to the quarterback on the play. His first thought is how to get the ball to X on the weakside. That is his number-one priority. When the X-receiver is gone, he goes to the sit receiver, who is the number-two choice. The pivot is the number-three choice, and the arrow route is the number-four choice for the quarterback. That is his progression straight across the board.

We can be in a 2x2 alignment and motion one of the backs across the formation to create the 3x1 look. We can get to the three-man side in different ways.

One thing we like to do, and you can do this in high school as well, we like to put our 3x1 formation into the boundary. That allows us to put the X-receiver to the openside of the field. That gives your best player a lot of room to make his best moves. Normally, he would be at a numbers split when the ball is in the middle of the field.

If the ball is on the opposite hash mark, he can split between the numbers and the hash mark. That gives him a lot of room to work with to the outside. He can run the hitch, slant, Sluggo, and hang loose, and he has all of the room from the tackle to the sideline to work with. It is a bit different with the hash marks college deals with, but it is good for us, and it is good for the high schools as well. We go back to our core rules. Play fast when you know what you are doing.

Each year we do a self-scout at the end of the year. It is good to do for the running game as well as the passing game. After the review, we could see where we made mistakes of adding plays that we did not have time to perfect. We have decided to stop running plays that we add late in the week, and we do not have enough reps where our players feel comfortable running them. We may add a play to take advantage of a team that widens their 3 technique. We work on that all week, and when we get into the game, the opponents do not widen the 3 technique, and we have wasted a lot of time working on something we did not need.

I want to encourage you to stay away from doing that next season. I am sure you will stay away from it, as I am. You see something you think will work, and you think it will help you in the next game. You get to the game, and you see it does not work. You need to go back and call the plays the players know; just call them from a different formation.

The split for our Z-receiver is four yards unless he moves out of that set. This four-yard split is the nasty split in most terminology.

We want to play fast with a lot of reps and a lot different formations. We talking about more personnel, more formations, but less plays. We can run our 2x2 personnel with running backs and two tight ends. We only have one receiver in the game. Obviously, this is a big run set for most people. However, here comes the same play we ran before because everyone knows what to do because of the system we run.

When we are installing the plays, the receivers, running backs, and tight ends all have to pay attention to all of the spots in the formation. We tell them, "The more you know, the more you can play. The more you know, the more spots you are going to be used in." All of the players want to catch the passes. We remind them the more they know, the more they are going to play. We challenge our receivers for all four of the receiver spots the first year they are with us.

Here is another great concept with the slant routes over the years. In the pros, they call the play "Sluggo win route" (Diagram #6). In the West Coast offense, it is a Sluggo seam route.

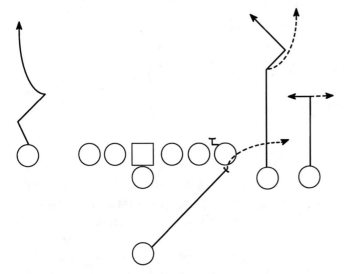

Diagram #6. Sluggo Seam Route

We have a Sluggo route by the X-receiver. He is the main receiver we have been getting the ball to on the pass. You do not have to signal the play to the X-end. We call the play in the huddle. We call a Sluggo win route. We have the maximum protection on the play. If X is pressed, he is going to run a hang-loose route. You do not have to signal him out of the route. We do not want to change the press if we are going to slant inside. If he gets too far inside, he gets too close to the free safety. We can automatically convert Sluggos to hang-loose or fade routes on presses.

The foot movement for the quarterback is the same as before. It is the three-step drop, weight shift. We do not want him to overstride. He kicks back on his last two steps and then strides into the throw.

The tight end can be involved in the protection. Stay tells him to stay in the protection. If we call 82 stay, the tight end is going to stay in and pass protect. He blocks the defensive end. The back makes his move off the tight end. From the frontside tackle, back it is all gap protection. It does not matter what type of pressure comes, you only have to identify these fronts. We do not have to put our back on the defensive tackle on gap protection.

On the win route, the split is eight-plus-two. Two yards outside the hash mark is the win route split. The receivers can nail this route. All they have to know is a single high safety versus two high safeties. If it is against a single high safety, he must use an outside release on any defender who comes to him. Then, he stays vertical on the route. If it is a two high safety alignment with a safety aligned over him, he must turn his route into a post route.

The idea of the whole play is to attack the two high safeties. To the X-receiver, the quarterback pumps the Sluggo route to force the deep safety to move to cover him. That leaves the win route open on the opposite side of the formation. The win route is a post to the inside where the safety lined up. He goes to cover the X-receiver on the Sluggo route, and it leaves the win route open on the post.

The route outside is a max split and is called a stop route. He wants to be as wide as he can be. The defense will take the corner on the three-man side and try to get him to cover the win route on the post. That leaves the stop man open on the outside on the progression of the play.

If the tailback is on a trickle as the play develops, then after his protection, if he does not have anyone to block, he trickles outside two yards deep. He is the fourth progression. The progression is: Sluggo, win, stop, and trickle. This call can be a good audible against pressure looks.

This can be a good play to motion into when you are getting late cover adjustments. We do not care what they do up front, because we are in gap protection. We run the slant to the single-receiver side, and they stay deep on the play. The inside receiver on the strongside has to win against the corner to the post to the inside.

We talk to our receivers a lot about going back to the days when they played football in the park. Back when they played in the parks or in the streets, no one could cover a receiver 1-on-1. Some players get too robotic when they get a little coaching. We do not want to overcoach them too much. The receivers need to have some freedom to develop releases and some different moves. Again, it is as it was when they were playing in the park.

We spend a lot of time in practice during the week working on the pre-shifts. We want to get the receivers in position to where they can run the routes we want.

Thanks for coming, guys.

BUILDING A PROGRAM WITH FUNDAMENTALS

University of Minnesota

I appreciate the opportunity to be with you today. I am a very blessed individual. I was talking to Brady Hoke, the new head coach at the University of Michigan, when I came in today. We were talking about the fact that most of you probably feel you have a good chance of becoming a Division I coach, when you see Brady and myself on the itinerary.

I am one of the few guys at this level that started out exactly as you are. I started coaching high school football in the state of Oklahoma 28 years ago. From there, I went on to be the head coach at Webb City High School in Missouri. I was fortunate enough to be around some very good coaches and players. We won a state championship in 1989. I decided I wanted to get into coaching college football and finally got an opportunity. To give you an idea of how you have to sacrifice when you are young, I worked for three years at a school called Pittsburg State University in Kansas. I made $250 a month and lived in a trailer house.

It has been a whirlwind ever since. I was also a head coach at Saginaw Valley State University in Michigan. It has been one of those things where you have no idea where you are going to be in the next job.

I am a cancer survivor. Six years ago, I was given a fifty-fifty shot to live or die. I will tell you guys something that is important. When you get a second chance, there are no bad days. I have been through a lot and I have been lucky as could be. I love to coach the game of football. I have been fortunate enough to turn some things around in my lifetime. What I would like to do today is to give you some ideas to help you turn a down football program into a winning program.

I have been very fortunate to have a lot of loyal people around me. It does not matter if you are in high school or college football, you need to have a great staff. If you think you can coach football by yourself, you are in trouble. This is probably why I got the job at the University of Minnesota. My defensive coordinator has been with me for 17 years. My strength coach has been with me for 17 years. They both worked with me at Saginaw Valley State. Rob Reeves, our tight ends and H-backs coach has been with me for 17 years and he played for me. We have all been through this together. That continuity is very important. I do not have to worry when I am on the road talking to people. My program is still going to run well without me.

When I walk into a new program, I do not change a great deal. I may change some things up offensively or defensively, but I have not changed coachingwise.

We build our program on these things. We want to play smart. We do not want to beat ourselves. If you think about any sport, whether it is football, basketball, or any sport, teams do not win. They find a way to lose. They turn over the football. Fundamentally, they are not sound. If it is basketball, they may not shoot free throws worth a darn. I will tell you that we have forgotten the fundamentals of the game. We have all gotten into these wild schemes and we try to trick people. The bottom line is you win with fundamentals and you have to play smart. In addition, you have to have smart kids.

You have to play tough. One of the first things I found out when I walked into Minnesota was the fact that we are not very tough. We do not know how to work. We are now doing some things in our workouts that will help define toughness for them.

When I talk about toughness to our kids, I talk about these points. Number one, you have to be able to run the ball. If you cannot run the ball, you are not going to win.

You better be able to stop the run. That is part of being tough. If you come to watch us in our spring practice, and you are certainly welcome, you are going to see us run the ball. We are going to get in the middle drill with nine up in the box and two safeties, and we are going to run the ball. That will never change. We are going to learn how to run the ball and our defense is going to learn how to stop the run. That is part of being tough. You cannot say you are a tough football team if you throw it 50 times a game. This is my opinion.

We are going to do a lot of different things in spring ball, in our two-a-day camp, and in our goal line situations. You may see me have players run gassers. Then, we may run our two-minute offense. You want to make them understand, mentally, that when they get tired, they need to concentrate. You have to practice those situations in practice.

We talk about toughness. We talk about giveaways and takeaways. We define to our kids that this is who we want to be. We want to be the best-conditioned team and we want to play fast. I am not talking about the no-huddle offense. I believe in repetition. I believe they need to hustle in practice. If I call the team together and they jog up, I make them turn around and we do it again. I want them to sprint up, get right on the line, and I want them to pay attention.

I want them to move fast all of the time. I think it is important because it sets the tempo. I tell our kids we want to practice fast. I currently will run two offensive huddles in our pass shell. When I get some depth, we will run three huddles at a time. It will go fast. We are going to bang it out as fast as we can. We want them to be able to process things very quickly. If you go back and look at your film, notice if you play as fast in the last game as you did in the first game. That is how I evaluate our kids.

In my past, I have pushed and worked my kids too hard. We ran out of gas at the end of the year. Kids are not what they used to be. You have to adjust a little more today. Conditioning is very important. How you practice is important because you want to play the last game with the same speed that you played the first game of the year. If you looked at the team I coached last year at Northern Illinois University, they played as fast in the bowl game as they played at the beginning of the year. The assistant coaches did a good job with that. You develop that mentality and you have to talk about it.

We talk about playing hard. It takes *no* talent to play hard. You need to understand that. You need to sell that to your team. I have been a high school coach where you could not find 22 players that were what you wanted. You might say I cannot win with this group. In the end, they are all that you have. If you can get them to play hard for you, then you have a chance to win. You can watch NFL films and see teams that do not play very hard. All coaches will talk about playing hard, whether it is NFL, college, or high school. Look at your films and see if you have players taking plays off.

Watch an NBA game and look at how many of those guys take plays off. It is all about playing hard. If you can get your kids to play hard, you have a chance to win.

You start that in the off-season. At the University of Minnesota, right now we are wearing their tails out. I am trying to break them. We do not go for very long, but we go hard and fast. We preach to them, "We are trying to help you, but you have to learn to play hard."

Consistency is important. I will meet with each kid before spring ball. I will tell them that we are going to have 15 practices. I will tell them they are going get graded for consistency over those 15 practices. Can they be consistent and compete every play?

I met with Matt Spaeth, who played at the University of Minnesota. He is currently playing for the Pittsburgh Steelers. I asked him what makes the Steelers so good. He said, "Coach, we just have a group of players that play hard." Matt talked about Dick LeBeau, one of the greatest defensive minds in all of football and the current defensive coordinator for the Pittsburgh Steelers. Dick will ask his players to play hard for just six seconds. He is always talking about playing hard for just six seconds. Men, if you can get your players to play hard for six seconds of every play, you are going to have a very good football team. There are a lot of players out there that cannot play hard for six seconds. When you do things in your spring practice or in your off-season, make it for six seconds. Make it a big deal. If you really get down to it, it is a six-second game.

The other thing is that we make no excuses. It is what it is. I can come in and take over a program or Coach Hoke can come in and take over a program and you never have things as good as you would like. We can say that we need more talent or we need to go recruit this and that. What you've got is what you've got. You cannot make excuses. If they hear you make an excuse, that is how they will play. You have to build confidence in them, and do not take any excuses. I tell our kids, "It does not matter what happens, there are no excuses here."

We talk about being a team. In this world today, it is hard to get players to play as a team. We live in an "I" society. The team concept is something that is hard to sell. At the end of our workout today, I told our team to go over and shake each other's hands. I told them that if they will care about their teammates more than they care about themselves, we will win. You have to talk about that. We also talk to them about being role models. We want them to be unselfish team players.

We try to lay down the ground rules right off the bat. I do not really have a lot of rules. Have you ever been to some of these schools that have 14,000 different slogans? I had a 2.5 grade point average and a 17 on the SAT test. Shoot, I cannot remember all those things. I asked Matt Spaeth about the Steelers and what slogans they have posted around their building. Matt said they have the following three C's posted:

• Common sense
• Courtesy
• Compete

He said those are the only things you will see in the entire building. For us, our slogan is *act right*. That covers an awful lot of areas. I guess that falls under the common sense rule. Everyone knows how to act right, and we tell our kids, "You know what that means."

We want our athletes to be on time. It is important to be on time. I learned when I was going through the fight with cancer that if I did not do things on time, I was in deep trouble. You only have so much time in your life. I am not worried about going to bed tonight, because someday I will get to sleep a lot. Do not waste time. It is disrespectful when people have to wait on you. These are the lessons kids are going to have to learn in life.

Our kids have to go to class. I was a walk-on player. I do not understand how or why, when you are given $25,000 a year to get a good education, you do not go to class. I do not understand it, and I do not accept it.

Play hard on game day. From the day I walked in, that was the first thing I said when we walked into the University of Minnesota. You have to teach your kids what you want.

I do not know if this is good or bad. If you get a kid that needs to be disciplined and you have a coach that gets up at 5:30 in the morning to run the kid, you are punishing the coach. I decided to do something different on this situation and it has been very effective. What we do if a kid misses an appointment, misses a class, or screws up he automatically goes into a brown shirt for practice. The brown shirt, at the University of Minnesota, says "Minnesota Loafers" on the front in bright fluorescent pink lettering. On the back it says, "I let my teammates down."

I know I am not the only coach that does this, but I think I may have been the coach that started it. They have to wear that in our football facility. The first time they get it, they wear it for a week. The second time they get it, they wear it for two weeks and they donate $20 to the children's hospital. We have athletes at the college level, and if you make them run, they can run. If you hit them in their pocketbooks, or in their playing time, or you embarrass them, they will stop that crap. The first week I was at Minnesota, we had 13 brown shirts. When I went in today, we only had two. We are getting better.

They do not like wearing the brown shirts. One of my players came up to me and said that he was not going to wear one of the brown shirts. I told him to call his parents and tell them that you are not going to wear a brown shirt because you did not go to class and you are giving up a $25,000 scholarship. I told him I did not care if that is what he wanted to do. He put a brown shirt on, by the way.

The third time they get it, they wear the shirt for three weeks and donate $30 to the children's hospital. If it happens a fourth time, we have a problem and we have to get things straightened out. If they do something wrong, I do not have to scold them and browbeat them. I also let them know that I have made mistakes before. Take a brown shirt, put it on, and take it like a man. They know up front what the deal is. If you do not tell them up front, they do not know what to expect. It is important to understand that. You want them to understand what your standards are for your program.

I give our kids a player policy manual when I walk into a new program, so they know exactly what to expect and what it is going to take to win. I tell them if they will do these things, then we are going to be in good shape. You have to tell them what you want.

In this day and age, you cannot tell a player to do a drill without telling them why they are doing the drill. In the old days, you would just tell them to do the drill. They are not going to do it until they know it is going to benefit them. We try to do that.

The other thing we have learned that we need to do is to get control of our kids and their use on the websites. We have forgotten how to communicate. When our kids enter the academic or athletic facility, they have to turn their cell phones off. I am old school; I want to be able to look you in the face and communicate with you. We tell our kids we want to be able to communicate with them one-on-one and not through a text message.

I talk to them about Facebook and websites. Our players do not understand that our alums will look at that stuff. They do not understand that they may put something on there that will cost them their college careers. I have told our kids that if any football information goes out from their website or their text messages, they are putting themselves in a situation where they may not be on the team. We want our football information in-house only.

I have somebody on my staff that goes through all of our players' information every day. That is all they do. This new technology can affect your job and is important that you get a grasp on it as soon as possible.

We put together a video of inspiration and motivation to show our kids. You have to show today's kids, through video, what you want. I started this when I was at Northern Illinois. We went 11-3 this past year. About every three weeks, we add to this video something that would show them what we expected or what it would take to win.

I am the most fortunate guy in the world in that I coach at the university where Tony Dungy played. I probably would not have gotten the opportunity to go to the University of Minnesota if Tony Dungy had not said, "This is the guy you need to hire at Minnesota." Before I even knew who Coach Dungy was, I read his book entitled *Uncommon*. It was the best thing I ever did. Two years ago at Northern Illinois during two-a-day camp, we read a chapter out of his book each day. I had the players stand up and report on the chapter that they had just read. We read the whole book through two-a-day camp.

It is the best thing I did in my life. There is no better book to read about character and what kids need to stand for in this day and age than his book. It is worth every penny your booster club can get you to get your players a copy. You can do it in the summer or you can do it during the year. The book, and what he stands for, and what he put in that book, I believe, helped us turn the program around at Northern Illinois. What the book is saying is that you have to be different to be good. You cannot be like everyone else.

I told our kids this year, "You have to give up something in order to be successful." To be a good team, you have to give up what some of those other kids are doing. It is hard to be different in this day and age. It is easier to go out and do the wrong things than it is to do the right things. That book will certainly help you.

We are going to do the same thing at the University of Minnesota. The thing that I have going for me now is the fact that Coach Dungy will come back to his alma mater and tell them why he wrote that book and what it stands for.

I firmly believe you turn programs around and you win with fundamentals. We have forgotten that in all sports. Some 20 years ago, you never missed a free throw. I could go out there right now and shoot free throws and hit 9 out of 10. I would go out with my dad and we would practice free throws all day long. It is all fundamentals. You get guys making millions of dollars who can run and dunk, but they cannot shoot a free throw.

If you just look at tackling in the game of football, it is terrible. You can look at your films, look at our films, or look at NFL films. We are all terrible at tackling. We have great athletes, but we forget to teach the fundamentals of the game. When I go back and look at tackling, I see what we need to do better. Here are some of the things I look at.

We start out every day on defense with a tackling circuit. You do not have to beat the heck out of each other to teach tackling, but we do it. The only way we really get better is to work on the fundamentals. We use about four base drills when we work on our tackling.

We run what we call a "shimmy drill." They come up with their body under control, they have their hips down, and they have their shoulders square. We want to get our head on the side of the bag and move the bag. We really focus on getting our kids to understand that you cannot tackle what you cannot see. We have all these concussions today because kids are ducking their heads. It is a safety factor. Play with your eyes up. Our offensive and defensive coaches are talking all the time about getting the head and eyes up. You have to coach the eyes. They learn by repetition, so we do it every day.

We teach roll tackling. When you are a mid-major, and you are playing teams like the University of Tennessee, who had a 240-pound running back, it is tough. We had a 190-pound safety that was going to be run support. If we hit him straight on, we are not going to win that war. We teach them, on the perimeter, to roll tackle. We do not want defensive backs to duck their heads and have the offensive players jump over them. We teach them roll tackling every day. What we are trying to do is to emphasize the run, the rap, and the roll. If you do that, you will not miss tackles. It also will keep your kids from getting concussions.

We do the same thing on offense for blocking. We will take five minutes for each of our circuits. Blocking is a lost art. If I am fired, I want to go coach as a high school offensive line coach. I will do it free. You can use your hands as lethal weapons. You can use your hands. Everything that we do in the off-season in our weight room and in our drill work is to teach them to shoot their hands out in front of them. When they come off the ball and take a short step, their hands come up and they can control the defensive linemen with their hands.

When you are on a down block, if you stick your hand up in his rib cage, you have him and you can control him. It is legal holding. You can control everything with your hands. I used to think it was always the feet. The feet are important. You do not want to take big steps. It is all about the eyes and the hands. If you can get your hands in the right place, you can be smaller and control a bigger guy. You have to work on that in practice. We want to work on technique and shooting the hands out.

We work on the cut block. There is going to be a time when a 320-pound lineman is going to have to do a cut block. You do not want his head down on the cut block. He has to keep his head up, extend his arm, and cut through. We teach them to get up and go get another defender. Those good offensive linemen will always block two men. You teach it and you get things done through repetition. We do this with our linemen and our backs and receivers.

We coach ball security. I have been very fortunate in that my teams have not turned the ball over very often. It is a fact that if you look at teams that are winning in the NFL or college, you will see that they do not turn the ball over. You have to teach it. If you do not turn over the ball often, you have a chance to win. We talk about ball security equals job security. I will not play a running back, no matter how good he is, if he turns the ball over. We go over it every day and we teach the techniques of holding on to the football.

On defense, you have to teach your players about taking the ball away. We teach it two different ways in our takeaway circuit. We try to come up underneath and punch it out, or we come over the top and try to chop it out. The important thing is that you teach them how to do these techniques. They will not do it unless you teach it. We spend about 40 minutes per practice in individual time and fundamentals. It might be group work, but we are going to spend time on the fundamentals. Certainly, we get it done in the spring and in our Tuesday and Wednesday workouts. We take a direct angle and chop it out.

Football is a game played with leverage and angles. That is the bottom line. You have to practice it. We are creatures of habit. My dad was a chain-smoker. He was good at it. He did it all of the time. It was a habit. It was not a good habit, but it was a habit.

Let me make one thing clear. You get what you emphasize. Coaches have to make poor plays unacceptable. If you are in practice and your quarterback throws a ball and the corner breaks on it and has a chance to intercept the ball but drops the ball, that is not acceptable. You cannot have that. When you pick it off in practice, you need to make a big deal out of it. If you tell them you want to get interceptions, they will get interceptions. The minute you forget about it, they will too. You have to figure out what the most important thing is that you do and how you are going to emphasize it.

Let me tell you how to win a few games. You are talking to a guy that went into a new program and won one game in that first year. The next year, we won four, and then we won 10 from there on out. I will tell you how we did it. I will tell you how we stole a couple of games. Special teams!

Nobody wants to work on special teams. I assign every coach to a portion of our kicking game. You win in the kicking game. We have blocked 26 punts over the last 10 years. We do not call our team "the punt return team." We call them "the punt block team." I like aggression. We want to be aggressive on offense and defense, and darn aggressive in the kicking game. Do not tell me you emphasize the kicking game or that it is important to you if you are the head coach and you are not involved in it. I am in every single special teams meeting. If your players know that you are sitting in on them, it will be important to them.

We watch your film and find the weakest guy on your punt protection team. We take the weakest guy, and we are going to go after him in some way, shape, or form. We are going to get our good punt block players in that spot.

We spend time working on our running form and 40-yard starts. All of our guys want to go pro. They watch the NFL Scouting Combine on TV. They all want to work on their 40-yard starts. I will tell you the reason why we spend time on this. It is to block punts. Every one of our kids on the punt block team will be able to get out of a stance and get after the ball.

We catch the ball every day. We do fundamental ball skills every day. Again, we are going to emphasize what we want to do.

You have to take some shots if you want to be successful in football today. Find somebody out there that can run fast. You can find somebody at the opponent's cornerback position that is weak. You want to get your best athlete on him. If the head of the school board's kid is out there playing football, you are likely to find him at defensive corner. The coach will put him out there at cornerback and tell him to start backpedaling and get the heck out of there.

I think you need to take four or five shots a game. However, you have to work on it. It is not easy to catch a deep ball. You have to train them, and you have to develop it. You cannot throw it just occasionally. When we practice our pass shell, we treat everything like it is a game situation. Every play that we have in practice has to be as if it is in a game. You have to coach it that way.

There is no substitute for playing hard. You have to teach that. The game is not as hard as we make it. If you can get them to play hard, you have a chance to win. To do that, you have to coach them hard in practice. You have to teach them to play hard. You cannot emphasize those things enough. Get them to play hard for six seconds. Make them compete and make them work. You need to find it out in the off-season if they are willing to work hard. You have to do things in the off-season to make them compete. Make up drills that will test their competitive level. Do not let them hide. You cannot win with a guy that is going to hide.

We spend a ton of time doing change-of-direction drills. You have to get from point A to point B and change direction. We start them running, make them plant that foot and get around the cone, and make them finish strong. Make everybody finish. Do not accept anyone not finishing. Make them finish every single drill. Make them do everything right.

Now, we have to change the culture at Minnesota. I have been fortunate to where I can bring in my guys and change a culture. There is no magical answer to changing the culture other than this. You have to roll up your sleeves and you have to go to work. You have to outwork people. You outwork people by taking your work ethic, and your staff's work ethic, and the kids have to see you put in the hours. What you get out of life, the game of football, and your team is what you invest in it. This is how we try to change the culture. We try to do it through fundamentals, the kicking game, and bringing people in that understand things. If you have an ex-player that has been successful, have them come back and talk to your kids. You have to reach out and do that. You cannot have an ego to where you think you have to do it all yourself.

The Twin Cities is a great place. We have a brand new stadium, and there may not be a nicer one in the country. It is an unbelievable facility. You are welcome to visit us during spring practice. We will try to help you any way we can.

In closing, I will tell you this. It is a great privilege for me to be here tonight. I love the game of football. I am glad just to be in the profession. To be honest with you, football saved my life. Six years ago, if it was not for the game of football, I would not be here. The doctors told me I had kidney cancer. I missed four days of work, and that was it.

The reason I was able to do what I did, was mentality. I felt sorry for myself. I sat in a La-Z-Boy® chair with tears running down my cheeks and I told my wife, "I do not know if I can do it anymore. I do not know if I can battle this disease and coach the great game of football." My wife said, "Jerry, that is not who you are. You have taught your kids how to battle through adversity and all that, and you are just going to sit in that La-Z-Boy chair. This is not like you." That was my wife talking to me like that.

I felt sorry for myself for that one day. After that day, I got up and I went to work. I fed off our athletes. If it were not for those kids at Southern Illinois University Carbondale, I would not be here today. I firmly believe that they helped me get through it. You have to understand, we coach the greatest game ever invented. Do not get away from your values and get into the bull crap. Make those kids accountable. Make them do the right things. You are their parents. A lot of the players I deal with do not have parents. I am old school and I am proud of it, and I am not changing. Coaches are the last hope a lot of those kids have.

Thank you very much. I appreciate your attention.

DEFENSIVE LINE PLAY A THROUGH Z

University of Virginia

Thank you. I appreciate that introduction. I want you to know I am a Virginia product. I went to high school at Bethel High School in Hampton, Virginia. I know many of you coaches from my days at William and Mary, Richmond, and the University of Virginia the first time I was there. My story is a humble story and I feel privileged to stand here in front of this group of coaches. I grew up in this area and associated with many people in this room. At the University of Virginia our door is always open to you. We welcome you warmly.

My career has been as a defensive line coach. Even though I am a defensive coach, I am concerned with what happens to the offense. Too many times, we do not communicate to our players what we actually want from them. When we talk about the defensive line, the first thing I want them to do is use their senses:

• What you see

• What you hear

• What you feel

• What you know

• Repetition is the mother of all learning.

The defensive linemen have to use their eyes when they play football. They must see formations, splits, and tight end alignment. You have to listen. I have seen linemen coming out of an offensive huddle asking one another what was the snap count. When you play defense, it is important to listen for the checks and automatics. They have to hear the calls and know what they are supposed to do. Listening is a skill much like tackling. You have to train yourself to be a good listener.

A defensive lineman must be able to feel the blocks. He has to recognize pressure when he feels it. They have to feel the difference between a true double-team and a combo block. They have

to know if the lineman is trying to drive you off the line of scrimmage or if he is trying to hit him and get somewhere else. The defensive technique we teach linemen is different for a double-team block and the combo block. If they do not know the difference, they cannot play the technique.

We teach the defensive lineman to drop to the ground when they have a double-team block. If they get the combo block and they drop to the ground, they block the linebacker. The overtake block is simple when the defensive lineman drops to the ground. The defensive lineman should be able to close his eyes and know what the offensive lineman is trying to do to him. He has to feel the blocks.

When you coach the defensive linemen, it is important to stand behind them and watch the footwork and reactions to block. That lets you know what the defensive lineman feels and sees. It also lets you know whether he understands the teaching.

The defensive lineman has to take the coaching that the coach provides. They have to know what to do as well as how to do it. Reaction, responsibility, gap control, and things like that are all part of knowing. We know that repetition is the mother of all learning. You have to do the skills repeatedly to make them a habit. However, I believe you drill the way you play the game. The drills you do in practice have to mimic the game.

TOP OF THE ARC

• Feet: pick them up and put them down

• Circle drill concept

• Flip the hips

• Ball awareness

When we talk about top of the arc, we are referring to a circle (Diagram #1). The top of the arc is where the quarterback sets up. We take an

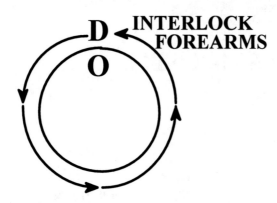

Diagram #1. Circle Drill

offensive blocker and a defender and lock them up with interlocking forearms. The defender uses his inside forearm, and the offensive lineman uses his outside forearm. They interlock at the elbow. The defender and blocker walk in a circle. The defender walks the arc with the offensive blocker applying pressure from the inside.

We want the defensive lineman to feel that pressure as he walks around the circle. What I do not want to happen is the offensive blocker pushing the defender off his path. The defensive lineman has to apply pressure on the offensive lineman to stay on his path. When the defensive lineman locks up with the offensive lineman, he wants to work on the positioning of the hips. Defensive linemen try to make a move around an offensive lineman without having their hips in position to do it. If the defensive lineman's hips are in front of the offensive lineman's hip, he cannot make a move.

If he tries, the offensive lineman simply slides in that direction and stays in front of him. If he is going to make a successful move, he has to be hip-to-hip with the offensive lineman. If he is, he can flip the hips. He can take his outside hip, flip it in the direction of the arc, and the blocker will fall off the defender.

The defender releases the offensive lineman's pressure by removing himself from the offensive lineman's push. That unbalances the blocker. It is the idea of pushing hard against something, which disappears quickly. With no pressure pushing back against him, the offensive lineman tips forward. The defensive lineman must gain ground and get hip-to-hip with the offensive blocker.

We talk about ball awareness. Anytime you do a drill with a defensive lineman, do it with a ball. Put the ball in front of the defensive lineman, and make it his key to reaction. Do not use cadence counts with a defensive lineman unless you are training him to ignore the cadence. If you want the defensive lineman to get his hands up in a pass drill, use a ball for him to knock down. Let him adjust the movement of the hands to knocking balls down. Knocking the ball down is a drill within itself. One point is not to raise the hands until the quarterback start to throw.

I want to show you a drill that trains flipping the hips. We call it step-over L drill (Diagram #2). We place four bags on the ground about two feet apart. Two yards past the last dummy is a stand-up dummy.

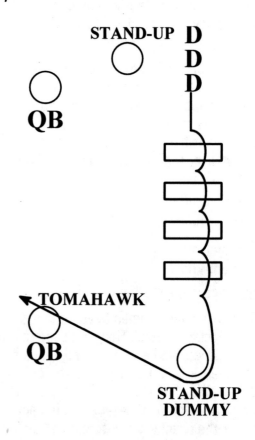

Diagram #2. Step Over L Drill

Two yards inside and slightly in front of the stand-up bag, we place another stand-up bag. The first bag represents the top of the arc. The second stand-up bag represents the quarterback. The defender runs over the bags on the ground. When he gets to the stand-up bag, he gets hip to hip on the bag, and flips his hips around the bag. The flip opens him up to the second dummy. He attacks the dummy and makes a tomahawk movement on the front side of the dummy.

The farther forward you move the second stand-up dummy, the more dramatically the defender has to turn his hips. We work down the bags, turn around, and work the other way. That gives them the opposite movement at the first stand-up dummy. You can put more bags on the ground or play around with the distance between the two stand-up dummies.

ON THE EDGE

- Attacking half a man
- Hand from the ground out
- Hand placement
- Shed and separate

We talk about being on the edge. When you come off the edge of a blocker, we want to attack only half the offensive blocker instead of taking him down the middle. When we begin to teach the pass rush, we tell them the bull rush is not an option. We want them to attack the edge of the blocker. That is why we use the hoops as one of our primary pass rush drills. The hoops drill puts the defender on the edge of a pass blocker and teaches him to lean to the quarterback. In playing the run, you do the same thing. We attack half a man.

When the defender attacks a blocker, he wants to attack with the hands from the ground out. We use a device called a hands lock. It fits over the wrist of the defensive lineman and acts as a spacer for the width of his hands. It keeps the hands at a width no wider than the armpits. When the defender pulls out against the locks, it brings his elbows into his side against his rib cage. That is the position you want in your hand placement on the offensive lineman. It allows your players to play with their hands within the framework of their body.

You do not need to buy something to do that. You can use a towel or elastic bands that serve the same purpose. It trains the hands to stay in position.

We teach attack angles in our drills (Diagram #3). The offensive player has a hand shield with a

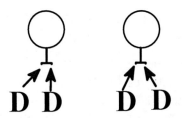

Diagram #3. Attack Angle Drill

defensive man in front of him. The drill is to hand punch into the shield. We work two defenders at the same time. What we do in the drill is to change the angle of the punch by making the defender realign each time they strike the shield.

The coach stands behind the defender and calls out the stance in which he wants the defender aligned. He calls right, and the defender aligns in a right-handed stance to the right side of the shield. The defenders strike with good hand placement on the right side of the shield. The coach calls left, and they realign in a left-handed stance to the left side of the shield and strike from that position.

Each time the defenders realign, they have to adjust their feet and hand placement on the ground to match the call of the coach. We do three reps on the strike. On the third rep, the defenders punch, shed, and rip off the blocker to the outside. It is a good drill because they must set each time and realign their stance, feet, and hands. It is a multiple skill drill. We work punch, footwork, angle of attack, attacking half a man, shed, and separate.

CROSS THE LINE

- Mirror drill run blocks
- Hands out in front of the face
- Lock out
- Push/pull
- Separate

We want to make sure that what we see on film is the same thing we are coaching on the field. When we talk about crossing the line, we talk in terms of an imaginary line. If we drew an imaginary line from the ground to the sky, we want to know where the offensive lineman's hat crossed the line. If his hat crosses the line, we play a run block. If his head comes straight ahead, that is a base block. If it crosses outside, that is a reach block. If it crosses inside, that is a cutoff block.

When the defensive lineman plays with his hands in front of his face, he has the consistent tool to keep him in front of the blocker. The hands become the eyes of the defender. The thing that is consistent regardless of the alignment is the placement of the hands.

Once we set the hands, we want to lock out on the offensive lineman. That gives us space to execute a push/pull technique. We push with one hand and pull down with the other. That leads to the separation from the blocker.

The mirror drill is an offensive man with a shield and a defensive man aligned in an outside shoulder alignment (Diagram #4). The offensive man with the shield makes one of three moves. He goes inside, outside, or straight ahead. The defender shoots his hands and mirrors the movement of the offensive man. He locks out with his arms and uses a push/pull move to disengage.

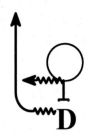

Diagram #4. Mirror Drill

The purpose of this drill is to get the hands out in front of the face and extend the arms. This is a basic block read drill. The emphasis of the drill is to get the hands into the blocker and locked out. We work on cross-the-line moves by the offensive blocker. We play the head and get control of the blocker.

When I coached at Virginia with Coach Groh, we played Wake Forest. We played the 3-4 defense and keyed the helmet of the offensive linemen to start our charge. Wake Forest's offensive linemen moved the head to the right and attacked back to the left or moved the head to the left and attack to the right. The offensive line did it in unison. They ran their plays that way. That is good for a reading team, but not good for a team that angles or slants.

OFF THE LINE

- Mirror drill Pass
- Hands, hips, and feet
- Shoulder Hump
- Spin move

The run situation is across the line and the pass play is off the line. The scheme may change, but having the hands in front of the face does not change. The defensive lineman plays down-and-distance, but having his hands in front of his face is the first part of all downs. In long-yardage situations, we can think pass rush, but for all other situations we have to react to what we see.

We drill the pass recognitions in a mirror drill, also. It is the same drill as the run react mirror drill except the offensive blocker shows high hat and a pass set. In the drill, the offensive lineman pass sets and the defender punches with his hands. We want fast hands into the offensive lineman and a pass rush move. In the drill, we use an outside move. We want them to swim or rip through the outside. He can flip his hips and get past the blocker.

The move I like is the shoulder hump (Diagram #5). On this move, the defender attacks the outside shoulder of the blocker. He drives two steps up the field, which gives the offensive blocker a chance to lean outside to stop the outside rush. When the blocker leans to the outside, the rusher reaches with his inside hand, grabs the inside shoulders of the blocker, and rips through the inside shoulder.

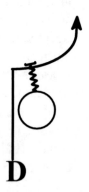

Diagram #5. Shoulder Hump

A move that can go with the shoulder hump is the spin move. The spin move could be the counter for the shoulder hump. The defender attacks the outside shoulder, grabs, and rips inside with the shoulder hump. If the blocker stays on the block, he spins back to the outside.

BIG BAG

- Active hands
- Fast hands
- When to and how to bet them off of you
- Arm's-length apart, near hand swat

In pass rushing, the defender does not make his move until he is arm's-length apart from the blocker. The blocker sets back off the ball, and the defender explodes off the ball and closes the distance between him and the blocker. When he gets to arm's length from the blocker, his hands come up in front of his face. The blocker will not try to punch the defender until he can reach him. If he tried to hit the rusher early, he tips forward and gets off balance. The blocker waits until he can get an active punch on the rusher.

When the blocker's hands come up to punch is the time the defender begins to make his move. The hand swat is a standard move we use.

In the big bag drill, we want to use the hand swat (Diagram #6). We align four big bags in a single line, two yards apart. We use the hand swat to knock the outside hand of the blocker off the defender.

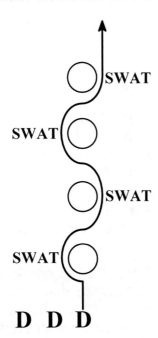

Diagram #6. Big Bag Drill

When the blocker puts up his arms and hands to punch the defender, the defender takes his outside hand and swats the outside hand of the blocker inside. Simultaneously, the inside hand and arm use a rip technique to get the defender past the hips of the blocker.

The defender pounds the bag with his outside hand and rips through with the inside hand. He wants to stay as close to the bag as he can. When he punches the bag, it tips to the side, and as he rips through he is almost on a straight line. He chops his steps in between the bags so he can align on the opposite side of the next bag. He swats the bag with his outside hand, rips through with the inside hand, and sets up to attack the next bag on the opposite side. We go through a sequence of four bags. The hands need to stay active and the movement fast and quick between the bags.

When the pass rusher comes off the line of scrimmage, he must have active hands. He is not running with his hands out in front of his face, but pumping his hands up and down in an active fashion. The target for the offensive blocker is the chest of the pass rusher. The pass rusher may misjudge the punch from the offensive lineman. He may think he is not close enough to make his move and tries to get closer. When he attempts to get closer, the offensive lineman hits him with a punch that stymies him.

That can kill the pass rush if the defender stops his feet. He has to keep the feet moving get his hands active and slap and swat at the offensive lineman's hands. He has to defend at all times for the hands of the offensive. He may not be arm's length from the blocker when all of a sudden the blocker stops retreating and punches.

If the defender does not have active hands, he runs into the hands, and the rush is over. When the offensive lineman's hands come up, the defender has to have actively pumping hands in the running motion and the readiness to slap and swat at an instance. The offensive and defensive linemen become involved with hand-to-hand combat in these situations. It is important to understand that when the hand fighting begins, the feet of the defender have to be alive. Under no circumstance can he stop his feet.

The sole object of the pass rusher is to get hip-to-hip with the blocker. If he can get to that position, the battle is over. When the defenders come through the big bag drill, their hands must pump up and down quickly in an active movement. We want to overemphasize that part of the drill.

We adapt the big bag drill and add a simple move. We call it "big bag, fake and combo." This is the big bag drill, except before we swat the bag, the defender head-fakes one way and attacks the other. The defender fakes with the head inside to get the offensive blocker to react to the inside. The best fake is to fake outside and go inside. The blocker has no help to the outside and will respect that movement more than the inside move.

In the pass set, most offensive blockers set to the inside and work to the outside. If you fake outside, they are more likely to lean or move that way. The defender head-fakes to the outside side, swats with the inside hand, and rips across with the outside hand.

COD

- Lateral movement
- Shifting of body weight
- Hand violence/recoil and strike
- Finish with a ball disruption

The COD stands for change of direction. In defensive line play, we must have lateral movement. The drill we use for lateral movement is a lateral shuffle and punch drill (Diagram #7). We align four players with shield held at chest level. The first three shields are almost shoulder-to-shoulder. The fourth shield holder stands two yards outside the third bag holder.

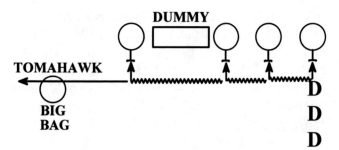

Diagram #7. Lateral Shuffle/Punch

Three yards past the last bag is a big stand-up bag like the one we used in the big bag drill. The defenders get into a good football position with their hands up. They shuffle down the shield line and punch the shields with their hands. When they reach the last shield, they punch it, turn toward the big bag, sprint, and tomahawk the dummy.

We want the hands up and the elbows tucked to the rib cage. When we punch, we never drop the hands to punch or load the hands past the body. The punch is short and quick. If the defender drops his hands or reaches back to punch, it takes too long to hit the target. Offensive drills and defensive drills are almost alike. In both cases, the players who get inside position with the hand generally win the battle. You have to beat the blocker to the punch and control him.

We do a similar drill called lateral shuffle/COD (Diagram #8). In this drill, we have three shield holders. The coach stands behind the defender. The defender does the shuffle/punch drill, except we number the bags and make him hit the bags in an order. We number the bags (one, two, and three).

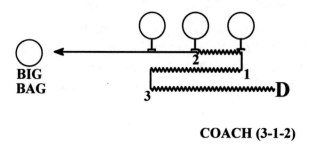

Diagram #8. Lateral Shuffle/COD

The defender starts outside of bag number one. On the coach's command, the defender punches the bags. The coach may say, "One, three, and two." The defender punches the first bag and shuffles to the third bag. After he punches the third bag, he shuffles back and punches bag number two. After he hits bag number two, he turns, sprints, and tomahawks the stand-up bag.

The purpose of the drill is to have the defender shuffle, hit, and change directions. The coaching points for this drill are punch, shuffle, and finish. In the punch, we want the short and quick punch delivered with the hands up and elbows tight. In the shuffle, we do not want them to cross over or click their heels as they shuffle up and down. When they turn to run, they want to sprint and finish with a hard tomahawk on the dummy. The coach can chose to use as many number as he sees fit. He can call a sequence of numbers or one number at a time. What we want to happen is a change of direction without coming out of the fundamental football position. We always want a good body position and footwork at all times.

TARGET PRACTICE

- See the big picture.
- Develop vision.
- Strike fast.
- Hand placement is always important.
- Keep the eyes straight ahead.
- Keep the eyes on the target.

When you coach the defensive line, you have to be consistent with the words you use. Be consistent in your language and nomenclature. When you say "Hands" or "Back," they know what movement they should perform. When the coach says, "Hand," that means quick hands. The meanings and actions mean the same things to every player on the team.

I like this drill, and you can use it for defensive line, linebackers, or backs. It is eyes, hands, and strike drill (Diagram #9). This drill involves three shield holders. The middle bag is square to the line, and the outside bags tilt in toward the middle bag. The defender is in a good fundamental position, facing the three shields.

COACH

Diagram #9. Eyes, Hand, and Strike

The coach stands behind the defender and cues the shield holders. The coach points to a one of the shields. The shield holder moves that shield toward the defender. It is a slight movement. The defender reacts to the movement of the shield. He has his hands up and punches the bag that moves. He resets his hands and waits for the next movement.

The first part of the drill is a hands-only movement. The defender keeps his eyes straight ahead and sees the outside shield with his peripheral vision. The defender strikes the shield that moves with his hands. You can go as fast as you need, but you must protect the integrity of the drill. You want them to do the skill correctly and not just for speed. We want the hands to strike each shield as it moves.

The second part of the drill has the defender rotate his shoulders and head, face the shield, and strike. He turns his shoulder and head to face the shield as they move. At each movement, he strikes the shield. This is a rapid hand-striking drill. We want the defender to strike as quickly as he can. He has to develop the reaction and cut the time it takes him to strike.

This drill develops the peripheral vision that a defensive lineman has to play with all the time. One of the most important assets of the defensive lineman is his vision. He has to see the big picture and play with his eyes.

The defenders have to recognize the feel of different blocks and be able to tell them apart. I want to show you some movements we use to get the offensive blocker's hand off the defender. We use these movements to defeat pass-blocking techniques. A defender will not do all of these movements, but we teach them a variety of things. They perfect and use the ones that suit them. The moves consider situations that occur in the pass rush. It teaches recovery from bad situations.

When we drill these movements, we face up to the blocker and defender in a fitted position. The defender's right hand is to the left hand of the blocker, and his left hand is to the right hand of the blocker. When we talk about the right hand of the defender going to the right hand of the blocker, it means the opposite hand.

We call the first movement "slice." In this example, the defender has his right hand locked out on the blockers chest and his left hand on the shoulder of the blocker. The blocker has an opposite hand position. The defender uses the slice move with his left hand. He takes the hand from the shoulder and makes a circular movement under the locked out arm of the blocker. He slices the hand off his chest with a hard downward movement with his left hand.

In the movie *The Karate Kid*, they called this move "wax on, wax off." The right hand forces the blocker away from the defender and allows him to disengage.

The next move is cut. In the example, the defender uses his right hand to do this move. The blocker has his hands locked out on the defender's chest. The defender takes his right hand and punches through the wrist of the blocker.

In this movement, he wants the right hand to end up grabbing the opposite wrist of the blocker. In one motion, he shoots the right hand through the left wrist of the blocker and rotates his shoulders to allow the right hand to come across his chest to grab the opposite wrist. In this action, he knocks both hands off his chest and can disengage and escape from the blocker into his pass rush technique.

The under and pin is similar to the slice movement. In this movement, the right hand comes under both arms of the blocker. He uses the circular motion to get his right hand under the opposite arm of the blocker. The defender uses his right hand to swipe off the right and left hands of the blocker. At the same time, he takes his left hand, grabs the blocker's right elbow, and shoves it to his right.

When we do these drills, we start out looking at each other. Once we perfect the skill, we look behind the blocker. Ninety-nine percent of the time, the lineman's hands in a pass set are in the same place. When the rusher reads the pass, he does not need to see where the blocker has his hands. He knows where they are. He attacks and uses the moves to escape the hands of the blocker.

If the defender faces a block with long arms, it presents a problem about getting to the chest. If the blocker has his hands into the chest of the rusher, we use a one-arm wrist pull. The defender takes his outside hand and slides down the arm of the blocker. We do not want to take the hand off the arm of the blocker. We slide it down the arm until he can grab the wrist of that arm. The wrist is the power base of the arms. The defender grabs the wrist and pulls down while stepping with his outside foot around the outside of the blocker.

I worked as a police officer for two years. In the police academy, they taught us self-defense. They teach how to get out of a grasp or break a grasp. Part of the defense class I was in was about angles and leverage. I found the skills I learned were adaptable to pass rush techniques.

The two-arm wrist pull is the same thing, except you slide the hands down to both wrists. You pull hard on both wrists and try to pull the blocker forward while you step around him.

We use the forearm collapse when the blocker gets his hands inside on the defender. The defender grabs the jersey of the blocker at the shoulders. With one hand or the other, he pulls hard on the shoulder of the blocker as if he were curling his shoulder into him. The shoulder of the blocker comes down and to the inside. The defender flips his hips and gets outside.

We use an arm-over collapse. The defender locks up with the blocker. The blocker has his hands inside. The defender grabs the jersey of the blocker at the shoulders. He takes his elbow and drives it across the blocker's chest over the opposite elbow of the blocker. He steps with his outside foot and rips through with the backside.

With the arm over collapse, we integrate the spin move. We work the first move through the rip-through step. We settle in the hips and spin back in the direction from which we came.

We do a tag drill, to work get-off. The blocker sets and retreats as fast as he can, and the defender chases him. We want to know how fast he can touch the outside shoulder of the blocker. It works on closing the distance between the blocker and rusher. We work the same tag drill with a bull rush. The blocker retreats, and the defender chase and touch the chest with both hands.

At the University of Virginia, we want to be as open and accessible as we can for coaches. I appreciate the opportunity to come to speak at this clinic. It is a great clinic. Thank you, and have a great evening.

PASS PROTECTION DRILLS AND FUNDAMENTALS

Syracuse University

This presentation is going to be a lot about pass protections. Everyone in here can learn some things about how to become a coordinator and head coach. I think you can relate what I am going to say to every facet of coaching. Whatever position you coach, this can apply to you.

PASS PROTECTION

- *Develop personal pride*. Pass protection is as simple as you having more desire to keep the man you are responsible for blocking from getting to the quarterback.

- *Develop unit pride*. Be the best in the business. No one touches our quarterback. The offensive line has dinner on Thursday with the quarterback.

We talk to our players about developing personal pride. Anything I do with our players, I try to be very simple. You have to develop pride within the offensive line. We want to be the best offensive line in the business.

I am a firm believer in never starting from where you stopped, but starting at the beginning. When you start fall practice, you do not start where you stopped in spring practice; you start at the beginning and teach everything anew.

At the beginning of each year, I sit down and write out my thoughts of what you need to do to be an offensive lineman. The tough part about being an offensive line coach is most of the coordinators are former quarterbacks or quarterback coaches. The problem with that is they scheme too much. They constantly work on protection schemes and plays. They want to add, add, and add some more.

I learned a method from Rex Ryan when he was the coordinator for the Baltimore Ravens. When he did his documentation of the play, he listed the scheme, the techniques you need from the players, and the drills that taught the techniques. I thought that was interesting.

Offensive line coaches are the best coaches in the world for stealing time. They may come on the field early or stay late to get it done.

PRACTICE PRINCIPLES

- Pre-practice (footwork)
- Strike drill
- Footwork
- Body position
- Redirection, redirection, redirection
- Stunts and games (finish)
- Dogs and blitzes (finish)
- Drill: heavy/squeeze/sort
- Drill: eye work (The faster we see things, the faster we react.)

In pre-practice, I did all my choreography footwork drills. Kick-slide movements or postdown moves were the types of movements I did. Those movements were strung together like a dance step. We repeated the movements several times in succession. That movement gets the linemen warmed up.

The number one mistake in football is not spending enough time on striking a blow. We play a violent game, which is a very high performance business. The offensive linemen strike someone on every play. They strike coming off the ball in the run game and they strike when they pass protect. You have to think about doing a striking drill for your players.

I did not play football until I got into high school. I was too fat to play in the little leagues. When I got to high school, I had a hard time learning how to control my body. I was as tall as I am now and weighed between 335 to 340 pounds. Running redirection drills helps the player control his body. The more redirection a lineman can do, the better he can react. It also improves his quickness.

We have to work on stunts and games. You do not want to wait until you play a team that moves the defensive line to teach stunt and movement. We work a couple of different drills on stunts and games.

We have to adjust to the type of quarterback we have and from where he starts the play. If he is under the center, we have to make sure we protect the A gaps. In the three-step passing game we have to do a good job of protecting the B gaps. You have to work those adjustments into your practice principles. You cannot wait until you play the heavy blitzing teams.

Coaches want to know how to improve the speed of offensive linemen. The defense usually has better athletes. Coaches build their defense on speed. We start coaching with the eyes. We do drill work on offensive lineman eye placement. We never want the lineman to see the whole picture. We want him to concentrate on small, little things. We want him to see the corner of the number on the jersey. That makes our player react faster on what we do.

INDIVIDUAL PRINCIPLES

• Head

• Shoulders

• Chest

The NFL Scouting Combine is coming up and college athletes will be there to participate. When I was in the NFL, I asked college linemen coming out of college what areas of their bodies they needed to protect. I got many different responses. I think there are three areas you have to protect. The first one is the head. If someone hits you in the head, the body will follow where the head goes. The second area is the shoulders. The third area the offensive lineman has to protect is his chest. The area on the offensive blocker that most defenders in today's football try to grab is the chest. Defensive players want to punch the offensive blocker in the chest to control him.

The blocker can protect all three of those areas in his initial set. The big advantage I have over most of you is we film our players all the time in every drill they do. In pro football, we made all our corrections on his pass set with the player in a film session.

We use a quick set drill to teach all the different pass sets we use. I am big on not wasting any movement. The lineman's hand should come from the ground or in an up position from the hips quickly. As his hands come up, the elbows may be down near the knees but the hands are ready to play right away. We have a heel-toe stagger in the feet. I want the shoulders back as he comes to the set position. If the shoulders lean forward, the defensive lineman has less distance to his chest.

I have the offensive line drill area marked with three-yard square boxes. I like to work the offensive linemen in those boxes. I like to work the unit rather than one or two at a time. When we do drills, I do not like anyone standing around.

In our running game, we strike with the thumbs up in the punch. We want to strike from underneath the defender and through him. When you pass protect it is the same theory. We want the thumbs up in the punch because of what it does to the elbows. When the thumbs come up in the punch, the elbows come tight to the body. With the elbow against the body, it acts as a back brace for the hands and arms. With the elbows away from the body, you cannot generate any force or power with the hands.

With the thumbs up in the punch, the lineman wants to hook up with the hands. The punch is the same for the running game as it is for the passing game. I do not have to double teach because I use the same punch in run and pass blocking. When you drill the set, the areas of correction are:

• Wasted motion with the hands coming from the ground

• Thumbs up

• Elbows in

• Body lean too far forward

• Head down—head back to improve posture in the set

• Hands too low and not protecting the chest

• Feet too close together

When I do individual drills, I work players hard and get them as tired as I possibly can. That is why we drill as a unit with five players going at once. I want them to work through the fatigue and concentrate on the job they have to do. I want the mental mistakes made in practice and not during the game. I fatigue them during the drills and make them concentrate and focus during the mental part of practice.

STANCE ELEMENTS

- Right toe to left instep (right-handed)
- Feet shoulder width apart
- Toes pointed inside
- Squat
- Left elbow to left knee (right-handed)
- Right hand extended in front of right eye (right-handed)
- Heels low to ground as possible

Our stance is not the lineman's base. We align in a right-handed stance to the right of the ball and a left-handed stance to the left of the ball. If your linemen have trouble getting into a left-handed stance, balance their feet with no stagger and let them get in a right-handed stance. The stagger of the feet is toe to instep. In a right-handed stance, the left foot is up and the right toe aligns level with the left instep. I am a big progression coach. We take the linemen through the progression in the previous list.

INDIVIDUAL PRINCIPLES

Footwork

- Heel to toe (post stagger)
- Knees inside ankles
- Feet stay low to the ground (sensitivity training)
- Power generated from the ground (feet in the ground when striking)
- Weight distribution
  - ✓ Inner part of the foot
  - ✓ Center line training

Everything we do outside our stance is heel to toe in the stagger. The post stagger is the inside foot being forward in the stance. Our inside foot is our post foot. I try to tell the players the reasoning

behind the techniques we use. The heel-to-toe stagger has good reasoning behind it. If we take a huge stagger with the right and left foot, we have great power with objects coming directly toward us. We can push and resist with force. However, if someone pushes the blocker from the side, he has no balance and falls down. All the power in that stance exerts vertically.

If the lineman expands the width of his feet, he has great power for objects coming from his right or left. However, an object that attacks him from the front pushes him over with no trouble. He has horizontal strength but no vertical strength.

We use the heel-to-toe stagger to get the best of both worlds. We want to be strong both vertically and horizontally.

An important point with our movement skills is knees inside the ankles. As a lineman moves laterally, he has to keep his knees inside the ankles. If the knees get outside the ankles, he cannot change direction without getting the knee in the proper place. The weight has to move from the outside of the foot to the inside of the foot before he can move the other direction. That is a waste of time in a redirection movement. We want our knees inside our ankles when we move laterally in a heel-to-toe stagger.

The feet must stay near the ground. When you train an offensive lineman, never do bag drills where they have to step over or jump over them. I never want to do two movements as offensive linemen. I never want high knee action or a crossover step. When the strength coach works with offensive linemen on their hips, I ask him not to do anything that requires them to cross their feet.

One thing I have found to be effective in this type of training is working the players barefoot over the grass. This is sensitivity training. It gives them a feel of the ground under their feet and they can feel the weight distribution much better. You generate the power in the strike from the ground. That is why the feet must stay near the ground. I do not have the same push from the ground if I am on my toes. I need the feet fully on the ground to get maximum push.

The power comes from the ground, through the leg, into the back, through the triceps, and into the defender. When I was at Georgia Tech, we had a motion analysis room. We found the more the heels were in contact with the ground the more force the linemen had. That is the difference you can get when the feet are flat on the ground when the linemen strike.

We want weight distribution to be on the inside of the feet. Centerline training is important when training players to move laterally and horizontally. We want the power in the center of the body. We drill this very simply. We put the linemen on a line and move them to the right and back to the center and then to the left and back to the center. The players want to move fast and start to sway with the weight going to the outside of their feet as they move off the line. If the weight gets to the outside of the foot, we lose power.

To drill this skill, we put them in the box and work a redirect drill (Diagram #1). The coach places a ball in front of the linemen. We work their set with the ball on the outside, head-up, and to the inside of the linemen. I want them setting to the ball and redirecting when the coach gives a change of direction. We partner up and let them work with each other. The linemen start with their hands on the ball. On the snap count, the lineman throws the ball to his partner with a one-motion move. Throwing the ball makes him snap his hands up. The partner catches the ball and uses it to redirect the blocker left, right, up, and back.

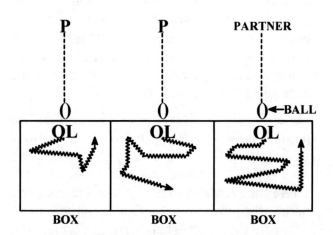

Diagram #1. Ball Redirect Drill

The thing I have always done from a principle standpoint is to work the power first. If an offensive lineman cannot stop a bull rush, he cannot become a good pass blocker. If he cannot knock defenders off the ball, he cannot be a good run blocker. Our progression is 1-on-1, 2-on-2, half-line, inside run, and, finally, team run. That is how we build their confidence.

The number one mistake I made when I started coaching was striking too much. My players started to get hurt on the inside of their elbows because we did too many striking drills.

We do a weight redirect drill. It is the same drill as the ball redirect except we use a weight plate in front of the body. This teaches a number of things. A lineman has to move with his hands in front of his body. If we use a 45-pound plate, we want the lineman to use the plate as leverage. He gets his elbows close to his body against his chest with the hands in a set position. In that position, the lineman can keep the weight in that position longer than a lineman that lets his elbows get away from his body. This forces the lineman to move his feet with his hands in front of his body. You do not have to use a weight plate. You can use anything that the lineman has to hold out in front of him.

When we give the redirect movement, we use a finger instead of a ball or verbal commands. That works on the eyes. It forces them to focus on something small. Sometimes I give them false signals to make sure they focus on fine targets and not react to someone else's movement.

We do many chest flexibility drills. Linemen that bench press develop barrel chests. Those players are difficult to coach because their hands are wide when they come to the set position. The hands have to get inside the chest of the defender. When we set, we want the elbows against the chest. As soon as the elbows get outside, the blocker loses his leverage.

Too many times, we go to clinics to pick up drills but never learn too much about the drill. The first thing you need to know about a drill is the tempo. You need to know the objective of it. You need to know the common problems of the drill. You have to know how this drill carries over to the football field.

In the NFL, we had three types of dress. It is probably the same in high school and college. The first dress is full pads. When I walked into the locker room and saw full pads, I knew the game was on. When we went out in helmets and shoulder pads, I thought the coach was throwing us a bone. It is a different mind-set. The third dress is no pads. When the coach told me the practice was a no-pads practice, that was a day off.

When I became a head coach, I made it the opposite for my players. When we had the pads on, I did more core drills. If we were in helmets and shoulder pads, I did more cardio drills and pushed them as hard as I could. With pads on, their individual period was the hardest I could make it. You can imagine the attitude of my players. When they walked in and we were in helmets only, they dreaded what was coming. I tried to create that mentality with my players because I always wanted them to be in pads and playing physical.

The softball drill is a good drill for redirection and centerline training (Diagram #2). I want the player working from side to side in the drill. The player tossing the ball stands in the middle of the box, two yards in front of the blocker. He rolls the softball one way or the other. The blocker shuffles to the ball, tries to field it in the middle of his body, and tosses it back to his partner. He shuffles back to the middle and the partner rolls the ball in the opposite direction or back in the same direction. I want the blocker to stay in good position with his head up. I want him to concentrate on a small object with his eyes and react. This is a good drill for movement and focus on the target.

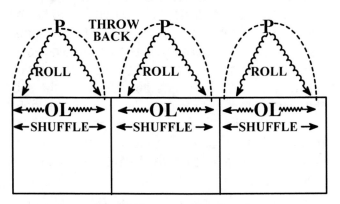

Diagram #2. Softball Drill

The next drill is more advanced. The offensive tackles at every level have trouble with speed rushers. The problem with the offensive line is the wear and tear of a long season. They start to wear down. When you play games, the level of effort by the defense kicks up. The linemen have to get used to that level of play. When I played with the Miami Dolphins, we got the wide receivers to rush against the tackles. If we had to play Lawrence Taylor, we needed to see the speed so we could be prepared.

There are a number of methods to help with the speed of the offensive linemen. People use resistive bands to improve speed.

The second thing you do is assistive training. That means you pull the offensive blocker into his set position. The blocker attaches the band and the coach stretches the band the other way. When the blocker drops into his vertical set, the band pulls him at an accelerated rate into his set. As with the resistive training, the blocker must maintain his form and technique. He must perform the technique without deviating from his technique.

That type of training can improve the set speed of the offensive linemen. Tackles in the NFL have gone from a set speed of 1.8 to 1.5 seconds. That is a tremendous amount of time. It does not matter whether you do the assistive or resistive drill first. However, make sure you always end the testing without the bands. We do the drills and test them every three weeks. They were all faster and it built confidence.

Hands

• Carry high (protect chest)
• Relaxed to hard (power)

There has always been discussion about where to carry the hands. I like to carry the hands high. That comes from a background in boxing and karate. Whatever I see, I want to hit in a short time frame. If I carry the hands high, I protect my chest.

The second part of the hands is tough to train. We talk about "relax to hard." Young linemen have a tendency to punch hard with a lot of effort. When they do that, they tighten the muscles in their entire bodies. Once that happens, he is susceptible to any blow knocking him off balance. If the defender pulls on the offensive lineman, the rest of his body will go down. We want to be relaxed to react to movement and keep the rest of the body in balance. The same thing is true with running and movement. The more relaxed, the faster the movement.

We call the next drill the "four-point punch drill." The players are facing one another on their knees. The four points are the knees and toes on the ground. The partners face one another in close proximity. The punch is a short, six-inch punch into the chest of the dummy player. The thumbs are up and the eyes look to the sky when we deliver the punch. This drill teaches hip movement. There is not a coach in here that has not said, "Roll your hips." When a blocker strikes, his hips drop lower and come forward. This is hard to teach because the blocker thinks that when he throws his hips, he gets run over by the defender.

When the hips move forward, we want the blocker to squeeze the buttocks tight. We punch through the defender but we never want to get to full extension with the arms. If the arms reach full extension and the defender moves, the blocker's entire body moves. We want a slight break in the arm and not fully extended. When we stand them up and strike, the look should be the same.

We do not want the blocker to wind up with his hands. The elbows cannot come behind the body. They shoot up and through the chest of the defender without reaching back with the elbows. The hands come from the ground up in one movement. When the blocker retracts his hands, he gives the defender a chance to get his hands on the blocker. The strike has to be four to six inches away from the target. If you retract the hands, the distance becomes greater and the chance of hitting the target lessens.

To train the players to not retract the elbows, we use an E-Z curl device. You probably have one in your weight room. It hangs from your neck and is molded so the elbows fit into it. If you curl a weight bar, the E-Z curl bar prevents the elbow from going backward and makes the curl exercise easier to do. It works in stopping the retracted elbow in blocking.

In this drill, there are certain things we look for. We look for the head and shoulders going back as we punch. We look for the elbows in and the thumbs up. However, the key is the hips going forward. If the hips are behind the blocker with someone running at him, he cannot stop him. The hips on the strike have to come forward in front of the feet. One of the big concepts as to why blockers get beat is they never meet power with power. We have to build confidence in our players that they can stop the bull rusher.

One of the problems offensive linemen have is understanding leverage. Coaches tell them to hit on the rise. The players want to hit the defender then redirect his power in an upward fashion instead of hitting through the defender. If you find a blocker that hits and climbs the defender too quickly or hits and ends up on his toes, the problem is he is trying to do what you tell him. You have to coach the blocker to drive up through the defender.

On the hit, we hook up on the defender. I do not want the blocker to let him go and then go block him again. We do not regrip in our technique. We lock the defender up the first time and do not turn him loose. If the hands get outside the framework of the body, we have to turn them loose. As long as we do not lock out completely with the arms, we can control the defender. If the defender tries to disengage to the right, the blocker can push out with his right arm and keep the defender on the block. If he locks out, he has no option. As long as the blocker controls the leverage of the defender, he can win the block.

The best way to handle a speed rusher is to do it with alignments and different personnel. I know the range of my tackles. I know when they cannot get deep enough in their set to take on a speed rusher. If that occurs, I put the fullback or a slot receiver on that speed rusher to slow him down. We take the tight end and put him in a nasty split to the speed rusher's side. The defender has to make a decision to go outside on the tight end or come back inside on the tackle. If he aligns outside the tight end, that puts him six yards outside. That is a big hole. Most of the time, he comes back inside and aligns on the offensive tackle. The farther the defensive end wants to go outside, the farther he is from the quarterback.

Coaching is difficult if you do not know what the player sees. I want to know what he sees and what he looks at. Many times, we do not listen to our players. I can never change or make him a better player until I know what he is thinking. I can make him a better player, but it may take changing the way he thinks.

This next drill is a visual drill. We align the defender three yards from the blocker and I stand behind the blocker. The defender shows three moves. The blocker identifies the move the defender runs by the movement of his hands and arms.

The defender does not attack the blocker. He simply makes an arm movement to indicate which defensive move he is going to attempt. The offensive blocker verbally calls out the move once he recognizes it. We give the blocker tips to use. If the left defensive end comes up the field and throws out his left hand, he will use an outside move. If the defender comes up the field and throws up his inside arm, that is a spin move. If the defensive end comes up the field and his hands come up from underneath, he uses the hand slap. If the defender comes up the field and the hands come up together, that is the bull rush.

There are counters off all those moves, but this is where we start. The blocker recognizes the arm and hand movements to evaluate the pass rush. When he can recognize those moves, he knows what move to stop. We do it from a distance to give them time to verbalize what they see. If the blocker does not pick up the movement quick enough, I ask him where he is looking. He looks at the inside part of the number covering the sternum but he sees the hand movement at the same time.

To be successful as a coach, you have to teach your players from a winning and losing position. You have to coach them how to execute the correct technique but you have to teach them what to do when things go wrong. If the lineman misses with his punch and the defender gets his hands inside on the blocker, the offensive blocker has to recover and make the block.

You have to teach pass-set combo moves. The first one we look at is the tight end combo. That is the defensive tackle penetrating the B gap and the defensive end looping to the inside. The problem is the penetrating tackle. We pass the two defenders in the twist from one lineman to the other. When the exchange occurs between the guard and tackle, the tackle has trouble leveraging the penetrating tackle working outside. If he cannot get leverage on the penetrating tackle, the defender has a straight shot at the quarterback. We drill this move.

When I work this drill, I work it on the hash marks (Diagram #3). On one hash mark, I put the center, right guard, and right tackle facing the sideline. On the opposite hash, I put a center, left guard, and left tackle facing the sideline. I stand between the two groups. The offensive group aligns on one side of the hash mark. Across the hash marks from the offensive blockers, I place three defensive linemen. Their job is to angle from the hash mark; they align to the next hash mark. They go from the tip of one hash mark to the tip of the adjacent hash mark.

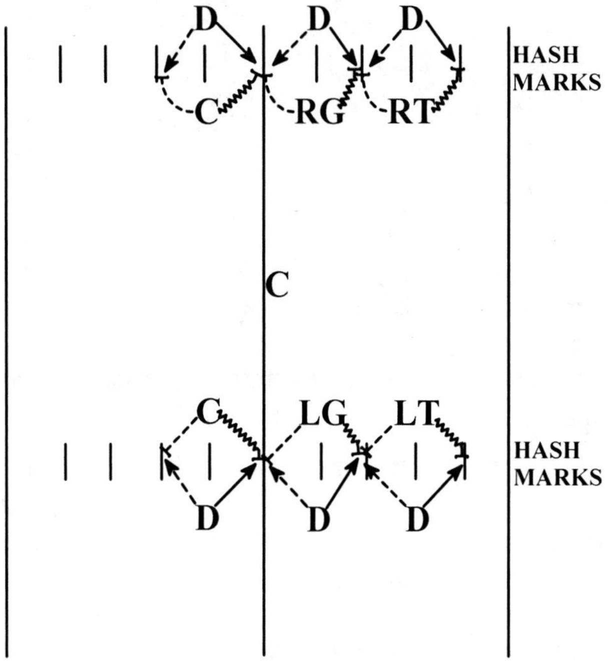

Diagram #3. Hash Mark Penetrator

They all go at the same time in the same direction. The offensive blockers have to flatten the penetrating defender and keep him from getting to the tip of the adjacent hash mark. When the first group finishes, I turn around and the group on the other hash mark does the same thing. When they finish, I turn around and work the other group in the opposite direction. It is rapid-fire and we get a ton of reps.

I do not work on the twist until I know the offensive linemen know how to stop the penetrating defender (Diagram #4). After I know the blockers can handle the penetrator, I add the twisting defender. When I do this part of the drill, I twist two defenders and bring the inside or outside defender straight up the field. The lineman blocking

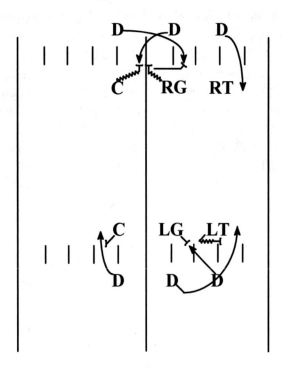

Diagram #4. Hash Mark Twist

the penetrator has to flatten him so the adjacent lineman can get inside leverage on him.

I work this drill every week. Eventually, I put all five linemen together and work against five defenders. We work three-man defensive stunts and things of that nature. We work the drills every week to prepare for the season. We do not wait until we play a team that gives us a heavy dose of twisting.

The offensive guard flattens the penetrator going outside and delivers him to the offensive tackle. When the exchange occurs, the guard shoves the defender onto the block of the tackle. The offensive tackle watches the defensive end. If the end stops or raises his shoulders, the tackle knows something is unusual. He wants to take a step backward and assess what is happening. He sees the end looping and knows the tackle is coming outside. He has depth, so as the guard shoves the defender, he drops his inside arm and pulls the defender across his body.

The defender wants to come inside the tackle's block and get to the quarterback. The guard shoves the tackle onto the tackle's block and sees the looping end coming inside. He has to gain ground back to the inside. He pushes hard off his outside

foot and jumps back inside. He wants to force the defender coming inside to go outside of him and not inside.

1-ON-1 PHILOSOPHY

- The most hated drill for the offensive linemen
- The coach must change the atmosphere
- Recognize how hard the situation appears
- Create goals
- No one gets bull rushed/beat inside (take a lap)
- Work on new techniques or sets
- Pick one thing for the players to work on (game plan)
- Keep a running total of wins and losses
- Prize at the end based on qualifying reps and winning percentage
- Be aware of match-ups
- Positive, positive, positive
- Make sure the group is encouraging each other

In 1-on-1 pass blocking drills, every advantage goes to the defense. The coach has to change the atmosphere. I tell my players they are at a disadvantage because the defense does not have to worry about anything except getting to the quarterback. However, there will come a time in a game where that is exactly what happens. Everyone in the stadium knows the offense has to throw the ball including the defense. This drill gets us ready to handle that situation.

We create goals. We tell them, "Today, no one gets beat with a power or bull rush." If they get beat with a bull rush, they have to run a lap. When I tell a player to take a lap, I do that for a couple of reasons. I want the player to think about what he did wrong. I want them to take a lap before I get angry and say something stupid because I love them and do not want to embarrass them.

During the 1-on-1 period, we can experiment on new and different ways of protecting. I pick a technique that I want a particular player to work on and give him a game plan. I tell him to work on keeping his elbows in or getting the thumbs up.

I saw something the defensive line coach did that made me think (Diagram #5). They set up a

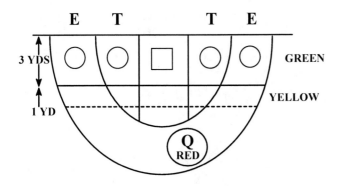

Diagram #5. Pass Rush Drill

drill and drew pass rush lanes on the turf with paint. They put their defensive line down and drew lanes for them to rush the quarterback. Where the quarterback stood in the pocket was a red circle. I use that drill and my own color-coding system. The first three yards, I colored green. The next yard was yellow. The area around the quarterback was red.

With the centers and guards, we wanted them to stay in the green area. We never wanted the guards walked back into the quarterback's lap by a bull rusher. I wanted the center and guards to keep the defenders on the line of scrimmage if they could. The yellow area was for caution and the red was a definite stop area. We wanted a point of reference for linemen in this drill.

When you do 1-on-1 drills, be aware of the match-ups. Having confidence is a big thing with offensive linemen. You do not want to match up a developing lineman with your best pass rusher. That is especially true in youth league football. If you embarrass him, you may drive him out of football. Make sure the match-ups are right so you do not ruin a player's confidence. When you coach in this drill, you must be super positive with the players. You want your players to think they can block anyone.

PROTECTING OUR THROWING AREA

- Depth of pocket guards and center
- Width of the pocket (tackles)
- No one runs through our A gap

The last rule of "no one runs through our A gap" applies for the quarterback under the center. If we are in the shotgun, we do not worry about that aspect. If we are under the center depending

on protection, we worry about the A gap and in the three-step game we have to worry about the B gap.

In the scheme of pass protection, we must know the launch position in the three-, five-, and seven-step drops. Everyone has to know the identifications of personnel. We make a declaration of the Mike linebacker and Will linebacker when we come to the line of scrimmage. We base our protection on knowing who the linebackers are.

You need a plan to handle four defenders to the weakside and four to the strongside (Diagram #6). We define four weak as a linebacker and defensive back in position to blitz on back to the weakside. In our normal protection scheme, the back has the Will linebacker to the weakside. If the defense brings the Will linebacker and the corner off the weakside, we have to do something. We can do two things in that situation. First, is to let the quarterback get rid of the ball with some kind of hot read. The second thing is to reidentify linebackers. If we designate the Will linebacker as the Mike linebacker, the center goes backside and blocks the Will linebacker. The back kicks outside one more defender and blocks the corner coming off the edge.

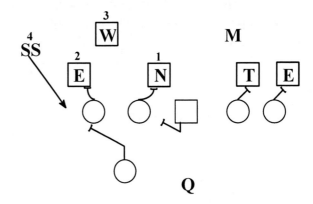

Diagram #6. Four Weakside Reidentify

We split our protections in half to help our leaning situation. If there is a back working to a side, we call it a "solidside." If there is no back working to a side we call that a "dualside." That means the quarterback throws hot off an unblocked defender. When the tight end stays in to block, we call that a "slow side."

In our 24-protection scheme, we have seven men in the scheme (Diagram #7). The five linemen have the four down linemen and the Mike linebacker.

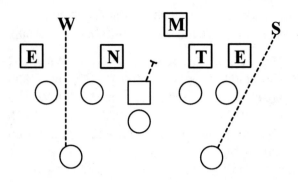

Diagram #7. 24 Solid

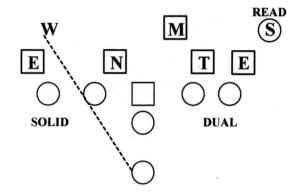

Diagram #8. 22 Dual

The fullback has the Sam linebacker and the tailback has the Will linebacker. We have two solid sides in the protection.

If we run 22 protection, it is a six-man protection (Diagram #8). The quarterback throws hot off the Sam linebacker. When we break the huddle, the right side calls dual and the left side calls solid.

During the week, the offensive lineman needs to make an individual game plan against the opponent. Defensive linemen tend to do the same things repeatedly in the pass rush. Get your linemen to chart what their defender does in game situations. They can watch films and chart what the defender does and prepare for them. Do not let the defender beat you with his best move. If you chart the pass rusher on third down, you can help your players. On third down, the pass rusher gives you his best stuff. Get your linemen to write down an individual game plan.

Every Thursday night, we do the chair drill. I sit my linemen down in a chair in an alignment and call a play. They clap as if they are breaking the huddle. I call the snap count and they all take their first step. We want to put mental pressure on them. I want them thinking about football and adjustments they have to make on game night. You go through all your running plays and protections without getting out of the chairs.

Thank you guys very much. I appreciate your time.

DEFENSIVE DRILLS AND SECONDARY SCHEMES

East Carolina University

I want to thank everyone for coming out this evening. I would like to thank Nike and the sponsors of this clinic. I want to thank you for taking time out of your day and spending the weekend studying football. Coming to clinics, you can always learn something. For all the young coaches out there, you need to hear as many of these lectures as you possibly can. You may hear many things that you already know, but you can always pick up something. If you can take one thing back to your program that helps you, the clinic is well worth the time.

I love the sport of football, and I love coaching. I think when you coach, you take someone to a place they could not go by themselves. There are many ways to skin a cat. My background is in special education. When you work with people with special needs, you learn how to teach and present things in different ways. Some kids you can tell one time, and they get it. Some of them you have to tell them, show it on the board, and show them on the field. In my first college experience as a graduate assistant, I worked for Danny Ford at Clemson. I learned so much from him, and I have been fortunate to work for some other good people. Everything you coach on the field is borrowed or stolen.

I coached high school football and still love the atmosphere of high school football. My coaching career has taken me many places. I played at East Carolina University and have gone full circle to come back home. I coached at Austin Peay State University, Appalachian State University twice, University of Nevada Las Vegas, Fresno State, Texas Tech University, and back to East Carolina. The first time I coached at East Carolina was in 1992, and I was the defensive line coach.

I went to Texas Tech and was there for 10 years. It was a good experience. I got a chance to recruit in Texas and became the defensive coordinator there.

Everything in this world happens for a reason. The last year I was at Texas Tech, we were getting ready to play in the Alamo Bowl game. I got a call on Monday, and the athletic director told me I was going to be the head coach for the bowl game. I was shocked and did not really understand. I decided I was going to do two things. I was going to be myself. I could not be Mike Leach. I wanted to win the bowl game for Texas Tech.

The storybook ended (and soon) after we won the bowl game. The team was happy in the locker room, and the bowl people presented us with the trophy. The next week, we went through interviews for the head coaching position, and the next week I was out of a job. We won a bunch of games and a bowl game, and I was out of a job. However, in this business, it works that way.

That reminds me of a story about a rattlesnake. The coach was driving down the road when he saw a rattlesnake beside the road. He stopped, and the rattlesnake asked him for a ride. The coach declined to give him a ride, but the snake continued to beg until the coach agreed to let him ride. When the coach put the snake in the truck and started down the road, the snake coiled up as if to strike the coach. The coach asked what the snake was about to do. The snake replied, "You knew what I was when you picked me up."

It is the same with coaching. You know what you are getting into when you take a job. When you take a job, you know what the consequences are. There are only two kinds of coaches in this world: those that have been fired, and those that are going to be fired. You do the best you can with the talent you have. I do not feel sorry for myself over the situations that occurred along the way. These situations led me back home. I am home where I started.

I talk to my coaches all the time about what we see on film. We can talk about the scheme and details of the game, but when we watch the film, we see what we are coaching. If you do not like what you see, you are coaching it that way, or you are allowing the players to play that way.

I have coached defense all my life. However, my offensive philosophy is throwing the football. We throw the ball for a living. We will run the ball, but our offense is based on the passing game.

Now that I am the head coach, I have to make sure we implement this philosophy to the entire team. When you watch us play, the first thing I want you to see is the effort our players exhibit on the field. I want them to play hard and play with great effort. The second thing I want you to see is the aggressiveness with which we play. I want my team to be physical on the field. I am not talking about taking a cheap shot on someone, but aggressive hitting.

The next thing we want to be is a fundamentally sound football team. We want to play with great pad level, hat and hands, and great technique. To accomplish what we want to do, we must have great discipline. It is not what you do; it is how you do it. The scheme is not important; it is how you play it. If you are responsible for the B gap, be responsible.

I am a DNA coach. I love good kids. Coaches tell me all the time that a player is not very fast, big, or strong, but he has a big heart. That will get you killed. I want the big, fast, and strong players with a lot of heart. I look at the parents to decide whether the player will grow into our expectations. That is DNA.

To be successful as a team, you must have players who make plays. I decide who plays and who does not play based on their production. If two players are on the field for 10 plays, I grade their production. If one player makes eight plays out of 10 attempts and the other makes six out of 10, the one with the most production starts. The player who made six plays will get some playing time, but the most productive player will start and get the most time.

The last thing it takes to be successful is players who know their job and the game. They know the down-and-distance, formation, what they do from the formation, and all the things that go into the game. I wanted you to know the things I believe in before we got into the football end of the lecture.

In our recruiting at East Carolina, we blanket North Carolina, and go into Virginia, Washington D.C., South Carolina, and Georgia. The key to our success is recruiting. We want to find those mommas who can run and the daddies who are big and recruit their kids. However, I want good players who want to go to college. I want players who go to class and do the right things. We want players with great talent, and that is what we recruit. We research recruits and find out who they are.

Three things in our program are important and non-negotiable:

• Trust
• Commitment
• Caring

I am going to hire coaches I trust and play players I trust. The other side of the coin is the coaches and players must trust me. If I can trust you, then we go to the second step. The second step is commitment. Commitment is like bacon and eggs. The hen is involved with the breakfast, but the hog is committed to the breakfast. The commitment in your program must come from everyone involved with your program. It starts with the coaches and players, but extends to the secretaries, equipment managers, training staff, custodians, and everyone who has anything to do with your program.

Within your program, you have to build caring for your fellow teammates. They are your brothers-in-arms. They will not care about your program until they know you care about them. If you care about them, they will return the feeling toward you. They have to feel as strongly about me as I feel about them.

I do not want to give the impression I am soft on players. I am not. Players want you to coach them hard because they all want to improve and win games. However, they want the dignity that comes from caring. I am an old school type of coach. If they do not do as I want them to do, I can bite. I wear a size 14 shoe, and it will fit most everyone's rear. If they do not do as I tell them to do, we can have some problems. However, at the end of the day, they are my players, and I love every one of them.

One of the things we established here is no entitlements. East Carolina has been very successful, and they have done some great things here. We had to establish that just because they played last year does not mean they play this year. If a player thinks he is entitled to a position, you have problems. I want everyone to be hungry. I want everyone working hard every day.

Another thing we preach and demand from the players is that team concept overrules everything. I believe the team is the more important than individuals. I believe in team, and I am not going to change the way I think. If the player is a team player, he can play for me. If a player thinks he is entitled and worries about himself instead of the team, he may not dress for the games. He definitely will not travel, and if he needs help with his transfer, I will help him. I do not get mad at them, but they will not be on the team.

The last thing I have listed is competitive spirit. Everything we do in this program will be a competition of some kind. In the weight room, we compete. We keep track of the wins and losses and make it important. The competitive spirit is what buoys us during the nonconference schedule. We play a tough nonconference schedule, and the conference is very competitive. If you do not want to compete against good football teams, you do not belong at East Carolina. We develop whatever we believe in, and we want to be known for those principles in practice. You should design your practices around those principles. If you want to have a competitive spirit, you have to practice that way.

If you want your team to be aggressive, you have to coach them aggressively. If you want them to have great enthusiasm, you have to coach with great enthusiasm. You play the way you practice. If you do not like the way you practice, you will not like the way you play in games. You are what you are. I had this same conversation with the team before I came down here.

The game of football has not changed. The team that blocks and tackles the best wins the game. The team that does the best job of blocking and tackling has a strong background in fundamentals. We lost many good players last year to graduation. Last year in Greenville, North Carolina, 28 NFL teams had representatives in here. There were not just assistant coaches, but some head coaches were there. We have to get better players, but we will never neglect the fundamental areas within our team.

FUNDAMENTALS

- Tackling drills
- Pursuit drill
- Individual drills
  ✓ Defensive back drills
  ✓ Linebacker drills
- Defensive line drills

We tackle every day. We run a tackling circuit. That allows the defensive coaches to coach all the players on defense.

The first drill in the tackling circuit is a two-man pursuit drill. We do this drill in a five-yard square area. The first man attacks the ballcarrier with outside leverage. The second man comes from the inside, keeps inside leverage, and attack the ballcarrier. The first tackler shoots for the outside armpit. He shoots his hips and never leaves his feet. He runs through the tackle. If he does not make the tackle, he forces the ball back to the second tackler.

The second drill is a shuffle tackle. We have four dummies on the ground. The tackler shuffles along the dummies, punching down on each one. At end of the dummies is a blocker. The tackler rips across the blocker and makes a tackle on the ballcarrier coming from the inside.

The third drill is a cut drill. The tackler aligns over an offensive blocker. The blocker shoots at the legs of the tackler. The tackler plays the cut block and comes outside for the tackle on the back.

The fourth drill is a shuffle over bags drill. The tackler has to run over four bags on the ground, keeping his shoulders square. At the end of the drill, he makes the tackle on the back. The back runs five yards behind the bags and cuts up at the end of the bags.

DEFENSIVE BACK DRILLS

- Double move
- Reach and grab
- Reaction

- Fade 'em
- Crossover and pedal
- Sequence

We work these drills with our defensive backs. I know most of you do the same drill. I want to talk about them briefly. The first drill is a double move drill. We start the defensive back backpedaling up the field. With an arm movement, we bring them forward. We give the second movement, and the back has to break back in a trail catch-up position. We throw the ball, and he intercepts.

The reach and grab drill is a position drill. We start the receiver and defensive back on the sidelines. The receiver faces the field, and the defender faces out-of-bounds. On the snap, the receiver runs across the field. The defensive back has to flip his hips and turn to the receiver. He gets into a run with him, and tries to knock the ball down. He reaches with his frontside hand for the ball, and the backside hand grabs around the receiver's waist.

The reaction drill in a mirror drill with the defender matching the receiver moves. It is a footwork drill. We start the drill with the hands behind the back. The defensive back mirrors the action of the receiver and maintains leverage. The receiver uses a series of three step cuts. After we do the drill with the hands behind the back, we work with the hands and footwork together. On each cut, the defender punches the receiver with his inside hand. Just remember, the DNA of a player may not let you play press coverage. If you do not have the players do not play the coverage.

The fade 'em drill is a reaction drill to the deep ball. The emphasis on this drill is to squeeze the receiver and cut the receiver off. We want to force him to the sidelines. We teach playing through the hands in this drill.

The crossover and pedal drill is mainly a safety drill. It teaches the safety to use a zone turn to get to the zone landmark and convert to a pedal once they are in position. We break them forward and throw them a ball on the end of the drill.

The sequence drill tests the memory of the defensive back. We set up four cones in the drill. The cones are set up in a vertical fashion and have

the numbers one through four assigned to them. The coach gives the backs a sequence of numbers, and the backs react to each number in sequence. The coach may say, "One, three, two, finish." The back pedals to the one cone, plants, and breaks up to the starting point. He changes direction and reacts to the three cone and returns. He backpedals again to the two cone and finishes. The back has to remember the numbers, react to the cones, and not look down. It teaches footwork, change of direction, reaction, and body position.

LINEBACKER DRILLS

- Sled punch
- Hat and hands
- Reroute
- Bags
- Drops
- Run step

The sled punch drill has the linebacker shoot his hands into a one-man sled dummy. He punches with the hands, rips off the dummy, and sprints to a cone behind the sled. At that point, he changes direction on the coach's signal. The coach stands at the rear of the sled and give him a right or left redirect movement as he rips off the sled.

We do the hat and hands drill in pads. We put blockers on linebackers. The blocker comes off at an angle at the linebacker. The linebacker reacts to the direction, strikes with his hat and hands, rips off the block, and makes a form tackle on a ballcarrier. Always finish the drill with some kind of skill. Do a tackle, pick up a fumble, or change directions. You want the linebacker to cross the face of the blocker.

We use the reroute drill in our pass defense scheme. At the college level, the defender can be very physical with the receivers all over the field as long as the ball is not in the air. In this drill, the linebacker drops, punches the tight end going out, and reacts back to an underneath receiver coming across the field. The linebacker has to stay square so he can see crossing routes. With our base personnel in the game, we play zone coverage. The linebacker wants to disrupt the route of tight end running through his zone. We must learn how to reroute the slot receiver in our zone coverage. The key is not to get off balance or overextended. He wants to stay behind his pads and under control.

In the drop drill, you teach the linebackers their landmarks in their zones. You have to teach them how to get to the landmark and what to do once they arrive. We start them out with a reaction shuffle to the coach's movement. His footwork is a read step, shuffle to identify, open to a 45-degree angle, and drop. Once he gets to the area, he squares his shoulders, feels the receivers, and keys the quarterback's eyes. Our linebackers key the backs instead of linemen.

For any position on the defense, if the players know what they are doing, they play faster. We know that clear minds lead to fast legs. Cloudy minds lead to slow legs. It is not what the coach knows; it is what he can teach the players. Coaches should remember, if the players make the same mistakes repeated, the coach is teaching that technique and allowing the player to play it. It is not a play problem. It is a coaching problem. If they are not clear what to do, the coach needs to try a new approach to saying the same thing.

DEFENSIVE LINE DRILL

- Shuffle and strike
- Hoop
- Hand punch
- Run reaction

The key to any defense is the defensive line. The best defensive line won the Super Bowl this year. It is the key to winning championships at any level. Auburn had the best defensive line in the country, and they won the national championship. It starts inside with the tackles. If the defense is a 3-4, you must have a great noseguard. If the defense is 4-3, you need two great tackles in the middle. It starts in there.

When you teach the defensive line, the first thing is the power step. You can work the shuffle and strike drill on a sled, hand shield, or people. We want the footwork coordinated with the punch. The punch comes from the ground into the target. It is a short, quick strike with the thumbs up with the elbows in tight to the ribs. The power comes

from the ankles through the knees into the hips. We want the shuffle low without the shoulder coming up and down as they shuffle to the right or left. We want the punch coming with the power step.

We run the hoop drill to teach body lean on the pass rush. It teaches the defensive lineman how to lean in to get to the quarterback. We use towels or scrimmage vests inside the hoop and make them pick them up as they run the hoop.

We use the hand punch drill to teach getting off blocks. We work this drill in a sequence of three repetitions. There are three dummy linemen standing in a staggered line two yards apart. The linemen shoot the hands and extend the arms. He shuffles up the field and repeats the drill on the second dummy. He does that rep three times. On the third time, he rips, swims, or shrugs to disengage from the block, and makes a tackle. We teach them to explode, play behind the pads, and punch with the same foot and same hand.

The run reaction drill teaches the defensive linemen reactions to special blocks. We teach them how to play a pull, trap, counter, double-team, as well as the single block. We teach them how to spill blocks and get to the second level. In this drill, we teach the entire blocking scheme.

When you teach a tight 3-technique defender, he cannot allow a reach block. It will happen. However, the defensive lineman is never wrong if he is attacking and creating a new line of scrimmage. The offense may reach the defensive lineman, but if he pushes the offensive lineman into the next gap, he is doing good work.

I want to get into some scheme talk. When you decide which players to play, I believe you need to put skills on the field. Our safeties are fast linebackers. A linebacker is a fast defensive end. A defensive end is a very fast tackle. You gain speed by substituting and moving the down linemen. A principle we never use is to take strength and try to fix a weakness. Substitute speed at your personnel positions. Players may not want to move at first, but they want to play and will accept it.

When we talk to our defense, we use the same language at each position. We name all the running plays and pass routes. We use that terminology with our players to identify schemes runs by the offense. We call the off-tackle power the power-O. The isolation play is an iso. We have China and smash routes. Everyone on the defense is on the same page, and they know a play when we call it. We do the same thing with techniques. We talk about armpits and numbers. That way, when a player comes to the sideline, the coach and player can talk and understand what the other one is saying. It is the language, lingo, and nomenclature.

Our base defense is Hawk. Hawk allows us to declare the strength of our defense toward the strength of the offensive formation via a Rip or Liz call. We can call the front to the tight end, receivers, toward the running back, away from the running back, or to the field or boundary.

The diagram shows the offense with 21 personnel (two backs, one tight end) with a strength of the defense to the left (Liz) (Diagram #1).

The left end is responsible for the D gap. The 3-technique tackle aligns on the outside shoulder of the guard and plays the B gap. The nose aligns in a weakside 1 technique and plays the weakside A gap. The right end is a C-gap player.

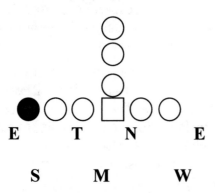

Diagram #1. Hawk

Position	Alignment	Key
Left end	9 technique	Tight end
Tackle	3 technique	Guard
Nose	1 technique	Guard
Right end	No tight end 5 technique	Tackle
Will	40 technique	Near back to block pattern
Mike	10 technique	Same as W
Sam	50 technique	Same as M

The Will linebacker aligns five yards off the ball and plays in a 40 technique head-up the weakside offensive tackle. If he has run toward him, he is a B-gap player. If the flow goes away, he flows to the strongside. On passes, he has the seam to flat on the #2 receiver to his side. The Mike linebacker is an A-gap play on runs toward him and a B-gap player on runs away. On a pass, he drops to the #3 receiver. The Sam linebacker has the C gap on runs to and flows to the A gap on runs away. His pass coverage is a seam to flat dropper on the #2 receiver to his side.

We play the 3 technique in an inside foot of the defender to the outside foot of the offensive lineman. The nose plays in a 1 technique on the backside guard. We call it a G technique. He aligns on the inside eye of the offensive guard. The reason we put him in a G technique is offenses attack the defense in the bubble areas of the defense. The 9-technique end must have D-gap integrity. That is his piece of ground. He has to defend, protect, and attack that piece of grass. The Sam linebacker aligns in a loose 50 technique, favoring the tight end.

We are an attacking front in our base defense. We do not sit back and read. We are in attack mode in the defensive line and from the linebackers. We attack our gap responsibilities and get downhill on the ball. When we blitz from this front, the intensity gets to another level. That is the general concept of the base defense.

In the secondary, we play cover 8 or quarters, with some variations. Our base cover is 83 (Diagram #2).

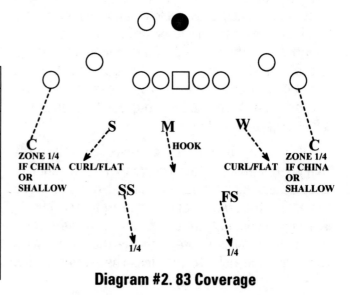

Diagram #2. 83 Coverage

Position	Alignment	Assignment	Technique
Sam	5 yards off nipple position cover #2	Drop on #2 see #3 curl/flat	Read guard to #2
Mike	4 yards off favor the back	Drop #3, see #2 hook to expand	Match #3 back
Will	Same as Sam	Sam as Sam	Same as Sam
LCB	7 yards off outside shade hard 8 press bail	Man #1 on all routes except shallow or China	Read step, press, press bail
SS	10 yards off 1 yard inside #2 WR	Pattern read, quarter defender	Read step
FS	Same as SS	Same as SS	Same as SS
RCB	Same as LCB	Same as LCB	Same as LCB

The coverage is four defensive backs playing four-deep coverage. We have eight-man support from a seven-man front. In this scheme, we involve the safeties in our support game because of their reads on the #2 receiver. From their reads, they can shuffle down into the box from the top.

We blend a cover 3 off the 83 coverage. We roll the strong safety or free safety down and play three-deep behind that scheme. We also play a quarter-quarter-half scheme from this base coverage. The coverage allows us to have flexibility of coverage against all plays, play-action passes, and designed to leverage all pass routes.

We walk off the Sam and Will linebackers, and they read the #2 receivers. They cover down on the #2 receivers, but they key the guard for their run key. If they get a high hat, they play pass. If the guard comes upfield, he plays run. We number the receivers the universal way. The nipple position is a slight inside leverage on that receiver. In the chart, if the defenders read two receivers, they exchange those receivers in a crossing type of pattern. If a defender reads #2 but sees #3, there is a chance he will play the #3 receiver.

The depths of the outside linebackers give them a chance to see the run keys and at the same time play the route patterns the receivers run. The Mike linebacker is a step closer to the line of scrimmage because he plays draw action by the running back (#3). The depth of the secondary depends on down-and-distance. Their number alignments are general rules. They may be closer or deeper, depending on the type of play.

TERMS IN COVER 83

Clue: A term used in conjunction with cover 8 versus a trips set with an open #1 backside. Clue allows us to defend three verticals to the trips with the strong safety taking #3's vertical and the corner splitting #1's and #2's vertical release. If no vertical threat from any of the three exists, go back to green rules with the corner and strong safety.

Red: A weak roll technique away from clue to assist the backside corners, or a call we can make if the wide receiver has a cut down split. Will is a curl player.

Shallow: Only to the single wide receiver side to the free safety. If the wide receiver goes under right now, free safety will drop in or drive the route.

Using the clue rule against the 3x1 set, the Sam linebacker aligns five yards off the #2 receiver with inside leverage (Diagram #3). He drops off the #2 receiver and is a curl/flat defender. If the receiver runs the wheel route, he carries it upfield. The Mike linebacker reads the #3 receiver and mirrors his drop. If #3 breaks outside, he looks for the #2 receiver coming inside. The corner aligns at nine yards and sees all three receivers.

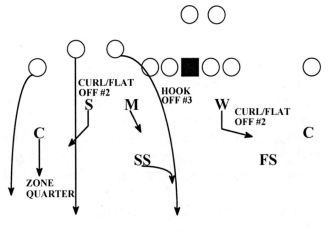

Diagram #3. Clue vs. 3x1

We refer to these rules as "green" rules. The strong safety aligns at 10 yards and pattern reads off the #3 receiver. If #3 runs an outside breaking pattern, he looks to the outside for a threat coming to him. If the #3 receiver releases vertical, he plays him. The backside defenders read the same keys, except there is no #2 receiver involved. The Will linebacker is a curl/flat defender, and the free safety pattern reads. His alignment is one yard outside the offensive tackle at a depth of 10 yards.

The "red" call is a cover-2 adjustment to the base coverage (Diagram #4). It is a cloud roll by the corner. The corner rolls up and becomes a flat defender. The red coverage does not affect anyone except the corner and Will linebacker. The Will linebacker is a curl defender and collisions all patterns coming to that area. He wants to collision the receiver or become inside force on a run. The corner aligns at seven yards or in a press alignment. He is the flat defender and forces the run his way. He wants to funnel the release of the #1 receiver. The free safety plays as a half defender. He uses a zone turn and crossover run to get into the half field behind the corner area. When he reaches his landmark, he backpedals.

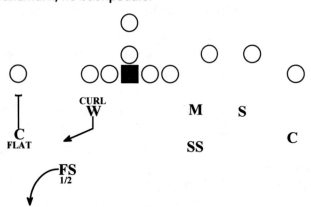

Diagram #4. Red

We have a shallow call to handle the crossing pattern by the #1 receiver (Diagram #5). The free safety has inside leverage on the #1 receiver and can intercept the route of the #1 receiver on a shallow drag route coming to the inside. The free safety jumps the underneath route. The corner sees the shallow and overlaps the backside half of the coverage. The Will linebacker has the #2 receiver coming out of the backfield.

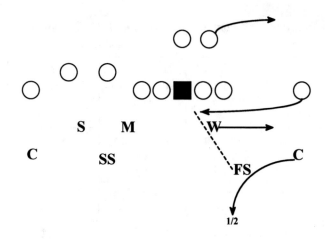

Diagram #5. Shallow

We have another variation called 83 special (Diagram #6), It is a three-under, four-deep concept designed to combat four verticals with all four defensive backs when the offense aligns in a 3x1 formation. The special has a built-in wheel call for the corner. The free safety reads the #3 receiver to the trips side of the formation. If he runs vertical, the free safety wants to get on top of his route. If he runs outside or across the field, the free safety looks back to the #1 receiver to his side.

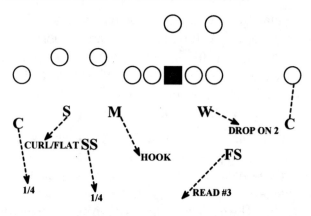

Diagram #6. 83 Special

The Will linebacker and backside corner are alone with no coverage over the top if #3 goes vertical. The backside corner plays aggressive man coverage on the #1 receiver. The Will linebacker matches the pattern of the #2 receiver in the backfield if he comes to his side. The Sam linebacker drops and sees #2 to #3 receivers. The Mike linebacker drops on the #3 receiver, but must see the #2 receiver on an inside breaking route. If #3 goes out, #2 probably comes in. The strong safety pattern reads off the route of the #2 receiver.

The corner has to play the outside quarter because he has to play the wheel route. If the wheel route is part of the combination pattern run by the receivers, the corner has to play it.

I want to go over the run fits quickly before I stop. If there is one back in the backfield, we are fitting one defender into one gap in the defensive line. If there are two backs in the backfield, we have two linebackers fitting into one gap on an isolation play (Diagram #7). In a two-back situation, on the backside isolation play, the Will linebacker attacks the fullback in the B gap with outside leverage. The Mike linebacker comes over the top and attacks the B gap with inside leverage. The Sam linebacker has C gap on runs toward him and A gap on runs away. Everyone else has a single gap responsibility.

If the isolation goes to the strongside, the Mike fills the A gap with outside leverage on the block, and the Will linebacker flows into the A gap and has inside leverage on the ballcarrier. We refer to the two defenders fit as "trapping the back."

Our door is always open if you would like to visit. I want you to come visit us at East Carolina because we do some good things at ECU. You have

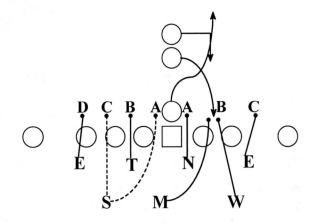

Diagram #7. Run Fits

been great, and it is a pleasure to talk football with you. The coaching profession is great, and I love it. I love the teaching, coaching, and preaching. Coaches are in a position to be a dad and counselor to your players. Some players come from environments that do not offer much for their development as a man. I know we talk about the winning, but the program is all about the development of the players as good people. That is our mission and duty. Thank you for your attention.

KICKOFF COVERAGE AND PUNT RETURNS

Louisiana State University

Thank you. I am proud to be here representing the Louisiana State University and our coaching staff. I was fortunate enough to hear Coach Bill Snyder speak today. I have sat in those chairs as you did and listened to a coach of his caliber and experience. I love listening to the coaches who have great experience in this game. I promise you, I sat in those chairs just like you did when he spoke.

The older you get, the more philosophic you get about the things we are doing. I do not know if coaching football is what we all are doing today. Some of us understand that. We are sharing the lives of the people around us. We are sharing the lives of our peers, assistant coaches, and the team. We are enjoying the laughs and sadness that comes with this game.

Every time I come to Las Vegas, it takes me back to my days with my father. He worked in the steel and trucking business in Ohio. He worked hard all his life and taught me how to play seven-card stud poker. We played cards at the Italian-American Club. He would give me 20 dollars and allow me to play. He told me if I lost the 20 dollars I had to sit there and watch him play. However, if I won anything over the 20 dollars it was mine.

When I coached at the University of Colorado, they assigned me to recruit Las Vegas. I felt like this was divine intervention for me to be recruiting in Las Vegas. When I recruited here, there were 10 schools in the city. In the early 1980s, I can remember going into Bishop Gorman High School when they had a grass field. This entire area has grown so much over the years.

The fact that LSU does not recruit in this state is a mistake. There are many good players here. This year at LSU, we won 11 football games. The players we had were competitive, tough, and great people. I have a great staff. It is amazing the kinds of things

that become newsworthy. How many coaches in here have plucked a blade of grass and put it in your mouth? I did that, and they asked my son in school if he ate grass, too.

The great thing about this sport is the people that coach it. It is the reason Coach Bill Snyder, you coaches, and I are here today. The biggest piece of advice I got was from my coach, Bo Schembechler, at Michigan. He believed we could get to the top. He set a level of performance so we had to fight like hell to get on top of the game. Once we got to it, he told us we had reached a goal. He told us we were tough and this was how we needed to operate. He told us this was our culture and this is what we do. I did not have any idea what he was doing for me.

In this profession, you can turn around and see friends and players you have coached. You realize that you have a shared experience with them. and they are taking the best from that experience through life with them.

I went to Coach Schembechler's funeral. I felt that summed up football for me. I was a very moderate player at Michigan and had to fight like hell to get on the field. At the funeral, I was at a church with 400 people connected to the coach by football. I truly enjoyed that relationship. I realized what had happened to me as a young man.

When I took my recruiting visit to Michigan, I showed up with a pair of blue jeans on a coat hanger with a sweater over the top of them. I did not even have a dop kit. At the funeral, I was with people that had fought for victory at Michigan on the fields and had learned so many valuable life lessons along the way.

Those are the lessons we talk about today. I am a better coach because of what I learned at Michigan. I believe I am a better coach because I am a father. I have four children. My oldest daughter,

Kathryn, is a 16-year-old swimmer. One of the toughest things I had to do was accept her goals and wants for her life.

We are a close-knit family and spend many weekends as a family doing family activities together. Kathryn told me she was not swimming with a coach who could motivate her or a swim club that could get the most out of her. She wanted to go to The Bolles School in Jacksonville, Florida, to swim for them. They have won 20 straight swimming titles in Florida. I asked her to quit swimming and play some other sport so we could keep the family together. She told me she wanted to swim fast and that was the best opportunity for her to do it. It was a tough decision, but I respected what she wanted to do and what she had to give up in the process of realizing her dreams.

I have a 14-year-old son, Manny, who just had an emergency appendectomy. I spent five days with him while he was fighting through it. I played a little Texas hold 'em poker last night. He texted me this morning and asked me how I did. I told him I was up a little and down a little, but ended up breaking even. He texted me back and told me, "Go big, or go home."

I have two other children. Macy is my seven-year-old. She plays basketball and recently tried out to sing the national anthem at a LSU baseball game. My other son is Ben. He is left-handed. Left-handed people are different. My wife played college point guard at Central Michigan and coached basketball for a time in college. I have an athletic family.

Ben was going to be the family's non-athlete. He was the one into Pokémon. The Miles family had weekend practices. Everyone got a ball and glove or bat, and we went out to play and have fun. This particular weekend, I felt it was time for Ben to learn to catch and throw. He had his glove on his right hand and had the glove down on the ground waiting for me to roll the ball to him. I rolled the ball slightly to the left of where his glove was on the ground. He looked at me and said, "If you cannot hit the glove, I quit."

I want to tell a story about my sons getting involved with a youth league football program. I was not worried about Manny because he was older and highly competitive. I was worried about Ben because he had never done anything that physical. At one practice, Ben left one of his football cleats at home. He played the entire practice with one shoe. After the practice was over, the coach called the team together, had Ben come to the front, and commended him for going the entire practice with only one shoe and doing everything the coach asked of him. He made a positive example of my son.

That gesture was a turning point in Ben's life. It changed his attitude completely. He became motivated and was totally involved with the program. He grew a chest and was proud of what he was doing. Had the coach made fun of him or given it a negative spin, Ben would never have played an organized sport again.

The reality of the whole deal is I owe that coach a debt of gratitude. The impact coaches have on the lives of your men and players is invaluable. Saying the right things can mean all the difference in a player's life and attitude about what he is doing. The encouragement and direction these coaches can give their players is priceless. This profession is an important one for the development of our children. They can grow up with the values we hope they cherish.

That youth league coach built a monument of success that day for my son. At the same time, he built that monument to the other players on that team. It was like Bo telling us we were tough, about our culture, and what we do. We do the same thing at LSU.

I have a number of things I want to do today. I have some ideas on special teams I want to share with you. I have a piece we put together for our team. It is how we reconcile our games. I will show you that and some of the recurring attitudes I talked about earlier. There are other clips included in the film that have become a part of LSU. (Film)

The idea is you paint the picture you want your team to be. You tell them how you expect them to play. They do not have to play perfectly, but they have to strive for it and play like it. When they do, you praise them for it, point it out, and make it a focal point.

In that film, you saw clips from the national championship game of 2008. You saw clips of LSU players who now play in the NFL. You saw starter and second-team players. The culture that football creates is a very violent one. The culture created says, "Football is different." It says we will work harder. You have heard the term "swagger." I was not sure what it meant until I got a feel for it the way it has developed at our place.

If you say you have swagger, you have to bust your butt. If you say you have swagger, you have to do hard things routinely. If you say you have swagger, you have to knock someone on his back. If you say you have swagger, you play for LSU. We want to celebrate great plays. We enjoy the event of celebrating with our team.

I have been on staffs and at places where they say, "We are not very good at that." When you make that statement, you are correct. It becomes a fact. When I arrived at LSU, we were 78th in the nation in special teams play. I coached for the Dallas Cowboys. Those experiences led me to believe that we could win with special teams alone. When I came to LSU, I used that approach. We knew we would play great offense and defense. The only thing left to do was to play great special teams. In four of the last five years, we finished in the top five in the country in overall special teams play. In that period, we led the SEC twice in total special teams play.

I am not telling you the scheme or players are perfect in the execution of special teams at LSU. I am telling you there is a want and a desire to play great special teams at LSU. It is the approach of the coaching staff and the approach of how you organize the day that makes a difference.

GOALS FOR ATTACK

- Hold the opponent to 20 yards or less on the return.
- We want the opponent to start inside the 25-yard line.
- Create a turnover with contact.
- Get a touchback.

When we refer to the kickoff coverage team, we call them "attack." We are not covering kickoffs; we are going downfield to attack someone. Before we leave the hotel to go to the game site, we have a team meeting. It is the last time the head coach can give an overview, which is not dressed with the emotion of the locker room. I tell the attack team what they do will set the tone physically for the game.

When Ryan Baker was a sophomore, he played on the attack team. He made his way onto the field as a starting linebacker with his play on special teams. He made great physical plays.

To get a touchback is the best way to cover a kickoff. If you can kick the ball out of the end zone, there is no return. We have a philosophy that goes with our special teams play.

GOALS FOR COVERAGE

- We want to have a complicated kicking chart.
- We want hang time on the kickoff.
- The target area for the ball is from the numbers to the hash marks.
- We look for the indicator as to what type of kickoff return is coming.

We can sky-kick the ball, which forces the return team to fair catch the football. It puts the ball in the hands of an up receiver who does not usually run back kicks. We use surprise onside kicks if the situation dictates that we do it. We kick the ball into voids in the kickoff return alignments. We kick ground balls and use any method to disrupt the timing of a return. We move the kick chart around and give calls that allow us to cover the ball.

We want to kick the ball toward the sidelines to cut the field down for the coverage team. If you kick the ball between the numbers and sideline, that is the place we want it. What you do not want to do is kick the ball out-of-bounds. We aim it down the hash marks. That gives a cushion against the sidelines. It allows the coverage team to squeeze and cut down the running lanes.

Teams will give indicators or tips to where the return will come. There is always something in the return team that gives you an idea about where they hope to run the ball. You have to look for it. Look for the depth of certain players. Look for players that move around in the alignment of the team. Watch the depth of the blockers in the scheme. The return team will always give you a clue. If you can find it and give it to your team, that is a big advantage.

If we can find the indicator after the ball kicks off, we yell that out as we run down the field. If all the blockers run in one direction or two blockers go together in one direction, that is the indictor. However, you have to stay in lanes and converge on the ball. If the kick returner stops, tries to redirect, or starts to dance around, we should punish him.

The two characteristics for a good kick coverage person are speed and violent contact. Our contain players are not trying to keep the ball inside of them. They will knock the ballcarrier out if they get the chance. Their purpose is not to turn the ball into the rest of the team. Their goal is to make the tackle.

When we cover, we have two contain players, and they contain at the level of the ball. We gave up a big return in the Cotton Bowl against Texas A&M University. The reason for it was the kickoff man. He was three yards less in his position to make the tackle. The vice players to the side of the ball want to keep the ball seven yards to the inside and seven yards to the outside as they cover wherever the ball goes. Once we reach a five-yard spot at the sideline, we work the vice slowly across that five-yard spot to close on the ball.

In the kickoff, the coverage team beats the return blockers with speed and avoidance. We do not take on blockers. We use our speed to run past them. The first part of the coverage is the speed zone (Diagram #1). In that zone, you do not take on any blockers. We avoid all blocks in that area if possible.

When we get within 10 yards of the football, that is the defensive zone or contact zone. In that area, you cannot avoid blocks. The coverage team has to play through the blocker to the ball. When we get into the defensive zone, the coverage team has to press on the blockers and get to the ball. If we attempt to run around a block in this area, we open holes in the coverage.

In my background, we did not do these drills. However, coverage players need to know how to get to the ball. When we drill these types of skills, we use dummies to knock the coverage players off their path (Diagram #2). What we want them to do as they avoid a blocker is get back in their coverage lane as quick as they can. We want to put

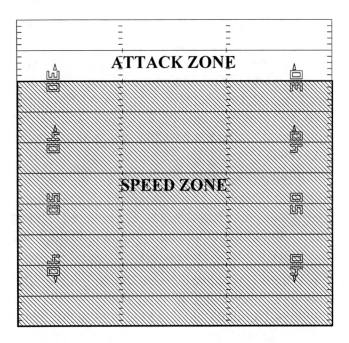

Diagram #1. Speed Zone/Attack Zone

the blocker behind us and in a position where he has to block us in the back. We call that stacking the blocker.

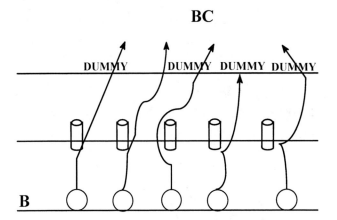

Diagram #2. Coverage Drill

In the speed zone, we want to avoid as much contact as possible, but we do not want to create holes in the coverage. We had a walk-on player who we used to block punts. He was the punt blocker against our punt team. He became so effective we gave him at shot at playing special teams. He is now on scholarship and one of our leaders on our special teams.

We run the live kick cover maybe three times a year. We do run it at least one time a year. We do the drill as an evaluation. In this drill, you find out who will kick the crap out of someone. In this drill, we have to see the want for contact, acceleration, and tackling ability. We want corners, safeties, walk-ons, and all the players who have to be tough. We want players who have to show and exhibit toughness. If you are a badass, you want to be on this team.

If the blocker turns and shows you his rear end, that means he will try to push the coverage players to the side away from his butt. The coverage player attacks to the butt side as he runs by. He does not cross in front of the hands and arms.

When the coverage personnel attack the blockers, they want to drop their shoulders to minimize the blocking surface. They want to rip through attempted blocks in the speed zone. We want to skim or rip through without losing speed and get back on the path.

The defensive zone occurs 10 yards from the ball. In this zone, the coverage player attacks the blocker with his hands (Diagram #3). He sinks his hips and gets leg drive through the blocker. He cannot run around the block to the ball. He has to play through the blocker. It is the same with a defender taking on an offensive blocker. He has to pound the blocker and drive with his legs. The technique used in this part of the coverage is striking with the hands, extending the arms, and getting off the block.

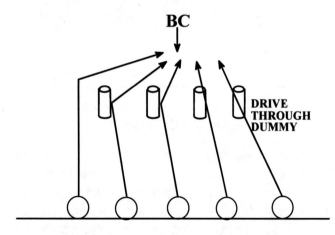

Diagram #3. Attack the Blocker

The contain coverage player takes the containment to the ball. He does not stand outside and wait for the ball to break to him. If he encounters a block, he keeps his outside arm free and squeezes

on the level with the ball. If he is unblocked, he squeezes and takes the containment to the ball. When he tackles the ballcarrier, he wants to put his head upfield on the ballcarrier. If he misses, he wants the ballcarrier to go back inside his tackle and not outside.

If there is a kick-out block coming from the inside, the contain player strikes him with his inside hand and keeps his outside hand free with the ability to have leverage to the field. If the ballcarrier bounces, the contain player has to get out and up into the field. If they try to double the contain man out of the play, the contain player takes on the outside blocker. The coverage player inside the contain player has to see the situation and play into that lane.

As the coverage players come down the field, they are communicating with one another. They are communicating the scouting report indicators or indicators they have picked up as the ball is in the air. When the coverage player raises his hand, he tells the coverage players around him what he intends to do.

If the contain runner raises his hand, he tells the man next to him that he is going to contain. That tells that runner that he must stay outside and he cannot knife to the inside and leave a lane between him and the contain runner.

When the coverage runner raises his hand, he bases it on an indication that comes from the game plan. Many times, the runner raising his hand is a reminder for him to scream out what he sees as he goes down the field. It is also a great opportunity for us as coaches to realize what they are doing on the field.

Communication on the kickoff is a tough. If the runner is going down the field and everyone calls right, the defender knows he can gain a coverage lane to his right. That is an advantage to the coverage team. The problem with that is losing lane integrity. If the coverage team knows the ball is going to the right, they cannot vacate their lanes and run to the right side of the field. The ball could start there and end up in some place totally different.

When we kick the ball, the target is deep right or left. We want the ball kicked between the hash marks and the numbers. We want it closer to the numbers if possible. If the coverage player beats the blockers and the ballcarrier is running undefended, we should kill him. That is the mentality of the coverage players coming downfield. If the ballcarrier does not explode into the blocking scheme, he does not have a chance of returning the ball. If he stops, delays, or stutters, he is dead. Even if he stops and you fly by him, he is dead.

GOALS FOR THE BANDITS

- Block a punt.
- Average 10 yards on the return.
- Never let the ball hit the ground.
- Allow no turnovers.
- Score or set up a score.
- Stop the gunner.

When we talk about bandits this is our punt block/return team. We want to take something away from the offense. We want to steal yardage or steal the ball by blocking the punt. We are not going to be the punt return team; we are going to be bandits.

We had the best punt returner in the country last year, but we had to teach him to field the ball. He had the best ball skills in the country. You have to teach return men that you field a bounding ball differently than the punted ball. If you do not have a return man you can trust, tell him to get out of the way. If you can stop a bounding ball from going 10 extra yards or time the bounce and get a seven-yard return, that is important field position. However, you have to use discretion with the return man. If you do not trust him to make the tough catch, tell him to get away from it.

If you can return a punt over the 50-yard line, that should set up a score. The offense has to gain 10 yards to put you in field goal range. If the gunners are making all the tackles on punt returns, you have to stop the gunners. If we can take them out of the play, we can return the ball for good yardage.

We use a technique called pop and drive. We do not do this every week because it is difficult to do. We want to take the line of scrimmage. If the defenders get their hands on the ground and show that they are coming after the punt, it puts the

fear of God in the punter. It also makes the blockers want to block the defenders.

The defender aligns looking into the gap, at the ball and not at the blocker who is supposed to block him. The defender shows an intention of going into the gap and not at the blocker. If we can accomplish that, the advantage goes to the punt return team. The blockers do not release as fast and do not expect the defender to be blocking him at the line of scrimmage.

If we do not think we can influence them into not covering as hard and fast, we use a shuffle block on them. It is a basketball shuffle technique to stay in front of the coverage. You need to chart the punt tackles. Find out who is making the tackles, and block him.

We coach a punt safe return. One third of our calls in the punt return game are punt-safe calls. A punt safe means we are playing for a fake by the punting team. We play regular defensive alignments against the punting team. We also can return out of a punt safe formation.

We also use a sit and fit drill (Diagram #4). When we punt the ball down the field, the coverage team may get in front of the punt returners. When we field the ball and start back up the field, the coverage team starts to sit down and gets ready to change directions to attack the ball. The return team trailing the coverage continues to run hard as the coverage team begins to sit down. As the coverage starts to change direction, the return blockers sit and fit into the defenders and block them. Coaches need to describe what the coverage

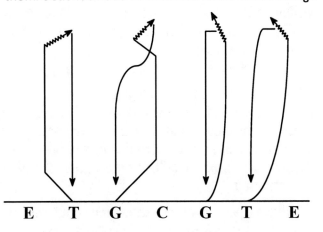

Diagram #4. Sit and Fit

team will do so the return team can get into position to fit their blocks on the coverage.

We use a technique we call "arm bar." This technique gives the blocker a chance to block a coverage player who has his back to him. If the blocker is in the trail position on his man, he can still block him without a clip. The coverage player will sit down some time during his approach on the ballcarrier. If he sits down early, the blocker hustles down, sits and fits on the coverage player, and blocks the coverage. If it looks as if the coverage player is not going to sit down, he may slow down. The blocker gets even with the defender and drives his outside hand across the chest of the coverage player. He will hit something that will help him move the coverage away from the back.

We time the players in this drill and evaluate them. We know who is busting his butt and who is putting in time. We work the drill in a half-line situation, and it is easy to identify the techniques.

When we talk to our punt team, we talk about reading intentions of the punt return team. If the defender is standing up and looking at the blocker, that means they intend to return the punt, and we release through the blocking assignment immediately. If there is a defender in front of the blocker with his hand on the ground and has his head down, we know he is trying to block the coverage. On that technique, we release quickly. We want to coach that to our return team so the punting team does not know whether we are coming for the block or blocking for the return.

On the pop and drive technique, we want to influence the blocker to sit back and block. When he does, we drive into him and push him back. That widens the coverage player out of his path and gives us a chance to return up the middle.

We practice in the half-line situation so we can put our good punt personnel against our good return team people. It lets us view them with good competition. First team offense versus first team defense is not a good drill, but it works in the half-line situation.

I have a piece I want to show you about who we are. We have a 20-hour rule in college and cannot spend the amount of time on films as we were able to before the 20-hour rule. In the old days when I was in high school and college, I watched every snap of the game film with my coach. The head coach stood in the middle of the room with the offense on one side of the room and the defense on the other side. Everyone gets to experience the game again together. With the 20-hour rule, you cannot do that.

If you do not let your position coaches coach their players in a timely fashion, it is not fair to them. You cannot have the offensive line watching the defense play as they would if they saw the entire game film. We have to allow the position coaches to make corrections on the aspect to their players.

When we watch film as a team, it is what coaches pick out for them to see. It says who we are as an offense, defense, and special teams unit. We do this every week no matter what the outcome of the game is.

This is not a highlight film. We show things that demonstrate who we are. We show the quarterback getting blasted and jumping up immediately. That shows his toughness. We show a substitute lineman playing for a player that went down in the game. We show an adjustment we made at halftime that helped us win a game. We show the protection schemes. It makes no difference what type of offense or defense you run; the choice of what you show is yours.

It is anything you want to show that tells your team what they are going to do to win. It defines us and tells the players who we are. We start practice at 6:30 in the morning. Around 7:15, we show them this film. You have the option of showing some things about who we are not as well. Excessive celebration penalties are bad penalties, particularly if it is in a tight game.

You show them plays made in critical situations. We show them plays that the defense knows is coming and they know the defense worked. We practice those plays, and the players expect them to work in a game when the defense knows what is coming. That is who we are.

The anticipations exceed the expectations. Thank you very much.

OFFENSIVE LINE DRILLS AND FUNDAMENTALS

The University of Iowa

It really is an honor to be here. This is your clinic. If you have a question, raise your hand, and I will give you anything we do. Regardless of what type of team you are, the same fundamentals will apply. For 26 years, I coached from junior high school through high school. I learned more from making mistakes and failing just like all good coaches have done over the years. I have a lot of respect and admiration for the job that you do. You guys are the trainer, the strength coach, you mark the field, you are the father figure, and you do so many things that are positive for young kids. You have a huge influence on them. More so than anybody at the college level.

I love my job. Can you believe I am paid to work on football all day? I do not have to teach classes, I do not have to put up with administrators. It is a great job.

My presentation is nuts and bolts and fundamentals for offensive linemen. That is who we are, and we are interested in player development. We want to take a player and make him better. We are not going to try to outsmart somebody. We are going to try to outexecute them.

Three people have had an input in my presentation. The first guy is Kirk Ferentz, our head football coach at The University of Iowa. Kirk was a longtime offensive line coach at The University of Iowa with Coach Hayden Fry for many years. Then, he went to the NFL and was a line coach for Bill Belichick while at Cleveland. He was the line coach and assistant head coach with Ted Marchibroda with the Baltimore Ravens. Then, Coach Ferentz came back to Iowa, where he took a chance on me. Everything we do trickles down and comes from Kirk Ferentz and from his background.

The second guy that had an influence is Joe Moore. Many of the young guys may not know who Joe Moore is. Joe Moore was the line coach at the University of Notre Dame when they won a national championship. He was the line coach at the University of Pittsburgh when they won a national championship. Joe coached Hall of Famer Russ Grimm, who is now the line coach for the Phoenix Cardinals. A lot of Coach Ferentz's stuff came from Joe Moore, who was Kirk's high school coach.

The third person of influence is Joe Philbin. I do not think anyone in here will know who Joe Philbin is. Joe was the line coach at Iowa during my first two years when I coached the tight ends. He is now the offensive coordinator for the Green Bay Packers.

Those three guys are the coaches all of this comes from. Also, there might be a few things that I figured out along the way.

I want to explain the *how*. I want to explain about the why, but we are going to mostly focus on the how. I am going to cover what we do at Iowa. This is not the only way to do it. You are going to see some things that you may not agree with. That is okay. It does not mean that it is either right or wrong. I am going to tell you how we teach it and why we teach it a certain way. I hope you have an open mind to that.

Let me start with some general comments:
- Coach people, not positions
- Be simple
- Teach *what* to do
- Teach *how* to do it
- Few drills, apply to game

We coach people and not positions. It is important that we do that. Not everybody has the same learning style. Some kids are very visual learners. Other kids have a kinesthetic sense. They have to go through that skill and move around to get the feel for it. Some people are verbal learners. You have to be able to react to everyone's learning style. Some kids do not learn as well as others.

You may have to take a kid in a little earlier and keep him later and spend time with them. Everybody wants to coach the all-star offensive lineman. Unfortunately, you do not always have an all-star offensive lineman. We have to take that lineman in high school and make him the best lineman we can.

Sometimes we spend most of our time working with those good players, and we do not spend enough time on those other guys that are an important part of our team. If you can find a way to include them and make their role of value to where they feel they are a significant contributor, you have become a master coach. They may not make a huge impact on the field, but if you can make it to where they feel that they are a better man because they played for you in high school, then you have done something good for them.

The next thing is to be *simple*. You are probably going to say there is no way they can be that simple at Iowa. However, we are that simple. I am not very smart. I did get a 30 on the ACT. I got a 15 on it the first time and a 15 on it the second time. That adds up to 30.

It is important to teach *what* to do. What to do really amounts to assignments. Anybody can teach assignments. This guy blocks this guy. This other guy will block this other guy. That is important. We all have to know how to do that. But, that is only a part of it.

The depth of this presentation is going to be teaching *how* to do it. The *how* is teaching the technique, the fundamentals, and the corrections.

I plan to talk about six drills today. We only run four of the drills every day. We do the same drills from the very first day of camp, when we are in shorts and T-shirts, until the day before the bowl game. We do the same exact thing on the drill. It will not change because fundamentals do not change. These drills apply to the game.

I heard a quote this past summer at the Hall of Fame induction of Russ Grimm. Russ Grimm was with the Washington Redskins and part of the Hogs offensive line. He is now the offensive line coach for the Arizona Cardinals. To me, this is what football is all about. A quote by the late Joe Moore about offensive line play is worthy of reviewing.

There's no greater feeling than moving a man from point A to point B, against his will.

—Joe Moore

This is how we feel about football. You better be physical. You better want to impose your will on somebody else. You better want to move somebody off the ball. That is how we try to teach football. We are going to have that physical mentality. Our guys may not be the biggest and the fastest, but they will come after you.

PRINCIPLES IN RUN BLOCKING

- Stay square
- Keep your feet underneath you
- Chest on chest
- Create muscle memory/repetition

What do we mean by square? We mean staying square to the line of scrimmage. We tell everybody to be square to the line. We do not want to move off the line. Why do we want to be square? It is because the running back has two ways to go off the square lineman. This is what we learned in junior high football.

You do not want to get overextended and you want to keep your feet underneath you. We want to have our feet, our chest, our knees, and our toes all in the same line, eventually. When we make contact initially, we are going to have some momentum forward, but we want to come into balance or in a balanced position.

This is where we may differ from some of you. We want to get chest on chest. In run blocking, we want to close the distance between us and the defender. We want to get as close to the defender as we can. We do not teach leading with the hands. I saw some heads pop up on that one. We teach old-fashioned shoulder blocking. We want to get our pad on his pad. After a few seconds, we will get our hands more involved.

In pass blocking, it is just the opposite. In pass blocking, we want to have separation. I do not want him near me. Those of you who coach the defensive line, what do you teach them to do once they make contact? You teach them to get their hands up and to separate.

We are trying to create muscle memory through repetition. We are trying to get our eyes, our brain, and our central nervous system to send a message to our muscles in order to execute a skill. Blocking is the most complex skill in football. You are teaching someone to do something they do not know much about doing.

What I would like to spend the rest of my time on is talking about our five keys to success.

FIVE KEYS TO SUCCESS

- Eyes on aiming point
- First two steps
- Vertical leverage
- Horizontal leverage
- Backside knee

Our players hear the same things repeatedly in our team meetings and in our practices. We are just talking about the fundamentals.

What do I mean by eyes on the aiming point? The *eye* is a muscle. You are going to train your muscle to pick out different things. The first thing you are going to do is to try to hit a target on that defender. You may have a narrow focus, where there is one guy on you, or it may be a wide focus where you are involved in a combination block between you and another player. You may have multiple targets. You have to have a real detailed focus on that aiming point. When I say aiming point and target, I use them interchangeably. Once you start your block, that aiming point may move. It could stay stationary, but it probably will not. We really have to start with the eyes.

At Iowa, we are a zone team and we run power. We will run the draw a little bit. Our first two steps are critical. Let's talk about the first two steps of a base block, or a reach block. My first step is a position step. I am going to take a lateral, and possibly a small forward step. It should never be backward.

What is that step for? A position step is to enable you to make your block. Our second step is a power step. What we are trying to do is to drive our knee through the defender's crotch. We want to get that second foot in the ground as fast as we can. We want to bring our pad and our knee at the same time.

Some of our kids ask how big of a step they should take. We do not take a four-inch, a six-inch, or an eight-inch step. It is simple. We take a step big enough to make the block. It depends on the defender's alignment. Where is he? If he is head-up on me, I am already there. If I have a reach block, my target is farther away. I have to step accordingly, in order to get to my target. I am just trying to get to my target. The wider the defender is, the more you are going to have to get width and depth.

When I talk about vertical leverage, I am talking about the low man wins. Everybody that has ever played or coached football has heard that. I want to get lower than the defender. I am going to be underneath him. I want my pads underneath his pads, and I want my pad underneath his chin. It is simple. You learn that when you are in junior high football.

When I talk about horizontal leverage, I am talking about having inside leverage. We do not want our elbows out. If you are watching your linemen block from behind, you should never see their elbows. We want our elbows inside and in tight. Horizontal leverage is where your strength comes from. A little guy can control a big guy if he has inside leverage.

I have one of those real man's push mowers. It is not a self-propelled mower used by soft people. We have some real hills in my backyard. When I get a chance to cut the grass, I enjoy doing it. I think about inside leverage cutting the grass. I am thinking, keep your elbows in and bring your knees up. It is physics, leverage, and it is fundamentals. That is all it is.

The last thing I want to talk about on this, you probably have not heard much before. I want to talk about the backside knee. If you run your backside knee, and get it in the defender's crotch, you will have a successful block regardless of where you are. If that backside knee gets weak and stiff, you have nothing. You want to keep that backside knee moving and strong.

STANCE AND STARTS

- Shoulder width
- Toes slightly out—squat

- Toes to instep relationship
- Bend knees, hips, ankles—catcher
- Hand down, balanced, flat back

We start just as you do on the very first day. We talk about the stance and the start. We want to get our feet shoulder width apart. We start with a toe-to-instep relationship. If you are in a right-handed stance, you want to have your right toe intersect your left instep. We point our toes outward slightly, just as we were getting ready to do a squat. Bend down just as you are going to get into a catcher's stance. Take your right hand and put it right out in front of you. You want to have a flat back. You want your knees bent at power-producing angles. You want to have a good bend at the hips and a good bend at the knees.

Next, I want to go over a few drills. In the first drill, stance and starts, we have our five offensive linemen lined up in a stance, one behind the other. They are parallel to the line of scrimmage (Diagram #1). The idea here is we want to get the second step in the ground as quick as possible. On the snap, the first step will be a position step with the right foot across a four-inch line to their right. The second step we want to hit the ground as quickly as possible on their side of the line.

We do not want to come up and get too high. The emphasis is to get the second foot down. We will do this drill with our right foot going first, and then we will turn it around and go with our left foot first. It takes just a couple of minutes to get this done. We do allow our center to take a little bit of a drop-step because of the proximity that he is to his block. He might look a little bit different on this drill. If we see a player not doing it right, we will do it over again. Not as punishment, we are going to do it because we are going to do things the right way every single time. We will not just move on to the next drill. We will do it right.

CHALLENGE DRILL

- Come off ball
- Teach leverage: vertical/horizontal
- Strain through block
- Compete/finish

The next drill is the challenge drill. If you like football, you are going to like this drill (Diagram #2). There is not a lot of coaching involved here. We are not teaching fundamentals right now, we are teaching the players to come off of the ball. We are trying to teach leverage, leverage, and leverage. You cannot be comfortable when run blocking. You have to strain. It is a physical thing. You have to compete and finish.

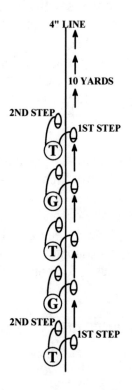

Diagram #1. Stance and Starts Drill

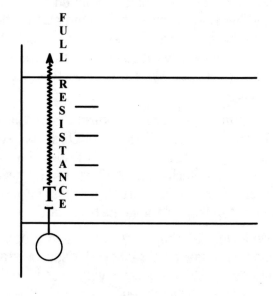

Diagram #2. Challenge Drill

This is just a 1-on-1 blocking drill. We tell the defensive lineman to get in a four-point stance and to stay in that stance until contact. Once contact occurs, the defender has to fight his tail off and not let the offensive guy drive him back.

We tell the offensive lineman to come off of the ball any way he wants to. We do not really talk about footwork here, but he better come off low, he better fight his tail off, and he better bring his knees and drive the defender back five yards. It is trying to move a guy against his will. If the offensive man comes to a standstill, he can reposition his hands, keep his elbows in tight, and sink his butt to get started again. He must keep straining and keep fighting.

This is a great drill for us. Our kids want to do the challenge drill. We will film it and coach it up. Of the days that we are in pads, we will use this drill about 75 percent of the time. Everyone will get a chance at the challenge drill.

TIGHT REACH DRILL

- Target playside number
- First two steps
- Aim backside pad
- Elbows in
- Hands up and under
- Run knees
- Finish

The tight reach is nothing more than a base block (Diagram #3). In a tight reach block, my target is the playside or far side number. We already talked about the first two steps. The first step is a position step and the second step is a power step. We aim at the backside pad. We want to bring our pad and our knee at the same time and make contact on the playside target. I want my elbows in and I want my hands up and under.

I do not want to lead with my hands. My hands naturally come up and under my body. We do not coach hands until we are into the development of the block. We feel that if you lead with the hands, you will give him bad habits. If you lead with the hands, you will overextend and you will be reaching and grabbing. We teach technique. If we see a guy holding, we will jump on his tail. That is something

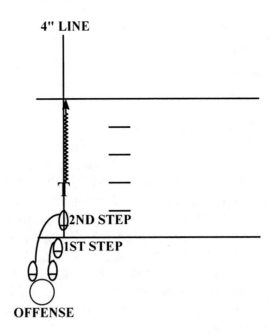

Diagram #3. Tight Reach Drill

that we will not allow. We are going to run our knees and we are going to finish.

We tell the defensive lineman to get into a four-point stance. The reason we do that is so that we can get low and we can get leverage. We think this is better than using sleds and shoots because we are blocking a real person. This is the way to go. We line up the defender's crotch on the line to see if our second step is in proper position. We tell the defender to anchor to the inside. What that means is the defensive lineman is to stay there until contact and then he will fight through the blocker's head as if he were trying to get to the ballcarrier. We coach the defensive linemen up a lot so that we can work on our proper technique.

We are coaching the first step as a position step and eyes at the aiming point. We want to get the second foot in the ground at the defender's crotch. We are making contact with our pads. We want to watch the elbows to make sure that they are in tight. We then want to run the backside knee and finish. At the end of the block, they start extending and creating separation. We will run one, two, or three players at a time, in order to be able to coach them on their technique.

TIGHT REACH WITH A BAG

- Target playside number
- First two steps

- Aim backside pad
- Elbows in
- Hands up and under
- Run knees
- Finish

We are going to do the same drill, but we are going to have a bag holder (Diagram #4). We are not going to hold the bag, as if any of you have ever held the bag. The reason that we are using the bag is for two things. Number one is we want the guys to get confidence in coming off the ball, really exploding, and making contact. If you have a big soft bag there, they will come off and really hit it. They think this is fun, and they want to really come off and hit that thing. The second thing is we want them to make contact with that pad.

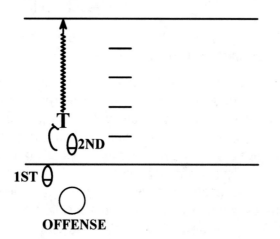

Diagram #4. Tight Reach With Bag Drill

We have to teach the bag holders how to hold the bag. We have the bag holder turn his butt at a 45-degree angle toward the boundary. He is going to squat down and take his outside hand and put it through the straps of the bag. We are going to get low and make that 6'6" tall guy get down low to about two or three feet. As contact is made, we give him some resistance and fight through his head.

We coach our offensive lineman to take his right pad and put it right on the aiming point. He has to keep his eyes on the aiming point because it will probably move. We tell him to take his right hand, as he is making contact, and put it up and underneath the bag. We want to put our hand underneath the bag in on the defensive player's chest. By putting that hand up and under onto the defensive

player's chest, it has put him chest to chest with the defender. We have made contact, we have leverage, and we are inside. The elbows have to stay in so we maintain leverage. It is important to bring that backside knee.

WIDE REACH DRILL

- Target playside armpit
- First two steps
- Aim backside pad
- Elbows in
- Hips down, playside arm, leverage
- Run knees
- Finish

This drill is for blocking on the perimeter play or outside play (Diagram #5). In this drill, we have the defender's inside foot lined up with the offensive player's outside foot. With my first step, I want to gain width and depth. I cannot go lateral because then I would have to cross over in order to reach my target. I have to gain some ground with my first step, and I am working to get to his crotch with my second step. I am going to aim my backside pad with my elbows in. We want to have our hips down, and as we get into the block, we will extend our playside arm. We are going to shoulder block the defender for about three seconds. We want to keep our butt down, run our knees, and finish.

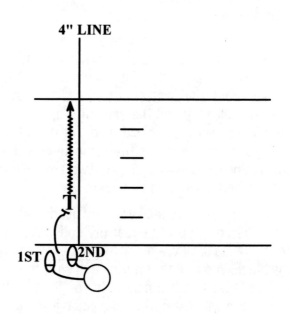

Diagram #5. Wide Reach Drill

Things do not always go as we plan them, or as we drill them. It is not always going to be clean. There are so many variables in football. If that guy is running, just take him with his momentum and drive him out of the play. Keep running and keep those knees moving.

THE BLADE DRILL

- Fundamentals of combo block
- Progression: 2 vs. 1/2 vs. 2
- Pad under chin
- Elbow in/flat back
- Foot to foot/hip to hip
- Drive knees vertical
- Come off for linebacker

The blade drill is nothing more than how we would teach the combination block (Diagram #6). We will start out with the fundamentals of it. What we are going to do is get our two offensive players with their hips together and on each side of the line. We have the defender with his crotch on the line. We will go from a stance and drive him back 10 or 15 yards down the field. The next progression is two versus two by adding a linebacker to the mix. We probably will not put a linebacker into the drill until after the first week of practice because we want to get movement. We will teach the scoop and slip blocks at a later time in practice. These are the fundamentals of this block.

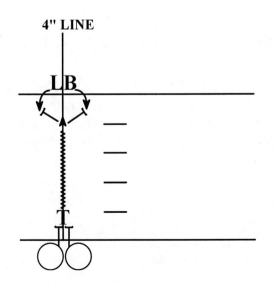

Diagram #6. Blade Drill

The main thing is to keep foot to foot and hip to hip. There should not be any space between the two offensive players. Our focus is getting the feel of getting hip to hip and moving the blocker back. We do not want our guys to get their butts separated. We would like our offensive linemen to both step with their inside foot first. The reason we call it the blade drill is because it is like the blade of a snowplow.

When we add a linebacker, we have him lined up about five yards from the defensive lineman. As the double-team gets to about a yard of him, we ask him to take a side. The offensive lineman to that side will pick him up. This drill is just to get the feel of a double-team block. We will work on the specific fundamentals of the scoop, slip, and the sting later in practice. The big problem we have is getting off of the double-team block too soon. That is why we go 2-on-1 to begin with. There is no one to go off. You want to get movement.

We were having trouble a couple of years ago of blocking second-level defenders. Our guys are big, fat guys that like to eat. Now we are asking them to go out and block an athlete. How do you teach that? I went back and got all of Coach Ferentz's drills when he was the offensive line coach back in the 1980s. I went through every one of those drills.

I found this drill that Joe Moore had taught him. We have a linebacker block drill, where we are just going to do a tight reach block with a bag from a distance (Diagram #7). We hold the bag down low, just as we do in the other bag drill. We are going to be about five yards away from the defender. We are going to coach technique. We are going to have the offensive lineman come off the ball, sink his hips, and get there, and then we are going to aim our pad under his chin. We are going to bend and then just run our knees. The big thing is to stay balanced. We have done a good job of blocking linebackers in the past two years. I believe this drill is one of the big reasons.

We have the same problems that you guys have. We have guys that are highly recruited and play in all-star games, but we have to coach the same things that you have to coach. If their eyes are not on the target, we have to coach that. If they do not have the proper footwork, we have to coach

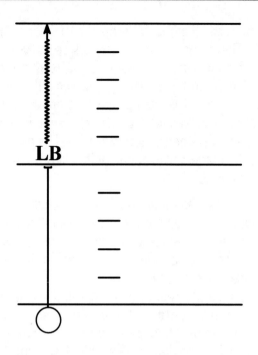

Diagram #7. Linebacker Block Drill

that. Our guys may be a little bigger than yours, but there is really no difference.

The blocks drill is a fundamental drill. We are running our number one offense against our number one defense (Diagram #8). We start out with a tight end, right tackle, and right guard, and put them on the hash mark. The defense has their Sam linebacker, a defensive tackle, and defensive end against them. In the middle, we will have a right guard, a center, and a left guard. They will have their two down tackles and a Mike backer. On the other hash mark, we will have a left tight end, a left tackle, and another left guard. They will block a 3 technique, a 6 or 7 technique, and another linebacker.

We have a manager at quarterback and a manager in the tailback position. We will run the drill on one side, then the middle, and then the other side. You can really work on fundamentals during this time, because you have good offensive players on good defensive players. I will make a hole call

so they know whom to block and I give them the cadence. The defense reads the running back and the heads of our offensive linemen. We are going live on both sides of the ball. Everyone spreads out so nobody gets hurt. We call it our "blocks drill." We run this for about eight minutes and get 35 to 40 reps out of it. Each group will have a chance to go a couple of times. The guys just rotate themselves through.

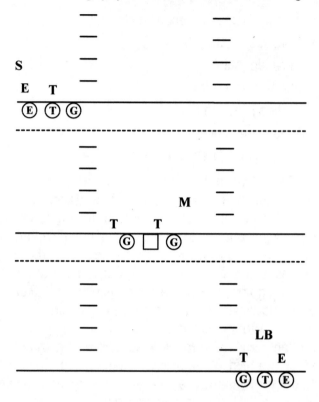

Diagram #8. Blocks Drill

Everything that I have talked about today is all fundamentals. Ultimately, though, what it comes down to is effort.

In summary, it has been an honor to be here. We are very humbled at Iowa. If there is anything that we can do for you, do not hesitate to give us a call. Thank you for your attention. This has been a lot of fun for me.

MAN COVERAGE CONCEPTS AND DRILLS

University of Florida

It is great to be here. My background is on defense and in the secondary. I want to talk about our defensive concepts. We teach everything by concepts, and once we teach, it we apply it to whatever scheme we decide to run. It does not matter what front or scheme we play, how we play the outside corner and middle field safeties is all the same. I am going to hit the drill work quickly.

I have been a defensive coordinator for a long time. I want the drill work we use in practice geared for whatever we are installing for that day. I want to work the linebacker on playing half a man and playing off blocks. I want the down lineman working on double-team blocks. Safeties will work on middle-of-the-field drops. We want to coordinate all our drill work for the installation of the day. We call that "practicing with a purpose."

We do not want to do our drill work just because we have done it that way for 30 years. In training camp, we go over our defense and teach special situations. It does not matter what we are working on in practice, we make sure the drill work matches what we are teaching. We want the carryover value that come with that type of coordination.

In the secondary, we work one-line drills. We also work two-line drills, which is ball reaction drills. Since we are a press man-to-man defensive team, we work those defensive type drills.

In our alignment, we want to be a two-shell team on everything we do. We want to show the quarterback a two-high safety look. We want to show the same look whether it is a six-man box against a one-back set or an eight-man box with a two-back set.

With our defensive backs, we work on middle-of-the-field drops and phase drills. That is one of the most difficult things to teach a defensive back. The hardest decision for a defensive back is when he plays the ball. We work those drills constantly because that is how we end up playing. There is a decision-making process on the back end.

DECISIONS FOR THE DEFENSIVE BACK

- When do I go for the ball?
- When do I try to make the interception?
- Where do I knock the ball down?
- When do they want to secure the ball?

When we start our drill work, we work one and two line drills every day. I want to go through the fundamentals we try to teach in our daily drill work. In the secondary, we constantly preach about their stance. We want them to be comfortable in the stance. We want them to get in a stance with their nose over their toes. If they work with their nose over their toes, they will be right. They need to work within the framework of their body. If you work outside the framework of your body, you have to step inside yourself.

The first drill we work is a simple down-the-line backpedal drill. We want the weight on the ball of the front foot. When the defensive back rolls back to start his pedal, we do not want him stepping forward. We do not want to see the pad level or helmet position change when we do this drill. When the players do this down-the-line backpedal drill, they are going on their own. I want to coach the drill instead of having to start each player with "set, hike."

The next thing we work on is a pedal weave (Diagram #1). We design the drill to teach the defensive back to maintain his leverage position on a receiver. It is a pedal drill, but the defensive back moves to the left or right of the line as he moves backward. We want him to observe the rules of the pedal, but he weaves left and right. He keeps his shoulder square at all times and does not tilt his hips.

Diagram #1. Pedal Weave

The defensive back wants to gain depth in his pedal but he want to maintain leverage. His posture and pad level are the same as in the backpedal drill. We use this skill when a receiver breaks off the line and stems in or out on the defensive back. If the back has an inside leverage position on the receiver and the receiver breaks to the inside, the defensive back uses his pedal weave to regain his inside leverage position without coming out of his backpedal.

When a player runs forward, he uses his arms. The same thing is true when he runs backward. He has to use his arm in his backpedal. The right arm is in direct relationship with the left leg, and the left arm with the right leg. We want the bend in the elbow at a 90-degree angle. We give the defensive back the analogy of having a hammer in his hand. The movement is like hammering a nail back into a wall. There is no difference in running forward and running backward. We work the pedal and pedal weave on a single yard line. We work as much as we can on technique in this situation.

The next down-the-line drill is the hip turn drill. We still work down the single line. We start the drill in a pedal. When we open the hips, I refer to it as giving yourself a contusion in the rib cage with your elbow. We make a violent move with the elbow to get turned 180 degrees in the other direction, running forward. After that movement, we want to turn in the other direction and get back to the forward running position, looking back. We want them to have fluid movement and work down the line.

When a defensive back gets beat, it is generally because he loses his cushion. If he does not know when to flip his hips, it is generally too late when he does.

From this drill, we go to a drive drill (Diagram #2). This is more of a half zone drill. This drill teaches the defensive back to open and drive at a 45-degree angle. If he goes from a two-high look to the middle of the field, he uses this drill. He opens his hips at 45 degrees and drives to a landmark in the middle of his zone. Once he reaches that point, he squares up to the quarterback and backpedals. When he squares up to the quarterback, we refer to that as fishtailing. The defensive back drives for depth and squares up when he reaches his middle zone.

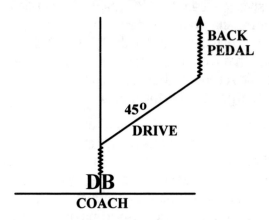

Diagram #2. Drive Drill

This next drill is a form of a W drill, and is important to our teaching progression. This is a change-of-direction drill. It gets us from the pedal to driving forward. On the drill, we teach a two-step (Diagram #3). If we are in the pedal and want to break up to the right, we turn the left foot to get as many cleats in the ground as possible. We want to point the toe of the right foot in the direction we want to go. We plant, point, and go. We do not put the toe of the cleat in the ground. When you do that, you have a tendency to slip. When we do the footwork, we want to stay within the framework of the body. We do not want the feet to get outside the shoulders. We want the feet under the body.

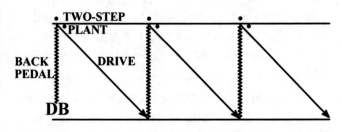

Diagram #3. Two-Step Drill

When we point the toe, it gets our hips going in the direction of the feet. If they do not get the hips pointed in the right direction, they round off the path of the defensive back's break. In the drill, the defensive man backpedals from one line and plants on the next line. They break up at a 45-degree angle. When they hit the line, they pedal back and repeat the drill. The difference between this drill and the W drill is the alternating pedal.

This drill is critical in the transition game for a defensive back. Defensive backs have to transition their movement from backward to forward. A back who cannot do this drill cannot play defensive back. The reaction time and drive on the ball is the difference between the good backs and the average ones.

The days we work two-line drills, we work a couple of one-line drills to loosen them up. The two-line drills are ball drills. We incorporate every drill with a ball throw of some kind. In every drill we do, we finish by catching a ball. That skill is the most important one for the defensive backs.

You can talk about all the different things you want to statistically, but the important stats are turnovers and big plays. You have to get turnovers on defense and prevent explosives plays. On offense, you have to produce explosive plays and change the momentum and field position. If you look at the NFL, the teams that win game and make the playoffs are the ones that do not turn the ball over and they make big plays. They all have great defenses that turn the other team over and do not allow explosive plays.

Turnovers and explosive plays are the things we try to emphasize in every drill we do. We chart turnovers in practice and record it every time a player gets his hands on the ball. We call them "ball hawks."

We do the two-step drill and break forward at a 45-degree angle. We throw them the ball. Sometimes, it is a low ball, and at other times, it is a high ball. We very seldom throw the ball to them. We want them to focus on the ball and make a tough catch. We throw it high, low, wide left, or wide right. Make him adjust and move.

We use all kinds of turns with the defensive backs. We put the back into a zone turn or a speed turn and break him back for the ball. We use the two-step drill from the pedal and break them downhill at a 45-degree angle. We use a zone turn, where the back opens his hips, retreats back at a 45-degree angle, and comes downhill to the ball. We put them in a zone drop, but instead of planting the outside foot and driving at a 45-angle in the opposite direction, we use the speed turn.

In the speed turn, the defensive back snaps his head and shoulders around, looks away from the ball shortly, and drives in the opposite direction. Off each turn, we throw the ball, and the defensive back goes to get it. We want him to high-point the ball each time.

In each drill, we try to get the planted toe coming downhill. In a zone turn drill, the defensive back zone turns and drives at a 45-degree angle to his zone (Diagram #4). When the defensive back gets to the middle of his zone, he fishtails and goes to the pedal. The coach gives him a direction, and he uses his two-step plant and breaks downhill at a 45-degree angle. We throw the ball, and he high-points the throw.

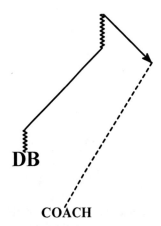

Diagram #4. Zone Turn

In our drills, we do work on individual patterns and movements. We work on an out and up drill, which teaches the footwork to play that type of pattern. Playing the ball in the air is the objective in our ball skill drills. To a defensive back, that is the most critical skill he can use. When we evaluate the defensive back, that is one asset he must have. We want to know if he can catch the ball and judge it in the air. He has to find it, adjust to its flight, and catch it. If he cannot do that, he cannot play in the secondary. Along with be physically tough, he must be in position to make plays and tackle.

When we teach press coverage, we teach it from a rock hard position. When we start teaching the drill, we go toe-to-toe with the receiver. The first thing we want to do is get the receiver off the plane. That means in the first three yards the receiver cannot get vertical on the defender. That is the worst thing to happen in press coverage. If the receiver can get vertical on the defensive back immediately, he has troubles. We want the defender to push the receiver east and west off the plane.

With a receiver breaking outside, the defensive back's first thoughts are to step with the outside foot. We use a kick-slide technique in our first movement to the receiver (Diagram #5). That means if the receiver tries to break outside the defender, he steps with his inside foot and kick-slides with his outside foot to get in front of him. It is the same step an offensive tackle uses on a speed pass rusher. When we kick-slide, we do not want the feet to get wide. We want them to stay within the frame of the body as he moves outside.

Diagram #5. Kick-Slide

That movement keeps the defender square on the receiver for a longer time. The defensive backs want to stay on the same plane with the receivers. Once the receiver breaks the plane, the defensive back opens his hips and runs with him. If the defensive back has trouble with his inside step, we use a replace step with the inside foot. We allow him to move the foot up and down quickly without gaining much ground. The thing that does is to keep his feet from getting too wide apart. It keeps him working within his frame.

The worst thing the defensive back can do is to widen his feet. That requires getting them back together before he pushes off and runs. If he does that, he is two steps behind the receiver. When we

play press coverage, we want to play with quiet feet. We do not want to move the feet a bunch. The defensive back needs to mirror the movement of the receiver and stay square on him. The objective of the drill is to get the receiver running east and west. If we can do that, we have a chance to win the match-up.

For the defensive back to win, he has to make plays on the line of scrimmage. That is the critical part of defensive back play. Big plays occur downfield.

The defensive back must win with his feet. When we start the drill, the defensive back has his hands behind his back. He mirrors the moves of the receiver and kick-slides with his feet. He moves inside and outside and stays square on the receiver. The objective of the footwork is to get a collision on the receiver. If we give the receiver a free release into the field, we are dead.

The defensive back gets nervous and wants to use his hands on the receiver, but the collision comes from using the feet. The defensive backs have to step with the foot opposite the movement of the receiver. If he moves the foot to the side of the movement, he has to step back into his frame to gain his balance. The outside step causes an extra step and gives the receiver the release.

The next part incorporates the hands into the drill. In our base technique, we teach an off-hand jam. When the receiver releases to the outside, the defender uses his inside hand to punch him. We deliver the punch with the elbow close to the body and the thumb up. The target is the inside breastplate of the receiver. It is no different from teaching an offensive lineman to choke down a defensive lineman's pass rush. The punch disrupts the timing in the pass route.

This technique is bump-and-run. If the receiver plants and tries to come back to the inside, we kick-slide inside and use the off-hand jam again. The bump is to disrupt the timing. If the receiver is good in his release technique and gives a lot of foot movement at the line of scrimmage, we use a quick-off technique. If he uses a footfire movement before the snap, we drop six to eight inches off the receiver. He uses the foot movement on air, and we engage him with our technique after he breaks off the line.

We have a quick-jam technique we use. However, we do not allow all the defensive backs to use this technique. We use this technique with long-armed defensive backs. We use the off-hand jam on the split end on the line and the flanker off the line. We incorporate the off-hand jam into the kick-slide drill and work up and down the line, mirroring the receivers. The receiver is making a chance-of-direction movement so the defensive back can kick-slide and uses the other side in the technique.

When we teach the middle-of-the-field safety, we teach them with a zone turn technique to begin our drills. The example I use is a pro set, which we do not see much anymore. We align in a two-deep look on every down. If the right safety has the middle-of-the-field coverage, on the snap of the ball he has to see ball on the line or ball off the line. He opens at a 45-degree angle and has to recognize whether the pass is a three- or five-step drop.

If he recognizes a three-step drop, he plants and starts downhill on the slant pattern. He has to see the midpoint of the formation. That means he has to know where the middle of the field is according to the X- and the Z-receivers. The seam area for the safety is two yards outside of each hash mark. At 18 yards, the safety has to be effective. He has to make plays from two yards outside the hash on one side to two yards outside the hash on the other side. When he gets to 18 yards, he has to be square up and make plays in those areas. If we play three-deep, man-free, or some kind of fire zone, he has to override the seam areas.

We do a three-step drill with the middle-of-the-field safety (Diagram #6). The safety reads the ball off the line and keys the quarterback. He breaks to his responsibility to the middle as his initial movement. When he reads the three-step drop, he plants and comes downhill on all slant patterns. If the quarterback looks to the left, he breaks down on the flanker coming inside. If the quarterback looks to the right, the safety plants and retraces his steps toward the split end on the slant.

The coaching points we look for in this drill are the plant and change of direction. We want him to point the toe and break straight downhill. We do not want him to round off the break back to the line. After we work the three-step, we go to the

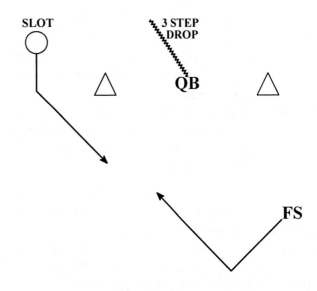

Diagram #6. Safety Three-Step Drop

five-step drop. He breaks at a 45-degree angle to the middle of his zone. Once he reaches the middle, he fishtails at 18 yards and breaks on the seam ball down the middle. If there is no immediate pressure up the seams, he slows his speed and plays the football.

His alignment is 10 to 12 yards off the line of scrimmage. We feel from that position, he can roll down into the box and be in position to make plays deep. The important thing for the safety to do when he plays the three-step drop is to get the first step coming out of the break correct. If he rounds off the break, he cannot get into the reception area of the receiver. The fundamentals of the one-line drill carry over to the middle-of-the-field drill.

If the ball is on the hash mark, we want the quarterback to make a decision as to where the coverage is going. I do not want to stand the middle-of-the-field defender in the middle of the field. I want him around the hash marks and moving when the quarterback puts his hands under the center or calls for the ball in the shotgun snap. I do not want that to happen unless that is what we want the quarterback to see. If the safety has an assignment out of the middle, he can align in that position. I want the quarterback to see two high safeties and have to make a decision. The safeties cannot let the quarterback get him out of position.

However, we want to get to our responsibility first. We do not want to hold the disguise at the risk of not getting in position to perform our responsibility.

The phase drill is the next thing I want to show you. There is an age-old question about "When do you play the ball?" If the defender runs with the receiver down the field, he is in-phase if he can hit the hip of the receiver. The defender is in-phase, and he can look back for the ball. When he looks for the ball, he turns into the receiver. That prevents separation between the receiver and himself when he starts to play the ball.

The hardest ball to play is the underthrown deep ball. The receiver sees the ball and the defender does not and overruns the ball. If the defender leans into the receiver, it is not pass interference as long as he looks back to the ball. If the defender is playing the ball, there can be contact.

If the defender cannot touch the receiver, he is out-of-phase. The defender cannot look for the ball. He has to play the eyes and hands of the receiver. I tell our players when the eyes and hands go up, the defender counts one second and secures the near elbow of the receiver. He sees the eyes and hands go up, he counts 1001, and rakes the hands across the elbows. It is a 15-yard penalty and not a spot foul.

The worst thing a defender can do is panic with his back to the ball. There is no guarantee the receiver can catch the ball. Keep the technique sound, and rake the arms. We play bump-and-run and do these drills every day. When we work the drill, we start out as an in-phase position. The defensive back runs down the field with the receiver, leans in, and plays the ball. However, in the course of the repetition, the receiver may put the defensive back in an out-of-phase position. If that happens, he uses the out-of-phase techniques.

In the drill, we work from an out-of-phase position. The defender starts two to three yards behind the receiver. He uses the technique for that position. The reverse is true if the defender gets in-phase in this part of the drill. If he is in-phase, he uses those techniques. Being out-of-phase is going to happen in a game. They cannot panic and play sound technique.

When we run the phase drill, on any outside release by the receiver, we want to play a high shoulder technique. He plays the high shoulder on the inside of the receiver. If the receiver runs the fade pattern toward the sidelines, the corner cannot depend on any help from the half-field safety. The corner plays from a high shoulder position, but must see the backside shoulder. If the offense throws the back-shoulder fade ball, the receiver's shoulder has to fall out for him to catch the ball. That is how the defensive back reacts to that throw. When the backside shoulder falls out, he knows the ball is on the way.

From this position, we have to play the comeback or stop pattern. They run that pattern at 16 to 18 yards deep. We read the outside shoulder up to 16 yards. At that distance, I want the defensive back to read the head. They must have a time clock in their heads. When the receiver gets past 15 yards, they will not run a back-shoulder fade. The defensive back's eyes go to the receiver's eyes, and we play the deep out or the comeback. If the receiver is going to run those routes, his head and eyes will tell the defensive back. If he passes 18 yards, he is going vertical.

The big problem with the in-phase position is the separation that may occur. If the defender is in-phase and turns to look for the ball, he has to lean in to keep the contact with the receiver. If he drifts away from him, the receiver has more room to catch the ball. The defender has to cup his body into the receiver. We do not want to create a situation where the receiver can collect his balance and jump over the defender to catch the ball. With the height of wide receivers in the game today, we do not need to give them the advantage of getting a jump ball.

As the receiver passes 16 yards, the in-phase defender wants to look back and find the quarterback or the ball. He always wants to go to the highest point of the ball. For in-phase, we want to press the receiver and play the ball.

When you teach ball drills, you have to make a decision on when to play the ball and when not to play the ball. You see it all the time in games. The back goes for the interception or tries to make a play on the ball and misses it. That snap decision can result in plays that are generally big yardage plays or touchdowns. I teach our players if they are in a press position, we want to swat and knock the ball down. If we are in position to intercept the ball, go for the interception. That is clinic talk.

You have to put your players in a situation so they understand what that position is. We drill the receiver coming back on an out cut. The technique we use is hook and swat. We run the drill as an in-phase drill. The receivers run an out or curl pattern. We play the patterns and react to the throw. If the defender can see the ball and is in position to intercept, that is what we do. If he can get under the throw, he goes for the interception.

The hook part of the technique is the upfield hand of the defender. The swat is with the downfield hand. If he breaks on a pattern to his left, his left hand is the hook and his right hand is the swat. If he misses the ball, he does not lose the receiver. Big yardage in football comes after the catch or a back running through a tackle. Teams will complete passes on you. We need to make the tackle at that point and not allow a run after the catch.

If we are in-phase, we want to intercept and swat. If we are out-of-phase except for the deep ball, we want to secure the area. The defensive back wants to break down on the pattern and secure the area. He does not want to look back at the quarterback. If he looks to the quarterback, all he will do is watch the quarterback complete passes all day. We do not want the ball to go any farther up the field.

The players who need to exercise judgment on the ball are the safeties. In most cases, they see the ball all the way. They have to make good decisions about when to play for the interception and when to knock the ball down.

When we talk in terms of boundary leverage, we refer to the corners. This concept does not matter whether you play press coverage or off coverage. If the ball is in the middle of the field, the divider for the corner is the top of the numbers. If the receiver aligns outside the divider, the corner plays him with inside leverage. The defender's outside eye aligns to the inside eye of the receiver. If the receiver is inside the divider, the corner has outside leverage because he is closer to the half-field safety.

If the ball moves to the hash mark, the corner into the shortside of the field has a divider at the bottom of the numbers (Diagram #7). The divider moves three yards into the sidelines. The wideside corner's divider is midway between the hash marks and the top of the numbers. That is six yards outside

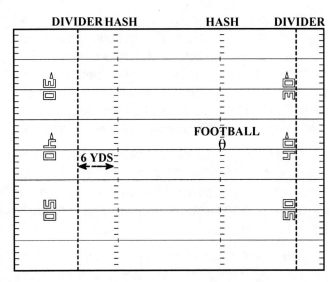

D Diagram #7. Dividers—Hash

the hash mark. If a receiver aligns on the hash, we have outside leverage on him. The dividers apply to the outside receiver only.

When we talk about covering a slot receiver, we talk about seam leverage. That could be a corner covering a slot receiver or safety. In our general rule and a base play, we play off the seam. The seam area is two yards outside the hash marks. If the slot receiver is inside the seam, we play outside leverage on him. We assume there is help down the middle. We want to be five to seven yards off the slot receiver. When they snap the ball, we want to be seven yards deep. That is to keep the slot from getting on top of the defender too quickly.

If the slot receiver splits outside the seam, we go to an inside leverage position. Because we are farther away from the half-field safety, the route combinations we get are inside routes. There are coaches who know we play the seams this way, and we have to change when we play them. However, this is our base way that we teach seam leverage.

We have some techniques we use in our man coverage to change up on the receiver. We have a show hand technique. This is a fake move by the defensive back. He loosens off the receiver on the snap of the ball and takes a short inside jab with his inside foot and an inside punch with his hand. It is a fake, and he quickly jumps back outside. The defensive back shows something to the receiver and does the opposite.

We use a quick hand move. We use these against bigger receivers. We jump him, get our hands on him quickly, and release him. That makes it hard for him to get on top of us. If the pitcher keeps throwing fastball, eventually the hitter will hit it out of the park. You have to show them a change-up to keep them off balance. We play wide receivers that way.

As a base rule for the outside leverage player, if he gets an outside release, he plays the high shoulder of the receiver. We want to lean on the route and play through the receiver's outside hip to his outside shoulder.

We do a release drill every day in our practice. We run 1-on-1 every day. You have to do that to play the scheme we play. If the receiver takes an inside release, the defensive back plays his low shoulder position. He plays the outside hip of the receiver. If the receiver runs an inside route, he leans to the outside before he breaks to the inside. We read that lean and overplay the inside portion of the route. If the receiver leans inside, the defensive back climbs for outside shoulder leverage. We try to overplay the route based on the lean of the receiver.

When you get an inside release by the receiver, you do not get many vertical routes from that move. The only outside route you get from an inside release is a seven pattern, which is the corner route. You can eliminate the route the defensive back gets based on the stem from the receivers coming off the line of scrimmage.

The key to playing bump-and-run is to keep the receiver on a horizontal plane. The problems are when the receiver gets on top of the defender early in the route. The reason you play bump-and-run is to disrupt the timing of the route and destroy the spacing they like to get.

In the seam area, the defender knows he has inside help. He does not pedal back. He uses a shuffle step, which is what we call a "step replace." He has a tilt to his leverage and steps with his outside foot and replaces it with his inside foot. If the receiver stays in the seam, at 10 yards the defender wants to be in a low hip position and outside of him. If he works out of the seam, we get a high shoulder position. In the low position, the defender has inside help and can undercut the routes. If the

receiver works away from the half-field safety, the defender gets a high shoulder position. We read the opposite hip and opposite shoulder, working inside the seam and outside the seam.

If a team uses motion in their scheme, we play it two different ways, depending on the motion. We bump motion in, but never bump it out. When we get inside motion, the defender wants to get back hip leverage. If the receiver runs a drag route across the field, he wants to get the defender on a different level so he can pick him off with another defender or the umpire. We use a technique called "tailpipe." We get directly behind the receiver and trail him across the formation. It is hard to hit a receiver with someone right on his heels.

If the offense motions into a stack position, the corner takes the man on the line of scrimmage, and the defensive back plays the man off the line of scrimmage.

If you are going to be a man-coverage team, you have to practice it every day and work on it. You have to practice what you want to get good doing. One last thing before I stop: players get so nervous about getting beat that the first thing they do is widen their feet. You have to work on that along with the off-hand jam.

When a player plays man coverage, he has to understand where he has help and where the problem areas are. If he understands the route combination that come from an inside stem and an outside stem, it give him an edge on the receivers. A huge part of his technique is his eye control. He has to know where to look on a receiver and what he can see. When you play bump-and-run, the hands are down at the line of scrimmage. The defensive back does not get his hand up because the wide receiver will grab them and use them for leverage.

The phase drill is critical because it give the defensive back a guide as when to look for the ball.

I appreciate the opportunity to talk with you. Our doors are always open, and we do not have any secrets. We have a good staff. I think we do some good things, and I am excited about the opportunity we have. I appreciate it, and thank you so much.

STOPPING THE RUN WITH THE 4-3 DEFENSE

Michigan State University

I appreciate being here today. If you want to talk fundamentals, we can do that as we go along. I want to talk briefly about the press box and what role that plays in the aspects of the game. At times I am in the press box, and at times I come down to the field. I can talk to you about the good and bad aspects of being in the press box. When the game goes poorly, it is a good place to be.

The first time I came down out of the press box was in a game against the University of Louisville. We had qualified for a bowl game and had one more game left to play. The day was cold—about 10 degrees—and drizzling rain. Louisville was smoking us. It got worse when I came down. That was my first time to come out of the box and call the plays from the sideline. I do not think it made any difference whether I was up or down for that game. Coach Mark Dantonio told the manager to shut the heaters down because the players were more interested in staying warm than what was going on in the game.

Coach Dantonio still controls the option of going to the press box or staying on the sideline today. He asks me to come down on some occasions, and others he wants me in the box. I come down from the press box now to give inspiration and an emotional spark for the players. Sometimes I can do better working with the players. Football is a game of emotions. It is not about X's and O's, it is about your team and their attitude.

Through the years, it has changed. Sometimes I come down for the last quarter or I come down in the last two minutes of a game to help celebrate with the defense when we put the game out of reach.

I enjoy coaching from the press box. If I had a choice, I would stay up there the entire time. As the defensive coordinator, I can see everything I need to from on top. I can see the down-and-distance, and I do not get emotionally involved as I do if I am on the field. One of the worst experiences was the first year we were at Michigan State University; we played The University of Iowa and were ahead at halftime. I came down for the second half and that was a bad move.

The game went to overtime. I made a dumb call and we ended up getting beat. If I had been in the press box, I would not have done it. I was not in the game with the right mind-set. I was too emotionally involved in the game.

My topic today is defending the running game. The first thing you have to do is stop the run. Two years ago, we were bad against the pass, but we were good at stopping the run. We won several games and it was because no one could run the football on us. The season is successful according to the wins and losses. However, if you want to be a good defense, it all starts with stopping the run.

STOP THE RUN

- Build a wall
- Make the offense one-dimensional
- Defend their favorite runs and passes
- Be fundamental in your approach
- Keep it simple
- Big hits
- Disguise
- Speed

The first thing you have to do to stop the run is to build a wall. The linebackers have to get down into the defense and fill their gaps. It is like a row of chairs. If I pull out one chair, there is a hole in the line. That makes a leak in your defense.

If we can stop the run, we can make the offense one-dimensional. If the offense can get the running game going, they can mix up their play calling enough that you cannot stop anything. That is a bad feeling. When I was at Northern Illinois University, we played Miami University (Ohio) when they had Ben Roethlisberger. He threw for 500 yards that day. They rushed for 32 yards and we won the game. We made them a one-dimensional football team and won the game.

When we play a team, we want to defend what they do best. We want to stop their favorite play. We want them to beat us left-handed, if they can. We are not going to spend time working on the things that they do not depend on with the game on the line. We want to take them out of what they do best and make them run something they do not do so well.

To do that, sometimes you must be fundamental in what you do. It is not our scheme or The Ohio State University's scheme that makes you a good football team. The scheme you play and the fundamentals that go with the defense are what make you a good defensive team. Defense is not about how many different fronts, stunts, or blitzes you can run. It comes down to doing the fundamental things correctly. If you run too many things, you cannot do them all well. There is not enough time to practice them.

We are big into fundamentals. We do it every day in the spring and fall practice. We have many individual periods where we work on the base fundamentals of playing defense. Too many times late in the season, coaches cut their individual time down and spend more time working team. We do not do that. We coach fundamentals and individual drills the entire season. Fundamentals win games and not schemes.

If you keep the scheme simple, the players can play fast. We coach all the little things and get them to play fast. If your defense is not playing fast, it means they do not know what they are doing. When the players know your defense, you can concentrate on coaching what the opponent is doing on offense rather than what you are doing on defense. If you spend more game-preparation time coaching what you do on defense instead of focusing on what they do on offense, you will not play well.

We want to get big hits on defense. You get big hits by playing fast. When you know what to do, you are there in a hurry and you can run through the ballcarrier and create that big hit. Our players get excited about big hits. On Sunday, our players come in and watch the film. We put together a big-hit film and show it to them. They want to see the big-hit film.

In the game of defensive football today, it is tremendously important to disguise what you intend to do. We want to make everything look the same. We show a four-man front, with three linebackers, pressed corners, and two deep safeties. It does not matter if it is first-and-ten or third-and-25, the alignment will look the same.

We are coaching speed to aid our defense. When we recruit, that is one of the main ingredients we look for in an athlete. We want players that can run on the football field. The reason we do not play the five-man front is that the Sam linebacker is a big linebacker that cannot run. When we recruit a big safety from high school, he may be a linebacker after we get him into the program. Football evolution is putting more speed on the field at every position. Corners become safeties, safeties become outside linebackers, outside linebackers become inside linebackers, a Mike linebacker becomes a defensive end, and a defensive end becomes a defensive tackle.

The slower, big players become offensive linemen. If we had a race of all our defensive players, the two defensive tackles are the losers in the race. The fastest players will be the corners and safeties. We recruit speed at every position on our defense. We have a defensive tackle that weighs 375 pounds and is a physical machine. The only problem is he cannot move. If the offense runs right by him, that leaves a hole in our defense. He has to lose weight and get faster to get on the field.

We play with a strong safety and a free safety. The free safety is the faster of the two. If you have two fast safeties, it does not matter where they play. We do not need to flip one because he is faster than the other player is. They can play left and right. In the bowl game, The University of Alabama found our slow safety. They got in the right formation, found the match-up they wanted, and scored a touchdown. Next year, we will not have a slow safety.

We have players that are athletes and can play a number of positions. What we have to do is get as many of the fast athletes on the field at the same time. It may take up to two years to move a player or he may move in two weeks.

If you recruit too many offensive linemen, they end up on the bench. The offensive linemen we have are not fast enough to play defense. They are probably athletic enough but not fast enough. In the evolution of football, the offensive line is the last stop for some of the big players before they find a home on the bench.

The evolution occurs every spring and fall. I am looking at a safety right now as possibly moving to outside linebacker. We do not have enough athletes at that position. Ultimately, what we are trying to do is get our best 11 football players on the field.

We play a 4-3 defense. I believe one defense can stop everything. I believe we could play a football game in our base defense. We have done that before. Two years ago when we played the University of Michigan, we zone blitzed three times and the rest of the time we played base defense. It will give up yardage, but you can stay in it and win games. I believe that if everyone lines up exactly right, reads their keys, and does all the fundamentals involved with the defense, it is enough to win games.

The secret is not to develop entirely new defensive schemes to stop the shortcomings of a defense. Focus on the one defense you have and fix all the problems with that defense and you will be successful. You cannot go to a new defense to stop one play.

In our defensive scheme, we want to get nine defenders in the box to stop the run (Diagram #1). If we do not need nine in the box, we can play with five, six, or seven in the box. We want to bounce all offensive runs. The fastest way for an offensive back to score is straight ahead. We want them to take the long way.

The defensive end and linebacker spill the run to the outside. We spill all inside runs to the sideline. We want to turn all outside runs back to the inside. When the running back turns inside, we go back to the evolution of our defense and have speed run you down.

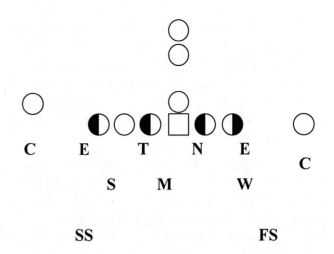

Diagram #1. Base Defense

The first thing we must do is align. The defensive line always aligns with the down hand to the offensive lineman we play against. If I am a 9 technique, I play with my right hand down. The right hand comes from the ground and makes contact with the blocker. We are an attacking defense. We do not read the blocker and slide up and down the line of scrimmage. We attack off the movement of the ball. The quickest get-off on our team is Jerel Worthy. He is a 295-pound defensive tackle. He is probably faster than most of our players in the 10-yard sprint.

He makes plays in the backfield. We want to cause havoc in the backfield with our defensive line. We want to do that by penetrating the offensive line. We want to penetrate and react to the block we get. There are not that many blocks for a 3-technique tackle to play. We play with a 9-technique defensive end, a 3-technique and 1-technique defensive tackle, and a 5-technique defensive end to the openside of the set.

The linebackers have to know their keys. If we play an I-back team, the linebackers will see the running back. They read their keys and attack the line of scrimmage. We are not a shuffling group of linebackers. One of my pet peeves is drilling something we do not use in a game. I do not want to see a shuffle drill in our practice because they used it at the NFL Scouting Combine. We do not shuffle; we play downhill and attack the line of scrimmage. We do not want to confuse our players with how we want to play.

Our linebackers align at five yards off the line of scrimmage and run downhill attacking what they see. If we align at three yards and attack the line of scrimmage, there is no way to adjust to a counter. We cannot get over the top of the defensive linemen when we are too close to the line of scrimmage.

The safeties align in our base coverage and play pass to run. They have to read their keys. Our base coverage is cover 4 or quarters coverage. We have a term we use in the secondary. We have to "verify key." The safeties read the slot or #2 receiver. Even if the offensive line lies to the safety with their key, he has to verify the key by looking at the slot receiver.

If the slot receiver runs by one of our safeties, it is a problem. The rules in cover 4 are the same as they are in cover 3. You must stay as deep as the deepest and do not let any receiver run past you, if you have a deep zone assignment. We play pass first and verify everything off the #2 receiver.

The corners are the key to what we do. If they can take the wide receiver out of the scheme of the offense, we can play great defense. If they can handle the wide receiver, it allows us to get nine defenders into the box. What they do defines our success as a defense. They align in a press alignment on the wide receivers.

Our corner may never make a tackle and play a great game. They must play great technique because they lock up with the #1 receiver. We press the wide receiver. It is easier to play press coverage on the wide receiver than it is to play off him. We do the easy thing and not the hard thing.

We call our defensive front an "over defense." We move the front to the strength of the formation (Diagram #2). If the offense has one tight end in the formation, that gives us the running strength of the set. If the tight end aligns to the left side, our call is "left." It is not "Larry or Lilly," it is what it is. It is "left."

The defensive end to the left aligns in a 9 technique on the outside shoulder of the tight end. The defensive end to the right side is the rush end and aligns in a 5 technique on the outside shoulder of the tackle. We do not flip-flop the ends. We do not have rush and drop defenders. If the call is right,

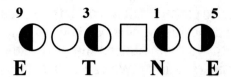

Diagram #2. Defensive Line Alignment

the right end is the 9-technique end and the left end is the 5-technique rush end.

If the call is left and there is no tight end to the left side, the 9-technique end aligns in a ghost position. He takes his alignment on air as if there were a tight end. He aligns in a loose 5 technique or a ghost 6 technique on the tight end. There is no reason to be tight because he does not have to protect an inside gap. We play him in a square stance and do not tilt him to the inside.

The defensive tackle to the side of the call plays a 3-technique alignment on the outside shoulder of the offensive guard. This is a specialty tackle. He is always the 3-technique tackle. He flip-flops with the 1-technique defensive tackle. We call the 1 technique a "nose tackle."

We align the Sam and Will linebackers in 50 techniques five yards off the line of scrimmage (Diagram #3). They align on the outside shoulder of the offensive tackles. The Mike linebacker aligns in a 10 technique to the callside. He aligns on the inside shoulder of the offensive guard.

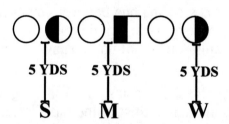

Diagram #3. Linebacker Alignment

I told you at the beginning, you must align correctly. You can have a great and talented player, but if he cannot line up, he will have trouble playing. We have a linebacker by the name of Greg Jones. He had many alignment problems. He was smart and very athletic and was what we call a "football player." He had great instincts. The one thing he did not have was great attention to detail. He would think he was in a 10 technique, but he was not and it hurt our defense. That goes back to the fundamentals of alignment. That is the alignment of the front seven.

The safeties align at 9 to 10 yards deep and one to two yards outside the alignment of the tight end or the offensive tackle with no tight end. The corners are in a press alignment.

I want to show you how we align against different formations. These are the problem alignments if you play a four-man front. The first formation is the pro set, which we talked about earlier.

If the formation is a two-tight end, one-back set, we do not change much in our alignment (Diagram #4). If the call is "left," the 9-, 3-, and 5-technique defenders align as they did previously. We make a "G" call for the nose tackle. He aligns on the offensive guard away from the call. That moves the 1-technique defender to a 2i technique on the inside eye of the right offensive guard to his side.

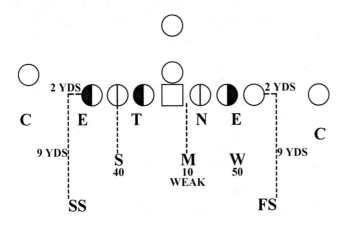

Diagram #4. Two Tight Ends, Two Backs

The secondary aligns using the same alignments. The difference may be the safety to the side of the second tight end. His alignment depends on what type of tight end aligns in that position. If it is a 290-pound tackle that has not caught a pass all year, we walk the alignment of the free safety down to seven yards. If it is a speed, pass receiving tight end, we may deepen the alignment.

The linebackers key the single back. The fullback, in our minds, moves from the backfield into the second tight end position. The Sam linebacker moves from a 50 alignment into a 40 alignment. The Mike linebacker goes from a 10-strong position

to a 10-weak alignment. The alignment of the Will linebacker does not change. If the offense offset the fullback in a weak set to the split end, that is the adjustment we make.

When I first played this defense, I walked the Will linebacker out to a 90 alignment on the second tight end. We played Kent State University and they aligned in this formation. They combo blocked the backside 5 technique and Will linebacker and bloodied our nose. We could not stop it. They started to the frontside and broke the ball back. We had to make a change. It was not the players' fault. It was our fault because we lined them up wrong. After that game, we were a better football team because we made the adjustment and got the alignment where it needed to be.

It was impossible for the Will linebacker to make that play. We made the adjustment and he can now make that play. We stopped the inside zone play coming back to that side. We treat it as the fullback aligns as the tight end and we stopped the inside run. We want all inside runs bounced to the sideline. We bounce the ball to the twelfth man and he makes the tackle. They run out of room and run out-of-bounds.

The next formation is the one-back set (Diagram #5). We do not consider the two-tight-end set as a one-back set. The second back lines up as the tight end. The one-back set has two detached receivers to the backside of the formation. In a left call with the tight end set to the field, the only adjustment is the Will linebacker to the slotside. He walks away to the slot receiver but he plays run first. He has a run fit and plays run first and pass second.

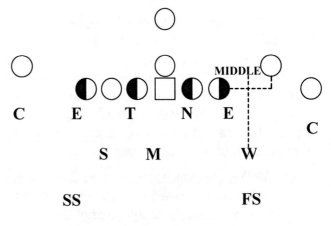

Diagram #5. One-Back Slot Formation

We align him at different positions in relation to the slot receiver. He can be head-up the slot or on his outside shoulder; however, his base alignment is halfway between the tackle and slot receiver. He keys the one-back in the backfield. If the running back comes his way, he is the D-gap defender. The linebacker can never let the slot receiver block him. The only way he should block him is clip him.

His job on the pass is to reroute the slot receiver if he tries to get vertical up the field. He has flat coverage on the slot receiver and we expect him to make the tackle on an out pattern run by the slot. We want to keep the gain to five yards or under. When we put the Will linebacker in that position, we make him one-dimensional in that alignment.

The next formation is the trips set (Diagram #6). It is a triple formation with the tight end to the three-receiver side. The front play their usually techniques. However, we want to kick the front to the weakside of the formation. The people that adjust are the linebackers.

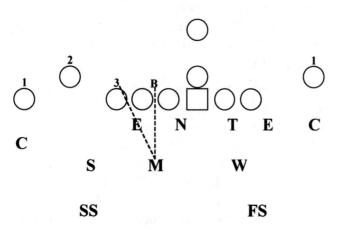

Diagram #6. Trips, Tight End

The Sam linebacker applies his base rule for a detached receiver. He walks out halfway between the tight end and slot receiver. The Mike linebacker bumps from a 10-technique alignment to a 30 alignment on the outside shoulder of the offensive guard. That puts him closer to the #3 receiver in this set, which is the tight end. In his pass coverage, he takes his drop off the #3 receiver.

The Will linebacker bumps into a 30 technique on the backside offensive guard. The strong safety alignment is an inside leverage position on the #2 receiver. His depth is 10 yards. I will talk about the coverage later.

I want to go over the rules for setting the front. If we have a tight end, we kick the front to the tight end. If there are two tight ends, we kick the front to the field. If the ball is in the middle of the field with two tight ends, we kick the front to the left. That is the offensive right. Most teams are right-handed teams. They usually run the ball to the right. A formation with no tight end, we kick the front to the field except for a trips set. We kick the linebackers to the three-receiver side and the secondary tilts in that direction. We kick the front to the weakside of the formation. We want to put the defensive line in a position to make plays.

Kicking the front to the weakside in the trips set helps our Mike linebacker. A trips formation is a passing set, but they can run the ball out of that set. If we kick the front to the trips, that means the Mike linebacker has a run responsibility in the A gap and a pass responsibility on the outside. That is too much for him to cover. By kicking the front to the weakside and moving him to a 3 technique, we move his run responsibility from the A gap to the B gap. That helps him play the #3 receiver and make a play in the B gap.

Putting the Mike linebacker in that position gives him a chance to be successful. Following are the reasons we run our press coverage:

• Attacks the receiver
• Forces bubble release by the receivers
• Gives away route tendencies
• Forces routes to take more time
• Forces routes to end inconsistently
• Keeps receivers off the safeties
• Forces the quarterback to throw the ball to a secondary receiver
• Gets in the receiver's mind
• Easy to coach
• Players love to play it

The front is an attacking front and the press corner fits the mentality of the defense. The receivers have to bubble around the corner. If they try to run a vertical route, the quarterback throws the ball on the numbers and the receiver is against the sideline. Our players want to play press coverage. They like the challenge and I like their attitude.

We play quarters coverage in the secondary. In this coverage, everyone has to be on the same page. We number the receivers from the sideline, moving in toward the formation. The wide receiver is the #1 receiver and the #2 receiver is the next receiver to the inside. It is usually a tight end or slot receiver. The #3 receiver is the receiver closest to the inside. It is the third receiver in the trips set or a back in the backfield.

The defenders have to know where those receivers are when they align in formation and when they go in motion. If a receiver goes in motion, he may start out as the #1 receiver but end up being the #3 receiver on the other side.

The wide receiver with an off coverage defender can run any route he wants to run. I took one of the least athletic corners we had, and made him a good press corner. He was not very fast, but he was coachable. One of the reasons we play press corner is because it is easy to coach. I have the confidence to put him in the game and let him play. He will play good technique and will do things right. He is not talented enough to play there, but he will be in position and get it done.

If the receiver takes an outside release against a press corner, he can run a fade or a comeback. If the receiver takes an inside release, he can run the slant, curl, dig, or post. In the Big Ten, the patterns we see are the fade and comeback.

Our corners press the #1 receiver (Diagram #7). We play an inside eye leverage position and make the receiver bubble to release around the corner.

In our alignment, we want to prevent the receiver from running by the corner. At times, the corners stay up in their coverage, but most of the time, they get depth. The corner aligns with his inside foot forward.

His first move is to kick-slide into the receiver and get his hands on him. We want the hips open to the pattern we give the receiver. We open up to the fade route. We open to the routes we see in the Big Ten. They run fades and comebacks. If the receiver releases inside, they try to crack the safety. The corner has to be alert for that possibility and make it tough on the receiver getting inside.

The safety aligns at nine yards deep by two yards outside the tight end. The tighter I can get them, the better I like it. The first step is a stick step. I want the safeties to stick their feet and not backpedal. He gets his run/pass key off the #2 receiver. He keys from the #2 receiver to the #1 receiver. He has vision of the quarterback but verifies his read off the #2 receiver.

The backside safety on a trips formation gives a "Yo, yo, yo" call to the corner on his side (Diagram #8). That means the corner is man-to-man on the #1 receiver and has no help over the top. The backside safety in the trips set plays the #3 receiver from the trips side on a vertical route.

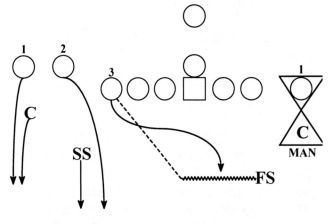

Diagram #8. Yo Call

Cover 4 is not a man coverage defense. It looks like man, but it is a pattern read, matched zone on receivers. If the corner gets an inside release by the #1 receiver, he has help from the Sam linebacker and safety to his side.

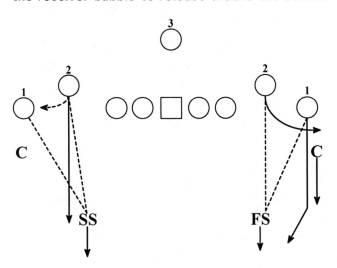

Diagram #7. Corners and Safeties

The safety has to be aware of the crack block from the #1 receiver. Once he has a run key, he has to attack up. The longer he hangs, the deeper the #1 receiver can get up the field. That makes his pattern look like a vertical and the corner has to respect that move.

The Mike linebacker takes his pass drop off the #3 receiver (Diagram #9). He has to play the run first and drop off the #3 receiver. In his pass scheme, he reads #3 to the #2 receiver. If the #3 receiver releases to the outside, the Mike linebacker gives and "Out, out, out" call to the outside linebacker to that side. He releases the #3 receiver to the outside and looks for the *new* #3 receiver coming inside from the outside.

The Mike linebacker exchanges receivers to the outside linebackers. If the #2 receiver runs across the field, the linebackers pass him from one area to the other.

If the #2 receiver goes vertical, the outside linebacker reroutes him and finds the #1 receiver (Diagram #10). If the #1 receiver runs a hitch, the outside linebacker expands to that route. When the corner sees the hitch, he bails off the #1 receiver and plays the smash route from the #2 receiver running to the flag. The safety sees the smash route and plays over the corner; however, the corner has to get under that route also.

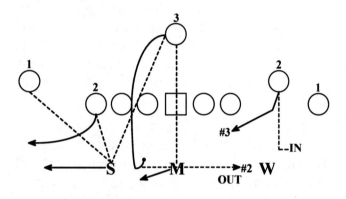

Diagram #9. Linebackers

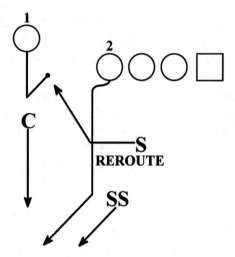

Diagram #10. Smash Coverage

If there is no receiver coming to the inside, he gets depth. That is the only time he drops for depth. He is the low-hole player most of the time. If the #3 receiver goes vertical, he takes him.

The outside linebackers read their keys for run/pass reactions. If it is a pass, the outside linebackers have to find the #2 receiver. If the #2 receiver releases outside, the outside linebacker sprints his butt off to get to that receiver. If the #2 receiver goes vertical, he reroutes his pattern, slows him down, and turns him over to the safety to that side. If the #2 receiver releases inside, he escorts him to the inside, passes him to the Mike linebacker, and looks for the *new #2* coming outside. He gives an "In, in, in" call to the Mike linebacker.

We play our coverage off the splits of the receivers. If the #1 and #2 receivers are regularly spaced, we play quarters coverage. However, if the splits between the #1 and #2 receiver get tight, we play a cover 2 type of roll.

If you are interested in a detailed explanation of quarters coverage, Coach Dantonio did a lecture for the *2009 Coach of the Year Clinics Football Manual*. Read that one and you will get the details of this coverage. I appreciate your attention.

COACHING TIPS AND THE WILD REBEL OFFENSE

The University of Mississippi

I grew up three blocks from the Arkansas School for the Blind & Visually Impaired and my parents taught at the Arkansas School for the Deaf. My dad was the head football coach, head baseball coach, head basketball coach, head bus driver, and he lined the fields. He did it all. As a kid, my main responsibility after the game was to hand out the bologna sandwiches, and there was always one left over. He would say to me, "That one is yours." They were big ole, thick bologna sandwiches. That job meant so much to me. It was awesome, and there was nothing like it on that bus, the camaraderie, especially after a victory. I got to pass out those bologna sandwiches.

What I could not understand was that after those boys spent the whole week with my dad, they would still come knocking on our door on the weekend. I asked my mama why that was, and she said, "Your dad is the coach." The first thing I want to say to you all is, *you* are the coach. What a role you have and what an awesome responsibility you have. My dad was the coach and he was looked up to by all the little deaf kids and he was "the guy." This is why I feel like the people in this room are so important. You are "the guy!"

In the past four years, probably 15 of 25 athletes we have signed each year are from a single parent home. I have a lot of respect for the mothers that have raised most of these kids. I think I have only had one kid whose father played both roles in a single parent household. We hand out a questionnaire to our team and ask this question: Who is the most influential role model in your life? And more times than not, they say "my coach."

The future depends on you. The great thing about coaching is that you can make a difference in a young man's life. You are going to be a difference maker.

Players are looking for the following characteristics in a coach:

- They are looking for somebody they can *trust*.
- They are looking for somebody they can *depend on*.
- They want to have someone *predictable* and *consistent*.
- They also want to have someone *committed* to them.
- They don't really care how much football you know until they know how much you *care*.

When you tell these young men something, they are looking for somebody that is going to see it through. We ask for five things from our players today:

Attitude. The first thing we ask for is a great attitude. Everywhere I've been, whether it is Murray State University, Boise State, the University of Arkansas, or The University of Mississippi, we had to change the attitude of the players to our way of thinking. I might see a player walking down the hall with a frown on his face and I will ask him, "What is wrong with you?" He might say, "Personal problems." I ask if he has cancer and he might say, "No." I would say, "Do you have a brother or family member in Iraq?" He says, "No." Is your mom sick, your dad sick? "No." Then I would say, "You cannot have any personal problems. These are the best days of your life. Put a smile on your face."

Pride. There is nothing like having pride in your school. It does not matter where you are; you have to have pride in your school.

Sacrifice. During your winter program when you are working hard in the weight room, it is all about sacrifice. You are making an investment in your future. You need to be able to take *constructive criticism*. This is one item that is different from what it used to be. Players must understand I am going to treat him as a person off and on the field. I want to know about where he likes to fish, who his girlfriend is, what he likes to do. But when he comes here as a player and he jumps out on the field, I am going to coach him and I want him to have the attitude that he wants me to coach him hard. He has to have the attitude of "teach me." This is the attitude he must have. I am going to coach him very, very hard. I'm going to teach him that he has to understand this, and he needs to put a good look on his face while I am doing it.

Football is important. Football has to be important to them. A lot of the times they go through the motions as pretenders. Do not let them be pretenders. Now, it's a man's man's game. As a coach, you make football important and you set the table.

Passion to win. You have to have a passion to win every day, even if it is during the winter program. We have some type of competition every day to see who is going to be the winner. We call out the winner and recognize him. We want to build within them a passion to win.

I believe young people are looking for two things—they are looking for *love* and *direction*. We try to smother them with love. I don't know if you all know this, but we do not have an athletic dorm anymore. I cannot overstate how much we miss that type of camaraderie. We ate together, we laughed together, and we cried together. In today's world, college presidents want to have the athletes be more a part of the student population and be more involved with them.

HOW DO WE WIN ON SATURDAY?

Win the Turnover Margin

Take care of the most important thing you have. Take care of the ball. I don't care if it is peewee, high school, college, or the tough SEC. Check out the turnover margin in the paper and see who wins. Usually, it is the team that took care of the ball the best on that given day.

No Foolish Penalties

When we first got to Ole Miss, we led the league in penalties. We had to convince and teach and persuade our guys that they cannot make foolish penalties. It is against the rules. Let's don't beat ourselves.

Win the Kicking Game

A lot of people talk about the kicking game, but you really have to practice it. You have to make it a part of your practice every single day. Punt and kickoff returns are hidden yardage that can help you win football games. Punt and kickoff coverage is important in winning the field position. Extra points and field goals can cost you a game or a championship. The kicking game is important and you have to put in the time on the field working on it to win it.

Have No Missed Assignments

To me, this is teaching. I have to tell you a story. Every time I think about missed assignments, I think of Lou Holtz. In 1983, Lou Holtz gave me the job of a graduate assistant to coach fullbacks. After every practice, Coach Holtz would bring each coach into a meeting room to critique the mistakes he had made that day. Coach Holtz would come into the room smoking his pipe. He would yell, "Who is coaching the fullbacks?" Now, I knew in my mind, even at age 22, Coach Holtz knew who was coaching the fullbacks because he gave me the job. I can still hear him say, "The fullback went the wrong way. The fullback did not take a six-inch step." For a guy that is 5'7" and speaks with a lisp, Coach Holtz is intimidating. "The fullback went the wrong way again. The fullback missed his assignment. Who is coaching the fullbacks?" I said meekly, "I am sir." He asked, "Did you work on these things?" I said, "Yes, Coach." He said, "Well, obviously, you're not a very good teacher."

He made me sick to my stomach. I thought there is no way I am ever going to coach. "The fullback went the wrong way. The fullback did not get the outside leg. The fullback did not hit the linebacker. Who is coaching the fullbacks? Did you go over any of that? Who is coaching the fullbacks?"

I blurted out by mistake, "I went over that play 500 times." The projector goes off. When the projector goes off, there is extreme silence. You know you are in some deep doo-doo and you are in bad shape. "What did you say?" "I went over that play 500 times." He said, "Obviously, you are a very, very poor teacher. I know how smart this young man is in the classroom. He is a smart kid." He asked me, "Mr. Nutt," he doesn't call me coach anymore, "what's so significant about the number 500? Why not 1,000? Why not 1,500? Do it until the job is done, Mr. Nutt." That is why I love Lou Holtz. I hated him then.

If the coach gives you a responsibility, then it is *your* responsibility. You have to do it as many times as it takes to get the job done. That is teaching, and that is coaching. It is easy to sit in the back of the room and say that player is not bright enough to do it, but he is. It is your responsibility to get him to do it. You have to have the attitude of perseverance in teaching. You have to want to make sure he gets it because it is your responsibility.

Must Play Great Goal Line Offense and Defense

There are going to be a few times during the year where winning comes down to great goal line offense and defense. You have to take great pride in that area.

No Cheap Long Touchdowns

We gave up way too many long plays this year during our games. Usually two to three missed tackles ends up resulting in cheap scores.

Honesty and Integrity

As a coach in today's society, you are under a microscope. The first thing you have to do is be honest. We are role models. You are an example in the town. You are an example in the city. You are an example at the school board. You are an example in your community. Everyone watches you. Everyone looks up to you. You go into a coffee shop and they are talking about you and your team. You go on an airplane and they are talking about you and your team. They look at a paper and they go to the sports page first. You are a role model and your players are role models. You may not want to be, but you are.

Coach the Player as if He Were Your Son

I know it is easy to get caught up in just the first teamers, but you have to coach everyone as if they were your son. That second-team guy may be in class or rooming with the first-team guy. Their attitude can become contagious. That enthusiasm and that passion can become contagious from one player to another.

Treat Them Fairly

Not all players will be treated the same. You get the respect that you earn. I may not treat someone that comes in late to a meeting the same. If someone comes into a meeting late one time during the entire year, I may come up to him and say, "Don't be late again," but somebody that is repeatedly late for meetings, I may get on them a little bit and be a lot tougher on them. I'm going to try to help him and I want him to "like it." I'm treating them fairly, but I may not be treating them the same. This is not a one-size-fits-all organization.

Coach, Coach, Coach, and Coach Before You Criticize

Do not be quick to give up on someone. He may be closer than you might think to getting the idea and to getting the job done. Don't give up on him. There is nothing better than coaching someone and watching him get better. This is where we have to become expert teachers. It is easy to say that he cannot do it or he will never be able to do it, but do not be too quick.

Repetition Is the Mother of Learning

Say it once, but do it a thousand times. This goes back to my story about Lou Holtz. We are going to go over, and over, and over it so they know what they are doing and can do it with their eyes closed.

Enthusiasm Is Contagious

When I go to a Friday night game, I like to see who is showing the most enthusiasm and effort. There is nothing like coaching a team and then getting told as a coach that your team plays hard. It's about effort.

Fundamentals

The most important factor you can teach is *fundamentals*. You must teach fundamentals every day. Do not let an opportunity go by to teach a kid the fundamentals of the game. It will save you time and keep you from being embarrassed later on.

Overcoach Effort

Never allow a player to *loaf*. That is one lesson you have to teach them. This world is too hard to let them loaf.

Don't Argue With Other Coaches in Front of Your Players

Sometimes you may have a disagreement with another coach, but you have to have the attitude that we will get this right but we're going to do it in the office after practice, rather than in front of the players. It is just like a husband and a wife. You can't argue in front of your kids because you lose credibility when you are arguing amongst yourselves. I've seen it happen on teams where they lose respect for their coaches.

Make the Game Fun

One thing Jimmy Johnson always did was he made it fun. When I played for him, it was really hot in Stillwater, Oklahoma. It hit 100 degrees for 10 straight days and I never will forget, in the second week of two-a-days, he told us to take off our pants and shoulder pads and to stack them neatly against the wall because we were going to go for a 200-yard walk to the swimming pool. I thought it was the neatest thing I had ever seen. Everybody just stood there. He had to tell us three times before we would believe him. But once we did, we sprinted to that swimming pool and boy that water felt good. The next day, I realized he got it out of us, but he made it fun. This is a hard, hard game we play, but make it fun and enjoy the competition.

Listen to Your Players—Balance Between Friends and Boss

It is always a good sign when former players come back to see you. There is not a greater feeling in the world than when one of your ex-players becomes a football coach. They are now coaches and teachers and making a difference in someone's life.

Try to Make All Players Feel Important

They all have to feel important, whether it is a scout team member or one of your starters. Everyone has a role. You need to let them know that they either need to lead, follow, or get out of the way. Everyone has to have a role, and everyone has to contribute. We are going to make everyone feel important.

Good Teams Get Better as the Season Goes On

They will either get better for you or they will get worse. Good teams always get better. I have a lot of respect for Coach Beamer at Virginia Tech. He lost his first two games this year to a tough Boise State team and then to James Madison University. Look how his team finished. They got better and better as the year went on, winning the remainder of their regular season schedule and the ACC Championship game. Commitment, attitude, and confidence grow as the season goes on for those great teams.

Coaching: Taking someone where they couldn't take themselves. This is what coaching is all about. It takes you, your staff, and their teammates. It takes everybody.

Let me talk about the Wild Rebel offense just a little bit. I will show some film and make comments as we go. At Ole Miss, we use what we call the "Wild Rebel." We get more credit than what we probably deserve for this. The single wing formation has been around for a long, long time.

I get asked all the time, "What would you do if you were starting a new offense from scratch?" Take any formation you want. I would take my best and fastest athlete, put him about five yards behind the center in a direct snap position, and run our plays. The same exact plays that the offensive line runs all year long, whether it be a power play, a counter play, or whatever. But when you do it, put your best player in that direct snap position. You can take your quarterback and put him outside as a wideout. The defense is going to have to cover him. We first started by taking our quarterback and putting him in that direct snap position, but he did not have the speed of Darren McFadden. We wanted our fastest athlete taking the snap.

We take the next fastest guy and send him in motion. You will have to work on this quite a bit to get the timing right, but you want the ball snapped when the man in motion is at the left tackle position. We want to hit this with the motion man going full speed, even if we are running power. It's funny because every time we called the Wild Rebel formation, our guys knew something big was about to happen. The defense has to respect the fast lightning sweep and we can still be running power.

Sometimes we did not even motion that guy. We might make him stationary, and we just take it and go with a direct snap and run the power. It is the same blocking scheme as before and the guard is still pulling to find a linebacker. We would mix it up and put the quarterback on one side and the next time, put him on the other side just to cause some confusion. The receivers have to still do a good job of blocking. We do not want our receivers to go to sleep on this. "We are getting ready to throw you a crumb here in a minute. Make sure you take care of your guy." The Wild Rebel really gave our guys our lift.

Take the fastest guy and let him take a direct snap. He is the guy that makes good things happen. We would run a counter off of that. And if he can throw just a little bit, he becomes a triple threat. If everyone crowded inside, we would bounce the counter play. We would use the word "bounce" just to tell the guy that he can use his speed and bounce it off to the outside.

Sometimes we would run the inside zone where the fullback would kick out the end defender on the line of scrimmage. He would put his head inside. Everyone else is going to run inside zone. A lot of times when we ran this play, we did not put the man in motion. If you put the man in motion, sometimes the defense will try to squeeze the edges. We kept him out there on the outside and ran it to give us more room inside. I think anyone in this room could take his best and fastest player who has some ball skills and can lift his leg and develop some timing and be successful in running these plays. It is even better if he can throw, just every now and then.

When we run the sweep, the man in motion has to be coming fast. Let him circle the defenders on the line of scrimmage. The receivers have to make sure that their defenders cover the field. I think this is just a fun set that everyone has confidence in. People are getting better at defending it by having their defenders come off the edges and hitting the quarterback in the mouth and blowing things up. Our quarterback this year was really good at rising up and throwing the quick hitches to offset those defenders coming hard off the edge.

The idea is to put your playmakers in a position to make plays. A variation that we run is to pull the guard to make the defense think it is power, but we hand the ball off. The defense is thinking power, but we have already hit the outside. We can do the same thing with the counter. We still have the

guard pull. We fake the straight handoff and in the end, our fastest guy has to make one person miss. The counter action freezes everybody on the inside.

With the same formation and same play-action, we can run the reverse and the reverse pass. With the reverse pass, we will have the X-receiver come all the way across, aiming for the pylon on the other side of the field. After the direct snap guy hands the ball off, he sprints out to the numbers and sits there as an outlet receiver. If anything goes wrong, you can just flip it to him.

We also will run a wheel route off of it after the fake. For all of these plays, if the ballhandling is good, it is hard to defend. When your quarterback can rise up and throw the quick pass, it makes the opponent defend the whole field. These are simple throws, slants, hitches, and wheel routes. A six-yard throw might turn into 12 or 13 yards and a first down. If we see the corner is sitting off seven yards or more, we would call smoke and throw it to the outside and let him go get 10 or 12 yards. We can also take the guy in motion, after we fake it to him, and let him be the lead blocker for a quick screen. There are a lot of variations that you can do off of the Wild Rebel.

If you feel the corners are squatting on you a little bit and you want to take a shot, you can take a chance down the field and run by somebody.

You are not really changing routes or schemes, you are running your plays with a little bit of variation. I would not change your offense a lot. I would do what you do with just a few minor adjustments. The good thing about it is the guys always felt that something big was about to happen when we got in the Wild Rebel formation. Everybody felt good about it.

There are many variations off of this. Sometimes we fake the run and run a naked bootleg off of it. We can run the fullback into the flat and the tight end runs a little flag on the backside. Then the quarterback can throw off of the naked bootleg. If you can keep a quarterback in there at the direct snap position, that is great, but he has to be a really good athlete and really fast.

I really appreciate you coming to the Nike Clinic and coming to hear me speak. I wish you all a lot of luck, and I appreciate everything that you do. Thank you.

NECK EXERCISES TO HELP REDUCE CONCUSSIONS

University of Kentucky

First, it is a privilege to be here today talking with coaches. I have my staff with me today. They are Dr. Ted Lambrinides and Brady Collins. Let me give you a background on Ted. He was one of my strength coaches at The Ohio State University. I was a defensive back at Ohio State, and Ted was one of my strength coaches. He is as knowledgeable as anyone in the United States in the area of strength and conditioning.

In addition, we have Brady Collins, who is a grad assistant with us this year. He is going to demonstrate some neck exercises today. We want to give you an idea on the techniques we use.

I am going to talk about some of the things we do *not* do. It will not help you if we just stand up here and tell you, "We do this at the University of Kentucky." It is not going to make much sense to you just to go over what we do in our program. I am going to cover some of the things I think are important. Ted will cover some points he feels are important. Brady will demonstrate a few exercises for you.

In strength training, as coaches we must understand exactly what our job is and what the role is for strength coaches. I was at a physical conditioning clinic at Michigan State University last week. A speaker I used to work with when I first started out in this profession gave a good definition of what a strength program should be like. Most people will say the strength program is a bunch of squats, clings, and bench press. It is whatever you feel you need to do to become stronger.

I want you to write this definition down, because if you do not understand this explanation, you can leave now. This is as close to being perfect to what a strength program is supposed to be. It is true for middle schools, although I think it is idiotic to have young kids lift weights, or high schools, or college, and at the highest level of strength training.

The job of the strength program is to physically prepare the players to play football. It is to physically prepare the players to play football. *It is to prepare the players for the stresses and rigors of a violent game.*

That is what we do. We prepare them physically to play football and prepare them for the stresses of a vigorous and violent game. When you review this statement, you have to think about what you are doing. You must decide what you are trying to accomplish. What are you spending the most of your time on? Whom is it benefitting? Are you turning kids on to strength training or turning them off from strength training?

You will have young athletes with long legs, long arms, and long torso who can play their rear end off. You are going to have some short-legged players like me, who can bench lift the whole weight rack. You must decide what you are going to try to accomplish, and who is going to benefit from the strength program you use? Is this going to help them become better players, and is this going to prepare them for a violent, violent, violent game?

I want to make sure you understand where we are in the game of football today. I just had a talk with some NFL people. I talked with a couple of college reps as well. These people have been talking to the people in Congress about our sport. We need to start reducing the concussions, understanding more about them, and we must understand we must get the neck a lot stronger.

Every neck of a football player should be larger than other individuals their age. Understand what I am saying to you. We are not close to where we need to be in terms of where we need to be in working with the football players' necks.

I want Dr. Ted Lambrinides to talk with you about this problem. This should give you a good idea of what we are talking about.

DR. TED LAMBRINIDES

Thank you, Rock. Along with the federal legislation that is coming down, we are getting more information from the medical field on concussions. This may help some of you coaching at schools where you do not have a lot of kids playing football. If one of your players has a concussion, how many games is he going to be out? Who knows that answer? Perhaps two games. Yes, provided the medical staff clear him. You are talking about two to three weeks for a player who sustains a concussion. If he is your best player, you are in trouble.

When someone asks us the most important things we do in our weight room, we talk about the neck. When we are queuing up the players to do their exercises, we let them know how important the neck is in our game. "You do these exercises as if your life depends on it! It does depend on the neck."

When you figure out how you are going to organize your program, this will shift the priority. It is not like, "We are going to fit the neck exercises into our weight program." No! It should be where we fit all of the other crap into the program after the neck exercises.

ROCK OLIVER

Do you understand where we are coming from? We are not going to talk about bench press or the squat all day. I am addressing this to all levels of football, including high school, college, and the pros. If we do not get this problem figured out, it will not matter about the squat or bench press anymore for football. How many of you know how to train the neck? How many muscles in the neck? You say 52 muscles in the neck. It is the most important thing you are going to do in your program. I always think that way myself. Before, I had head coaches getting on my butt about getting the players to increase their number of squats or bench presses. I do not care about that anymore. That is going to take care of itself.

The most important thing you are going to do in football is to strengthen the neck muscles. The second-most important thing you are going to do is to teach the players how to tackle. I am not kidding you, now. If we do not do this, our game of football is going to disappear.

Coaches tell me they did four sets of bench press, five sets of squats, 10 sets of triceps pushdowns, and 500 sprints. I ask them why they did not work the neck. I tell them not to give me the bull story that they did shrugs.

The first thing you should do when you get back to your school is to get a tape measure and measure the player's necks. No one ever broke a "pec muscle." You get into a game, and the player makes a tackle with his head down. The player is on the ground, and everyone is quiet. That is not your son, but it is someone else's son. What I am telling you is that we must get this situation corrected. In our program, we have to get it right as well. If we do not get it right, then shame on us. I am sorry, Ted; go ahead.

DR. TED LAMBRINIDES

It is important for the coaches to document what you are doing in your program. If you look at the headlines of the major magazines, including *Time Magazine, The New Yorker, Outside the Lines* on ESPN, and other publications, it is important to document what you are doing in football. When you have soccer moms saying, "Kids should not be playing football," every job in football is in jeopardy. You have to document what is your neck program. You better have it spelled out, what you are going to do and how you are going to administrate the program. If one of your players goes down on the field, and you end up sitting in front of an attorney, he will drill your butt on the stand.

You had a case in Louisville a few years ago when a kid went down on the field and died later in the hospital. That case went to court. If you have 80 players on the team, some of them are going to be on special medications. You better make sure you red flag those players at risk with their problems and the medications they are taking. These players will be more susceptible to head ailments.

If you have kids who have sickle-cell traits, you need to red flag them. If you start chewing out a kid who has sickle-cell traits, he is having a bad day, and he dies, guess what? Ask University of Mississippi, ask the University of Central Florida, ask Rice University. All of those cases were settled out of court for 10 million dollars. If a player breaks his neck during a football game and dies, those are 50-million-dollar cases to settle.

When you are playing in a game, and you see these head injuries, and the player is struck on the side of his helmet, the bowl of jelly inside the player's skull bangs off the side of the player's skull. If the player has a larger neck, it decreases the massive forces in the brain. Why is this important? First, you are protecting the kid, and second, if you had not increased the size of the player's neck, the player may have gotten a full-blown concussion. Then, he is out two games, and you lose those two games. Guess what? At the end of the year, they fire the coach. Make no doubt about it; it all comes down to wins and losses. We must make sure our players are doing the proper neck exercises.

The other benefit of working the player's neck is this: research shows when you strengthen the necks of the players and make the neck stronger, the players' vertical jump goes up, and they can run faster. What a great side effect. How about that! Can we explain this? We can't explain it. It just happens. I do not want to date myself, but it goes back to the days of Woody Hayes, former head coach at Ohio State. This is what he used to say: "You should be able to tell who the players are on campus by the size of their neck."

We want the neck starting behind the ears, and coming down toward the shoulders. Players must be able to absorb the forces to the head that occur in football. Also, make sure when you are teaching tackling to show the players the incorrect way to tackle, and what the side effects are. When you look at some of the lawsuits that have occurred, when coaches are on trial, this is what the lawyers ask the coach: "Coach, did you show the individual players the 'incorrect' way to tackle?" So be sure to show the players the incorrect way to tackle and the side effects of an incorrect tackle.

It is the same thing in the weight room. There is a case where an individual sued a strength coach in high school. The player threw out his back doing squats. The case went to court, and the attorney asked the coach if he showed the individual the correct way to squat. The coach assured the attorney he did show the individual the correct way to squat.

Next, the attorney asked the coach if he had shown the individual the incorrect way to squat. He was asked if the coach told the player what the side effects would be if the individual did the exercise incorrectly. Therefore, in everything you do, you should show the players the correct way to do an exercise, and the incorrect way to do the exercise, and the effects of doing the exercise incorrectly. Then they want to know if you told them, what the consequences were if they did the exercise wrong.

ROCK OLIVER

Later, we are going to have Brady Collins demonstrate some neck exercises. Before we do that, I want to make some additional comments about the neck. If you work the neck correctly, you should feel as if you are about to pass out if you work the neck hard enough. When I watch players do neck exercises, and they have partners, they do not apply the pressure needed on the neck. How do you address the neck? How many of you have four-way neck machines? If you do not have them, what do you use?

I want to add a couple more things to this lecture. If you talk to athletic trainers at the NFL level, they will tell you it is a scary thing going on today. They cannot stay on top of all of the things going on with the forces of football that the game has become.

What is happening now is this: they have come up with a machine, similar to an MRI, where they can look at players with concussions and look at the brain to see what is happening with the injuries to the head. They can look at the brain and determine when the injuries occurred. Today, the difference in a 5-million-dollar lawsuit and a 50-million-dollar lawsuit is this: an 18-year-old kid was injured, and he did not train his neck. That kid will be in a wheelchair for the rest of his life. This is because he did not train the neck. Don't think when they start questioning you in court you can tell them what really happened. You will not have the right answer. You will not be able to satisfy the attorney and the jury in court.

What you can do is to document and make the neck an essential part of your program. That is a must in today's world. I know coaches who do not address the neck in their program. They are shooting craps with this situation in their programs. It is that important! Does everyone understand what I am saying? We will sit down and talk strength training all you want. We can talk about the bench press, squats, or any other phase of our program. We can talk with you about all of the silly stuff that we know everyone is going to work on.

What I want to talk about is my nephew. He is 14 years old. He is a good player. I am talking about this age group. I am going to talk with his coach and the players on his team. I am talking to you about the neck problem. This is important to me at the University of Kentucky that we get this message out to you. If we get nothing else across to you, we want to stress the neck problem. The University of Kentucky wants to convey the message to everyone how important this situation is today. It is our job to make sure before we leave here today that you understand the most significant part of a strength program is to get players prepared for the rigors of the program. The most dangerous aspect of this sport is how violent it is, and the injuries that come to the head, and the neck.

We can help these young people survive and enjoy the game. We can have parents who are not afraid and save our life at the end if we ever have to appear in court. We need to make this our number-one priority. You make the neck program number one, and then figure out where you are going to work in the squats and other exercises.

The bench press is one of the most stupid exercises I have ever seen. It is stupid. We used the bench press for 12 years. We had players who could not bench press 225 pounds eight times. Those players could play for us. But, don't get caught up in an exercise. The bench press does helps players get stronger. Who is going to be good at doing the bench press? The short players and players with short levers are good doing the bench press.

We get the genetics all twisted. Most coaches think the strength program is going to dictate how big, fast, and strong players are going to be. No! Genetics does this. I can personally tell you this. My father was a good athlete, and my mother was fast and a good athlete. She was a good volleyball player. My brother was strong in the weight program and a good football player. My uncle benched pressed 500 pounds. All of my genetics pointed to being able to do those types of activities. It was in my genes. We were all good at those exercises. What did that mean? It did not mean crap. I was not very good at

football. I was good at bench pressing. How much did the bench press really help me? I finally figured it out when I was at Ohio State. I was one of the strongest players at Ohio State as a freshman. On Saturdays, I was sitting on the bench. Of course, I was confused.

What all of us need to do is to get everyone in our programs involved in working on the neck. Turn them into training sessions to make the neck stronger.

Now, we want Brady Collins, our GA, to demonstrate some neck exercises. Before he gets going, I want to add a few points. We know how to train the neck. A long time ago, we learned about the strength of the neck. After 28 years working in this area, I think we are good at strengthening the neck. For those in the back of the room, get your butts up here where you can see. I want you to see this.

I do not want you to leave this clinic and say we did not teach you how to train the neck the proper way. That is not going to happen. If you do not want to learn how to strengthen the neck, you can leave now. This issue is that important to me. We want to make sure everyone knows how to train the neck.

A lot of the times, you are on a practice field in doing these exercises. However, we can do them inside as well.

First, we want to do is to work neck extensions. We are down on all fours with the weight on the forearms. If the players are on the hands, they start using their arms to do the exercise. By bending the arms, you cannot push off.

You have one player with his hand on the low back, with the other hand on the back of the head of the player doing the exercise. He brings up the head, and then out. The player doing the exercise is going to resist and press his head down. It is up, and resist down. Again, it is up, and resist down. When Brady gets done, his face is going to look as red as the shirt there. When you are queuing it up, you want to fill a pinch the whole way. The player helping on the drill is pushing the players head up, and the player doing the exercise is pushing his head down.

Now, you can do a couple of things. You can do reps, or you can time the exercise on the practice field.

Now, he is going to flip on his back. He takes his hands and raises them up just as he would be making a goalpost. We do a neck flexion. When you do this, you are trapped. If you have a weak neck, your trapezius is trying to do most of the work. By putting the arms up, it takes the trapezius out of the exercise.

We must understand that, on every repetition, Brad is going to get weaker. The helper in this case must understand this. He must understand that on every repetition less force is going to be needed.

The keys in the weight room are going to be the same as it is on the practice field. It is a matter of organization and execution.

I was listening to a coach lecture. He said they had to run four or five plays before they could run the multiple formations. The point I am making is this: whatever you do in the weight room, do it well. We do not do a lot of fancy stuff, but what we do, we coach up.

DR. TED LAMBRINIDES

When we sat down before our off-season this year, we asked the question, "What do we have to do better?" Rock and I both said, "Coach better." Each time the players came to the weight room, we assumed they had never done the exercises we were working on before. We coached them up as if it were the first time they had ever been in our weight room. We do this every time they come into the weight room. Is that hard to do? Yes! Was it necessary? Yes, it was necessary. It is repetition. You do the same things with your players. It is repetition, and you execute the basics. On this drill, we take the helmet off.

Next, if we are going to do lateral moves, we are going to have the player assisting the exerciser to put one hand on the shoulder, and the other hand on the side of the head. He brings it over, keeping the shoulders square. Power up, fight it all the way back.

The key thing on this is to make sure he does not cheat on the exercises. As he gets tired, he is going to want to cheat on the exercise. He is not going to want to go through a lot of extra motions. He wants to keep the shoulders square during the entire exercise.

Question: Are you going to do this exercise on a chair?

You can do it on a chair, but if you are in-season, you may have to do it on the practice field, sitting down on the ground. If you can do as much work on the field as possible, the better it is.

We do these exercises twice a week. We start at 30 seconds and add to that each day. We may go up to one minute. If you are doing reps, you can go from 8 to 12 reps. If you do it right, and you are honest, and you have not really concentrated on the neck, you should do 6 to 7 reps on this exercise.

The players must understand the importance on the exercises and the emphasis put on the neck because it is the most important part of our program. If they understand that, and we can convey that message to them, we can do our jobs. We want to be honest in letting them know this is our job and why we are doing the exercises.

If you want to use the NFL as a model, you can because all of the young players think they are going to play in the NFL. You can show them what is going on with all of the injuries and let them know it is important to do the exercises correctly. All of the players can understand the situation. We want them to know this is why we are starting to work on the neck immediately in our programs. The greatest thing about high school players is that they listen to the coaches. By the time they get to us at the college level, they stop listening. When they get to the NFL, they get their own trainer.

Because the high school players will listen to coaches, we must be very exact in what we are teaching the players. The techniques and fundamentals of what you are teaching must be sound. The high school players can spot do-do through the fog on the Hudson River.

I want to share with you what we do in our manual resistance training program.

RESPONSIBILITIES OF THE COACH

Thoroughly understand the responsibilities of the spotter and lifter. The coach should develop an in-depth understanding of how to apply the manual resistance concepts. These exercises cannot be spotted and performed in a haphazard manner.

Unfortunately, more often than not, this is the rule rather than the exception. If this occurs, the potential results from the exercise will be reduced and the risk of injury to the lifter will be increased.

Note: Thoroughly read the guidelines enclosed and develop a detailed understanding of how to safely and effectively spot and perform each exercise.

Perform the exercises with another coach in order to develop the skills needed to spot and perform each exercise. It's obvious to every coach and physical educator that doing something is better than talking about it. Unfortunately, few coaches are willing to actually practice doing the MR exercises. The exact skills to apply the resistance and perform the exercises will not be developed unless the coach practices what he preaches.

Note: There is nothing overly demanding about the skills needed to spot and perform each exercise. Something will be lost, however, from the instructor to the student if the coach doesn't experience of the problems encountered.

Minimize the loss in the interpretation of this information from the coach to the student. The coach's first responsibility is to adhere to the aforementioned rules. The eventual quality of MR exercise performed by the participants will be determined by how well the instructor prepares himself and by how well that information is taught to the students. This is not the type of information posted on the weight room bulletin board. Initially, constant supervision by the coach is necessary to eliminate any confusion. Ideally, the coach should discuss all of the concepts enclosed and then spot each student through the exercises until they have mastered the skills required.

Note: The coach can teach one thing, and the student may interpret it differently. Coaches must minimize the loss in translation to the students.

RESPONSIBILITIES OF THE LIFTER

For manual resistance to be safe and effective, the lifter must assume some responsibilities during the execution of each repetition. These responsibilities include the following four rules.

Communication with the spotter is essential. Total cooperation and coordination between the lifter and the spotter are essential. For maximum gains and safety, you may have to tell the spotter how to provide resistance that is more efficient. Cooperation with the spotter is necessary for smooth and even resistance. Until the spotting and lifting skills have been mastered, the lifter may have to talk to the spotter. For example, "You're not providing enough resistance on the lowering phase" or "You're pulling too hard in the stretched position."

Keep tension on the muscles. The relief of muscle tension for just an instant will allow the muscle to momentarily rest and make the exercise less productive. Allowing the muscles to relax briefly is a common occurrence during the lateral raise if the hands are allowed to touch the sides of the legs. This gives the muscles a brief rest and makes the exercise less productive. Another example would be the conventional push-up exercise. The muscles are allowed a brief rest if the chest, thighs, or mid-section touch the ground. Ideally, the hands should be elevated off the ground to prevent resting between repetitions.

Pause momentarily in the contracted position. The lifter should hold the contracted position momentarily during the execution of each repetition. If the lifter doesn't hold this position momentarily, he will not maximally develop the muscle at each point during that range of motion. The pause also gives the spotter time to begin applying the more resistance required for the lowering phase while in the transition from the raising phase of the exercise to the lowering phase.

An example of this concept is the bent-over side lateral raise. The lifter must stop and hold the contracted position momentarily. A good guideline would be to hold the position for a count 1001. If the lifter does not concentrate on pausing the contracted position of any exercise, there will be a bouncing effect or recoil from the raising to the lowering phase.

Note: Hold any contracted position for a count of 1001, and allow the muscles to develop maximally throughout their full range of motion.

Exert an all-out effort. A sub-maximal effort will produce sub-maximal results. The lifter must work as hard as possible if maximum gains are to be obtained. If the lifter exerts an all-out effort and the training partner applies the MR correctly, the lifter will be assured of obtaining maximum benefits.

Allow four seconds for the lowering phase. The lifter can lower more resistance than he can raise. During the lowering phase of some exercises, the lifter may be capable of exerting more force than the spotter can apply during the first few reps. The lifter must cooperate with the spotter and perform the lowering phase of the exercise. During the lowering phase of some exercises, the lifter could stop at any point, if he so desired, and hold that position, not allowing the spotter to push him down. This could invite injury and make the exercise less effective. Remember that in each succeeding repetition, the person exercising will grow weaker. Eventually, the spotter will be capable of applying more than enough resistance during the lowering phase. Until this point is reached, the exerciser must cooperate with the spotter during the lowering phase.

RESPONSIBILITIES OF THE SPOTTER

It should be more than obvious to anyone interested in MR of the value of a properly educated training partner. The effectiveness of MR exercise is almost totally dependent on the abilities of the spotter. It cannot be emphasized enough how important it is for the instructor to thoroughly educate the participants. For the exercise to be safe and effective, the spotter should strictly adhere to the following guidelines. The major responsibilities of the spotter include the following.

Communicate whenever necessary, and maintain constant coordination with the lifter. Pay attention to the execution of every repetition. *The lifter's safety is the spotter's primary concern.* How the spotter applies the MR dictates the quality and safety of the exercise. The spotter should make corrections, if needed, and provide verbal encouragement for motivation. If the lifter is not strictly adhering to the exact methods prescribed, the spotter should correct the lifter immediately.

Do not apply maximum resistance during the first few reps. The first few reps of each exercise should be used to warm up the involved muscles. This will also help to begin gradual fatiguing the

muscles so that when the lifter does exert an all-out effort, the muscle will be weaker. This will decrease the potential for injury.

Note: If maximum resistance is applied on the first few reps, injury could result. Less than maximum resistance is required on the first few reps.

Vary the resistance of each rep during the raising phase. Once the muscles are warmed up, the spotter should learn to apply as much resistance as the lifter can safely and effectively handle at each point during the raising phase. All movements should be smooth and controlled. This is the most difficult aspect of manual resistance to master. The amount of resistance that a lifter needs during the raising phase of one rep will actually vary. The bones and musculature are a system of levers. The changing positions of the bone and muscles create leverage advantages and disadvantages. These advantages and disadvantages will require more or less resistance by the spotter.

An example of the leverage system is the conventional push-up exercise. The lifter requires more resistance as the arms straighten. He requires less resistance as the arms bend. Another example of the leverage system can be observed while spotting the side lateral raise. It's obvious that the lifter gradually grows weaker (requires less resistance) as the arms are raised away from the body and weakest in the contracted position.

The spotter should learn to gradually increase or decrease the resistance accordingly to accommodate these changing "strength curves." If the resistance is being applied correctly, the resistance should feel constant to the lifter. The spotter is adding exactly as much resistance as the lifter can raise at each point during the raising phase. If too much resistance is applied at any point, the lifter will be unable to move momentarily. He will be forced to stop the exercise, jerk, or use cheating movements to continue the exercise. If not enough resistance is applied, the exercise will be less productive than it could be.

The spotter should also be aware that the lifter is gradually fatiguing with each succeeding repetition. If the resistance is properly applied, the amount of resistance will decrease with each rep. If the spotter applies the resistance correctly, he will only have to apply a few pounds of resistance on the last rep or two. On some exercises, the lifter may be unable to raise even the weight of his arms.

Note: It is the spotter's job to apply just the right amount of resistance at each point during the raising phase.

Maintain a smooth transition from the raising phase to the lowering phase. The person applying the resistance should adjust the amount of resistance at the point of transition from the raising phase to the lowering phase. It should be realized that the lifter can lower more weight than he can raise. This is why it is important for the lifter to pause momentarily in the contracted position. This gives the spotter time to begin smoothly applying the additional workload for the lowering phase.

Spotters cannot make a sudden change from the raising to the lowering phase, or the lifter will be unable to hold the contracted position momentarily. The lifter will not make a smooth transition. There will be a sudden drop, which will not allow the muscle to be exercised maximally at each point. It may also invite injury.

Add more resistance during the lowering phase. Due primarily to friction, the lifter can lower more weight than he can raise. The spotter should learn to apply more resistance during the lowering phase. If not enough resistance is applied, the lifter could stop at any point during the lowering phase and hold that position for several seconds.

Because the lifter is so much stronger during the lowering phases, there must be mutual cooperation between the lifter and spotter. The same leverage advantages and disadvantages that exist during the raising phase of each exercise apply to the lowering phase. The person applying the MR must also be aware that the lifter is gradually fatiguing each rep.

The spotter should learn to apply as much resistance as the lifter can resist while allowing four seconds to lower the weight. If too much resistance is applied during the lowering phase, the lifter will be unable to allow four seconds to perform the lowering movement. This could invite possible injury.

Change the angle of resistance being applied. Most movements in the body are rotary in nature.

Most muscles contract about an axis of rotation. They pull on the bones to form movements that form an arc. For the muscles to be most effectively exercised, the angle of resistance must change through the execution of each repetition. This must be done to accommodate the changing angle that the muscle is pulling on the bone.

The MR must be supplied to coincide with the changing angles of each arc formed by the muscles involved. The changing angle resistance applied can be observed while performing the side lateral raise. In the starting position, the angle of resistance will be almost perpendicular to the floor. As the lifter raises his arms, the spotter should gradually adjust the angle of resistance. This concept will apply almost any time a single muscle group is isolated. The spotter should develop the ability to recognize the correct angle of resistance.

Provide enough resistance to stimulate strength gains. For maximum gains, the spotter needs to apply as much resistance as the lifter can exert during the execution of both the raising and lowering phase of each repetition.

Do not apply maximum resistance for any exercise in an all-out manner during the first few workouts. Gradually increase the intensity of exercise in each succeeding workout until the techniques required for each exercise have been mastered.

When necessary, apply less resistance as the lifter approaches the muscle's stretched position. While performing some exercises, the spotter should learn to gradually decrease the amount of MR being applied as the lifter approaches and eventually reaches the joint's stretched position. Injury could result if too much resistance is applied in the stretched position of the muscles being exercised.

The spotter should sacrifice the application of maximum resistance to gain maximum stretching and prevent injury. A good example is the neck flexion exercise. The lifter will not relax and stretch the neck if too much resistance is applied. To get the lifter into a relaxed and stretched position safely, the spotter should begin to gradually decrease the amount of manual resistance as the lifter approaches the neck stretched position. It should be a smooth and gradual transition. The spotter is applying too much resistance near or at the stretched position if the lifter:

- Doesn't reach a completely relaxed and stretched position at the end of each rep.
- Stops short of the stretched position.
- Feels the need to pull back in the stretched position to prevent hyper stretching.

PERFORMING MANUAL RESISTANCE EXERCISES

While performing MR exercises, the following guidelines should be used to perform each exercise:

- Perform 12 repetitions or continue exercising for approximately 40 to 70 seconds.
- Perform only one set per exercise.
- Take four seconds for the lowering phase.
- Allow three to four seconds to execute the raising phase of each exercise. This will include moving from the starting position and pausing in the contracted position momentarily.
- Exercise two to three times a week while alternating days.
- Change the order regularly.

The most important aspect of MR is knowing the proper way to spot and to lift. All of you have been through our MR program from time to time, but for those of you who might have missed something along the way, here is a quick review of the MR exercises we perform at the University of Kentucky.

The following exercises will be explained (e.g., starting position, description of movement, and spotting form) on the next few pages:

- Neck flexion
- Neck extension
- Lateral flexion (right and left)

MANUAL RESISTANCE NECK EXERCISES

There are a variety of MR exercises that can be performed. A brief description of each exercise will follow. For maximum gains, reduce the lifter's strength level to zero. We do this by performing approximately 10 to 12 repetitions on each exercise.

Remember to follow the guidelines we discussed earlier for the lifter and spotter.

Note: Be especially cautious with neck exercises.

Exercise #1. Neck Flexion (Neck Flexors)

Starting: Lying flat on the ground, the legs are bent with the feet flat, and the arms are at 90 degrees. It is important to keep the back of the hand in contact with the ground. At the beginning of each rep, the neck muscles must be totally relaxed.

Movement: Flexing only the neck muscles, raise the head forward and upward so that the chin is resting on the chest. Pause momentarily, and recover to the starting position.

Spotting: Place the dominant hand on the lifter's forehead and the non-dominant hand on the lifter's chin. Apply as much pressure as is needed to accommodate for the strength curve of the neck flexors.

Exercise #2. Neck Extension (Neck Extensors)

Starting: Kneeling down with the knees and forearms resting on the ground and the chin touching the chest.

Movement: Raise the head upward and backward until it is fully extended. Pause momentarily before recovering to starting position

Spotting: With the right hand on the back of the head and the left hand on the lifter's lower back, begin the exercise with mild pressure to stretch the neck, and continue to carry the resistance according to the strength curve on the neck extensors.

Exercise #3. Lateral Neck Flexion (Right and Left)

Starting: Sit up with straight legs and arms extended behind the body. The shoulders should be square and the head flexed to the right.

Movement: Flexing the neck only, move the head from all the way to the left shoulder while keeping the shoulders square. Pause momentarily before returning to the starting position. Repeat exercise to opposite side.

Spotting: Standing behind the lifter, have your right hand on the lifter's right shoulder and the left hand on the left side of the lifter's head. Apply as much pressure as is needed to accommodate for the strength curve of the lateral neck flexors. Make sure that the lifter keeps the shoulders square, and vary the resistance to allow for a full range of motion.

I want to repeat the most important part of this lecture. Measure the neck when you get back to your school. Some necks may not develop as quickly as the necks of other athletes. But, because you are recording it, they are going to get stronger. You will see a stronger and faster athlete as a result.

The job of the strength program is to physically prepare the players to play football. It is to physically prepare the players to play football. *It is to prepare the players for the stresses and rigors of a violent game.*

If we do this, we can save our sport. If we do not get the concussions and cervical injuries under control and see them start to decrease, we can continue to coach. We love this game, and you are coaching because you love football. I can look at a coach and tell that person loves the teaching and coaching and loves the game. The game is going to be taken away from us if we do not change what is happening to our athletes.

If you do not understand what is happening, go online at NFL.com. Just go there and type in "concussions." See what Congress has to say about football. They are talking about making us play football without helmets.

Don't fit the neck into your program. Get the neck into the program, and then fit the other parts into the program. I do not want a coach coming to me, asking me how to bench-press. I do not care about that. Get the neck exercises into your program. This is our state, these are our kids, and if we do not recruit them all, wherever they go, we want them to know how important the neck is related to football and other sports. If they go to another school and they do not emphasize the neck, that athlete can ask the coach about the neck exercises. This will not be because of what I have done; it will be because of what you have done.

If we are lucky enough to get one of your kids in our program, we are going to make sure we address that issue. If they come to us, they are going to be fit, stronger, tougher, and we are going to love them. Moreover, we are going to get them ready to play football because we know it is a tough game. It is a violent game, but we love it. It is intoxicating. I know it is to you, and it is to me. I can't think of anything else I would rather do. But we must remember it is someone's son we are talking about.

Let's give Brady Collins a hand for his demonstrations of the neck muscles. You are always welcome to visit our program. If we tell you we are doing something in our program, and you come to see us, we are going to be doing those things we said we would do. We do what we tell you we are going to do.

If you have a question, come to us. We have a lot of experience. However, if we do not have the answer, we will find it. Whatever you do, do it well. The one thing I want you to get out of this lecture today is this: the neck is the most important thing in your program. Men, it has to be that way. You know how to do all of the other things related to your program.

God bless you, and thanks a lot.

DEFENDING THE SPREAD OFFENSE

University of Connecticut

It is great to be here. I had a great time in the NFL, but I am excited to be back in college football. The thing I missed when I left college coaching was the camaraderie with high school coaches and being around events like this. During the off-season, you get to talk football. You can do something with the research and development of ideas you may have. You start to make plans for next year and begin to collect tapes and films about next year's opponents. For a teacher and coach, this is a great time of the year.

For my family, it is good to be back in college coaching. I have 12-, 11- and 9-year-old children. For me, to have my children on a college campus around college football and college students is good for both them and me. To have my family be a part of that environment is an exciting thing.

I want to give you a brief defensive philosophy, which includes sound principles regardless of the system you may run.

PHILOSOPHY OF DEFENSE

Stop the Run

- Average three yards or less per carry.
- Limit explosive gains 12 to 19 yards.
- Eliminate big plays over 20 yards.
- No rushing touchdowns.

Control the Pass

- Do not let the quarterback beat you.
- Pressure with four-, five-, and six-man pressure schemes.
- Blitz (cover zero)
- 35 percent or less on the third down
- 40 percent or less in the red zone

I am going to talk about defending the spread offense and the zone read. I want to talk about the fundamentals and go into the concepts of doing that along with that topic. The NFL is beginning to see some of those concepts on their level. Before we get into that, I want to share something about the philosophy of teaching.

PHILOSOPHY OF TEACHING

- Always teach in progression.
- Progress comes a little at a time (breakthrough).
- Build the confidence of players.
  - ✓ Do not challenge his courage.
  - ✓ Do not break his will.

One thing we must be aware of and careful with is the issue of head injuries. That issue is a hot topic everywhere you go today. It is a serious issue in the NFL. If you have a player go down with a concussion or some head-related issue, your chance of getting him back quickly is slim. You have to jump through many hoops, and they do not allow players to come back until they are sure they are able to play.

When we talk about teaching, we want to teach in a progression. You must have a progression of thoughts about how you are going to play the blocks in the zone play. The zone play is the heart and soul of the spread offense. You must have a basic concept of how to defend the spread. It starts with the fundamentals, drilling the skills, and putting together a package to reflect your thoughts. After I go through this initial segment, I want to show you how we play from a linebacker and defensive line prospective.

When you teach, the progress the players make comes a little at a time. Position coaches look for breakthroughs in players understanding what they are teaching. When you teach the players a new scheme, the understanding does not happen overnight. When you coach players, you have to teach the older and younger players differently. In both types of players, you have to build their confidence. If a player has played in the program, he has more confidence from simply knowing what you expect. If you coach junior high football, that point is critical. The confidence factor follows him all the way through high school. Part of our job is promoting the game of football. It is the responsibility of the coach to promote the game of football.

The commissioner of the NFL is doing a tremendous job of promoting football. He is doing an unbelievable job. It is the job of the football coach to promote football. It is not our responsibility as head coaches to create an environment where we challenge the courage of the players. Coaches have to be careful not to break the will of a player to play the game.

I have two sons who are about to become involved with youth football. I'm not sure I want them to play football. If I let them play, I will make sure I know how the coaches intend to teach them. The last thing we want to do at any level is to challenge the courage of our players. I have taught and coached at every level of football. I coached sixth grade, junior high, freshman, JV, varsity, Division I, II, III, and two professional NFL teams. I coached them all the same way. I taught with a progression and built their confidence. The skills and tools used in the game come a bit at a time and not overnight. Impatience is not an option. You must teach, teach, and teach some more. You must have a passion for teaching to coach football.

PHILOSOPHY OF DEFENDING THE RUN

- Use the hands.
- Do not give up one for one.
- Everyone is responsible for the ball.

The first items in teaching defending the run are using the hands. Everyone used to refer to this step as "hat and hands." We do not use that term any more. It is not part of the terminology when teaching this part of run defense. If you use that phrase, that is what you will get. You get the player leading with his head and bringing the hands later.

When the player defends blocks, he uses his hands. His hat may get involved, but he is using his hands. We want an explosion with the punch inside the framework of the body. When I taught a six-year professional linebacker how to take on a block, I taught him to punch with his hands and explode through the blocker. I did not teach him to butt the blocker. In fact, I am teaching the same technique on defense that I previously taught on offense. It is the same technique. Offensive and defensive drills today involve the same teaching. Both sides of the ball punch and look for inside position with their hands.

When a player defends the zone play, you do not want him stuck on an offensive player's block. It is not enough to protect your gap. You have to defend your gap and pursue back to the ball to play the zone play. The offense builds the zone play on the cutback run and the outside bounce.

We do not involve the shoulder in the technique unless that is the last alternative. We want to play more than our gap so we do not give one defender for one blocker. We must force two blocks on one defender to play effective defense. If the offense can block everyone with a 1-on-1 block, they win. That principle is true with every defense. It does not matter if it is a 4-3 or a 3-4 front. Not giving up one for one is a big deal with the defensive scheme.

The defensive scheme has to figure out a way to get more defenders into the box area to stop these types of runs. Everyone on the defense has to be responsible for the running game. In your meetings, you have to tell your players that it is their responsibility to stop the run. It is not negotiable. It is an absolute fact, and we write it on the wall. Their number-one responsibility is to control their gap, but they are all responsible for the ball.

LINEBACKER PROGRESSION

- Hands
- Steer (leverage)
- Stance, start, shuffle, hands
- Blood drill
- Reads

The first thing in the linebacker progression is how to use the hands. It is important that we teach leverage because so many players do not understand it. We have to show them how to get into and use a leverage position. The players today are stronger, faster, better coached, work better in the weight room, and are in great shape. Coaches are doing a great job because the players coming out of high school today are unbelievable. Coming out of high school, the players are better. Coming out of college, the players are better. The game is in better shape than it ever was in modern times.

The first thing the coach has to do is make sure the player understands what you want him to do. I want to utilize everything the coaches taught our players in the weight room. I use the bench press, squat, and clear lifts to teach techniques in football.

When we teach the punch, we teach it the same way you teach them to bench and squat. We punch with the heels of the hands. We want to use the explosiveness you taught him in doing the bench press. He punches into the framework of the body with the heels of his palm. He turns the thumbs of the hand up as if he were gripping the bar. When he punches, he locks out his arms as he would with the bench press.

We teach the punch in a simple drill (Diagram #1). The defensive player gets on his knees in a two-point stance. His knees and his toes are in contact with the ground. The offensive player aligns in front of him in an offensive stance. The distance between the two players is slightly more than arm's length. On the command, the blocker moves up from his stance, and the defensive player punches him in the chest with his hands. He punches with the heels of the palms. As he punches, the hips come forward and the arms lock out.

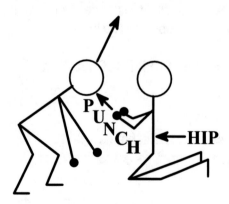

Diagram #1. Two-Point Punch

He does the repetition three times. On the third rep, he pushes with one hand and pulls with the other as the beginning of the separation of the block.

We do not align the players five yards apart and make them run into one another. There is a time and place for drills of that nature but it comes with the skill that it takes to perform the drill and the confidence to do it. At no time do we teach anything that involves butting with the head. My solemn advice to all coaches is: *do not* teach any drill that requires the use of the head as the primary weapon. When I was growing up, that was the accepted way to teach the drill, but not today.

The head will become involved with these types of drills, but the hands stop the momentum of the blocker and not the head. When you teach leverage to your players, use the fit drill. You put the player into a leverage position on the blocker. It is a fitted position. We want the palms into the chest of the blocker. The knees bend with the weight of the body on the inside of the feet. The elbows have a slight lock, and the eyes are below the hands. He wants his butt down and the back flat. That is the leverage position. That is the position we want the players to work for in the games. The blocker places his hands on the shoulders of the defender.

From the fitted position, the blocker moves to the right and to the left. When the blocker moves, the defender pushes up with the hand to that side and pulls with the opposite hand. He attempts to turn the blocker's shoulders as he shuffles in that direction. As the blocker changes direction and moves the opposite way, the defender reverses his leverage points on the chest. When the blocker moves, the defender shuffles in the same direction.

The linebacker has to play with his hands, and he has to be tough with the use of them. We call it playing with heavy hands. The punch is short and quick. In the leverage position, we teach them to steer the blocker. That is the movement and pressure of the hands. The defender moves in the direction of the blocker's movement. He pushes on the shoulder to that side and steers the blocker backward in the direction of the push. If the movement goes the other way, the defender extends the other arm and steers the blocker back.

The stance is a necessity for playing linebacker. We want his feet parallel with a good knee bend. His feet are under his armpits, and he is in a good fundamental football position. When the linebacker moves, we never cross over with our footwork.

We want him to shuffle as he goes downhill so he can redirect and track the ball. If the ball cuts back, the linebacker can move to the backside. If the ball stays frontside, he continues on his path. If he ball comes to him, he meets the blocker and executes the punch and separation techniques.

When you defend the spread, it is not as hard if all they do is run the ball. However, when you start to put a good wide receiver into the mix, you have problems. Cover zero does not look so good when the corner has to cover a good wide receiver alone. When you play a good spread team, you have to play the wide receivers with two people.

We use a simple step drill to teach the punch from depth (Diagram #2). The blocker aligns on the sideline. He steps with his right foot or left foot out of his stance. The linebacker aligns three yards away from the blocker. As the blocker moves his foot, the linebacker reacts toward the blocker. He closes on the blocker, punches him in the chest, and sheds the blocker to the inside.

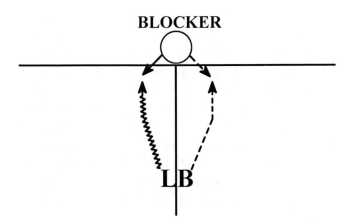

BLOCKER

Diagram #2. Step Drill

The linebacker reads the movement of the blocker and reacts downhill toward the blocker. He does not shuffle laterally. He shuffles downhill at the blocker. When the linebacker takes on a blocker, he delivers the blow on the same foot with the same shoulder. He wants that foot in the ground

so he can deliver maximum force on the hand shiver or the shoulder. If you have to stop the blocker, the linebacker shuffles down and with both feet in the ground, he explodes through the blocker.

The explosion is the same movement you use in the squat exercise. You have both feet on the ground and explode off both feet into the blocker.

The linebacker has to be first with his punch. If the blocker punches the linebacker, the first thing he does is grab the jersey with his hands inside. That is within the rules of holding. If the linebacker does not play with heavy hands, the blocker will grab and hold on to him. We cannot spend time locked into a blocker. We have to punch and separate from the block immediately. When we work the step drill, the blocker will vary with the width of his path. On one movement, he comes tight to the linebacker. On the next movement, the blocker takes a wider step. This makes the linebacker work at different angle on the blocker.

We do a punch and separate drill (Diagram #3). The linebacker aligns between two blockers. The blockers are one yard from the linebacker or defender. The coach stands behind the linebacker and cues the blockers to move forward. He points to one blocker, and he moves toward the linebacker. The linebacker reacts up, punches the blocker in the chest, and resets in his position. The coach cues another blocker, and the linebacker repeats the punch and reset. On the third movement, a running back behind the two blockers moves toward the line of scrimmage. The linebacker punches the blocks, separates, and attacks the running back. It is not a live tackle unless you have advanced to that point.

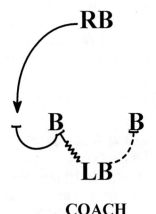

COACH
Diagram #3. Punch and Separate

The next drill is the same drill, except we have three blockers instead of two. The coach cues the blocker one at a time. The linebacker reacts to the movement and delivers the punch into the blocker. We watch the feet of the linebacker to make sure he is punching off both feet or at least with one foot. Reacting to the outside blocker, he may punch off one foot. However, we want him to punch off the foot to that side.

DEFENSIVE LINE PROGRESSION

- Stance and start
- Hands
- Steer (leverage)
- Shiver bomb
- Sled
- Bags
- 1-on-1 reads (1 count)
- 2-on-2 reads (2 count)

We coach the defensive line the same as we coach the linebackers. The first thing in the progression is stance and start. An offensive lineman blocks the defensive lineman on the second step. He cannot block the defender on his first step. He comes off on the first step, loads his hand, and readies for contact on the second step. He makes contact on that step and starts to climb the defender. The defensive lineman has to get off, get his second step down, and get his hands inside before the offensive lineman gets his second step down.

When we work on stance and the first two steps, we always work with a ball to trigger the get-off. We never go with a cadence. We want to get as close to the ball as we can. However, in our drill, we never work the defensive line off a yard line. The defensive line does not align according to a line. They align according to the ball. They have to align without being offside, but be as close as possible to the ball.

The stance on the first and second down is more balanced, and the first step from the stance is shorter. However, on third down, the stance has more stagger, and the first step is up the field. Third down is the pass rush down in the NFL.

The second progression on the list is the same as for the linebacker. The hand punch and steer are the same teaching for the defensive line as it is for the linebackers. The hands in this drill come in one movement from the thigh area. We do not put the hands on the ground or on the thighs in the punch drill. They do not rest them on anything. They are in front of the defender and shot from that position. They cannot draw back and try to deliver a hard punch. If the elbows go back before the hands come forward, he is slow to the target. We emphasize the hips coming forward and lock-out extension of the arm after the punch.

The steer drill is the same for the defensive line as it is for the linebacker. We put the defensive line into the fitted position. We make sure the heels are on the ground. In the fitted position, we do not want anyone on his toes. The power comes from ground traction. The more cleats you have in the ground, the more power you can generate.

We want the toes slightly outside and the weight on the inside of the feet. It is like pushing a car up a hill. You have no power if you are on the toes. You must have the feet on the ground and have a good base. In the steer drill, the defensive lineman shuffles and keeps the feet close to the ground.

We work on the sled to work the power punch. We have a two-man sled to work two players at a time. It is my job as the coach to make sure the defensive players are equipped to handle how they have to play. Their play is like a toolbox. It is my job as the coach to make sure they have the right tools in the toolbox. I must train them to play in the games. I have to make sure they have a chance to be successful by giving them the skills to play in the game. We repeat the drill until they gain confidence in what they are doing. That loads their toolbox with more tools.

The 1-on-1 drill is a read and react drill. When we work the 1-on-1 drill, it starts out as a two-count drill. That means the defender and the blocker start the drill with their first step. The step is the first count. After the first step, we say "Two," and they complete the drill. There is a pause between the first and second step.

We film all our drills and evaluate the players from those films. The big mistake the players make in the first step is letting the hands get behind the body. The hands have to stay in striking position. When we shoot the hands, they have to get there quickly. The more distance they have to travel, the slower the punch occurs.

When we go to a one-count progression, there is no delay in the movement. They start and finish the drill repetition with no delay. We work the 2-on-2 drills as one and two-count drills. We work two-on-two with combination blocks and double teams.

I want to get into some of my thoughts about defending the spread offense. The defense I use is base cover-4 quarter coverage (Diagram #4). The offensive formation is a standard 2x2 tight end set with the back aligned to the open slot side of the formation. We are not talking about outnumbering the offense in the box. The first thing we do is align our 3-technique defender away from the alignment of the running back.

the ball went wide, it had to bounce around him. If it came up inside, he discarded the tight end and fell back inside and made the play. If you have a defensive end who can play the C gap from a 9 technique, that is where you align him.

The 5-technique end comes across the line and has to play the quarterback as his first read. If the quarterback does not have the ball, he pursues down the line.

The 3-technique tackle gets penetration up the field in the B gap (Diagram #5). The dive back running the zone play can never get outside the 3-technique defender. The Mike linebacker technically plays downhill into the strongside A gap. On the snap of the ball, the Sam linebacker starts downhill, looking for the zone combination block from the tight end and strongside tackle. The 3 technique gets penetration into the backfield and looks inside. The Sam linebacker knows the ball cannot get to the outside and retraces and fills the strongside A gap. The Mike linebacker starts to the A gap, but retraces and plays to the openside C gap.

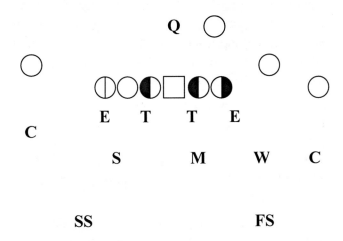

Diagram #4. Base Cover 4

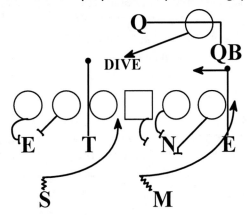

Diagram #5. Defensive Movement

The shade tackle plays on the inside shoulder of the openside offensive guard. The 5-technique end goes to the openside or the side where the running back aligns. The 6-technique defender plays over the tight end on the closed side of the formation. At Dallas, I never played DeMarcus Ware at 6 technique or a 7 technique. If he aligns over the tight end, he aligns in a 9 technique. The reason for that was there was not a tight end in the league who could block him.

DeMarcus Ware could take the tight end two yards deep in the backfield and play from there. If

Spread teams like to tie the bubble screen with the zone play. To the slot receivers, we are playing quarters coverage (Diagram #6). We read the receivers involved in the coverage. The Will linebacker aligns on the slot and reads the bubble screen to his side. The corner and free safety involved in cover 4 get their reaction off the #2 receiver, which is the slot receiver. The corner reads the wide receiver to the slot receiver. Once they see the bubble scheme, the coverage goes from cover 4 to cover 2.

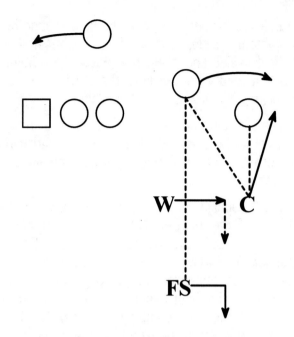

Diagram #6. Quarters to Cover 2

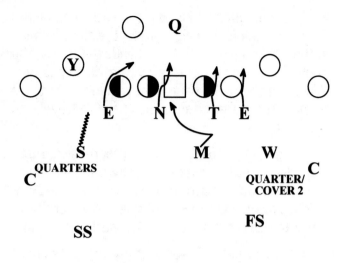

Diagram #7. Double Slot Tight End

The corner rolls to the bubble screen, and the free safety plays over the top. The Will linebacker in a cover-2 scheme plays from the #2 receiver to the #1 receiver. If the #2 receiver runs the bubble, the Will linebacker is working to the #1 receiver. If he blocks, the Will linebacker plays football. If he is running a pattern, the Will linebacker plays him for the inside curl. The free safety is over the top, and the corner rolls to the flat.

If the slot receiver runs vertical, the coverage stays in quarter coverage. The free safety takes the slot receiver on the vertical, and the corner plays his read off the slot receiver. Once the slot goes vertical, the corner locks on to the wide receiver.

If the offense flexes the tight end and become a double slot formation, we have to make an adjustment (Diagram #7). We want to align the 3-technique defender away from the alignment of the running back. The shade tackle plays 1 technique on the guard to the side of the running back. The Sam linebacker walks out on the tight end slot. The 5-technique end to the tight end side closes inside down the line off the butt of the offensive tackle. If there is a tight end as the slot, he is generally not

an option for a bubble screen. If the tackle turns back on the 5-technique tackle, the Sam linebacker becomes the B-gap player to that side.

They may show a bubble action to the tight end, but the bubble will go to the wide receiver in the opposite slot. To the tight end, we stay in quarter coverage. The Mike linebacker aligns to the 3-technique side and plays to the backside of the play. If they bring the center out to block the Mike linebacker, the 1-technique tackle has a free run to anyone running in that area.

You cannot play a good zone-read team in base defense all the time. You must have some change-ups and adjustments to use. You have to make the quarterback uncomfortable. If the offense knows what you are doing, the chances are you will be in for a long night.

We play quarter coverage in our secondary. The problem with quarters is what happens in vertical patterns. If the wide receiver and slot both go vertical, quarter coverage becomes man-to-man.

If you would like to come to visit us, we are always available. I hope I gave you something today that will help you. If you need anything from a football standpoint, we are there. Thank you for your attention.

PLAY-ACTION PASSING GAME

Penn State

I would like to thank you for being here. Pittsburgh is a great football town, as we all know, and it is great to be here. I love coming to this clinic because it is so organized and they do a great job of running the sessions. The coaches attending this clinic are here to learn. They are not just here for the fun of getting away.

What I would like to do tonight is give you an idea about our play-action passing game. As most of you know, my father, Coach Joe Paterno, has been at Penn State for decades and has always been committed to a balanced attack. Each year as we plan our offensive attack, the play-action pass is a very important part of that plan. When we talk about our offensive plan going into a game, we will talk about the running game, the dropback passing game, gimmick plays, the screen game, and play-action passes.

The play-action passing game does two things for us. Number one, it helps keep the run going; and number two, it also becomes like a counter play in our offense. One thing that we always want to make sure of is that we have some type of counter play off of our normal running plays. We will run counters, but we can also use the play-action pass and treat it like a counter. When we talk about all aspects of the offense, whether it is a dropback pass, running game, or screens, all those things have to be coordinated so that they are in sync with each other. Over the years, we have been a very effective play-action passing team. Our system is variable and flexible, and it allows us to use the element of surprise to keep defenses off balance. What I believe makes us unique is that we have developed a system that is simple enough for the quarterbacks and the receivers to learn, but has built-in flexibility to allow us to present multiple problems for the defense. We have minimized the amount of learning for our quarterbacks and

receivers, and maximized the amount of learning for their linebackers and secondary players.

I started my coaching career as a graduate assistant coach working with the secondary at Penn State. Part of my job was to look at the opponent's film and diagram all of their pass plays for our defense. I want our opponent's graduate assistant, who is trying to draw diagrams for our plays, to be ready to jump off a bridge because he has so many of our plays to draw up. We want to do a whole bunch of stuff without having to learn a bunch of different reads. We do that by creating a lot of different personnel groups, formations, and motions, combined with play fakes and a different range of running plays.

When we develop a pass play, there are four factors that we can throw into the mix. It starts with what we call "modular learning." We compartmentalize our play-action pass game routes so that they are simple and flexible. Our system breaks down our play-action passing game into separate reads. We have standard reads that we use across a wide range of different formations and personnel groups that will give the defense a lot of things to look at. We want to give the defense a lot of things that they have to work on during the week leading up to our game.

During a game, we may utilize as many as 10 different personnel groups. We want to create positive match-ups. We utilize our formations and our motion to have the ability to take our best players and put them into match-ups on your worst players. If we can get one of our great wideouts in the slot on your linebacker, we feel like we have a great pass game match-up. The other thing we want to do with our motion and formations is to outflank you. We do a lot of different things to try to gain an advantage.

The thing that we have to guard against as coaches is overdoing it. We can watch an opponent's film and come up with 50 or 60 different things that we think we can be successful with, but there is no way that we can teach them in one week. The hardest part is knowing how much we can teach in any given week so we can become proficient in executing on game day. That is why we came up with a system to compartmentalize our passing game. We would like to be able to bundle up a series of plays in our read packages for our quarterbacks and skilled players. We are teaching our quarterback a limited number of plays.

We break the game down into about 8 to 10 reads for them. As an example, we might have a curl read, a four vertical read, a smash read, a crossing route read, an under read, a triangle read, and a post wheel read. We have 8 to 10 of them. They learn those reads and they know what is happening. Some weeks, we will use more reads than others because of the types of coverages we will face. Each week, we will choose the packages that will match up best for us.

The important teaching part of this package is taught during the off-season. During spring training and during the pre-season, we will really hammer on those reads. This way we can learn it when there are not any upcoming games that are imminent. I have been told it is like playing jazz music. I am not a jazz aficionado but I have been told that jazz will have a base melody. On any given night, the jazz musician can improvise and create something a little different and new, but with that same base melody as the foundation. That is kind of what we are doing with our pass game. We have our base read and then we have all kinds of things off of it.

Let me show you how flexible we can be with our offense. If we have five formations, five basic reads, and three different personnel groups, we can have 75 different combinations out there. So, you can see the real danger is expanding the package and giving them too much to understand in a given week. Each week, we will provide them with a read spreadsheet. The read spreadsheet will have 10 categories listed on it. The quarterback will know that on a particular week, we may run the out pass two different ways. We are going to run four or five play-action passes. We are going to have two

or three triangle reads and three smash reads. We cannot get too many because we have to be able to implement this in our practices, and we are limited on the amount of time that we can practice.

This is how we develop our plans for the game. We will have 10 different reads on this, but this will give us about 25 to 30 different combinations. We like to go through everything that we plan on running in the game that week in practice every day that week. So, if we have 50 combinations and we try to run those every day, our wideout's legs will be shot before the game starts. At the high school level, it might be even worse because you have guys going both ways.

When we come in on Monday, we pretty much know what we are going to do. We give our players off on Sunday because of the NCAA requirement to give players a day off. We have to maximize our time and be ready to go on Monday. I need to know what we are doing in the running game that week so that I can coordinate our play-action. If we are going to run the inside zone a lot, we want to be able to keep the backside end from closing, and we want to keep the safeties honest. We want to design our play-action pass to keep the defense from becoming too aggressive.

We have two types of play-action passes that we use. The first is a hard play-action fake with our offensive line run blocking. If we run a play-action pass off of the sweep, our guard is going to pull. The tight end is going to block the end, and the tackle is going to block down on the 3 technique. We are going to block exactly like a sweep. It makes it really simple for the offensive line. If we call sweep naked, the offensive line knows that they are going to block like a normal sweep. Obviously, they cannot go downfield. It makes it easy for them to learn.

The other type of play-action passes we use are called "run-action passes." These are not hard fakes and the protection may be built into the play. We still make the run fake. It might be something like a draw or an inside counter where the quarterback stays in the pocket and doesn't move.

The play-action pass gives us a chance to create a big play. It gives us a chance on first or second down to take a shot down the field and set the tone to keep the safety back. That helps us with our running game. The quarterbacks have to understand that there is a risk and reward factor with our play-action passing attack. There is a risk of a big loss, but there is a chance for a big gain. The quarterback has to understand that. If we run a naked and the backside end does not get fooled, the quarterback has to get rid of the ball. He cannot take that sack. He knows where the risks and the rewards are.

We have a chance to make an explosive play, and by that I mean a play of 20 yards or more. Last year, we had 26 plays from our play-action pass game that resulted in 20 yards or more. Nine of them were touchdowns. That is an average of two explosive plays per game from our play-action pass scheme. If our goal is to have five explosive plays per game and we are getting two of them from the play-action pass scheme, that is a high percentage. The 26 play-action explosive plays we have came from the 65 or 70 play-action pass plays we ran throughout the season. That is a pretty good percentage as well.

It is critical that we coach everyone involved in the play-action passing scheme. It is not just the quarterback and the running back carrying out their fakes. We have to coach the offensive linemen to carry out the fake as well. The secondary coaches teach their safeties to read hats and hear the sound of the offensive line. If the safety is sitting back there looking for hats that are high and they do not hear any impact at the line of scrimmage, the safeties start bailing out of there, right now, and they are not buying the play fake or the run-action. The offensive linemen are a big part of it. We tell the offensive line that we want to hear the play-action pass. We want to hear a smack at the line of scrimmage when the ball is snapped and we want to see their heads going down. The safeties have to hear run and see run. It has to look exactly the same as a run play. That is the biggest factor—it has to be believable.

We have to keep the routes simple so that we can apply them to any run play. We may want to run a naked off the inside zone play this week, and the next week we may want to run it off of the power play. We want to keep the routes the same so the receivers do not have to relearn them from week to week. The quarterback will have the same read.

The offensive linemen are blocking an offensive play that they already know. Essentially, any week, we can have a new pass play without having anybody learn something new. The defenders that we see every week will see something different from week to week.

When a team sees something different than what they have been practicing against all week, it creates some type of confusion for them. This system also allows us to make in-game adjustments. All five of our skilled players must understand our play-action schemes and all positions of those schemes. We may want to plug in a #2 receiver into the #3 spot to get the match-up we want. They have to be interchangeable and know all of the positions within the scheme.

Let me draw up a few plays to give you an idea of what I am talking about with this concept. First is the naked post (Diagram #1). With the naked post, the #1 receiver is going to run a post. The #2 receiver is going to delay that contain rusher for a two count and then release to the flat. The #3 receiver will run a crossing route on the backside. It does not matter what formation or what personnel we have in the game, the quarterback knows he has a naked post, a man out in the flat, and a man crossing on the backside.

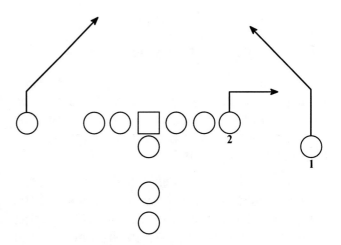

Diagram #1. Naked Post

It does not matter if it is I right, twins, three wideouts, or four wideouts; if the quarterback can learn that concept, we can plug naked post into anything we want. We teach the quarterback that if we have fooled the defense, he can read high to low. Obviously, if we call this on third-and-one and the receiver in the flat is open, he better get it to that guy so we can move the chains. We talk about those types of situations prior to the game so there is no confusion about what to do for a particular down-and-distance.

The next thing that we can call is the naked bench (Diagram #2). Our #1 receiver will run a bench. The #2 receiver is in the flat again, and the #3 receiver is running the backside cross. When the quarterback comes off his fake, no matter what running play we are running from, he will have a bench in front of him and a guy out in the flat. It does not matter what the running play is that we are faking from; we can run it with any play. This is very simple.

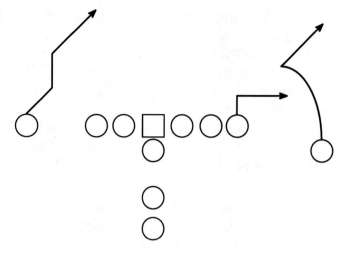

Diagram #3. Naked Corner

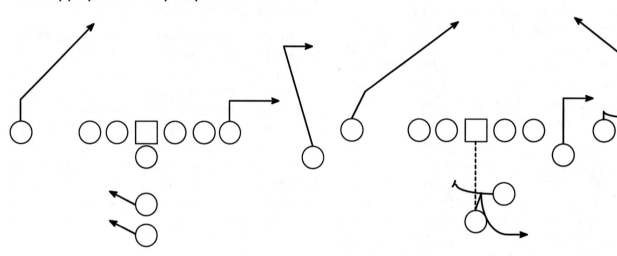

Diagram #2. Naked Bench

We can run a naked corner with the same concept (Diagram #3). With the naked corner, the #1 receiver runs a corner. The #2 receiver still runs his route to the flat, and the #3 receiver runs his backside crossing route.

The fourth play in this scheme is the naked wheel route (Diagram #4). Our #1 receiver will run the post. Now, our #2 receiver will run a wheel route. Our #3 receiver goes to the flat, and the backside receiver runs his cross again.

Our quarterback runs the fake for whatever play we call. If we call stretch naked post, we are faking the stretch to the weakside and coming out. If we were to call blast naked bench or blast naked corner, we are faking our blast play and running our play-action pass. These are the four basic concepts that we use.

Diagram #4. Naked Wheel

We teach our quarterback that if after their fake we are getting pressure, they can dump it off down low. If they are not getting pressure, then they can take a shot down the field high to low. We believe that this process helps it become clearer in the quarterback's mind. No matter what the formation or play call is, if they hear naked post, they know that they have somebody running the post, somebody in the flat, and somebody crossing.

The next step in this process, after the baseline, is to attach routes and structure to the series. Let's say we have 21 personnel. We will be in an I right stretch naked post (Diagram #5). We are faking the outside stretch play. We have two backs, a tight end, and two wideouts. Our #1 receiver goes to the post. The tight end will be out in the flat. The backside receiver runs his cross.

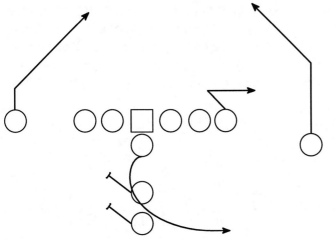

**Diagram #5. 21 Personnel I Right
Stretch Naked Post**

We can run this from our 20 personnel (Diagram #6). In the 20 personnel, we will have a wideout playing tight end. We will motion the tight end wide. It really does not matter to the quarterback that he has a different personnel group. The motion does not matter to him. This just helps us get a receiver out there that has a little bit more speed.

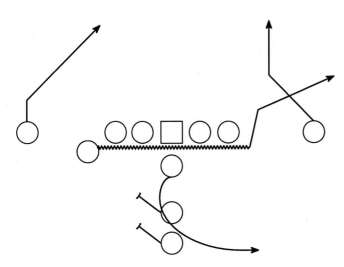

Diagram #6. 20 Personnel

If we are in 12 personnel, we can go ace right, blast, naked post (Diagram #7). The quarterback is faking the blast play inside zone. Now, we have two tight ends in the game. We fake the inside zone and the quarterback has the same type of read. He knows that when he comes off the fake, he has a man running the post, a man in the flat, and a guy

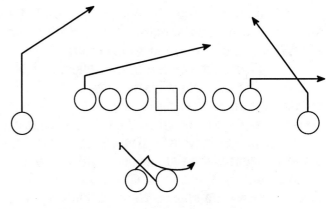

**Diagram #7. 12 Personnel Ace
Right Blast Naked Post**

crossing. That is three different personnel groups, three different formations, three different things for a defensive coordinator to look at during the week, but it is the same play.

We can go to the 11 personnel group. We can run spread right gun blast naked post (Diagram #8). Now, we are going to fake the blast. The difference here is that the quarterback does not have the tight end slamming the defensive end for protection. By being in the gun, he can look right at that defensive end. He will know immediately whether the end went for the fake or not. It is very simple for the quarterback. He has the same look no matter what formation or package we are in. We teach our backs that after they fake the run, they need to look to pick somebody up. Hopefully, the fake will be good enough to where they get tackled and that will take care of that.

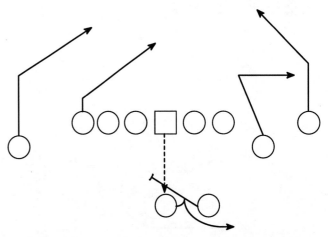

Diagram #8. Spread Right Gun Blast Naked Post

Let's go to a naked wheel post concept. Let's start from a trey gun formation this time (Diagram #9). With this concept, the #1 man runs his post. The #2 man runs the wheel route. The tight end will go out to the flat. We will still have the backside crossing route. If that middle defender does not take the fake and goes out to the flat, our receiver will turn it up on the wheel and he will be open. If the defender vacates the flat and goes with our wheel receiver, our third receiver will be open in the flat. This is just a little change to our naked, but it is not a big change. Our quarterback knows he has a receiver running a post and a receiver in the flat, but we have just added a wheel route to the equation.

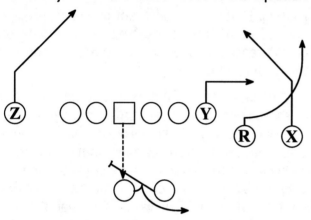

**Diagram #9. Trey Right Gun Blast
Naked Wheel Post**

We can run it from the slot formation. We might call slot right blast naked wheel post (Diagram #10). We motion our X into the tight end position. We fake the blast or inside zone. We still have a post, a wheel route, somebody out in the flat, with a guy crossing on the backside.

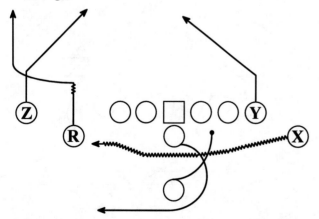

Diagram #10. Slot Right Blast Naked Wheel Post

We can also run the throwback from this look. We tell the quarterback we want a bad fake when we run the throwback (Diagram #11). We want the defense to think that it is a play-action pass, but then we slip the tailback out and down the sideline.

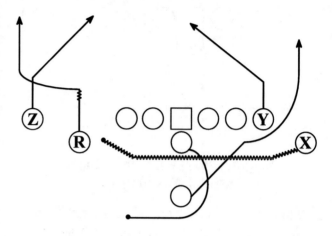

Diagram #11. Throwback

If you are going to guard us defensively, you are going to have a pretty hard time. We have a way to give you a lot of different looks but using very simple concepts for us.

Let's look at the film of these plays so you can get a better idea of what we are trying to accomplish with our play-action passing game.

Thank you for your attention and thank you for having me here. You are welcome to come and visit us. Thank you.

BUILDING THE 4-2-5 DEFENSE

Texas Christian University

Thank you. It is has been a long time coming. I spent a lot of my younger years in California. I coached at California Lutheran University, Sonoma State University, and I coached at University of California at Davis. I recruited California when I was at Utah State University. It has been great to see a lot of people I know. It is a pleasure for me to be here. I spoke in Dallas earlier this morning, got on a flight, and arrived here late.

This is my 14th year at Texas Christian University. I was there as a coordinator for two years before I became the head coach. It has been a situation where my staff has been very loyal to our program. Most of them have stayed on through the years.

I will tell you X's and O's are not the reason we have become successful at TCU. They have helped. As it is in all of the other successful programs, including high schools, it starts in the off-season. I am the CEO of our program. I have seen head coaches who do not take part in the off-season program. They do not think they need to be involved. I talk to corporate people all of the time. The bottom line is this: success is harder to deal with than failure is. Some people who have success, they think they are a better person than what they were in the first place.

We all deal with failures. You have to give Boise State University a lot of credit for doing what they have with their program and all of the wins they have recorded. Chris Petersen was the quarterback when I was the linebacker coach at UC Davis. We all go away back with a lot of successful coaches.

Kids can go across the street, and people will tell them how good they are. How do we handle this situation? This year is going to be a lot easier for me. We have won 33 games and lost three games over the last three years. Those three losses have been to some good football teams. In 2008, we lost against the University of Oklahoma who played for the national championship that year. We lost to Boise State last year in the Fiesta Bowl. However, we defeated them the year before. We lost to the University of Utah who went on to defeat the University of Alabama in the Sugar Bowl that year.

The media was asking me on Friday before the Rose Bowl why I thought we had a chance against the University of Wisconsin. My response was, "You do not know what our kids have handled, and where they have been." This is the thing those people must understand. From the very beginning, when we start our off-season program, I do the running groups. I do not send our coordinators on the road recruiting during the off-season program.

Our strength coaches are good with numbers. I have an unbelievable staff. However, in these days, I have to grow the team up. I know many of the high school coaches do the same thing. We have to have a number of young players ready to play in the fall. I have to see to it they get the work they need to enable them to help us in the fall.

I am not one of these coaches who try to kill the players in the off-season. Is it hard? Yes! It is hard. The bottom line is this: instead of going for six minutes in a county-fair situation, we go two-and-a-half minutes at each station. We are going to teach them in that time span. We want them to believe we are not going to leave them out to dry. A lot of the exercises we are going to do only take six to eight seconds. This is the amount of time a play lasts in football.

In January and February, we do what I have been doing for 17 years as far as speed workouts, hips and feet workouts, and then lifting weights. Why do we run this type of program? At the end of February, I can sit down and compare the football team to any other football team I've ever had. I will be able to evaluate where we are in our hips, how well we run, and how mentally tough are we.

Our strength coach will get the players in the summer. He can use the parachute exercises with them, and make them do all the other things the strength coaches do with their athletes. We take our players to a one-rep max. Last year, we had seven players who squatted over 880 pounds, for one rep. We had 12 players who bench pressed almost 500 pounds. We do not use creatine or any other type of strength builders. You can get the program done, and you can do the things you need to do to build up your athletes.

If we are going to be a smaller defense, we must be faster, and we must be stronger. We use a pyramid in our program. Going back to Coach Pat Hill and talking about his program, we do a lot of the same things. The bottom of our pyramid never changes. At the bottom is: attitude, chemistry, family, and accountability. The second level has the code of purple with MTXE, which stands for mental toughness and extra effort. We do not color the block purple unless they achieve it. In 13 years, we have gone to 12 bowl games. We had one bad year where we had a few bad apples who prevented us from reaching our goals.

We always come back to start the year by starting at the beginning. We have not been as big or as fast in many of those 13 years. A lot of our kids came back to our team because they needed a second chance. That is the way our place is. That is what I think you have to do to be successful. Two years ago, we had 13 seniors on the team. Two of them were in the first and second rounds of the NFL draft. All of them received their degrees. This year, we have 20 seniors, and before we played in the Rose Bowl, 17 of those 20 seniors had their degrees.

I am one of those guys who has learned to flip the switch. When I walk on the field, I am intent. I tell this story to my players all of the time: "When you get married, your wife is not going to let you bring work home. When you leave home going to work, your boss does not care what happened at home. You have to learn how to flip the switch."

I want a player who wants to rip the head off the opponents when we walk onto that field. I want the players to have one girlfriend, go to church, go to class, get a degree, and do the things they need to do.

I have three boys at home who have probably taught me more than I have taught them. Nevertheless, I told the team this: "If I am going to spend more time in my life raising you than I do in raising my three boys at home, then I better try to do a better job at it."

Now that I have been at TCU for 14 years, we have some players in their early 30s who have been successful. Some of them own their own business, have built their own houses, and have their own families. This is well worth the effort we put into the program with them. I believe coaching is like being a great carpenter. You are going to build your business on referrals.

I am one of those guys who is not going to tell you what you want to hear. I lost recruits when I first started coaching. In Texas, we are known for being great evaluators of talent. My mother can pick out a great player, gentlemen. She benched me (laughs). Once you get those players, you have to know what you want to do with those players. You have to fit players into position. I do not mind doing that. It may be a lot easier to do that as the head coach than as a coordinator because I do not have anyone yelling at me.

The talent we recruited is how we made our program successful at TCU. I keep a tape of every recruiting class that we have brought into our program. I am not sure why we are still coaching at TCU. The first three or four years, it was hard to get good players. We were able to build a program that was tough. After the 2004 season, we came back and went to work. We drug-tested every one of our kids. We worked hard and got ready for the 2005 season. We beat Adrian Peterson and Oklahoma at Norman. Since that time, we have won a lot of football games.

I learned a lesson in dealing with kids, and how important great players are if they do not play within a team concept. Coaches address their teams and tell them what they want to hear. Then the kids go out and play the game, and they get beat. They tell the coach that he did not tell them what they needed to hear about the game. When kids come to our place, we tell them that is not the way things are going to work. The player will know from the beginning what we expect of them. I call them "paper tigers." First, we have to recruit them, and the sooner we do that, the better chance they have of being successful.

The two areas where we have problems with kids coming into college are reading and writing skills and math. There is as program called ALEKS®. You can find it on the Internet. It is a program online for 30 dollars. You can be tested in those special areas. It is a type of program where you must get the answer right to move forward. Every freshman who comes into our program must enroll in ALEK. By doing this, we can evaluate who they are and how they do things. This system helps us to deal with the students and how we can help them to become successful.

Another program that you can download is the Kurzweil 3000®. You can order their books, put on a headset, and the program reads the books to the student. The audio tells the students what a paragraph means and how to use it. If I want my athletes to play for me, I must prove I can be successful to get them to where they need to be as a student.

Outside of that aspect of dealing with the athletes, the rest is all of the soapbox stuff. I apologize. People ask me about our defense. When I talk about our statistics, people comment that we do not play the schedule that some of the other top 10 schools play. Not many of those teams want to play us anymore. In the last 10 years, we have been number one in the nation in total defense five times.

Going back to the last three years, we have been very successful on defense. To understand our defense you need to look at our base alignment (Diagram #1). We play a 4-2-5 defense. We have five defensive backs in our alignment. We have to have one player more than the offense can block on our defense. You may say that we blitz a lot. No, that is not what I said. On defense, if you want to have one more player than what the offense can block, you must have a man-to-man side. We play quarter coverage so we can play man principles on one side of our defense.

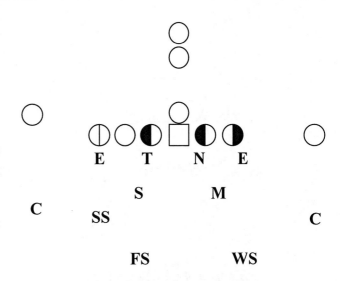

Diagram #1. Base Alignment

On the other side of our defense, we are going to be playing zone coverage. They are playing zone coverage and looking for the play-action passing game. If you are playing a three-deep secondary, and the offense runs three vertical receivers deep, you are going to cover them in man coverage. We teach our kids man-clue coverages. We match the receivers with our defensive coverage.

We teach three zone coverages. We play quarters. We are one of the few teams that runs an excessive man blitz package. We also run a zone blitz out of a two-shell alignment, and not out of a three-deep alignment.

If we face a team that likes to play with two backs in the backfield, we have to be able to stop the run. Teams use the eight-man front against the two-back set. I went to Texas Tech University several years ago to see their defensive scheme. The defensive coordinator was John Goodner. They were playing the 4-2 scheme. They used something in their package they called a "slide backs" move (Diagram #2). What they were doing was sliding a safety into the box when they played against a two-back team. They played a man-free coverage scheme. We play a little three-deep scheme with our package, but not much.

This is what I look at the end of the season. Obviously, scoring defense is important. The other thing I look at is stopping the run. In 2008, we held teams to 47.8 yards per game running the football. Immediately, you say, "You loaded the box to stop the run." We only gave up eight touchdown passes.

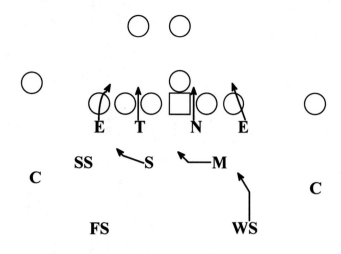

Diagram #2. Slide Backs

This is what you must look at if you are a blitz team. In 2009, we gave up 80 yards rushing per game, and touchdown on passes. This past season, 2010, we gave up 99 yards per game, and that includes the Rose Bowl against Wisconsin. We gave up 10 touchdown passes last year.

The key is the KISS method: Keep it simple, stupid. On defense, we want to have enough in our package that will allow us to be successful. How do you do that? We do it the same way as most of you do with your team. We have written down information on teams we play this coming season. It is: "New Game—Boise State."

We have the U.S. Air Force Academy on our schedule next season, and they are a triple option team. We run the weak zone play on offense. We are multiple in our offense. We go from the empty set to three backs in the offense. Because of that, we do not have to work on a lot facing their defense. All of the different types of offenses we are going to face next year, we are facing them every day in practice.

I am going to pick out Air Force, Boise State, and Baylor University, which is our first game next year. I know all the plays they like to run in the red zone. We have played Boise State the last two years, and we have only allowed one offensive touchdown in those two games. Boise State is good at what they do, and you better give them the respect they deserve. They are very good at what they do.

In our 15 days of practice in the spring training, we are going to take 15 to 20 minutes a day and work on the half-line option. We are going to spend time on the things we expect to see from Boise State. We are going have a team script, and we are going to work on Baylor as well. They are our first game of the season.

When we get into our two-a-day practice sessions, we are going to work on the half-line option, and we are going to work on Boise State every day. We do not play Boise State until the end of the season. When we get to that game, I want to have a game plan of what we want to do. If we do not prepare for them this way, we will not have a chance against Boise State. Offenses have been doing this type of planning for years because they can see what they want to do. A coach taught me the principle in preparing for teams. We back up, and we are going to prepare for the very best.

Today, most of the highly ranked teams play with two down defensive tackles. We do not play with two down defensive tackles. I believe in the one-gap principle. I want to let you know that I do not believe the 4-2-5 defense is the best defense ever made. I believe the 50 defensive front has strength. I believe the 4-2-5 defensive front has strength. We use all principles. The bottom line is this: does your defense fit your personnel, and can you fix that defense? When you are in a game and the offense causes you a problem, do you have the answer so you can do something to correct the problem?

I still call the defense at TCU as the head coach. It takes more time, but it is something I like to do. Put me in shorts and a t-shirt and give me a whistle, and I am happy at practice.

Most teams think TCU is an eight-man front defensive team. We are not an eight-man front team. If you watch us on film, you will see that we play more 4-3 concepts than we play an eight-man front. We do zone blitz, and we do man blitz.

The defense has to make the offense play their hole card. That is what we did in the Wisconsin game in the Rose Bowl. The linebacker had a big hit on a blitz. We had been keeping one man free in our dog package, where we bring four defenders from the off side. The way we were able to get the linebacker free to get the big hit was by running an all-out blitz, where we sent all five men on the same side. You have to have that in your package if you want to be successful.

If I can stop you with six men and play the run, it will make it easier on me in the secondary. If I can't stop you with six men, I will have to use seven men to stop you. If I can't stop you with seven men, I will have to use eight. If I can't stop you with eight men, I will have to use nine men. Against Wisconsin, it looked like we were using 15 men to stop them on the run. You saw the film, and you know they were a lot bigger than we were. Wisconsin was a very good football team.

It does not matter what I think about our team. If you can't get the team to take ownership, things are never going to change. Let me give you a great example. In 2009, we got beat by Boise State in the Fiesta Bowl. Our seniors came back and went to work. They ended up winning 44 games in their four years.

Soon after we found out we were going to play Wisconsin in the Rose Bowl, I had a meeting with the team. I always lay out a calendar of what our plans are so everyone can plan accordingly. In that meeting, I discussed our schedule for the bowl game. We would practice on the morning of December 24. We would take off after that workout and report to school on the afternoon of December 25 and head for Pasadena for the Rose Bowl.

Several hands went up, and most of them were seniors. I figured they wanted more time off for Christmas. I was surprised. "Coach, we have the rest of our life to get a chance to spend Christmas with our family. We are only going to get one chance to go to the Rose Bowl."

We left for Pasadena on Christmas morning and had a practice scheduled soon after we arrived. Usually, that first practice is the worst practice during the entire trip. Everything is different, from the dressing rooms to the hotel to the practice field. The surroundings are so different they just don't practice very well. We practiced on Christmas later in the morning and got that out of our system. We took the rest of the day off and had some activities set up for them for the evening.

The next morning, we had a great practice, and later in the day, we went to Disneyland®. I learned this from Coach Petersen. We usually give our team off on the Monday before a game. We game the team off on Monday and went to visit the Rose

Bowl. We let them take pictures and let them get all of that out of their system. We came back and got in our other practices the rest of the week, and you know the rest of the story.

In the Rose Bowl, the player who blocked the two-point play in the end zone did not play that well for the rest of the game. Like most of the time with the defense, it is the play we remember the most. However, he is a good defensive player.

Coach Lou Holtz had a saying that went something like this: "Inside and in front." Inside and in front means this: if I am a defensive tackle and the ball comes toward me, if I stay inside the ball, as long as the ball does not cut back across my face, I have a chance to make the play. If the defensive man outside the ball keeps the ball to his inside and does not let it cross his face, he has a chance to make the play. You would be surprised how often that happens in football. Just think about it; how often do we break that rule? We break it all the time.

Where we are different from other teams is on our rule for our safeties: "Don't go till you know." Other teams have their safeties backpedal in quarters, and we sit there and flat-foot shuffle. We want you to try to throw vertical. That is what we want you to do. This past year, we led the nation in three-and-out. Teams have an average of 12 to 13 possessions per game. We had three-and-out for an average of seven times per game. We want to take away the short game, we want to take away the combination routes, and we want to stop the run.

What are offensive teams going to try to do if we are successful in stopping these three categories? When I am talking about these situations, I am talking about first downs. If it is third-and-13, I am not going to be playing flat-footed. I am talking about first down. Here is the thing: most teams run their three-deep zone blitz, or their man blitz to stop the run. We will zone-blitz and run a two-shell with the blitz. We have played base with quarters the last couple of years. However, we do flat-foot on the coverage. You will get a chance to see that on film.

You saw us in the Rose Bowl. We did not tackle very well. This is what I want you to know about talking. That is for the off-season program. Good tacklers are strong players. If you do not have strength in your arms, shoulders, and legs, you do not have confidence. We can do all of the tackling circuits you want to do. The bottom line for us is the fact we are going to teach tackling last. The big back has become too big to tackle unless we hit him right in the hole. We are going to tackle less on anything on the edge. The little backs can outrun you. You have to go through the thigh and knee and go down the leg to the ankles. Running backs do not like to get tackled around the knees and ankles. The other point is that you will miss less tackles by going for the lower leg. In zone concepts, we want our kids to take the first shot. We do not want them to hesitate.

I talk to young coaches all of the time, and they want to know how to get to the next level. I apply the answer to that question to the corporate world as well. If you want to be good at something, you should not care how much money they pay you. The thing about it is the fact that I just got lucky in getting to the next level.

Do the best job you can, but go somewhere where people are good at what they do. Find the people who do things the way you think they should be done, and go work with them. You should not be so concerned about the other things. You are in it for the long haul. I am talking to the younger people here. I am talking about the long haul.

I came up the low road. I am not saying anything bad about UC Davis, but in South Carolina, they do not know where UC Davis is. I would not change anything I did, I would not want better people to work with, and I would not change how I was able to advance my career. I want you to know I learned more football in my first seven years than I have since that time. The principles I learned to live with are still there.

I can bring in a 220-pound player in as a freshman and I can add 35 pounds on him and still have him run as fast as he could when he weighed 220 pounds. I believe you kill with speed. If I could recruit a player who was 6'4", weighed 260 pounds, and could run a 4.5 40-yard dash, I would do it. If I can recruit speed, I can add the strength. I can't make them faster.

Here is what I have to teach the assistant coaches: it is not about winning. It is about when I watch the film, does everyone fit where they are

supposed to fit when the offense runs a divide zone? Does the defense get into their gaps? If the ballcarrier breaks back on the play, does the man who is supposed to fit that area to make the tackle make it? If the offense gets three yards, they win because we have more. It is not about winning; it is about learning to play as a team. Do you do your job every play?

We have young players to work with this spring. We want to get to where someone wins because he made a better play than his opponent did. He made the play not because someone did not cover his gap, or cover his man, or did not block the right person.

1-on-1 and 7-on-7—those are offensive drills. You have no pass rush on those drills. A defensive man could technically cover an offensive man in a 1-on-1 deal, and 50 percent of the time he could be successful without a pass rush or a blitz, he is going to win. We are working on technique and not about who won.

We run a drill we call rapid fire. We do 18 plays in about eight minutes. One defense stays on the field for three plays. To show you how I have changed, a long time ago when we did this drill, we would go ones versus ones, and we would run 15 plays. Then we would go twos versus twos. What happened is this: all we did was to teach them how to survive. At the time, we thought we were getting a lot of reps.

We changed the drill now so we have a different result. We start on the left hash mark, and then go to the middle, and then we go to the right hash mark. We start with the #1 defense versus the #2 offense. Then we have the #1 defense versus the #2 offense. Then we have the #1 defense go against the #1 offense on their third play. We have one group going rapid fire. We have to script the plays because it goes too fast.

Here is what the players have not figured out. If I am the #1 defensive team that starts out with the #1 offense, they are going to get two reps against the #1 offense and one rep against the #2 offense. Your #2 offense is getting better working against your #1 defense.

Then, when the #2 defense comes into the drill and starts with the #2 offense, they are getting two reps against the #2 offense, and one rep against the #1 offense.

I am finding out by the third play if they can play tired. I am talking about playing in Texas heat. I am talking about 115 degrees and in the 14th period of the practice. We are going to get 18 plays in eight minutes. Can they do it?

People talk about why TCU plays hard. The first thing is because we have good players. The second point is this: if you want them to play hard, they have to get to the point where they trust you. You have to make them tough enough to play hard, and they will do it in those conditions. I am not saying we have all of the answers, at all.

We use 55-gallon barrel trashcans with rope on the four cans in practice. There is a four-foot gap between each can. We put a person in the middle of the four cans as the center with a ball. The cans represent the offensive line. We have a manager, who has offensive cards for the scout team. We only have five offensive linemen for the scout team. From there, we run the play against the defense.

We still do the middle drill. We try to get an eight-play script, with #1 and #2 for 16 plays in 10 minutes. We have a 45-minute team practice period where we have 16, 16, 16, 16, and 10 plays. Each of those periods is done in eight minutes. I train the #1 and #2 to make sure they can play our scheme. We play base defense, and we do all of the personnel groups. We zone-blitz, and we man-blitz, and we do what we need to do.

When we get to game week, I do not want to be just working on our base defense. When we face the triple option, I want to be able to work on our other aspects of our blitz defense.

As a defensive coach, I know I was only going to get one chance. I was not a fair-haired boy. No offense to the offensive guys. You are always better looking, and the guy with the best-looking girlfriend. We can go down the list.

I believe you coach defense as if you are coaching offense. Offense has gotten so good, we must do this: we must teach our team what the offense is trying to do to our defense. We are going to check our coverages by what the offense does.

You must do this today because the offenses are so good.

We averaged 55.6 plays per game this year. That has a little to do with our offense. We had not allowed 50 plays in a game in four previous years. I know the offense cannot throw touchdowns if they are standing over on the sideline. You must be able to get the defense off the field. If the offense is running man pass routes, I need to be playing zone coverage. If they are running zone routes, I need to be playing man coverage. We still want to be able to come back and play great leverage defense.

I do not want to offend anyone, but I believe you must be a salesman to be a coach. If you want your kids to believe in what you are teaching them, you need to make them think you are good at what you do.

I believe when you do a drill, you are teaching. Instead of doing five minutes of the circuit drills, I am only going to do two-and-a-half minutes. I want to make sure my players know that we have to be in condition, we have to be tough, and mentally we have to have an edge.

We run a circuit drill we call the Colorado circuit. When we first started using it, we took about 45 minutes to complete. It has seven different stations. By the end of the third week, we have it down where it only takes us 28 minutes to finish. Once they do an exercise, if I see they are not doing the techniques and they are not in shape, we work them longer.

The better shape they are in, the less time I give them between drills. We cut the time down from 45 minutes to 28 minutes. All of the time we are doing these drills, we are building confidence within the players. We tell them how much better they are getting. You have to be careful in the drill. I am pushing them to their "wall" each day. The next day, their "wall" expands, and they can do the drill better. They never know how far they can go in the drills.

If you want your kids to practice hard, you have to put them in a position physically and mentally where they are challenged. You build them up to a point where they can do what you need them to do in the games.

We have two types of tackling circuits, and we have two types of takeaway circuits. We teach them how to strip the ball and how to recover fumbles, and how to pick balls up and run with them. We do all kinds of drills related to working with the fumble.

We developed a special teams circuit at the beginning of practice. We do two parts of the special teams that you never work on. For example, sky kicks to the up people on the kickoff return. There is an art to red zone punting. On Tuesday, we punt the regular type of punt down the field. On Wednesday, we are going to red zone punt. We have two lines of gunners going toward the goal line. How many times have you seen players running down the field on punts, and they never look up to find the ball? This is part of that drill. I am not saying we work on keeping the ball from going into the end zone. We are working on finding the ball.

On Thursday, we cover all of the aspects of the kicking game that will give our kids the chance to be successful. At times, we overlook those aspects of the game. Head coaches are worse than the assistance on this.

You are always welcome to come to see us practice in the spring. Call our office, and we will set up a time for you to visit. You can come on the field to see and hear what we are doing. You can see what we teach and what we do. The reason I am standing here today is because of our relationship with high school coaches. Without them, we are nothing. High school programs give so much to the college programs. In a lot of ways, high school coaching is a better job than college coaching. High school coaches can make a bigger difference in a kid's life. I know a lot of you will argue about the money signs. I will promise you this for college coaches: the only good day is July 7.

For you young coaches, don't forget about what I said about learning. Go somewhere that you can learn from the best of what you want to learn because that is how you can become successful. I used to think you needed to be good in a lot of things. I think you have to become great at something. In this profession, you have to be known for something to the point where you are a commodity and to where people want to hire you. If you can do that, success will follow.

No one in this room came from a lower road than I did. I am not going to forget where I came from, nor will I forget those who helped me along the way.

I just hired a grad assistant as my safety coach. I will tell you why I hired him. He made us a better football team. He was a walk-on wide receiver at Texas Tech. He was a high school coach, then a junior college coach, and then he came to work for us as a grad assistant. He understood what a secondary coach had to teach the players. Last year, he left our program to become a Division III coordinator.

I hired him to help us with our safeties. He is doing a great job as a recruiter. I asked him why he was working so hard. He said he did not want to lose his job. He has not made over 10,000 dollars in his whole life. Now, he is making a lot more than 10,000 dollars today. He knows his opportunity, but I know what I have with him. I did not have to go get a named person for that job. I needed someone who knew how we do things at TCU.

The coach I lost went to Texas Tech as the defensive coordinator. He is a good coach. However, the coach I hired is going to be special.

The older I get, the more I realize this game is not all about the fluff. When I was at the Rose Bowl, I realized I may never get a chance to enjoy that experience again. As soon as the game was over, they rushed me to the media room. I spent the next two hours telling people why we won the Rose Bowl. I did not get much of a chance to enjoy the victory after the game. Occasionally, I see something from the Rose Bowl game, and I tear up. I get a chance to enjoy it later, but I did not have much fun after the game. Our fans had a great time, and our players had a great time.

It has been a lot of fun visiting with you. Thanks for letting me come back to visit.

DEFENSIVE PHASES AND ALL-IN FOOTBALL

Iowa State University

I appreciate the opportunity to come here and speak tonight. It is a lot of fun for me to be back in Pittsburgh. I see a lot of faces I know, and I enjoy talking football with you. It is great for me to represent Iowa State University. I happened to grow up about 20 minutes away from Ames, Iowa. My father was a high school football coach, and is in the State of Iowa Football Hall of Fame. It is an honor for me to have my father come to our practice at Iowa State every Wednesday and critique me and to be around our program.

It was good for me to meet the coaches I have coached with and coached against, while here in Pittsburgh. It reminds me of the importance of hiring a great coaching staff made up of great coaches. When I put my coaching staff together, I always look for three things. First, I am looking for guys who can recruit well in specific areas of the country. We are going to recruit the state of Iowa in the Midwest. We are going to recruit in California, Texas, and Pennsylvania.

Secondly, I want coaches who are great teachers in the classroom and great teachers on the field. Thirdly, and most importantly, I am looking for coaches who are concerned with the welfare and well-being of our student-athletes. I have a group that is this way now at Iowa State.

Upon hiring this group of guys, something happened that I never expected. My defensive coordinator is Wally Burnham. Wally is pushing 70 years of age. He was a longtime defensive coordinator at the University of South Florida while I was coaching at University of Pittsburgh. I got the opportunity, and I hired him away from South Florida. We had a great first year. However, the next year, our schedule was rougher. We had our usual tough Big 12 schedule, and we were playing Iowa, who was picked to compete for a national championship. We also had to play the University of Utah and the University of Connecticut. We had 11 BCS teams we had to play.

It was time for us to get started for the season. We were getting ready for our first day of fall camp. I wanted to see Wally and our defensive staff. I could not find Wally anywhere. Wally's son, Shane, coaches the defensive tackles. I asked Shane, "Where is your dad?" Shane tells me that he must not be coming in today. I get real concerned, so I pick up the phone and I call Wally. Wally answered, and I said, "Wally, where are you? We have to get going today." Wally says, "Paul, I went to see the doctor, and I have been diagnosed with a very rare disease." I am thinking, *Wally is up in years; this might be serious.* Wally says, "I've got anal glaucoma." Now, I know glaucoma deals with the eyes. I know Wally does have some vision problems, because he is always taking off his glasses and holding papers close to his face and in front of his eyes, but I have never heard of anal glaucoma. I tell Wally that I feel kind of embarrassed, that I will do anything I can for him, but I do not know what anal glaucoma is. Wally replied, "Paul, I just don't see my ass coming in to work today."

Nevertheless, we battled through that schedule, and we are proud about where our program is going. On anything that I talk about today, do not hesitate to get back to me if you have any questions.

Tonight, I would like to talk to you about some philosophical things that we use in our program on the defensive side of the ball—things that I think are important as a head coach. After I took the job at Iowa State, I held my first team meeting on the first day of school in January. It was the greatest experience I have ever had as a football coach. It was the first time I had stood up in front of a group of young men as a head football coach. To be able to look them in the eye and have a chance to be able to lead a program was great. It still makes the hairs stand up on the back of my neck. At the end of that meeting, after I had told them the direction the program was going, I told them, "Take a hard look at what you truly expect to get out of life, because that is what you will get." You will get what you expect. Sometimes, we will exceed our expectations, and when we do, we are surprised.

Barry Bonds was coming home from losing the World Series. He was sitting next to his wife on the airplane, he was hanging his head, and he was dejected. He was mourning the San Francisco Giants loss in the World Series. His wife leans over and says to him, "I do not know why you are so upset. Your expectations were to go to the World Series. There was never anything about winning the World Series. Your expectations were only to go to the World Series. That is exactly what you fulfilled."

I ended our meeting with that story. I told our team, "The expectations of the 2009 Iowa State Cyclones football team are to win a bowl game." I said this to a group of roughly 100 football players who had just come off 10 straight losses. They finished up 2-10. They did not win a Big 12 football game. They had the longest road losing streak in the country. I told them the expectations in 2009 were to win a bowl game. They did not laugh, they did not panic, and they did not snicker, but I know they were thinking that.

As we went through the season, we got bowl-eligible against the University of Colorado. Word started to leak out that we had that conversation in the beginning of the year. As we got ready for the Insight Bowl game, it became a bigger story. We beat the University of Minnesota 14-13 in the Insight Bowl Championship, and everybody wanted to talk about that first day's conversation.

One day I was sitting in a meeting of one of our booster groups, and I was asked this question, "Did you really believe your football team could win a bowl game in your first season?" My easy answer to that question was, "It did not matter." It did not matter whether I thought we could win a bowl game. What mattered is that we set the bar high. We establish the expectation of our program so that those kids had to go out there and try to achieve it.

It would have been easy to talk about winning a game. They had lost 10 in a row. "Let's go win a

football game." "Let's go win a game on the road." We were playing Kent State University in Ohio, and I could have said, "Let's go win a road game at Kent State." If we had just done that, we would not have gone into Lincoln, Nebraska, and upset the University of Nebraska Cornhuskers for the first time in 32 years. It did not matter if I thought we could do it or not. What mattered is the fact I set the bar high for our football team.

That goal is what I ended our meeting with on that first day. What I had done before that was to begin to teach them what we were going to do in order to accomplish that goal. I included an old Vince Lombardi thought about unity and about building togetherness. We talked about a team of one. Gene Chizik was the coach of the team I had just inherited, and he had just left to take the job at Auburn University—a great career move, obviously. He had to move on. He had been at Iowa State for just two seasons, and they had not performed well, and he basically left in the middle of the night.

I had kids who were upset and bitter because of his leaving. I had players in the room who were recruited and coached by the previous coach, before Coach Chizik. I had those same players who were coached by Coach Chizik, and then here I come along. I told them when we left that day it had to be as *our team*. We could not be a disjointed team. We could not be concerned with who had brought them to Iowa State. It did not matter to me who they were or where they came from or what they looked like; we had to be *one*. The kids embraced that as we went forward.

We established three blocks as the foundation of our program. These blocks pertain to both on and off the football field. We talk about these blocks all of the time. The first block is being smart. I am talking about being smart as individuals. I want guys who are smart to be playing football. If we are running our two-minute offense and we throw the ball to our receiver, you are going to see him catch the ball, get as many yards as he can, and get out-of-bounds to stop the clock. If we are playing a deep zone on defense, you are going to see our defensive backs deeper than the deepest receiver is. They are going to keep the receiver in front of them.

We are going to play smart football. We are going to make smart decisions off the field as well.

If one of our players is about to get into trouble around campus, one of our other players has to grab him by the shirt collar and get him out of there. He is going to get him back to the dormitory. We want them to be smart off of the field as well. We talk about it all of the time.

We want to be accountable. We want to be accountable as football players. If you have the responsibility for the A gap, then it is your responsibility to take the area between the center and the guard. That is where you are expected to be. If it is your job to block the perimeter player, you are going to go and get that block, so we can execute and be efficient on offense.

We are going to be accountable on and off the football field. If you are supposed to be in class at 9 a.m., you are going to be in class at 9 a.m. If you are supposed to get six hours of tutor time or study hall, that is what you are going to get. If you do not do those things, there is going to be a consequence for it. I talk all the time about choices, decisions, and consequences. Our consequence for not getting something done that you are accountable for academically is this: you are going to get up at 5:30 a.m. on Monday morning, and we will have punishment for you. We do not have many problems in that area, and I believe it is because we set the blocks of this foundation, on day one, when we met as a football program. Now it is part of our culture as kids come into our program.

The third thing we talk about is trust. To me, there are two types of trust. There is blind trust, and there is earned trust. When I took over the job, I asked our players to have blind trust. We might ask a player to do something a little differently than what he was used to doing with one of his other coaches. He may be doing it well, but we may want it done just a little differently. I asked them not to question it, but to do it the way we teach them to do it. That is blind trust.

Over time, by being accountable as coaches and players and making good decisions, we would earn trust. That is exactly what took place. As we moved forward, I asked them for a complete commitment. I asked them to be all in for everything that we do. It is a very powerful phrase in our program. We started using this phrase when I was an assistant coach at the University of Pittsburgh.

I continued to use it as a defensive coordinator at Auburn, and I have brought it to Iowa State. I wanted it to become more powerful and grow. We talk about it as a football program. We have it posted on signs around our training facility and in our locker room. We even take it with us on the road and put it above the door of the dressing room. When we leave the locker room or at halftime, our kids slap that sign, going onto the field. When we have a group breakdown, nine out of 10 times, it ends with "One, two, three, all in."

Most teams will hold up four fingers going into the fourth quarter. I thought that we needed something more unique. When we go from the third quarter to the fourth quarter, our players will go to each other, look each other in the eye, and say, "All in." Then they will go to the next guy, and the next guy, reconfirming the commitment they have to each other.

As we built this culture, things started taking care of themselves. As we went into this winter, I decided to have the team select a panel of players to talk about who was all in and who was not. I divided the players into four groups. I told the players to vote for two seniors, two juniors, and so forth. We have two players from every class who sit on this panel. The panel meets every two weeks, and they go through every player on the roster, and we ask if they are all in or not.

The meetings have been very informative. They might say that so-and-so cannot be all in because he was on campus smoking cigarettes. How can he be all in if he is doing that? They might say this guy is drinking too much, or this guy is skipping reps in the weight room, this guy does not get out of bed. They are just as open and as honest as can be on the issues.

After the meetings, I go around to every one of those named players and tell them, "This is what your peers are saying about you, and this is why they are saying it." Those players want to have their name removed from this list. They must go out and prove to everyone that they are all in. By the time we get to spring ball, we do not want anybody on that list. I want to be able to say that every player on our roster is fully committed to Iowa State University football, academics, and everything that we are doing.

Let's talk about mental toughness. Our definition of mental toughness is the ability to prepare, practice, and play at a maximum level. We are talking about giving everything that you possible can, in concentration and effort, in order to perform like a champion. We drive this home with our players all the time. Mental toughness, to me, is winning on third down. Mental toughness, to me, is when it is cold out, you play through it. Mental toughness, to me, is when you are in the middle of camp and you feel hot as hell, you practice through it. Mental toughness is studying for that exam, even though you are tired or you want to play the new video game. Being mentally tough overcomes that.

One of my favorite words I like to use is "strain." Hopefully an image pops into your mind. As soon as I say the word "strain," I picture sweat running down a player's face. I see the veins popping out of his neck. I see his teeth gripping as he goes to finish that repetition. We want our kids to strain. The phrase "give it up" to me means the same thing. I use that phrase a lot as well. Give everything that you got. Give it up for the program. We want to have a sense of urgency. We want to have a sense of urgency to get the job done. We want to have a sense of urgency in accomplishing our assignment.

I think it is very important to keep the players aware and informed. I want them to know what is going to take place in practice and what to expect out of it. When we start our fourth-quarter program, the stations are going to last three minutes. We are going to have six stations. We tell them what they are expected to do for each station. If we make adjustments to that, we let them know ahead of time. We may work the same amount of time, but the length of the stations may be different. If you are out on the football field, you may have a long drive, that lasts a long period of time, or you may have a short drive that lasts a short period of time. You have to be able to adjust to what the game is going to be.

If we go to play Notre Dame University, we want them to know that they are going to be staying in an old hotel. We want them to know that Notre Dame has the worst visiting locker room in the whole country. When you put on your jock, you are going to put your ass in your teammate's face. It is a small locker room. You are not going to enjoy

that. If I know what they are going to face, I want them to know it. When they walk in to do battle, if I can have them prepared, I am going to tell them as much as I can. I think they will perform better when I do that.

There are five phases to every play. We talk about playing one play at a time. We talk about not being too high or being too low, emotionally. It is hard to pat yourself on the back when you make a good play. It is hard to kick yourself in the butt when you make a poor play. We want to play one play at a time and stay at an even keel.

The first phase of a play is to know and understand the call. I have to see the signal, and I have to hear the linebacker tell me what the call is. How many times have you heard in a film session when you ask a kid why he did something wrong, he responds, "Coach. I did not know what the call was." They have to know what the defense is. That is their responsibility. There are a lot of no-huddle offenses out there. I have to be able to see what the signal is. If I do not see what the signal is, there is somebody standing right next to me. Ask. There is no excuse for not knowing what the play is.

You must also understand what that call is. I want them to understand why we might make a call. If we run a defense with an eight-man front, they have to know that we intend to stop the run. I want them to know what the guy next to them is responsible for and how it relates to them.

The second phase is to recognize the formation. Is it a one-back set, or is it a two-back set? Is it I-backs, or is it split backs? I want them to recognize the formation for two reasons. Number one, I want them to eliminate guesswork. I want them to recognize what the tendencies are. I may know that if they line up in a pro I, there is going to be a good chance that they should run the football, based on their tendencies. I may know that if they run the football, they are going to run it to the tight end side. If I have studied a team's formations, and there are some tendencies, I want my players to know.

The second reason I want them to recognize the formation is so we can line up properly. The third phase of the play is to align properly. If I am a deep third corner, and the widest receiver is outside of the numbers, I am going to line up inside the numbers. If that receiver has a short split, I am going to line up on the outside. If I have two receivers who are tight together, I am moving outside of the corner and inside of the safety, and we are going to make a switch call because there is a good chance that they are going to run a scissor route when they come up the field.

If I am a defensive end, and the offensive guard and tackle take a wide split, I am going to get heavy on that offensive tackle. I want them to recognize the formation so that they can align properly. Offensive success is more a result of poor defensive alignment than anything else is. We can pass the chalk around all we want.

We have been through the first three phases and 60 percent of the play. What has not happened yet? We have not had the snap. 60 percent of our success is based on what we do before the ball is snapped.

The fourth phase is to key: run or pass. I am not going to stand up here and go through all of our keys; you have your own keys. The important part is you have to key. You may want to key the quarterback. You may want them to key the man in front of them. You may want to key the ball. You may want to key a receiver. If he does this, you do one thing. If he does something else, you do another technique. That is up to you. They have to read their key. If I notice we have a breakdown in how our defense is reading their keys, I go to the offensive side of the ball so I can see what they are keying before the ball was snapped.

I want to know if they are looking where I want them to look. I want them to do this so they can play fast. You will find that if a player is not reading his key, he is looking straight at the quarterback. He does this because he thinks that is going to allow him to play the fastest. That is not the truth. They have to key what you want them to key. In order to coach that, you have to see their eyes.

The fifth phase is to execute. Execute your responsibility. Do your job. If the B gap is yours, take care of it. If contain belongs to you, take care of it. If you have the outside shoulder, take care of it. Execute your responsibility one play at a time.

I was a position coach for 20 years. For 18 of those years, I coached the secondary. Two years, I coached linebackers. I went from coaching at the University of the Pacific to Iowa State. I was in charge of coaching the linebackers. I had never coached linebackers before. I applied every bit of football knowledge I had. I drilled the heck out of them. We did all kinds of different drills. I thought I was at best, a very, very average linebacker coach.

A few years later, my last year at Pitt, Dave Wannstedt decided to switch things up a little, and he moved me from coaching the secondary to coaching linebackers. The first thing I did was to watch films of our linebackers. I watched the linebackers and to learn what they had to do. I did not worry about the scheme because the scheme was not going to change. I knew what their responsibilities were.

I wanted to see what linebackers had to actually do. What exactly did they have to do in order to execute our defense? Then, everything we did from a defensive standpoint and a teaching standpoint was based on every snap of the films I had watched.

I thought I was the best linebacker coach in the country that year. That time spent, watching exactly what the films showed, allowed me to coach the heck out of them for that season. It was my favorite year as a position coach.

The first thing that I did when we got together the next spring practice was to develop the big three. Everybody on our defense had this for their positions. It is the priority and the things they have to do as a position player in order for us to have success. The first thing we had to do was to be sure tacklers. If a ballcarrier confronts us in our gap, or if we are attempting to stop the ballcarrier in the open field, we have to make the tackle.

The second thing was to make no mental mistakes. If we are responsible for the B gap, that is where we should be. We are not cheating over somewhere else. If we have the hook/curl responsibility, we are in the hook/curl area.

Lastly, we needed to fit properly. Our job is to fit the isolation to the outside, and that is where we need to be. If it is our job to match up with the #3 receiver, and he goes vertical, that is what we are going to fit on that pass play. We needed to fit properly in order to be successful as a defensive unit.

This is how I set up our individual drills in our practices. The first thing we are going to do is to move. We are going to move, and we are going to change direction. Again, it is going to reflect in what we have to do within the defensive scheme, in order to be successful.

Secondly, we are going to be physical. We are going to take on blocks, and we are going to tackle. Lastly, we are going to do key drills. We line up the garbage cans, put a manager at quarterback and put in a running back, and we are going to read what we are going to see. Of those three things, if I was going to cheat an area, it is going to be the read keys. We can get most of that done in film work, or we can get that work done in team drills.

If we have a team that is going to run a lot of misdirection, then we will do it more and make sure we get it in. We are not going to cheat movement, we are not going to cheat defeating blocks, and we are not going to cheat tackling during that individual time.

We do the same thing on the bag drills that you do. We run over the top of them. The first thing that we do is get in line and start running over those bags with one foot in the hole. I am going to stand at the end, and give them a direction. They are given a direction as if they are reacting to the ballcarrier

(Diagram #1). What is important about this drill is that I talked about it to them. I let them know what we are defending during this drill. I tell them that they have dropped into pass coverage, and it has turned into a draw.

You have to run full speed for 10 yards in order to get to the ballcarrier as fast as you can. They may have dropped back and you are in pass coverage, and now they drop it off to a back, slipping out of the backfield on a screen play. You have to get there fast by running full speed, one foot over those bags at a time.

Then at the end, you are going to have to break down, with two feet, as if you have gotten to that back, and he is going to make a move on you. I want them to understand why they are doing the drill. We are never going to do drills just to get them tired and leg heavy. Every drill that we do is going to have a point to it.

The next drill over the bags is with two feet in the hole (Diagram #2). This might be as if they are tighter in the hole with an isolation play, where we are running with short strides and getting ready to take on a blocker, or adjust to a quicker tackle. We have to be under control. Our numbers have to be over our knees. Our knees have to be over our feet.

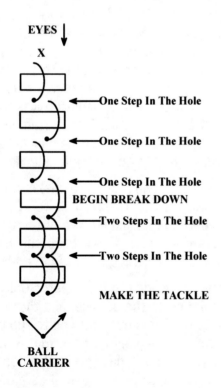

Diagram #1. Bag Drill, One Foot

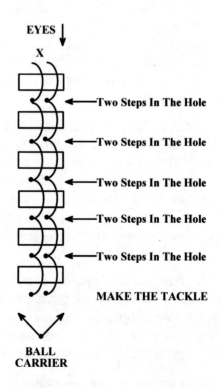

Diagram #2. Bag Drill, Two Step

We have to be taking control steps. This is why we are doing two steps in the hole.

The next drill that we are going to do with the bags is to line up, face forward, and go over the bags laterally (Diagram #3). We are going to step over those bags laterally with two feet in every hole. We tell them that we have an inside play. The play is not coming downhill, it is moving to the outside. It is starting out like a zone play. As the play starts, I want to match the ball movement, through the dummies. I am in control. I am not making up a lot of distance, but I am seeing the ball, and I am staying within that box.

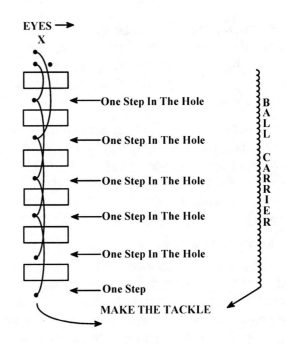

Diagram #4. Bag Drill Lateral Crossover

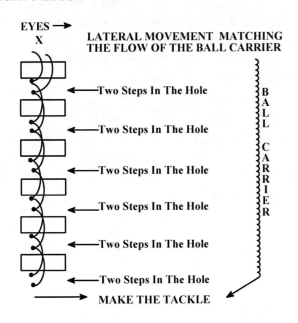

Diagram #3. Bag Drill, Lateral Two Step

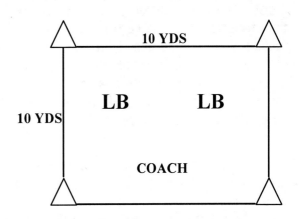

Diagram #5. Box Drill

We are facing the same way on the fourth drill. We are going to cross over and run through the bags (Diagram #4). Now, we have a toss play. I have an option play, where I have to get out on the perimeter. I want our players to know that every one of the drills is based on a play that we may face.

We can stagger the bags and run some drills based on other plays the offense may run. One might be as a response to a play-action pass. Another might be as a response to a counter play. All these drills are based off what I saw the linebackers doing on that game film.

For change of direction, I will use the box drill (Diagram #5). We start with four cones about 10 yards apart. We do this drill with both our linebackers and our secondary. To me, this is the best change-of-direction drill that you can do. If you take one drill back, take this one with you. You put two players in the box, and put them in stances. I get in the box, and I want them to move based on the step that I take. As I step, I want them to shuffle first.

We are going to start changing direction from this point. From there, I point to one of the four cones. What I want them to do is to sprint in the direction of that cone. They do not touch it, or even put their eyes on it. They are just running in that direction. Their eyes are staying on me as the coach.

Then, I am going to point at another cone. They are going to open up their hips, and they are going to run toward that cone. Their eyes always stay on me, and their chest is always open to me. They step up, responding to the run; then I point to a cone, they plant, their chest goes open, and they sprint in a direction like a dropback pass.

If I point to one of the front cones, they are going to put a cleat in the ground and drive forward in the direction of the cone, to play the dump-down pass or draw. I am going to turn them three to five times, and then I am going to pull them out. I always believe in two-part drills.

At the end of this drill, I will throw the ball, and they will have to intercept it. I may put the ball on the ground, and they have to recover the fumble. I may have a guy with a bag out there, and they have to make a tackle. We have a multipart drill of changing direction and then finishing with something else.

Let's talk about tackling. I think there are four characteristics that make a great tackler. The first is vision. You have to see what you are tackling. You cannot have your eyes on the ground. We want them to "sky the eyes." We talk about having eyes open and seeing the target. I cannot blink, and I cannot turn my head. I have to physically see the guy I am tackling.

If we are coming from an angle, we may not be able to see the ballcarrier's eyes or the ball. We focus on the near hip. That is where most tackles occur. More times than not, you are going to be coming from an angle. We want to physically look at that near hip.

The second characteristic is feet. Take the extra step to get to the ballcarrier. Do not start reaching. Take the extra step to get yourself all the way to the ballcarrier. Step on his toes. Get all the way to him, and run your hips through the tackle. Never talk about tackling with a shoulder. Shoulder pads were designed to protect the player. Do not teach them to tackle with the shoulder pads. We talk about bringing the hips to the tackle.

The contact will occur with the chest but without leaning, and I can get myself all the way to the tackle. The drill that I learned from the Green Bay Packers was a two-hand tackle drill. This drill is executed without pads or when we are not

tackling to the ground. The requirement is to tackle with two hands, below the waist, palms up, and in perfect tackling position. This forces them to take the extra step and to bring the hips to the tackle. This is the right way to practice in the off-season.

The third characteristic of tackling is desire. Whatever it takes—perfect form or shoestring tackle; get the guy to the ground. Everything is not going to work out just right every time. To be a great tackler, you have to have the desire to get the guy onto the ground.

The last characteristic is toughness. You have to have courage and want to put your face in there. You have to be willing to keep your eyes open. You have to be willing to go hit a guy who is running full speed. You have to have great toughness and courage to be a great tackler.

One of the tackling drills we run is the run, balance, hit drill (Diagram #6). We do this drill every Wednesday during the first period of individual drills. More teams lose games because their defensive players are poor tacklers. I believe that tackling is not emphasized enough.

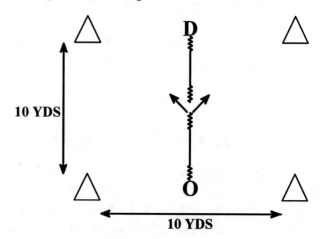

Diagram #6. Run, Balance, Hit

We coach the heck out of tackling. We are going to be 10 yards apart with a defensive player and an offensive player. I am going to say go, and both guys are going to move their feet. I am going to say go again, and the defensive player starts closing down on the offensive player, who is going to start working up the field. They are working straight at each other, and it is with speed.

It is like the bag drill that I talked to you about. I have dropped back in coverage, and now I am coming and putting one foot in every hole. I am making up ground. I have to close the distance between me and the ballcarrier just as fast as I can. As I do that, I get to a distance of about three yards. I then have to balance. I have to widen my base a little bit, and I have to holster my hands.

I need to keep from rushing toward the ballcarrier. I am not breaking down and stopping. I am still coming forward. I am doing it under control. I want a wide base and short choppy steps. If I do not get balance at that point, and I keep going with long strides, the ballcarrier makes a move, and I am going to reach out and miss him.

We want to run and close down the distance. When we are at that cushion position, we want to get balanced, but keep moving forward. Then we want to hit. Most ballcarriers are going to make a move left or right. If he makes a move to his right, after we are balanced, we want to match that step. I want to move laterally with that step of the ballcarrier.

I do not want to balance and then step toward him. If I step toward him, he goes away, I lose my angle, and I have to try to arm tackle. We want to take a step laterally with him. When he continues on, I am right where I want to be in our angle form tackle position. I am going to go tackle the hip. I am going to put my hips on him, and I am going to finish. We can run some slight variations off this drill by positioning them differently.

I appreciate you taking the time to listen to me. It really is a kick for me. Thank you very much.

RECEIVER FUNDAMENTALS AND PASSING CONCEPTS

Arkansas State University

I have been a high school coach before. That is probably the best thing that ever happened to me. When you are coaching in college, it is more like a business.

In high school coaching, you are constantly checking the time elements. It is difficult to get everything done in the time frame that you have in college. In the time that you have in high school, there are things you can teach and things that you cannot teach because of the time restraints.

We start every single practice with "stance and starts." The main reason we do this is because there is one thing guaranteed that is going to happen to all of our receivers. They are going to get into their stance and they are going to start running our play. They may run a route or they may go downfield to make a block. On every play, the receivers start with our stance and start techniques.

I am not sure I have ever had a freshman that knew what he was doing when he arrived on campus as far as proper stance and start techniques. The way I explain to them what we want is this. The first thing I ask the receivers is, "Have you ever been in a fistfight?" I want everyone to raise his hand because we do not want anyone that has not been in a fight of some type in his life. I explain to them that they need to be balanced if they are going to punch someone in the nose. They have to be balanced to hit someone in front of them.

We always start with our feet shoulder-width apart in our stance. That is zero power to us. We go from there to a plumb line. I will ask how many of them know what a plumb line is. I look at them and they have no clue what I have asked them. I take my whistle and a string and I put it in the center of my chest. When they get into their stance, they should be able to drop a plumb line and the line will go over the top of the knee and down to the top of the toes. This stance is best to generate power.

The second thing this does is it closes your chest. When I was coaching in high school, we only saw a few games where we faced press coverage. You do see it from time to time, and you do not want to give up your chest area as a receiver.

I tell the players they have to load up on the front toes. We want them to have 80 percent of their weight on the front toe. We do not want any part of the heel hitting the ground. We run a no-huddle offense and we line up as fast as we can go and we do not want any weight on the heel. We try to play as fast as we possibly can play. I have heard our head coach, Hugh Freeze, yell out 50 times a game, "Snap it! Snap it!" The receivers are running up and down the field and it takes a lot out of them.

I can tell when they get tired because their heels start hitting the ground when they line up. When they have their weight on the heels and they think they are ready to go, all of a sudden, you are playing a team like the University of Louisville and they line up eight yards off the receivers. When the quarterback leg kicks, the defender comes up and gets in the face of the receiver, and that receiver is done because his chest is open to the defender. We want to get our weight on our toes and close our chest to the defender.

The other part of the 80/20 theory is that it eliminates a false step. When you have your weight up on your toes, it is hard to do anything but drive and drive. We work on this every single day. That is the first thing we do when we start practice.

When we get into fall practice, I take the freshmen and work on closing the chest and picking up their hands. We have them in their stance and have them relaxing their hands. When they pick up their foot, we want to make sure they are balanced. We want to make sure they understand the front load has to be on their front toe.

We ask them to close their chest and to relax their hands. The favorite part of the year for me is the fall camp and then the summer camps. I am by no means a receiver guru, but I have a personal preference in some of the pass receiving techniques. I just believe in what I coach. I am anti when it comes to the hands and the chest. My reasoning is this. Once you get into your stance, you have your hands up high, and the defense knows what they are doing on the press; he is going to use his hands and his feet. He is not just lunging at you and punching at you. He is punching and recoiling, and he will hit you four or five times before you get downfield.

The receiver must be physical back. If the defense can get through your hands and to the chest, you have to drop your hands to come back against him.

The big mistake, on any level, when a receiver gets a press defensive back on him is that they shoot to get their hand on the chest of the receiver. Everyone works the hand drills, right? The weakest point on the human body to try to hold on to someone is the wrist. This is good for the offensive linemen as well. The weakest part of the body is the wrist. The big mistake is when the offensive players try to slap at the elbow. You can be more effective by slapping the wrist and getting the defender's hand off the chest. It takes very little effort to get the hand off the chest by grabbing the wrist. If you try to grab the elbow, it will not go anywhere.

Once we come off the ball and we have our hands down and a defensive back shoots his hands at our chest, we are going to flip our hands. We punch the air. We punch the defensive back in the chest. We do not do anything but rip after that. We rip and try to get up underneath the arm of the defensive back.

We see a lot of different cover 2 coverage. If the receiver opens his shoulders against this coverage, he is done. He may as well go to the bench and get a drink of water because he is not going to recover from the defensive back. That is where he is going to be sitting after the play is over if he lets the defender get to his chest.

The hands are the main thing in shooting to the impact point. We do not shoot at where we think his hands are going to be. By the time you shoot at his hands he will be in your chest. Shoot your hands toward your chest because that is where the defender is going with his hands.

CATCHING FUNDAMENTALS

- Catch the ball with your eyes
- Follow the ball with your eyes all the way to the tuck
- Strong hands and surface area
- Secure the catch
- On bad position balls, stop the bullet
- Catch the ball
- Play the next play

I know that everyone here knows how to teach catching fundamentals. I have a few things I stress to the receivers. Catch the football with your eyes. We have players coming to us from high schools and they do not catch the ball with their eyes. They are gifted athletes but still have problems catching the football with their eyes. They have been told repeatedly to watch the ball with their eyes. "Watch the T-ball, watch the golf ball, and watch the pitch." We stress catching the ball first. They should know to catch the ball first because they are going to be hit as soon as they do catch the ball. We see the receivers come across the middle and a pass comes to them. Soon, when they come across the middle, they start watching the defense as they catch the ball. We want them to follow the ball all the way live and we want them to tuck the ball into their body.

I have a joke I tell my receivers, and they think I am telling the truth. I tell them, "When you catch the pass, it does not hurt as bad when you get hit by the defense. So, make sure you catch the football."

We want to develop strong hands and surface area to catch the football. I do not allow our wide receivers to use straps in the weight room. I want them to develop strong hands. They can do a lot of exercises to strengthen the hands. They can squeeze a tennis ball.

I tell the players to develop a strong surface area. I tell the players it is as if they were going out in the snow and they were going to put on snowshoes before they went out. If the snow was

10 inches deep, they would have to put on a huge snowshoe. They would do that so they could walk across the snow. If they just wore their boots out in the 10-inch snow, they would sink down in the snow. It is the same theory.

We want them to spread the fingers and the hands to create a surface area to catch the football. We are going to create the areas with our hands in the shape of a football. We want to make sure our palms are facing up toward the sky when we catch the ball that is out in front of us or slightly over our head. We call it "catching the bullet." We know there is going to be some bad passes. We know that is going to happen. Other passes are coming at different angles. When the receiver has to leave his feet, we want him to make sure his palms are facing the area the spiral is coming from.

We teach our receivers they have to be ready to catch poorly thrown balls. Not all passes are going to be perfect. They must have their palms in position to catch the bullet. They must have their palms at the angle the spiral of the ball is coming from.

We run the fade drill every day. You run the fade route and you have the quarterback that can turn the ball over on the throw. On that throw, we want the receiver to catch the ball with his palms up over his head.

Next, we get a quarterback that cannot throw the ball over the receiver's head on the fade. He cannot get a turnover. We want the receiver to have his palms in position to catch the bullet. We work on the bad ball drill as well as the good passes.

One of my pet peeves concerns yelling at the kids when they drop a pass. Everyone in the stadium, including my mother, knows the receivers are supposed to catch the ball. I make it a habit not to yell, "Catch the ball," when one of our receivers drops a pass. The receivers feel bad about not catching the pass and we do not need to get them thinking negative. Along with that phrase is the next point that follows this same thought process.

"Play the next play." We can develop confidence in the players if we simply remind them to play the next play when they drop a pass. "I know you did not mean to drop that pass. Play the next play. Let's go." This is the way we can develop self-confidence with the receivers. Football is a mental game. It is the same as playing golf. When good golfers get into a zone, they can strike the ball. If you only hit a ball 30 feet and you start getting mad at yourself, the next ball may go to the right or to the left. It does not help to get upset. It is a mental game and we have to let them play.

Next, we want to talk about the top of the route. I want to remind you that these points are things I work with my young players especially hard on and we work on them every day. Entrance to the breakpoint must be natural. I do not want them to leave the ground when they enter the breakpoint and are ready to receive the pass. If they are a fast runner, they just need to be natural. We want them to keep the body movements natural just as they do when they are running.

It is a natural thing to look a person in the eye if they are looking at you. The first thing we do as a receiver when we come off the ball is to look the corner dead in the eye. He is looking at our eyes. He is not looking at our chest or hips. He is looking at our eyes. We want the receiver into the breakpoint before the defender can figure out where he is going. We want to look him in the eyes.

When we are coming off the ball and we are getting ready to stop, we call it "air brakes." The longer the route, the more pressure we have to use to stop. It is just common sense. It has to end with a start. How do we start? We start in our stance with our plumb line. It has to end where it starts. When we are coming into our break and we get ready to hit the air brakes, depending if it is an inside or outside break, the weight needs to be on the opposite foot. The first step has to be there and it has to end where it started. It is the same as the stance with the plumb line. Boom! It has to end there with their foot in the ground.

At first, the receivers think putting on the brakes is going to hurt them. It is not going to hurt them. I played receiver for a long time and I never turned an ankle running a route. The shorter the route, the less pressure you need. On the longer routes, you better put the air brakes on.

We use a simple move we call the "sprinkler head" route. We are moving around as the water does on the sprinkler in my front yard throwing water around. The longer the route, the more pressure you have to put on the foot opposite of the direction you are going. If the defender does not stop us, we keep on running by him. We practice applying the brakes in all of our drills. When we go into a drill, we want to finish where we start.

I want to touch on speed and zone cuts. Every day, we do a type of cone drill to illustrate the man breaks and we do zone breaks. The first point on step number one is to keep your pivot step inside your framework. The next step has to be at a 45-degree angle in the direction you are going. Most of our speed cuts are into zone coverage.

When we come out of the zone cut, we want them to get their body under control. There is nothing worse than coming out of a speed break out of control. If the receiver comes out of the speed break, he is going to round the pattern off and the defender is going to run underneath him and make the play on the ball. We have to get on the top, and run the hoop, and hit back downhill.

Once we catch the football, we are going vertical. I hate to see guys trying to imitate Randy Moss and some of the other NFL receivers. When they try one of those NFL imitations, I remind them who they are and who they are playing for. We want to go vertical and get up field. We want them to catch the ball and trap it. After they catch the ball in practice, they can give me 5 or 10 extra yards and I will leave them alone. We want to catch the football and get up field, but we must protect the football.

A word about my "shut up rule." If a receiver catches the ball at a five-yard gain and then turns it into a 15-yard gain, I will not say anything to him. If he catches the ball at five yards, runs sideways, and ends up with a three-yard gain, I will say something to him. He could have stuck his head up in the hole and gained 14 yards. I am going to let him know he needs to move the ball downfield and not across the field.

I want to move to our go route techniques. When I was coaching high school football, this is one phase of the game I would like to have been more involved with. What we did when we say "one deep safety" was to send our two fastest receivers deep, throw the ball deep, and hope one of them could run under the ball and make the catch.

There was not a lot of technique involved in the go route. Probably the least amount of coaching I ever did when I coached in high school was the year we won the state championship. When you play with players with talent, you can overcome a lot of what you lack in technique. If you are not as good as the team you are playing, you must be good at technique.

We use the fade line, which I know a lot of you use. On our practice fields, we have a red line between the bottom of the numbers and the sideline. That is our fade line. That is the aiming point for the quarterback on the go or fade route. Our job as a receiver is to control the fade line. When I coached in high school and I had the good quarterback, I had to make sure the receivers and the quarterbacks were on the same page.

There are two basic positions on the fade route. It may be a 1-on-1, a cover 3, or quarter coverage, and it is 1-on-1 outside. You can take the side position or you can take the top position. If the receiver is on the side position, he must squeeze the defender back and fight pressure with pressure. We do not allow the receivers to use their hands on the play. The defensive back will try to control the receiver with his hands, and we must not let that happen. We want to keep the hands in tight and fight pressure with pressure.

If we are running side by side with the defender, we have to be ready to expect one of two things. We must expect the back shoulder pass or the fade pass. We control the fade line and the quarterback makes the decision on throwing the ball on the fade.

If we are not even on the fade route and we do not have control of the fade line, I have told the quarterback to throw the ball on a line drive and try to hit the cornerback in the back of the head. We do not want to try to throw the ball to the receiver because that is a mistake if he does not have the fade line under control. We want him to throw the ball hard because the speed of the ball does not give the defensive back time to react.

We want to get on top of the fade route if possible. That is our number one rule. We love to get on top on that route. How do you get on top of the fade route if you are not as fast as the defender? It is hard to find receivers that can get over the top on the defensive corners. If you are not fast, how are you going to attack the cornerback? You do it by mixing up the routes. Test the corner out on downs when we are running the football. If we are running against man coverage, and running the read zone play the other way, and he is not involved in the blocking scheme, we want him to give that defensive back a scare. Speed release against him and get on top of him. Does the defensive back remember that was a run play? No. He remembers the receiver beat him off the ball. Now, he starts to play cautious.

If you are facing a press team and you are aware your man is not as good as the man that is pressing you, we want the receiver to speed release against him every time he is not involved in the play. We want to loosen up the defensive back.

The second thing we do is to have a change of pace. I understand you want the receivers running full speed. Use a change of pace and then run by the defensive back. Again, does he remember that was a running play? No. He just remembers that he got beat on the release.

We want to get on top of the defender. We are going to fight the stack. We fight the stack when the defender gets alongside the receiver. When the defensive man brings the inside arm down to his side, we can grab his inside wrist and get on top of him. We are not telling them to hold or to yank the defender but to use his leverage and use the defender's wrist to give him the push-off to get on top of the defender. We do not want the tempo to stop, and we want to keep going. The official should not call that as a penalty.

Once we get on top, if the ball is late or low, we must change gears. If we get downfield about 20 yards and are on top of the defender, we may cut our speed down to three-quarters so the quarterback can get the ball deep enough for us on the throw.

We teach the superman technique. We have our receiver running with the defensive back and it is going to be a jump-ball situation. This is usually in the corner of the end zone and it is a jump-ball situation. The ball is on our inside. We take the outside foot and plant, and we attempt to jump backward. If we are running even with the defender, we want the receiver to shoot straight up in the air, even if the receiver is thinking he is going to go

backward. If the defender runs buy us, we want to get our body in position on the inside.

After the catch, no matter where the catch is, he tries to get by the defender going away from pressure. We work on that leverage drill every day. We want the receiver to turn his back away from the pressure because we do not want him to get him in the front.

To help our receivers to catch the ball up high, we have them work with a tennis ball on a high wall. We have them throw the ball on the wall, go up, and catch it with two hands as the ball comes down. We use the tennis ball because it will bounce back into the player's hands, and that will strengthen the hands. In addition, it will get them used to going up to catch the football with two hands.

Then, we add a partner to the drill. We have the receiver go up and catch the tennis ball and then turn away from pressure applied by his partner. They can do this drill repeatedly. This is one way to get the receivers to catch the ball at its highest point. It is hard to practice this drill on the practice field, but you can work on the drill where you have a high wall.

We are going to talk about the scat. I have three things I want to cover here. We are a no-huddle team. We do not know what a huddle is. Our run game is the same as the run game that Auburn University runs. Everything is the same except we try to play a little faster. We try to play as fast as the University of Oregon does. However, our passing game is a lot different. We have nine concepts of the passing game. A concept to us is this: They are plays that tell everyone what to do on the play. Our scat concept tells everyone what to do on the play. We also have 63 combo plays. We have 63 combos and nine concepts. Scat is our number one concept. Coach Freeze talks about the scat concept about 50 times per year.

One thing you need to know about Scat is that it is a five-man protection scheme. If you are not a five-man protection team, I do not encourage you to run this play. You do not want to run it with a six-man protection scheme.

Let me show you the play from a 2x2 formation to start with (Diagram #1). We start with the three-man side of the formation. The two outside receivers on both sides run a scat route. The two

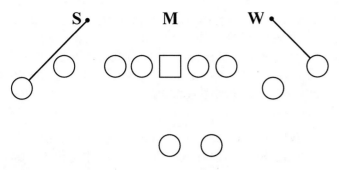

Diagram #1. Outside Receivers

outside receivers are going to run to the original alignments of the flat/curl defenders. Notice I said *original alignments*.

The #2 receivers on the inside run different routes. The inside slot on the three-man side runs a flag route (Diagram #2). The #2 receiver on the opposite side runs the bubble route to the outside.

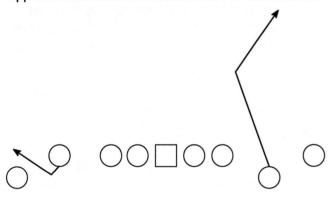

Diagram #2. Inside Receivers

The running back on the three-man side runs a bubble route outside (Diagram #3). On both sides of the formation, we have a scat route and a bubble route. Again, the middle man on the three-man side runs the flag route.

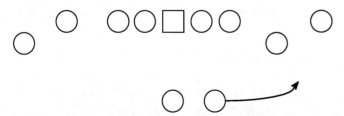

Diagram #3. Running Back, Bubble

You can run the scat from every formation you have as long as you have a two-man side and a three-man side (Diagram #4). Here we have all of the receivers in the pattern on the scat play.

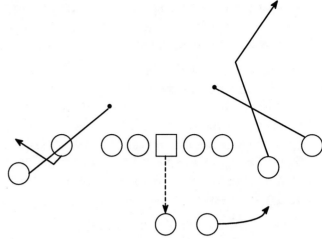

Diagram #4. Scat Pass, 2x2

In a 3x1 formation, the middleman has the flag. The outside man has the scat route. The inside man in the slot runs a scat. The back has the bubble. The end on the backside runs a flare. We have a two-man scat and a three-man scat route.

Let me get into the pre-snap reads on the scat. If we see no more than two high safeties, we go to the three-man side. Period. If it is only one high safety, we go to the two-man side. Period. That is the pre-snap read. This is a *KISS* play—keep it simple stupid. I love this play.

Now, the most important thing after the pre-snap read is this. Do not miss the scat! Do not miss the scat! Do not miss the scat! The quarterback has to make the scat receiver get covered. I mean get hammer covered. If the scat receiver has a defender trailing him, we want to get him the ball. If he has position on his man, it is a five-yard pass and we can get our first down on the pass. We will take that play. Do not miss the scat! We run scat to high/low. If the scat receiver is open, we want to get him the ball on the two-man side.

If we see only one safety or a one-high read, we are going to read scat, scat, scat (Do not miss the scat!) to the flat route. We will see this route in our films later.

We can tag any route to any receiver on scat. On scat, the basic route is our dig route. It is an eight-yard speed cut inside. All we are trying to do is to hit the middle zone of the field.

Again, this is a five-man protection scheme. If you are a six-man protection team, don't run the scat. I learned a long time ago about drawing up pass plays. You must think in terms of the protection that goes with the pass plays.

If we play a team that gives us a lot of one high safeties, we go to a concept we call "mesh." The mesh basic is this. The mesh play is the exact same play as scat, except for the scat receivers. They keep coming across the field and become the mesh receivers. Everything else is the same as the scat play. It is an easy play and you can teach both the scat and the mesh in about five minutes.

The big thing in our offense is that we tell them to stay on schedule. Keep us in a positive play. We do not want negative plays. We want to keep on schedule in our tempo.

Our next point is our nine concept. Everyone runs this route. How many of you run a four-vertical route? We call our four-vertical game the "nine concept." We can run the play out of any formation we use. When we run the play and we are in a 2x2 set, we must have a bender. One of the receivers is going to release downfield and then bend it back inside.

Our basic rules are simple. We have a man on the fade line on both sides of the formation, and we are going to have a man two yards outside the hash mark. Those are our landmarks. In high school, the hash marks are wider than they are in college. We had the high school players line up on the fade line and a man on each hash mark. We ran the mesh out of this set because I had a quarterback that could get the ball to the receivers.

If we see one high safety, we hit the man in the hole on the pass. If it is a two high safety, this is where the bender comes into play. We can tag the A-back, the H-back, or the X-, Y-, or Z-receiver. The receiver that we tag has to become the bender on the play. We try to tag the receiver that is going to give us the best match-up on the play. If you have a receiver that can go get the ball, we want to put him on the same side of the bender. It becomes a bender to the "big dog" play.

The big point about the nine concept is this. Quarterbacks give your receivers a chance to make a play.

When you are in five-man protection, you must tag one of the receivers. We have five possible receivers but only four landmarks. Tell the man you

tag what to do on the play. One of the plays I like is our choice route. It is a five out route. If we call Z choice, we run the two inside receivers deep and the Z-receiver comes down inside. It is a rub down play. We can call the choice route to any of the receivers.

We do run a sail route with this alignment. We are working on a few other routes for the future on this same concept.

We like our nine switch and over route when we run the 3x1 alignment. We tell the inside man he has to go underneath the #1 receiver and over the top of the #2 receiver. If the defense has a safety setting on the hash mark, then the hole is not on the hash mark, it is in the middle of the hash marks. We do not want to break the route too high. If we get too high, the safeties will pick the pass off.

If the defense has only one high safety, now we have a hole on the hash mark. We adjust our over route on the nine concept. We run the over concept a lot.

Let me talk about the bubble route. I could talk on this one play for a week. We tag our screen passes to runs. From every single run play we have, we can tag a screen pass to it. On 90 percent of our runs, we have a tag for the screen pass. We have five basic screens that we use. The bubble is the most important and the number one screen that we use. The first thing we must talk about relates to the base blocking rules. We want to know how teams are going to screen the bubble pass. We want to know this from week to week and use this to our advantage. On most defenses, the corner is the contain defender. Most corners want to hold leverage outside on the receivers. If the defense is playing man coverage, we run past them. Why block them when we don't need to block them?

When we come off the bubble screen, we understand the corner's job is to contain. When we come off the ball, we cut his body in half. The defender will stretch the entire field for us. He has containment on the play.

When it comes to contact, we tell our receiver that he better be "sitting in the chair." He better put his big boy britches on because the defense is coming. The contain man will come to our blocking receiver. He does not need to turn out on the defender. He will take us downfield. We do not want to drift with the man. We want a body on a body.

You must be committed to running the bubble screen pass. It is the same as it is on anything else you do to make it work.

We want the receivers and the quarterback to be comfortable on the play. I want the receiver to take a jab-step with the first step, and then they open. They want to do everything they can to keep the shoulders square to the line of scrimmage. Now it is a catch-and-go drill.

The drill we use is with the JUGS machine. I put the ball on a line, and I line the players up on that line coming to the ball. I crank it up to about 55 and they must stay on the line to catch the ball. This forces them to stay square to the line of scrimmage. We rep this play every day. It is easy for the quarterback to run this play. If it is on a straight line, it becomes consistent.

The one error on the bubble screen pass is the angle of departure. If the receiver does not go upfield after the catch, it stretches the blockers out. We call this the "team four rule." The first four yards are mine. We have not failed to gain at least four yards on a bubble screen in 79 attempts in a game. We average close to eight yards per play on the screen. Again, we tag the screens to running plays.

If the defense is anxious and triggers the corner, we want the quarterback ready to pump the ball as if he is going to throw the ball deep. We are not afraid to pump the ball. We run it anytime, anyplace, and on any play.

I am running out of time. I hope I have given you some ideas that will help you with your receivers. If you want to know more about our passing game, you are welcome to visit us.

THE 3-4 PRESSURE DEFENSE AND COACHING POINTS

The University of Oklahoma

It is great to be here. I am the son of a high school football coach. I grew up in a locker room watching my father watch reel-to-reel tapes. My father was the defensive coordinator for 28 years with the same head coach. He passed away in 1988 on the sideline at 54 years old. He was not overweight, never smoked, and did not drink much at all. He played softball until the day he died. That is a reminder to all of you to be checked regularly by a doctor. You owe it to your family and today's medicine and technology is too good to neglect it.

I was fortunate to grow up in that kind of environment. I appreciate all that coaches do working with young people. What you do matters. We do not do it for the money. That is hard for me to say because of the situation I am in and the money I make. Someone asked me what I would be doing if I were not coaching. My reply was, "I would be coaching." It might be in high school, but this is my passion. I am just like most of you coaches. It is almost as if we do not work. We just go to school and play a game all day.

We enjoy the players, helping them and developing them into what they want to be. The things we teach them have more to do with the way they live than with playing football. It is exciting, has great passion, and we are involved in it. The competition is exciting and fun. That is why we do it. Always embrace that part of the game. Do not let all the people, fans, media, and other outside influences take away from what you do. Do not allow them to take away your joy for the game. I promise you, I do not let that affect me because at the end of the day, I am in this profession for the same reasons you are in it.

When I walk around looking into all the breakout sessions, there are coaches in there talking football. I enjoy that part of this game. I get together with my brother, Mike, Coach Saban, and other coaches and we hash out different ideas. Everyone does things a little different with their terminology and schemes. The game of football is always evolving. I respect you coaches in here today trying to get better at what you do.

When coaches come to a clinic, they look for different things from the speakers. Some people want the technical aspects of the game and some people want to know how you do it. I am involved with the offense, but my background is on the other side of the ball. I am going to talk about our 50 defense and some of the pressures we use with it.

Some of those pressures are good against the run and some are good against the pass. Some of them are good against both the pass and run. I will spend the first part of the lecture talking about the technical end of what we do. The last part, I will talk about how we do what we do. During that time, I will give you some of our philosophy.

Our base front is a 3-4 look with the outside linebackers dropped off in the spread formation (Diagram #1). We play with a Sam linebacker to the strongside of the set and a Jack linebacker to the boundary side of the formation. These are personnel positions. If we have a long-yardage situation, we replace the Sam linebacker with a nickel back.

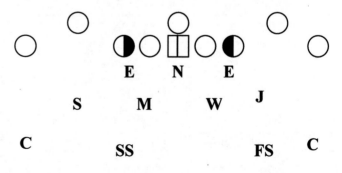

Diagram #1. Base 50 Defense

The Jack and Sam linebacker either expand or reduce, depending on what the #2 receiver is doing. The Jack plays into the boundary or weakside of the formation. He has the skills to play that position. He is more of a blitzing or coverage linebacker. The nose tackle is head-up on the center in a 0 technique. The defensive ends align in a 4i technique in running situations and 5 techniques in passing situations. Their gap responsibility is primarily to the inside in the B gap.

If there is a tight end, our defensive end can go to a 6 technique head-up the tight end (Diagram #2). The first thing I will show you is the strong blitz package we use. We declare the strongside of the formation by using a number of factors. We can declare to the wideside of the field, running strength, or number of receivers.

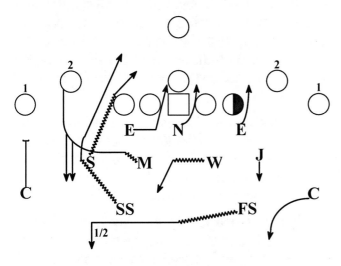

Diagram #2. Strike

We call this blitz "strike." We blitz from the strongside and the nose slants into the backside A gap. The weakside defensive end moves from a 4i technique to a 5 technique. We bring the strongside 4i defender on a long stick to the A gap. He takes a flat step with his inside foot and comes at a 45-degree angle on his second step to the A gap. The Sam linebacker cheats to the line of scrimmage, keys the offensive tackle, and reacts off his movement. If the tackle blocks inside on a running play, the Sam linebacker comes off his butt and spills everything to the outside. He becomes the B-gap defender. The strong safety walks down and blitzes outside off the edge. He is the contain player. He is the C-gap defender.

The strong corner rolls down and plays the flat zone. The free safety cheats to the middle of the field and plays the half-field behind the strong corner. The Mike linebacker has to play under the #2 receiver if he releases vertical.

This is not a magic stunt. The defense knows we come on blitzes. We mix up our stunts to come from the strongside, weakside, and up the middle. When we run the stunts, we try to disguise the stunt. It may look as if we will come from one side and then we come from the other side. We do that with movement of the secondary people and linebackers. We do not want to get predictable as to where we are coming from.

There are some coaching points to this blitz. We protect the Mike linebacker in this stunt. The long stick is the A-gap defender. The Sam linebacker closes on a down block by the tackle and becomes the B-gap defender. The strong safety comes off the edge and contains. The Mike linebacker fits outside. He works from the inside out and plays football.

The Jack linebacker to the weakside reads the block of the weakside tackle. The defensive end moves into a 5-technique alignment. If the offensive tackle blocks out on the defensive end, the Jack can fill to the inside along with the Will linebacker. The Will linebacker plays with inside leverage and the Jack linebacker plays with outside leverage. On the strongside, we appear to have a soft corner to the field, when actually it is a rolled up hard corner.

We can bring different people from the strongside (Diagram #3). On this blitz, we bring the Mike linebacker instead of the strong safety. On the spice blitz, the Mike linebacker blitzes the A gap and the Sam linebacker blitzes the B gap. The defensive end moves into a 5 technique and becomes a C-gap defender.

We can move the front to the strongside (Diagram #4). We use this alignment in a long-yardage situation where we expect the pass. On this blitz, we move the strongside defensive end into a wide 5 technique. The nose moves to a strongside 3 technique and the backside defensive end moves to a 2i technique on the guard. The Jack linebacker moves up on the line in a stand-up 5 technique.

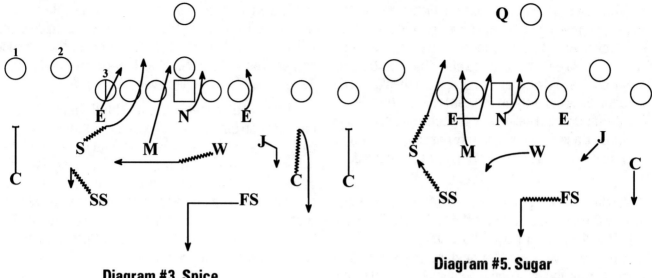

Diagram #3. Spice

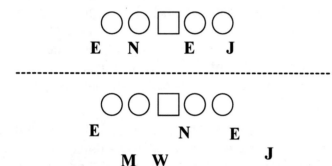

Diagram #4. Adjustments (Nose)

We can also move the nose to the weakside off the center into a shade or 2i technique; that pushes the defensive end back to a 5 technique.

We can change the gaps of the blitz runners; we call this "sugar" (Diagram #5). If we want to take advantage of a pass blocking scheme or a particular player, we can change the blitz responsibilities. On this blitz, we bring the defensive end on a long stick into the A gap. The Mike linebacker blitzes the B gap and the Sam linebacker comes off the edge. He is the C-gap defender. The nose and backside play their normal adjustments to the spice blitz.

We game plan the blitzes. We decide what we want to do and coach them up. On the sugar blitz, the same three people come but their gaps change. The coaching point for the Mike linebacker is he goes first and blitzes the B gap. The defensive end comes behind the Mike linebacker and long sticks into the A gap. The Sam linebacker comes off the edge and is the C-gap defender.

Diagram #5. Sugar

In the secondary, we have a number of different ways we can cover. We can play cover 3 with the strong safety rolled down into the strong flat area. We can roll the corners in a cover 2 look. We can play a free safety in the middle and play man under. In situations like that, we cheat the Will linebacker to the strongside and play him on the #3 receiver in a 3x1 formation.

The next series of blitzes come from the weakside. The blitz runners from the boundary are the Will, Jack, and boundary corner. The defensive end to that side can run the long stick to the A gap. This is the same type of three-man game coming from the boundary.

The first one is the Will linebacker blitzing the B gap (Diagram #6). The nose slants into the strongside A gap. The Will linebacker blitzes the B gap. The defensive end runs the long stick behind the Will linebacker and the Jack linebacker comes off the edge.

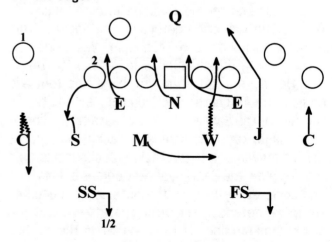

Diagram #6. Boundary Blitz Will B

The next combination is a blitz involving the corner (Diagram #7). The Jack linebacker blitzes the B gap. The defensive end takes a long stick to the A gap and the corner comes off the edge as the C-gap defender. The nose takes the strongside A gap. He has to be aware of the guard to the strongside. If we play a zone read team, the nose has to be aware to which side the running back aligns. If he is away from where the back is going, he has to play the block of the strongside guard if he comes down on him.

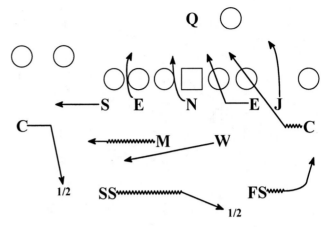

Diagram #8. Boundary Blitz Corner B

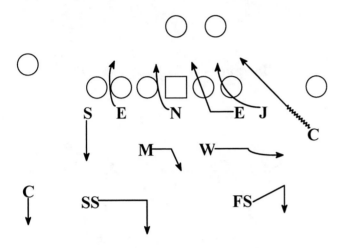

Diagram #7. Boundary Blitz Corner

The Will linebacker on this blitz is a free hitter. The outside defenders fill the A and B gaps and the corner comes off the edge. If the ball runs into the boundary, there is no one left to block him. He has an outside fit.

The last movement off the boundary side is to the corner in the B gap (Diagram #8). On this blitz, the Jack linebacker comes up the field and the defensive end long sticks into the A gap. The corner comes off the boundary side and into the B gap. Everything to the strongside is the same. The nose slants into the strongside A gap.

When we face a triple set into the wideside of the field, the offense likes to work to the single receiver into the boundary (Diagram #9). If the offense has an outstanding receiver at the single receiver position, we can give the free safety help. When the corner blitzes, the free safety has coverage on the single receiver. The strong safety aligns to the wideside of the field but works his way back to the backside hash mark before they snap the ball. He can play over the top of the free safety to the boundary.

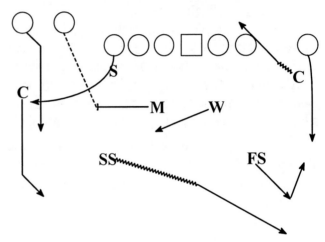

Diagram #9. Weakside Roll

To the wideside of the field, the corner comes off and plays the half-field. The Sam linebacker works to the outside into the flat area. The Mike linebacker widens and works under the #2 receiver. The Will linebacker cheats to the trips side and works the middle hook. We play three underneath zones to the wideside of the field and two-deep zones with help into the boundary. This allows the free safety to play tight coverage on the single receiver.

The next blitz comes up the middle (Diagram #10). There are many ways to send the inside linebackers. One way is to bring both linebackers to the strongside of the formation. The defensive ends play outside technique and charge up the field. The nose slants into the backside A gap. The Mike linebacker blitzes the strongside A gap and the Will linebacker blitzes the strongside B gap.

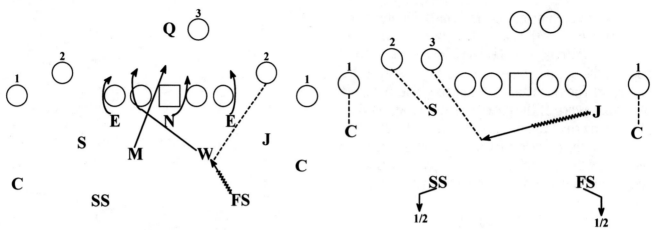

Diagram #10. Middle Blitz

The gap that is not covered is the weakside B gap. We can walk the free safety down into the scheme and he replaces the Will linebacker. He is the B-gap defender and runs under the #2 receiver to that side. The Sam linebacker plays under the #2 receiver to the strongside. The Sam and Jack linebackers play the flat zones and the free safety is the low-hole defender in the middle of the field.

We can bring both inside linebackers from the weakside in the same pattern. We can change the gap responsibility and blitz them in any fashion we can imagine.

In a 3x1 set, the free safety has to find the #3 receiver to the trips side. If the #3 receiver goes vertical, he picks him up on the seam. However, if the #3 receiver works to the outside, he becomes the low-hole player in the middle for crossing patterns coming from the outside into the middle.

If it is a passing situation and a 3x1 formation, we like to play a true two-deep secondary (Diagram #11). The corners play the wide receivers in tight coverage. The Sam linebacker works under the #2 receiver to the trips side. The Jack linebacker cheats over the center and plays under the #3 receiver. We can also match the patterns of those receivers and play man under two deep.

The last blitz is an outside blitz (Diagram #12). We can bring the blitz from the strong or weakside. We can bring it up the middle and we can bring it from both sides. This is the outside blitz coming off both edges. We bring the Sam and Jack linebackers off the edges of the defense. We can play a number of coverages behind the blitz. We can play man free or two deep with no problem.

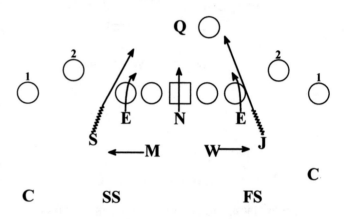

Diagram #11. Coverage vs. 3x1

Diagram #12. Outside Blitz

If we play man free, the corners lock up on the wide receivers. The strong safety and Will linebacker match the #2 receivers to their sides. The Mike linebacker takes the back in the backfield and the free safety is down the middle of the coverage in a free position.

If we play two-deep coverage, the corners roll up and play the flat zone. The Mike and Will linebackers are the seam players under the #2 receivers to their sides and the strong and free safeties play the deep halves of the field.

If we play two deep against the trips set, the Mike and Will linebackers play under the #2 and #3 receivers to the trips side.

If we are in man free coverage, we have an adjustment we can make (Diagram #13). In the 2x2 formation, we lock the corner on the wide receivers. The strong safety walks down and takes the #2 receiver strong. The Will linebacker has the

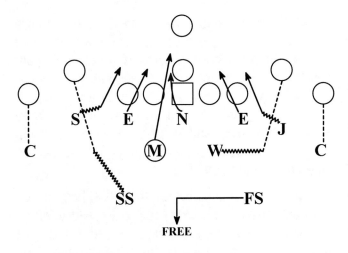

Diagram #13. Mike Linebacker Add-On

#2 receiver weak. The Mike linebacker has the #3 receiver in the backfield. If the #3 receiver blocks, the Mike linebacker adds on to the blitz and rushes the quarterback.

In man coverage, we can add on any defender whose man becomes part of the blocking pattern. However, the problem in the secondary is the distance to get to the quarterback. If the strong safety has a tight end in man coverage, he could stay in and block. Unless the strong safety is in close proximity to the line of scrimmage, he will not get home if he comes on the blitz. He would be better off playing a low-hole zone in the middle.

A change-up we use comes from our zone blitz package (Diagram #14). We reduce the weakside and bring the defensive end into a 3 technique on the guard. The Will linebacker walks outside in a 5-technique alignment on the offensive tackle.

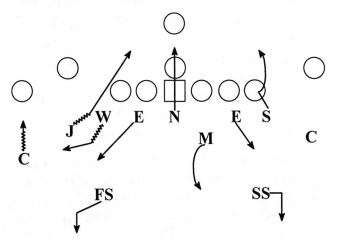

Diagram #14. Zone Blitz

The Jack linebacker aligns on the slot receiver, cheats inside, and blitzes from the outside. The Sam linebacker comes off the other edge. The Will linebacker drops into the area vacated by the Jack linebacker. The Mike is a middle hook dropper. We drop the 3- and 5-technique defensive ends into short coverage. They engage the blockers at the line of scrimmage and drop into coverage.

The scheme is not that complicated and is easy to run. The communication at the line of scrimmage is simple. The secondary coverage is execution. We have to know the coverage and execute the coverage.

I want to cover a few things that are part of our philosophy at The University of Oklahoma. These first things I will let you read them and we will go on.

BUILDING A TEAM

- *Establish trust:* To lead players, they must trust you and believe you care for them. You cannot fool players; you must care for them for more than just their football abilities. They must trust each other and depend on each other.

- *Establish discipline:* All young men want it, be strong enough to give it to them. John Wooden said, "Do not treat all players the same, treat them the way they deserve to be treated." (Make players be accountable to each other.)

- Establish work ethic (effort): Grade their effort the same way you grade technique. Demand it.

- *Create team unity:* Teach them how to respect one another and pull for one another. They must understand that not everyone can be a star, but everyone has an important role on the team.

- *Play to your players' and team's strengths:* In all phases of the game, avoid their weaknesses and plan for ways to protect their weaknesses when possible.

- *Create a positive learning environment:* Be sure players have some fun while they work. Talk confidently and positively to players; they begin to believe what you're saying, whether they should or not.

- *Acknowledge performance, not potential:* We will play the players who work within the system the hardest and who make the most plays. Players will earn their way onto the field and will have to compete throughout the year to stay on the field.
- *Respect fellow coaches:* Coaches must have a great respect for one another and a great working relationship. Keep egos out of the office and be willing to help each position or side of the ball improve.
- *Share the responsibility:* Be sure players take responsibility for winning and losing with coaches. We are one team, all pulling for each other with no excuses. There will be no excuse not to play our best and win.
- *No excuses:* They only try to justify failure. You either succeed or not. It is black or white.
- If we will play *smarter, harder,* and more *technical* than our opponent, we'll win.

COACHING

- Be positive with your corrections
- Have some fun; let them laugh
- No excuses
- Have great expectations
- Be specific in your teaching
- Play smart, play hard, play physical
- Win the turnover battle
- Play great defense
- Keep balance on offense
- Have great special teams
- Win the fourth quarter

In our coaching meetings, I talk to my coaches about these points. When they correct a player, always try to put a positive spin on the correction. At our level, that changes everything for the player. They will remember it and they will listen to the coach more.

You have to let your players have some fun. I listened to Mark Dantonio speak at the AFCA convention. He is a great friend of mind and a good football coach at Michigan State University. He said you have to keep everything fresh for the players.

I tell my coaches all the time that the players must have fun. The players have to want to come to practice. They have to want to go to your team meetings. They have to drop in and see you at your office for no reason at all. They just want to talk to you about nothing. The coaches have to keep what they do fresh and when it is possible, let them laugh. We do not want them to just goof off, but we do want them to have fun.

I want no excuses for anything that happens on the field. All it does is to try to justify failure. When you start to say we are inexperienced or we have too many injuries, you can begin to write off the season. If you have five or six games to go on the schedule, you can forget about the season. It does not matter what the circumstances are, we expect to play well and win.

Having great expectations goes beyond football. If you are going to achieve your goals in life, you must have great expectations. If you expect a lot, you will either reach your goal or come closer to it. Either way, you will be successful. We expect a lot in our program. I talk to the players all the time about this point. I tell them they will achieve, in life and in the games, what they expect to achieve. To play in our program, you had better expect a lot.

Nothing is worse than the coach being very general about what he wants a player to do. Be very specific in what you want from a player and tell him exactly what you want him to do. Make sure he knows what his assignment is and how to execute it. There is no gray area when the pocket collapses and the defense sacks the quarterback.

When I got to Oklahoma, I said it takes no talent to play smart, play hard, and be physical. If you can get your players to do those three things, you will win most of your games. It takes no talent to not commit dumb penalties or know your assignment. It takes no talent to perform the job hard. There is no substitute in this game for being tough.

If you want to be competitive, do not turn the ball over. Take the ball away from the offense. You have to work on it in practice, and it will always be a telling statistic in winning and losing games. You have to protect the ball. I do not think anyone has a chance to win a national championship if they do not play great defense.

You must have balance on offense. We had a Heisman Trophy winner in Sam Bradford two years ago and an outstanding quarterback this year by the name of Landry Jones. We also had an All-American receiver by the name of Ryan Broyles. However, if you watch us play, we will run the football. We did not run it as well as I would have liked, but it was not because we did not call it. We will work harder this year in spring practice to get that part of the game to where I want it.

I think it is important to have great special teams. I never miss a special teams meeting. I am at every one of them and I want to contribute in those meetings. The team knows it is important.

These are some principles that I absolutely believe in and talk to my staff about all the time.

STAFF

- Work the job you have—don't be looking for another (phone coaches).
- You must believe you can win—wherever you are and regardless of the circumstances.
- Never worry or complain about what other coaches on your staff or other staffs have.
- Never stop learning—always be looking for new or better ways to play or teach.
- Be willing to be criticized—make decisions in games based on gut instinct and what you believe is necessary to win, not on what the book says or to avoid being criticized.
- Coach players hard—never personal—always laugh with them and let them laugh with you as much as possible.
- Always coach and instruct in a positive, confident manner.
- Whatever you say to a player, always be prepared to back it up and follow through.
- Be prepared—do not second-guess yourself.
- Recruit every day.
- Do not stress. Enjoy the challenge. Enjoy the game. Do the best you can and let it be.
- Include family—be rested—be confident. Work out every day.

- Never allow winning and losing to define you—always realize what is most important in your life.
- Never allow excuses or reasons to justify failure.

In my eyes, this is how success happens. Do not look for a job when you have one. If you do the job well, you will always have an opportunity to find another job. I finished the job at Kansas State University before I took the job at the University of Florida. We had an outstanding year at Florida and we led the nation in defense. I got another opportunity at Oklahoma. Be loyal to your head coach.

When we went to Kansas State, you would not believe how bad the program was. I coached with Coach Snyder at The University of Iowa. There was no doubt in either of our minds when we arrived at Kansas State that we were going to win. People will try to convince you that you cannot win. If they convince you, you will not have a chance.

The game of football never stops. It continues to evolve and you have to continue to learn and study. I make decisions that I believe need to happen for us to win. The example is when we played The University of Alabama in Tuscaloosa and we were ahead 14-7. The momentum had changed and they were coming hard. They had us backed up and we had to punt the ball. Our punter was standing on the eight-yard line. I felt if we punted the ball that they were going to block it. I called a fake and the play went to the their 45-yard line. We scored on the next play and we went on to win the game. I knew if that play failed, we were beat. I felt the only way to stem the tide was to make something happen. I did not care if someone criticized me because that is what needed to happen for us to win the game.

Nothing is worse than a coach that says things and never follows through on them. I tell my coaches all the time not to give players an ultimatum. Do not tell them it is either you or me. That puts me in a bad position. The coach can never back himself into a corner with no alternatives.

I do not spend time worrying about what we do. I feel if we worked all week and practiced well, then I do not see any reason to worry. There is no need to second-guess what you did. What is done is done, and there is no changing the results.

There is nothing better than being at the game site 10 minutes before the kickoff. When you walk on the field, you do not know what is going to happen. That is the best part of the entire experience. I enjoy that feeling. The players catch your energy and if you are uptight, they have a tendency to do the same thing. You have to stay loose and have fun.

I lift and work out for 45 minutes every day. It does not matter who we play, I still go work out.

I want the families of our players and coaches around our practices. People laugh at me because we moved a drill 10 yards up the field so the kids could play a pickup game of football. All our kids come to our practices. We want to make sure they are included in our program.

I know who I am. I do not let people define what I am. I have been around success and failure. The reality of my life and the things that are important to me are clear.

It is fun to be in the DC area. I am from Youngstown, Ohio and it is a little ways from here. However, it is a heck of a lot closer than Oklahoma. I enjoyed being here and I thank you for your attention. We are always open to you if you want to come out and watch us in the spring. You are always welcome and our coaches do a good job of working with high school coaches. I want to thank you for having me here. Best of luck to you next year. I hope you all win state championships.

DEFENDING THE SPREAD ZONE OPTION

University of Arizona

Thank you very much. I want to give you something to think about in simplifying what you do. I want to give you some ideas I think are important to having some success. I was fortunate to be around many great people growing up. My father was a football coach and I grew up going to football clinics. There are four Stoops brothers in college coaching today. Mark is the defensive coordinator at Florida State University, Bob is the head coach at the University of Oklahoma, I am the head coach at the University of Arizona, and Rob Stoops is now coaching at Youngstown State University. Rob is our oldest brother. We grew up watching tape with my father. He was quite successful in this profession.

I hope I can pass on some things that will help you in your program. I do not want to talk a lot of philosophy. I know you get that from many head coaches. They want to talk about structure and motivation. I am different from them. Our style is hands-on with the offense and defense. My expertise is on the defensive side of the ball. Good high school coaches become great college coaches because you have to coach so much in high school on both sides of the ball.

I want to give you some basic thought about how we build our team. I want to give you some of the ingredients that are important to building a winning program. When I took the job at Arizona, we had some problems. I had to instill certain characteristics, values, and discipline into our program so we could become a winner. Football is one of the hardest areas to make wholesale changes because there are so many players involved. We had to recruit quality football players that fit into our system.

ELEMENTS FOR SUCCESS

- Great defense
- Turnover margin
- Red zone offense
- Special teams

For you to have a successful team, it is important to have a good defense. Being good on defense gives you an opportunity to win. I believe having a balanced football team is important. However, I believe the entire team's attitude and durability to play with the best teams has to come from within the structure of your defense. Arizona has always played good defense.

It goes back to the old adage, which says, "Offense sells tickets, and defense wins championships." When you look at the University of Oregon, they were good offensively but the thing that made them a great team was their defense. If you watch the evolution of Oregon in the past couple of years, it has been their ability to play good defense. They have one of the fastest defenses in the country. Their defense gives them an opportunity to go to the next level.

The turnover margin is something that we talk about all the time. This year, we ended up fourth in the PAC 10. Statistically, we were third in total defense and total offense. We were eighth in turnover margin. That was different and the lowest ranking we have had in the last four years. We do not read much into statistics. However, turnover margin is a telling statistic when it comes to evaluating your season. It is critical and something we must address with our team.

Last year, we had six turnovers in the red zone. They were lost opportunities and momentum changers. Those mistakes are difficult from which to recover. You have the chance to go in, get points, and end up with nothing. That is a good statistic at which to look. The previous year we finished first in the PAC 10 in that statistic, and we finished second in the league.

The PAC 10 has never been as competitive for teams one through 10 as it is now. The competition in the league has never been better. Special teams are more important than ever before. The special teams can decide the game in a closely competitive contest. We scored with 26 seconds to go against Arizona State University and missed the extra point to win the game. We went into overtime and lost the game on a missed extra point in the second overtime period.

You must stress those areas within your program. You have to be able to punt and return the ball. All those areas become invaluable when you are in tight football games. We have to do a better job on special teams, and we will direct our attention to those things in the spring.

In those four statistics, we were third in total defense and in the bottom half of the league in the other categories. Those are not good statistics, and that tells us why we finished where we did in the PAC 10.

We have to improve in those areas, and the keys to doing it starts with leadership.

HOW DO YOU ACCOMPLISH THESE THINGS?

• Leadership (seniors)
• Play hard every snap; average play 4 to 7 seconds
• Preparation: Do your job.
• Team first: Don't be selfish; maintain positive energy.

The leadership on your team comes from your seniors, hopefully the best players on your team. A good team with good leadership can win 7 or 8 games. A good team with great leadership can win 9 or 10 games. That stat is critical when you look at your overall team. You look to your seniors for leadership. You look at your seniors and try to see if there is a correlation for the past couple of years. Trying to build leadership is something we talk about continuously over the course of the year.

It takes no talent to play hard. Each play is 4 to 7 seconds in length. That is not a tremendous amount of time. In our back seven players, we do not substitute many times with them. However, in the front four, we play seven to eight players each game. We build the linebackers and defense to play hard and the front four get enough rest that they should play hard every snap. We grade every play for effort. Getting a team running to the ball and giving maximum effort is paramount to your success as a football team.

The preparation you put into the game is tremendously important. The preparation of your team is the key any time you step on the field. We have the same preparation for each game, and we want to show great respect for each opponent we play. We want to be prepared to play the best team in the league or the worst team in the league. The balance in the league means you must be prepared every time you step on the field.

The last thing is putting the team first. Football is the ultimate team sport. You have stars, and you want them to have individual goals, but that cannot overshadow the importance of putting the team first.

Those are some brief philosophical points that I think are important to being successful and certainly to being good on defense. If your players are accountability for those areas, you have a chance to be a good team.

When I was a player, we played many spread teams. Today, I want to talk about how we play a three- or four-wide formation team. Our approach has not changed much as to the way we play a 2x2 set or a 3x1 set. In those sets, the quarterback is in the shotgun 70 percent of the time. Oregon and Arizona State are in the shotgun almost 100 percent of the time. Few teams in our league align in a conventional set, and most of them are in the spread formations. Stanford University and the University of Southern California are predominantly under the center.

When we teach defense, we start with the three- and four-wide formations and work our way into the more conventional sets. We build everything we talk about on numbers. We teach from a 2x2 or a 3x1 formation. Because of the zone read concept in football today, it is important to have the extra defender on the quarterback.

At Arizona, we structure our defense to gap control with the nickel, Mike linebacker, or Will linebacker based on where the running back sets. In the first example, the back sets away from the nickel back (Diagram #1). After we set the front, the nickel widens outside the B gap and splits the difference between the slot receiver and the offensive tackle. He reads through the B gap for the zone play.

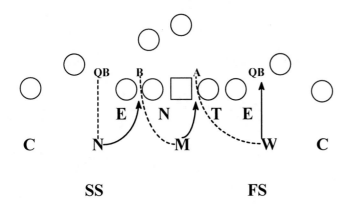

Diagram #1. Back Away From Nickel

If they run the zone play, the nickel back fills the B gap to the backside. The Mike is the A-gap player to the ballside. The Will linebacker becomes the extra defender on the quarterback if he pulls the ball. If there were a tight end to that side, the Will linebacker moves out over the tight end, and nothing else would change.

If they brought the back to the other side, the Will linebacker plays the A gap to the backside. The Mike linebacker takes the B gap to the playside, and the nickel back is the extra player on the quarterback if he pulls the ball.

When we call a double palms defense, the corners read the #2 receivers (Diagram #2). They take their alignment off the #1 receiver, but they read the #2 receiver. They are at a depth of six

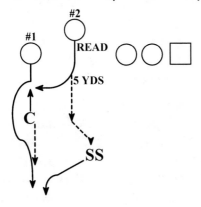

Diagram #2. Corner Key

yards off the wide receiver with an inside leverage position. They read the release of the #2 receiver. On a vertical release, anything past five yards turns the corner's coverage into quarter coverage with the safety to his side. If the receiver releases off the line and at five yards goes to the flat, the corner jumps the flat route, and the safety plays over the top of the corner.

The safeties alignment is at 10 yards on the outside eye of the #2 receiver into the wide field. If he is into the boundary, he plays at 10 yards on the inside eye of the #2 receiver.

It is a basic two-read concept on the release on the #2 receiver. If the offense runs the smash route, the corner plays the hitch. He tries to buy time for the safety to get over to the 7 route (flag route) by the #2 receiver. He plays midway between the corner route and the hitch by the wide receiver. The safety reads the seven route by the #2 receiver, gets over the top of the corner, and takes the #2 receiver going long into the sidelines.

This is a double palms call, so the backside of the defense plays the same type of coverage. When the corner reads the outside move by the #2 receiver, he tries to buy the safety time to get over the top of the wide receiver. He holds on the wide receiver and disrupts his release going vertical before he jumps the slot coming to the flat.

The rule for the corner is he has the wide receiver going vertical unless the slot receiver runs an out breaking pattern at five or less yards. If the slot runs vertical, the corner stays on the wide receiver. People like to try to cross the receivers with the slot going up the field and the wide receiver breaking to the post behind the slot. When the corner and safety are on two different levels, the corner takes the wide receiver going to the post, and the safety stays on the scissors route of the slot receiver up the field.

If the back sets into the wideside of the field, we play the nose to the back and the 3 technique away from him. If they run the inside zone, the Mike linebacker fills the B gap to the playside. The Will linebacker aligns in a mid-alignment on the slot receiver and offensive tackle. He stays wide. If the offense run the zone read, he does not need to fill the A gap to the backside of the play immediately. He lets the A gap work to him as the play develops. The nickel back playing to the field plays the quarterback on the zone option, if he pulls the ball.

We do not want to bring the Will linebacker back inside because the bubble screen is a part of the zone read play. He has to stay in position to support and attack the bubble to his side. That is the first thing the offense wants to see. They want to know if you are respecting the bubble screen. That is the reason for the strong safety's alignment on the slot receiver to his side.

We play the nickel back, Mike linebacker, corner, and strong safety on the three possible receivers to their side. On the backside, the Will linebacker, corner, and free safety play the slot and wide receiver. To the field, we play four defenders over three receivers, and to the boundary, we play three defenders over two receivers. It is a match-up concept based on the release of the slot or #2 receiver (Diagram #3).

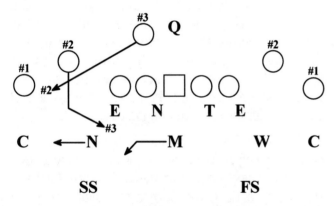

Diagram #3. Match-Up Coverage

The running back in the backfield is the #3 receiver. The Mike linebacker has coverage on an inside release by the #3 receiver. If the running back releases to the flat, the #3 receiver can never outflank the nickel. As soon as the running back gets outside of the slot receiver, the nickel plays the running back, and the Mike linebacker expands to the slot receiver.

The thing I do not like is the fact the front is into the boundary. That puts the nickel having to cover the A gap from the wide field. That becomes a difficult task to ask him to play the A gap with the wide field to his outside. Play-action schemes

put him in a bad situation. If the offense aligns with 10 personnel (zero tight ends/one back), we want the nose into the field (Diagram #4). That puts the nickel one gap closer to his responsible for action away from him.

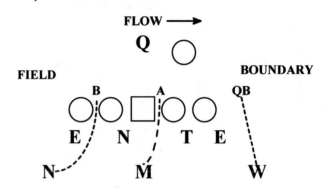

Diagram #4. 10 Personnel Alignment

That allows the nickel to stay wide to give help to the outside. He has to stare through the B gap because that is his gap on run flow away. If you have to bring him all the way to the A gap, he is no help in coverage to the wideside of the field. That alignment leaves too much ground to cover without severely cutting his alignment to the inside.

In our adjustments, the overhang defender to the side of the running back is the extra defender on the quarterback. He has to take the quarterback if he pulls the ball on the zone option. The Will linebacker or nickel is the overhang player. The overhand defender plays the quarterback, and the other two defenders play the A gaps and B gaps.

In a straight dropback pass, the Mike linebacker takes his drop off the #3 receiver. If the #3 receiver goes away, the Mike linebacker sets in the curl to that side. The nickel splits the difference between the slot receiver and the offensive tackle. The strong safety aligns on the slot receiver. The corner takes an inside alignment on the wide receiver. We are 4-on-3 strong and 3-on-2 weak.

If the pattern is a shallow cross coming underneath the coverage, we make an adjustment (Diagram #5). The Will linebacker reads from the slot receiver to the running back or the inside receiver in a trips formation. If the slot receiver runs under the Will linebacker going inside, he releases him to the Mike linebacker. If the running back goes to the outside, the Will linebacker takes that coverage.

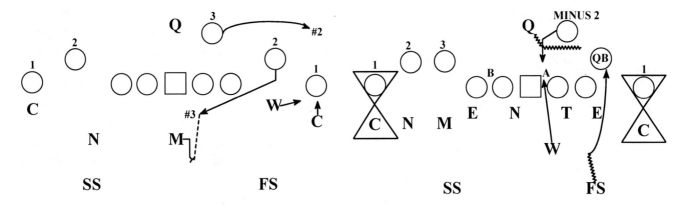

Diagram #5. Shallow Cross

Diagram #7. 3x1 Minus Alignment

We go from covering four to the strongside to cover 4 to the weakside.

The Mike linebacker reacts off the pattern of the #3 receiver. If he goes strong or weak, he looks from #3 to the #2 receiver. If #3 goes out, #2 is probably coming in. If #3 blocks, the Mike linebacker zones off, looking for the crossing routes.

With the trips formation, we can get a 3x1 or a 3x2, which is the empty set (Diagram #6). It does not matter if the personnel group is 10 or 11. To the trips side of the formation, we eliminate the wide receiver to that side by locking the corner in 1-on-1 man coverage. The Mike linebacker, nickel, and strong safety play the same coverage as they did in the base coverage. If we play a pistol set in the backfield, we treat that as a home set. A home set is an I formation alignment to us.

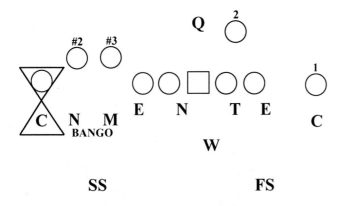

Diagram #6. 3x1 Coverage

If the offense aligns in the trips set to the wide field and puts the running back in a "minus position" to the boundary, we kick the linebackers over to the field (Diagram #7). The nose aligns into

the field in a 1 technique on the fieldside guard, and the 3-technique tackle is into the boundary. The Mike linebacker moves outside and aligns inside the #3 receiver. He plays the nickel's responsibility on flow away on the zone play. He is the B-gap player with the ball going away. The Will linebacker becomes the A-gap player to the boundary side of the alignment. The extra player on the quarterback becomes the free safety moving down from his alignment.

The free safety reads the offensive tackle to his side. If the tackle blocks down or scoops to the inside, he plays the zone option play. If the tackle pass-sets, he looks for the #3 receiver strong coming up the field on a vertical route. If the #3 receiver releases outside or comes shallow across the field, he zones off and helps the corner to his side.

If the #3 receiver is trying to get deep, it is a mismatch unless we have a dime package in the game. The free safety is more of a free runner to this formation. He has to be the support with the running back set to his side, but gives help on a vertical from #3 trying to get down the middle.

If the running back aligns into the trips formation, we call that a "plus position" (Diagram #8). In this alignment, the free safety becomes a gap control defender. The Will linebacker has the B gap to the trips side of the formation. The Mike linebacker does not have a gap to control. He is the extra player on the quarterback, if he runs the zone option. With this adjustment, the corner to the single-receiver side is playing man coverage on the wide receiver. In any trips formation, the corner playing the single receiver is on the island most of the time.

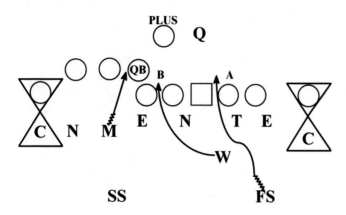

Diagram #8. 3x1 Plus Alignment

The corner away from the trips has very little over the top help his way unless we game plan it.

Against Arizona State, they did not run the zone read too much. The free safety played deeper and looked to help the Mike linebacker on the #3 receiver going vertical. If he went to the outside, the free safety worked over the top of the corner to his side. Against Oregon, it was a different alignment for him. Oregon is a big zone option team. The free safety has to cheat toward the line to handle the quarterback coming out that way with the ball.

The Mike linebacker on the trips set has to play the alignment the nickel plays on the 2x2 formation. He aligns splitting the difference between the #3 receiver and the offensive tackle.

With the run flow away from him, he fills in the B gap. If he has quarterback option his way, he is the extra defender on the quarterback. The nickel back to the trips side plays the #2 receiver like the corner played the #1 receiver in a 2x2 formation. If the #3 receiver breaks to the outside, he jams the #2 receiver going up the field and sits on the #3 receiver coming to him.

The strong safety plays over the top of the nickel back just as he did in quarter coverage. The safeties drop and try to find work in their area of the field. When we play teams that are primary zone read and passing teams, we play five and six defensive backs.

In the PAC 10, teams align in the empty set and motion back into a 2x2 set or a 3x1 formation. They want the defensive back to adjust and to think. They use a number of return motion schemes and flipping the back from a plus to a minus side

of the quarterback. They feel they can get a miscommunication in the secondary and break someone open in the deep zone. We do the same thing. We very seldom see plays where there is not some kind of movement. It is either a shift or some type of motion. We do not align in a stationary front anymore. The game has become so multiple, and players are moving every play. There are very few plays where the offense just lines up and snaps the ball.

We play several man concepts in our defensive scheme. When playing teams with a four-wide receiver package, we play with six defensive backs. That allows us to play a number of ways in the man schemes. We can bracket receivers on either side. We can bring six defenders into the box and play gap control with the four down linemen and two linebackers. We can match the four wide receivers with a free safety or with a four-under, two-deep scheme. When we play six defensive backs, we generally take the Mike linebacker off the field.

We play two-man coverage with two different leverages (Diagram #9). It is part of our third-down package. If we want to force the ball to the outside, we align with inside leverage and force all the receivers to the outside. When we use this coverage, we must be aware of the splits of the receivers. If the receiver starts to tighten his split, he is trying to get inside. We consider a split tight when the receiver gets inside the hash mark.

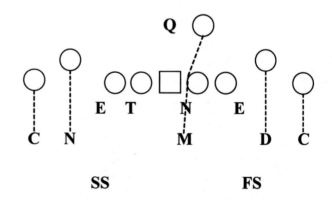

Diagram #9. Two Over Man

We play this type of adjustment in a third down and medium yardage. We want to stop the quick slant to the inside. If we have a third-and-long situation, we want to force the ball the other way. We want the receiver to break to the inside and into our coverage. We play a two-deep zone behind this coverage.

We bracket receivers when they cut their splits down. If we stand a chance to get a pick off the man coverage, we bracket the coverage. The two defensive backs zone off the receiver and take the receivers the way they break. If the receivers split, the inside defender takes the inside receiver, and the outside receiver takes the outside receiver. If the receivers cross, the defenders switch their men.

My time is getting close, and it is almost happy hour. You have done a great job of hanging in here.

I appreciate speaking and share ideas with you. I know there is a lot of great football played in this area.

I have great appreciation for what you coaches do. I know you are strong men of faith and character, and teaching is what we do. We have a great influence on young men that participate in our programs. Teach them the right things, and keep it simple. That way, they can understand and play aggressively. The game of football has become a game of movement at the college level, and I am sure it is working that way in the high school level. It is not 22 players in a shoebox anymore. The teams spread out, and so does the game. Thank you.

DEVELOPING THE QUARTERBACK AND LEADERSHIP

University of California, Berkeley

It is an honor to be here representing Nike, and it is honor to be here and to talk to you guys. I admire you all for taking the time to come out to learn some new techniques and maybe something that you can use to better your young men. I have been at the University of California going on 10 seasons now. It is hard to believe the time has gone by that fast. When I got to Cal, they had just come off a 1-10 season and had not been to a bowl game in many, many years. I can remember our first team meeting, where I was explaining to our team about the importance of running the ball off-tackle. Most games are won and lost by your ability to run the ball off-tackle. We can create an identity by running the ball off-tackle. That is where most games are lost. I asked one of our players, who was half asleep during our meeting, "Where are most games won and lost?" He woke up real quick and said, "Right here at Cal, coach." At that point, I knew we had a big job to do.

Fortunately, I have been able to assemble a great coaching staff, and we have been able to recruit very well. The first team we had at Cal was very, very hungry for success. Our quarterback was going into his final season, and his name was Kyle Boller. Kyle Boller ended up being a first-round draft pick and played for the Ravens. He was going to quit football. I watched some of his tape and has fundamentals were terrible. He had come to Cal and started as a freshman, but he was beat down. He was supposed to be the savior, but he had a 47 percent completion percentage. He had more interceptions than he had touchdowns. He was a mess, and he was going to quit football. He was able to turn it around and become a first-round draft pick in just one year. He deserves all of the credit because he did all of the work. We just gave him some direction.

I admire what you all do, and we coach the greatest game in the world. You coaches make a huge difference in these young people's lives. I am living proof of this. I was from a single-parent home. My father left us when I was nine years old, and I didn't have a great upbringing. I remember when I was a freshman, I was a little skinny kid, and I walked up to our varsity football coach's office after school. I could have gone in one direction or the other. I could have gotten into trouble very easily. But as I was pacing in front of the coach's office, he called me in and sat me down. He asked me what I wanted to do with my life and what my goals were. He had no idea I was going to be a good football player because I was just this little scrawny kid. He took the time to sit me down and talk to me. That made all the difference in my life. If that coach had not taken the time to do that with me, there is no way I would have ended up in the coaching business. By the time I left his office, I knew what I wanted to do. I wanted to be a football coach, and I wanted to be just like him. What you guys do is to provide a lot more than just X's and O's. If you see that little skinny kid out front of your office walking around, take the time to call him in and sit him down and talk to him.

We do some teambuilding exercises at Cal where we may take something like the topic of trust, and we will talk about it. We ask them, "Who do you trust and why, and who don't you trust and why?" You will not believe how many times a kid will say their football coach. Whether it is the person he trusts, or the person he does not trust, you guys play a very important role in what goes on in these kids' lives.

What I would like to talk about today is the development of a young quarterback. I have been very fortunate in that I have coached six first-round draft picks, and just recently was thrilled to see that I am a two-time Super Bowl winner. Aaron Rodgers went to Cal and just recently won a Super Bowl, and Trent Dilfer went to Cal as well. I am very proud of all those guys. One thing that is consistent with those guys is that they are all very competitive and all students of the game. They have a great drive and a great passion to understand what they are doing. If you watched Aaron Rodgers play during the season, it was not just the pinpoint passing and the quick release, but he has a great understanding of what is happening on the football field, conceptually. He gets it, and he knows what is happening around him. He will go to the right place with the football all of the time.

I want to preface everything I am saying by telling you that this is just one way to do it. What we will talk about today is what we feel is important and what we do with fundamentals. Other people may feel it is important to do it differently, and that is fine, but I am going to give you what we have done and what we feel good about.

The first thing you think about when you think about quarterback play is arm strength and throwing the football. A lot of people think that is all that the quarterback is made up of. As we go through the characteristics that we are looking for, first, we want to see physical and mental toughness in our quarterback position. It is imperative to have great physical and mental toughness. The mental toughness to be able to stand in there after you have thrown three interceptions, when the fans are booing you, and be mentally tough enough to get back in that huddle and lead your team down the field. Physical toughness is very important, because when you get hit and you are bleeding from the chin, are you going to be the guy that gets back in that huddle and gets it done? Can you demand the respect of your teammates by your mental toughness? Everybody on the other team wants to get after the quarterback. You have to have the physical toughness to be able to play through an injury like a cracked rib or a hurt ankle.

The next thing we look for is intelligence. It is critical to have a quarterback who can put you in, or get you out of, the right play. Can he comprehend things in the huddle? Can he communicate with clarity in the huddle and understand the vision and the concept of what is going on?

The next thing we look for is competitiveness and leadership. Is he the guy that wants the ball in his hands and that your team can rely on to be a competitor. He has to have leadership qualities that are infectious to the whole team, not just to the receivers and the running backs, but the whole team. Before the Super Bowl this year, I sent a text to Aaron Rodgers and told him I had done more interviews about him that week than I had about our team all year long. What people wanted to know was, "How is Aaron going to perform on the big stage?" I felt very confident in saying that he was going to perform great because of what I saw Aaron Rodgers do while he was quarterback at Cal. When we were playing Southern Cal in 2003, at our home when they were ranked number two in the country, we beat them in triple overtime.

The next year, we had to go to their place, and they were ranked number one with 100,000 screaming fans, and it was the biggest stage by far that Aaron Rodgers had ever played on. He came from Butte Community College as a junior college kid. I saw him on tape while I was looking for a tight end and asked who that kid was throwing the ball, because he looked pretty good. I will never forget in that locker room scene, the type of leadership qualities that Aaron had. I was watching him before that game; he was just walking around in the locker room with a smile on his face, slapping guys on the butt and getting them going, but also getting them relaxed. He was not going haywire and yelling and screaming. He had this confidence about himself because of his leadership ability that was unbelievable. It was infectious to everyone when they took the field with that feeling. Aaron went out and completed 23 straight passes in the Coliseum with all those people yelling and screaming. That is hard to do any time, yet alone with the USC defense coming at you and in a hostile environment. We want to make sure all of our quarterbacks have this type of capability.

The next thing we look for is their escape dimension and athletic ability. We want someone who can move the pocket and someone who can get out of a bad situation. We want somebody who can manufacture a play, be it with a scramble or resetting the pocket by using his athletic ability. I have coached both types of players—those that could go out and make something happen, and those that were stiff and could only sit back in the pocket.

I will tell you the players who can make something happen will make more plays for you and win more games. The athletic dimension of the quarterback is very important. It is amazing when I look at college football these days, and look at how it has changed over the years. What has really changed is the ability of the quarterback to run. With all the read zones and quarterback powers and moving the pocket with boots and nakeds, it is very important to have a quarterback with athletic play-making capability.

From there, finally, we look at the throwing motion. Let's talk a little bit about the mechanics that we teach, and I do believe they can be taught. I believe passing efficiency can be taught. Our goal is to be accurate and consistent. Following are the five different points we will look at during this discussion:

• Ball placement
• Separation
• Cocking the ball
• Release
• Finish

The first thing we talk about in the mechanics of throwing the football is ball placement. We want two hands on the football and on the shelf. When we talk about the shelf, we are talking about coming right off his top number. We want the ball past the midline and the point of the football slightly outward. That is the ball placement that we like to start with. From there, we want to make sure the elbow placement is where we want it to be. We want to make sure that he is comfortable with his elbows down. To give the quarterback a feel of what I am looking for, I will put my fists under his armpits. I do not want him to squeeze my fist, but I want him to be able to just barely feel them. That is our starting point.

We then look at separation. To me, separation is one of the biggest things that there is, as far as being efficient at throwing the football. What I mean by separation is when they take the ball away, the lowest possible point that the ball is. I want the ball above the shoulder. What I have found out is the ball will mirror their front wrist on separation. What I am looking for is their front arm angle. If I see someone who is dropping the ball, I do not tell him to

keep the ball up; I tell him to keep his left wrist up. If the ball is held down, it takes too much time to get the ball out, and you cannot hit your receiver while running the post for a touchdown. If I have the ball up, I may take a hit, but I am able to get the ball out, and I will take a hit for a touchdown. The front wrist will mirror the ball. Separation is very important in being able to get the ball out quickly and being efficient. Timing is critical, and the higher level you play, the more timing is critical. Because of the speed of the game at the higher levels, you have to have more speed and efficiency in getting the ball out quickly. The higher level of competition you go, the faster they are playing and jumping on things. It is really important to get the ball out quickly, and the separation part we teach helps us do that.

We then look at cocking the ball. We want to make sure the elbow is at least shoulder height. We may have good separation, but then we have to make sure we have the ball at shoulder height. When cocking the ball, do not cock it down low. We then look to make sure that we have at least a 90-degree angle in our arm to throw. The tighter we bend our arm, the more the ball is going to spin. If we have our arm out like a javelin, then we are not going to spin the ball very well, and it is going to come out like a knuckleball. Quarterbacks who have their arm open do not throw a tight ball, and typically, they will have shoulder problems to go along with it. We then will look at the release. We would like to have the elbow at eye level on the release.

Next, we look at the finish. When we finished the throw, we look at what we call "exchange of shoulders." We take our throwing shoulder and put it where our off shoulder was. We want to take our throwing hand and put it in our opposite pocket. We also want to make sure we keep our head in there with our shoulder underneath our chin.

We will now get into some drills. We have a seated drill and a knee drill. If we have a young quarterback who is having a hard time getting the feel of putting his hand in his pocket, we put him on the ground on his butt with his legs spread across and have him throw the ball. Now when he throws, if his hand comes straight down, it is going to hit the ground. He will have to come across his body to make a throw. In the beginning we do not want to be very far apart, maybe eight yards apart. We are still working on the five points we discussed earlier. This helps, especially with the finish. When we go to two knees, it simulates getting the hips involved a little bit. If we want to simulate throwing from the pocket, we will throw from the right knee. If we want to simulate throwing on the run, you go to your left knee, then right knee. The ball is in the same spot all of the time.

Let us talk about the drop. Not everybody does the same thing, but I am going to tell you what we do and why we do it. First of all, we start with our stance and getting away from the center. We have our feet parallel; we do not stagger. The reasons why we do not stagger are we want to get out of the box cleanly and we are creating our angle with our punch step. The punch step is going to create our angle. If I was going to drop straight back and always going to throw to the right, I would be fine with being a stagger guy. Sometimes, you go left and then you have to spin the foot in the hole to create an angle to where you are going. What we do is use a punch step, which is a little six-inch step with our off foot to get going. That little punch step creates an angle to where we are going. We use one little quick punch step to get out of the hole. If we are going right, we want our weight on our right foot, because that is where we are pushing off of because your left foot is going to be your angle step and your get-out-of-the-hole step. The last thing we want to do is have a false step. The punch step is not used just in the passing game. It helps him get out fast and at the correct angle, in both our passing and running game. It needs to be consistent so we are not giving the play away.

When we look at our profile when throwing a pass, we want to make sure our shoulders are slightly open and parallel, and we are standing erect so we can see the whole field. We have to be able to see the weakside flat and the weakside corner. How do we do it? It starts with our feet. Almost every single kid who comes to our summer camp takes a runback from the center, not a dropback, and the shoulders are closed. How do you get them to open their shoulders? You get them to open their shoulders by opening their hips. You do that by opening their front foot. The front foot is slightly open, and the back foot pretty much has to be parallel with the front foot. We want to be in a heel-to-ball-of-the-foot relationship. I do not get

into being exactly seven yards on a five-step drop. I do not say you have to be this or you have to be that, because the last thing I want our quarterback to do is to look at the ground on his drop. If he does, he will be neither accurate nor consistent. It is not about being seven yards deep. It is about being under control and completing passes and doing what we need to do. If we can keep the heel of the front foot to the ball of the back foot and keep our knees bent, we are going to get our depth. We will be able to get back there as fast as we need and see what we need to see.

The drill that helps us with our profile is what we call the line drill. We put him on a line, and we do not care about anything other than footwork. We are watching the front foot. We are going to use the line to stay in a heel-to-ball-of-the-foot relationship. When you do this with your quarterbacks, I promise you, their front foot is going to close because it is just not natural to keep it open. This drill will help you, and you are sacrificing a little bit of speed for the proper mechanic. In this drill, watch the front foot—period. Do not worry about ball placement or any of that stuff; just watch the front foot. Make sure that the back foot is with it.

The next drill in the progression is the hold the shoulder open drill. I am going to stand in front of the quarterback and put my hand on his front shoulder and hold it open, and I want to take my backhand and push him open. As he steps and crosses over, if his front foot is not open, he will start falling down. He may think his shoulder is open, but with this drill, he can feel it. If his feet are not in the right place, he is going to fall down. With this drill, we can take 80 kids in our camp and teach this in about two days.

The next phase of this drill is to get in their blind spot. Now we are going to run with him and show him why we need to have that shoulder open. We need to be able to see the backside if we are going to throw a hot read when the backside blitz is coming.

One drill we run every day is the board drill (Diagram #1). When we go through the boards, we work on ball placement, shoulder placement, and the whole profile. We are going to simulate stepping up into the pocket. We want to stay in a throwing stance the whole time because once we get into the pocket and we switch our feet over,

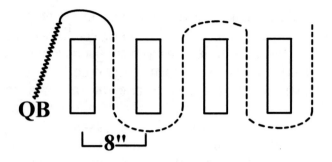

Diagram #1. Board Drill

the play is pretty much over. We either had better take off and run, or we better have a real short checkdown. Once our hips turn, it is over, unless we have a whole lot of time to reset our hips. The boards are about a yard apart, or you can just use the hash marks. As the quarterback is going through the boards, when I clap my hands, he has to get the ball out. We want him to keep his feet underneath, like a boxer. We will also swat the ball on the board drill in order to make sure that he is keeping both hands on the ball.

Okay, let's talk about the drop a little bit. Previously, we talked about loading the leg, and we talked about the hitch. We are going to load the leg on our timing routes. When we are throwing timed routes, we are loading the leg. When we are loading the leg, as in a three-step drop, we are throwing a hitch, a slant, or possibly a timing post off of a five-step drop. We are going to have everything the same. We are going to have a punch step as the first step, the second step is a break step, and the third step is an angle step. A lot of times, a young quarterback will make the mistake of getting too extended and not taking that angle step by the third step. At this point, they have no power. So when we are loading the leg, we are always teaching punch, break step, which is where your weight is.

The third step is the position and power step, like we are pushing off a pitcher's mound. In that third step, we have our foot angled in the direction that we want to throw the ball. This third step positions the foot so we will have some power behind it and so we can drive, open our hip, and throw. When we take that punch step and that break step, we want everything to look the same no matter which direction we are going. Defensive backs will start to read shoulders, and we want to keep everything the same until the last second so

they do not know which direction we are going. We cannot do that if our third step is our break step. If our break step is our second step, we can create the angle with our third step and get our hips in the right position. The feet are very critical.

If we are running a five-step drop and loading the leg, the break step becomes the fourth step. It is punch, two, three, break, and five is my angle and power step. Our profile is the same all the way until we take that angle step. We want to make sure that we are not overstriding, we are keeping under control, and we are doing it all with our feet. Keeping our feet underneath us is the key to being accurate and consistent.

Let's talk about the hitch a little bit. We do not want to overstride with our hitch. What we want is to make sure we keep our shoulders parallel and our spine erect. I do not want to have a big hitch because the farther our feet get out from under us, the more it throws our shoulders off plane. Kyle Boller was really long, so I had to put him in tennis shoes on the grass to help them with that. It helped to wet the grass a little bit, too. Every time he did not have his feet underneath him, he slipped down. He got used to keeping his feet up underneath him and staying in good position to be able to throw an accurate ball. With all of the intermediate throws, you want to make sure you keep your shoulder plane parallel. As soon as the throws start going further, the shoulder plane has got to change. If I am going to throw a go route, where we should take a five-step drop and a hitch, of between 43 and 48 yards, we have to change our shoulder profile. If you watch a long ball thrower whose ball never turns over, it is because he never changes his shoulder plane. If we get him to change his shoulder plane, we can get the ball to turn over. The further we throw the ball, the more we have to change our shoulder plane a little bit.

If we decide we want to throw the ball to the right on the run, we want to make sure we keep the ball on the shelf. We are going to shorten our stride toward the end, before the throw. We are going to cock the ball and keep it on the shelf. We exchange our hips, throw it off the right foot, and we bring our left knee to our right elbow as we throw the ball on the run. The arm still goes across the body. We do not want the arm to go straight down after the throw. We still want to finish coming across our body with our shoulder underneath our chin. If I am going left, I want to make sure I get the ball back on the shelf and cocked and use the same mechanics. We want to get them used to running like that.

I do a lot of different drills with the quarterbacks, including one I do that is not a throwing drill. Quarterbacks are not used to going to the ground with the ball. One reason is because they are not allowed to get hit during practice. The running backs and receivers all have time on the ground because we tackle them in practice, but we do not tackle the quarterbacks. The natural thing for the quarterback to do, as he is going to the ground, is to let his elbow fly out so he can land on it, and roll. This is when the ball will get ripped out. What I will do is put a pad on the ground and make the quarterback dive over it, as if he is trying to get a first down over the pad. I will have another pad that I can whack at the ball with, to make him keep the ball tight and roll on his shoulder. That is critical for our quarterbacks. Quarterbacks will fumble all of the time, because they are not used to going to the ground with the ball.

Years ago, ESPN did a story on us at Cal about our use of checkers. I learned this from my high school coach, who did this with me. I would take my lunch and go up into his office, and we would get out the box of checkers. I would be the offense, and he would be the defense. We would line up our checkers, and he would move things around and start asking questions about what adjustments needed to be made. I have continued to use this with our quarterbacks. You can teach your entire playbook with it. You can teach your formations with it. This is a great, great tool because you start from the basics, and then you go to the different types of fronts that you will be facing. You can teach protections, coverages, pre-snap reads, the whole bit. I will take regular black and red checkers and paint white letters on them for the positions. We will get to the point where I will have the quarterback turn his head and call a play. When he turns around, I will be the defense and position my pieces in order to make him make a call. He will have to explain everything that he is doing to me and verbalize why. That way, I know he understands what to do. I will have him move the pieces for

the routes so he knows exactly where the routes are going and how they change, depending on what I do on defense. It is a great learning tool for the quarterback and the coach. You can teach everything: running game, protections, fronts, you name it. They love it. It is very easy to do.

Part of my topic today is to talk about leadership. I am finding it harder and harder these days for kids to be leaders. Often, when I call a player in and tell him I need him to be a leader, he might say, I lead by example. I hear that more and more and more all the time. I believe kids these days think that a leader has to be perfect and cannot make any mistakes, or they have to be a bad guy and chew people out to be a leader. They think to be a leader you have to get up and make speeches. What we are working on this year is having team leadership. That is where everyone is accountable toward each other. I think some leaders will emerge from this, but it is impossible to get a leader from someone who will not accept it. Accepting leadership is just as important as providing leadership. This year, we are focusing on team leadership and vision. "Where do you want to go, where are you now, and how are you going to get there?" We are going to have them write all of this stuff down.

I have read an awesome book called *My Orange Duffel Bag* by Sam Bracken. It is an orange canvas bag, if you go to a bookstore and look for it. It will take you about an hour to read it. It is about a guy who had a really rough upbringing and was a mess. He ended up being an academic All-American at Georgia Tech. It has some great exercises in it, and we are going to have our kids use it. We are going to have our team write important goals down because it first crystallizes their thinking. They have to sit down and put some thought into it. Second, they have to have a written plan. Third, they have to have iron will and determination to get it done. And fourth, they have to have the competence to do it.

I had a rough upbringing myself. I came from a single-parent home. Then, my mom got married, and my stepdad was a jerk. I moved out when my sister heard him cussing me, and she called my mom to tell her that I was not going to be living there anymore. My last two years of high school I lived with my sister. I remember during my 10th grade year I was sitting in my room, and I took out a pad of paper and wrote down a bunch of goals that I wanted to achieve. I wanted to be all-conference. I wanted to be player of the year. I wanted to play in the shrine game. I wrote down all of this stuff. When I moved to my sisters, I left it in my old closet. When it was time for me to go to college, I cleaned out my closet. I found this old notebook, and I looked at my goals, and it almost came exactly the way I had set my goals, and almost to the yard of what my goals were. All of the things that I had written down came true. It was unbelievable. When you crystallize your thinking, it makes you have a burning desire to succeed and get it done.

When I got cut from the CFL, when I was with Hamilton, I wanted another shot. I got back into serious training. One night I was sitting in my apartment and I decided to write down all of this stuff again. I wanted to make another team. I wanted to get married, and all of this other stuff. About a year-and-a-half later, I am about to get married, when a buddy that I am living with who is going to be in my wedding, brings me this piece of paper that I had written before. Everything that I had written down before was about to become true. My point is that if you crystallize your thinking enough to write it down in a plan, it means something to you. That is what we are going to do with our kids this year. I do not think they take enough time to sit down and put thought into what they are doing and why they are doing what they are doing. They do not know why we are getting up at seven o'clock in the morning and working out. They do not know why we are lifting weights. They do not know why we are going to study hall. I do not think they ever think about why we are doing all the things that we are doing. If you get this book, *My Orange Duffel Bag*, read through it. I think you will get some insight as to what some of these kids are going through and what they are thinking. The person that turned Sam around was Bill Curry, when he was coaching at Georgia Tech. Bill gave him all the tools to figure out who he was and what he wanted to be.

Guys, I admire what you do because we coach the best sport in the world. More than just X's and O's, you have the ability to make a difference in your kids' lives. Take the time to sit down with them and give them good, positive direction. Be enthusiastic with them because they need to have fun at what they are doing. Sometimes, we are so much into it as coaches and making corrections and telling them not do this and do not do that that we forget to find them doing something right. Tell them about it when they do something right. Give them some positive feedback that will make them want to keep on keeping on. Give them a little love sometimes. Make them feel appreciated, and make them feel important. Again, I appreciate you being here tonight. I wish you all the best, and thank you very much.

2011
COACH OF THE YEAR CLINICS
Football Manual

Featuring lectures from several of America's most renowned coaches. Edited by Earl Browning.

$29.95 • 295 pages • 978-1-60679-171-4

NEW!

Edited by Earl Browning

Also available:

2005	2006	2007	2008	2009	2010

1-58518-932-4	1-58518-969-3	978-1-58518-073-8	978-1-58518-719-5	978-1-60679-062-5	978-1-60679-104-2
288 pp. • $24.95	304 pp. • $24.95	288 pp. • $24.95	272 pp. • $24.95	288 pp. • $29.95	313 pp. • $29.95

Title	Item #	Price	Qty	Total
Tax on materials for California residents only. Shipping & Handling: $7.50 for first item $1.50 for each additional item	PLUS	CA Tax 9.25%		
	PLUS	Shipping		
		TOTAL		

Name _____ Organization/School _____

Address _____

City _____ State _____ ZIP _____ Phone ( ) _____

Method of Payment: ☐ **VISA** ☐ MasterCard ☐ American Express Cards ☐ DISCOVER ☐ Check #_____ ☐ P.O. #_____

Account # ☐☐☐☐ ☐☐☐☐ ☐☐☐☐ ☐☐☐☐ ☐☐☐☐ Expiration: ___/___ CVC #: __ __ __

Signature: _____ Email Address: _____

COACHES CHOICE
www.coacheschoice.com

Send check or money order to: **Coaches Choice**
P.O. Box 1828 Monterey, CA 93942
or call toll-free: (888) 229-5745 or fax: (831) 372-6075

2011
CLINIC NOTES
Lectures by Premier High School Coaches

Edited by Earl Browning.

$29.95 • 265 pages • 978-1-60679-172-1

NEW!

2011 COACH OF THE YEAR CLINIC NOTES
LECTURES BY PREMIER HIGH SCHOOL COACHES
EDITED BY EARL BROWNING

Also available:

2006	2007	2008	2009	2010

1-58518-982-0	978-1-58518-074-5	978-1-58518-740-9	978-1-60679-065-6	978-1-60679-109-7
256 pp. • $24.95	268 pp. • $24.95	256 pp. • $24.95	272 pp. • $29.95	260 pp. • $29.95